JOHN ROBERTS is Professor of Art and Aesthetics at the University of Wolverhampton. His recent books include *The Intangibilities of Form*, *The Philistine Controversy* (with Dave Beech), and *Philosophizing the Everyday*. He contributes to *Radical Philosophy*, *New Left Review*, *Historical Materialism*, *Third Text*, *Oxford Art Journal*, and *Chto Delat*. He lives in London.

THE NECESSITY
OF ERRORS

JOHN ROBERTS

VERSO
London • New York

First published by Verso 2011
© John Roberts 2011

All rights reserved

1 3 5 7 9 10 8 6 4 2

Verso
UK: 6 Meard Street, London W1F 0EG
US: 20 Jay Street, Suite 1010, Brooklyn, NY 11201
www.versobooks.com

Verso is the imprint of New Left Books

ISBN-13: 978-1-84467-739-9

British Library Cataloguing in Publication Data
A catalogue record for this book is available from the British Library

Library of Congress Cataloging-in-Publication Data
A catalog record for this book is available from the Library of Congress

Typeset in Garamond by Hewer Text UK Ltd, Edinburgh
Printed in the US by Maple Vail

CONTENTS

PREFACE

The Necessity of Errors has its distant origins in a book I published in 1993, *Selected Errors*, a collection of essays on art and politics. Although the title suggests a certain familiarity with the philosophy of errors, there was no discussion at all of the errors in the collection; my own errors and the errors of my interlocutors and targets were merely assumed. Yet the concept of the error, as a factor both constitutive and destabilizing in thought and practice, never left my work. Indeed, in retrospect the concept seems to have operated in various cognate ways throughout my writing. So, I felt the time had to come for me to 'think' the error directly and systematically, but more importantly, address what increasingly appeared to me to be one of its singularly defining characteristics: its *productiveness*. But productiveness, of course, means many things, and is not generalisable, given the different role and function of errors across practices and disciplines. The driving question of *The Necessity of Errors* has been quite simple therefore: how, and under what conditions, is the error productive, and is there anything consistent to its productiveness? Consequently the book covers what I take to be the key sites of this productiveness (or lack of productiveness): the philosophy of the subject, the philosophy of science, psychoanalysis, political praxis and art. In this sense the book moves deliberately beyond various localized responses to the status and the function of the error in various disciplines, to produce a critically synoptic and historical account of the error. As such it breaks with what we might call, loosely, a philosophy *of* the error (although, to be honest, we would be hard pressed to find such a thing in philosophy) in order to formulate a dialectical theory of the error and errancy. In these terms *The Necessity of Errors* is as much a reflection on the presence of error *in* dialectic as it is an engagement with the philosophical content of the error and dialectic.

I would like to thank John Timberlake and Ben Noys for their close readings of the text and for their support; and also thanks to Tom Penn at Verso for his faith in the project and the University of Wolverhampton for awarding me a sabbatical to finish the book. And finally thanks to my wife, Michelle, and my daughter, Gilda, for putting up with all my lengthy sojourns into 'philosophical abstraction'.

INTRODUCTION: THE RENEWAL OF TRUTH

PURE PERCIPIENCE

Imagine a world in which everything you said was right, and everything everyone else said was also right, a world, in fact, in which there was no error, only instant and transparent veracity. What an impossible burden that would be: with no space for dispute, argumentation or qualification, or scope for the development of knowledge, conversation would dry up to the exchange of veridical statements and declaratives and their endless confirmation.

> (a): 'This ball is 10.769 centimetres in circumference and will travel at 39.43 miles per hour, when I throw it.'
> (b): 'Yes, that's indisputable.'

Judgements of value might offer more scope for dispute (within a given range of shared approbation or criticism), yet, essentially, no opinion would appear opaque or untoward, and as such nothing exchanged by the addressor would be learned by the addressee.

> (a): 'César Vallejo is one of my favourite writers; it is a shame he died so young. The early poems are the best.'
> (b): 'Yes, he was only forty-eight; the early *Trilce* is one of the great poems of the twentieth century.'

Predicting the ball's trajectory – particularly after it bounced – might be a bit more difficult, but perfect percipience about the ball's size, weight, and pressure exerted per square inch by the thrust of the arm would go some way to compensating for this uncertainty. Consequently, this kind of percipience would transform all our social relations: knowing every-thing, everyone would share with everyone else a full complement of what is judged to be knowledge. Although *judged to be knowledge* is perhaps the wrong phrase here. For in a world of transparent and instant veracity there is no sense that truth can be the *possession* of thinking and judging subjects at all. On the contrary, as the mouthpiece of indisputable and indefatigable knowledge, the subject could be said to exist not as the subject of truth, but, rather, as the bearer of truth as an external, de-subjectivised process. Because consciousness operates here as cognate with truth – on the basis of that which is transparently true – truth, thereby, is not subject to a process of self-reflection and collective scrutiny. Transparent knowledge in this imagined exchange *is* consciousness, and, therefore, no gap exists between consciousness and knowledge, knowledge and truth. The world exists as a perfected Cartesian realm of pure and absolute understanding.

Why is this imaginary scenario of super-percipience so dismal and so implausible? In many ways it is not hard to understand why. Perfect percipience and instant and transparent veracity produce epistemologi-cal closure and the death of communication. As a shared set of veridi-cal statements and declaratives conversation becomes frozen in its own petrified and perfected rationality. At the point of their confirmation by others, therefore, instant truth, paradoxically, encloses its opposite: the forces of reification, heteronomy and untruth. In 'knowing' omnipotently consciousness exists only in pure form because there is no prior sense of 'not knowing'. The self has no history as a 'knowing subject' or a 'not knowing' subject; that is, it has never experienced 'knowing' as a state following or preceding 'not knowing'. Or, to put it in a more dialecti-cal fashion, it has never experienced the pleasure of 'knowing' as 'not knowing', and 'not knowing' as the precondition of 'knowing'. 'Knowing' can never be what is emergent as knowledge, because 'knowing' is not possessed and repossessed as an uncertain, discursive process. Rational subjects on this basis are pure non-reflexive, non-historical entities whose possession of knowledge is utterly abstracted and naturalized, a process as unconscious as breathing or walking.

The perfected rationalism of this subject is thus fanciful and impos-sible. The embrace and inclusion of error and 'not knowing' is a constitu-tive part of 'knowing'. But what kind of embrace and inclusion is this?

What kinds of errors and mistakes constitute knowledge and truth? What kinds of errors and mistakes are constitutive, for instance, of science, political praxis, art, philosophy and psychoanalysis? In this book I want to look, therefore, at what we might call the *different theoretical and practical orders of error*. For it is one thing to say that 'not-knowing' is constitutive of 'knowing', it is another to determine on what basis and under what conditions errors produce their effects across the domains of knowledge.

ERROR AND ENLIGHTENMENT

Now, of course, on one level this project appears, philosophically, to be grossly naive and negligent, even tautological. A book on *errors*? Isn't the history of philosophy precisely this from Plato to Locke to Wittgenstein and Quine? Isn't philosophy, conspicuously, a reflection on the presence or absence of truth, its conditionality and possibility, its particularity or universality, its emergence or disappearance, its partiality or totality? Of course. My presumption here, therefore, is not to write a philosophy of error in order to explain philosophy's relationship to truth all the better, as if a book on 'errors' will clarify where the errors in philosophy's reflection on errors lie. Rather, the aim is more practical, hesitant, circumscribed and dialectical – to place the 'error' back in practice in order to reflect on the condition of practice and the movement of thought and practice itself. In this it offers a broader social and political understanding of the function and role of the error than Nicholas Rescher's *Error* (2007). Rescher's book, for all its incisiveness in stressing the productiveness of the error, remains locked in pre-Hegelian logic, using the error, in pragmatist fashion, to shore up a very delimited account of consciousness and praxis. The 'salient feature of error', he states, 'lies in its role as a characterizing hallmark of human finitude and imperfection.'[1] Consequently, *The Necessity of Errors* brings a wider theoretical and historical compass to bear on the epistemological and critical status of error than is usually subscribed to. For let us be clear: the theorization of the error has had a strange half-lit life, that is, although it is ubiquitous – in passing – as a knotty site of problems in philosophy, the philosophy of science, psychoanalysis, art theory, and political praxis, it nonetheless remains a subfusc, shadowy presence theoretically.[2] In this sense there is no systematic, materialist and synoptic analysis of the productiveness of the error across these domains. This is not surprising, because the status of the error has represented a profound problem for Marxism in the twentieth century, in so far as the thing that truth is designed to expunge or challenge has continually mocked Marxism's claims to reason; Marxism has seemingly been a home to a thousand (unproductive) errors and the hubris of scientific objectivity. As such on this basis we can link Rescher's defence of human finitiude to the two broader and explicit functions of the analysis of error in the modern period: generally, as a critique of reason, and specifically, as a critique of Marxism (or a certain, instrumental, collectivist, technocratic, Stalinized version of Marxism) and revolutionary praxis. In this sense the key figures in this history of the error have been its modern inaugurators: Nietzsche, Freud, Heidegger, Wittgenstein, Foucault and Georges Canguilhem. All have talked in passing about the significance of the error in order to invoke the error as the productive site of reason's failure to be equal to its own demands for universal truth and progress. However, this critique of reason's transparency has three distinct trajectories here: a Nietzschian *relativism* of truth as error – as Nietzsche argues in *The Will To Power*, truth is no more than a variety of error;[3] a Heideggerian ontology of error – 'Man errs. Man does not merely stray into errancy. He is always astray in errancy'[4] – and a Wittgensteinian-Freudian-Foucauldian-Canguilhemian understanding of the material and epistemological interrelationship of truth and error as a condition of praxis. In this sense the error here broadly signifies the point of truth's emergence, although it takes quite different emphases across these authors' writings. In Wittgenstein, in both *On Certainty* and *Culture and Value*, the error is where truth hides, so to speak, but it is also the place where truth is renewed. 'Don't *for heaven's sake*, be afraid of talking nonsense! But you must pay attention to your nonsense.'[5] 'Our greatest stupidities may be very wise.'[6] In Freud, in *The Psychopathology of Everyday Life*, specifically the chapter 'Errors', the error, of course, is the means by which the unconscious speaks – 'where an error makes its appearance a repression lies behind it'[7] – and as such psychoanalysis derives its interpretative powers from making a distinction between the error of consequence and the error that is based on what Freud calls 'genuine ignorance.'[8] And in Foucault and Canguilhem the productiveness of the error, its constitutivensss for truth, is given a kind of universal bio-political drive. That is, as Foucault argues in his 'Introduction' to Canguilhem's *The Normal and the Pathological*, 'error . . . is the permanent chance around which the history of life and that of man develops.'[9] Indeed, for Canguilhem the study of pathology reveals how metabolic errors – the production of innate chemical malformations in humans – produce a body born of error, or on the edge of 'error'. In this there is a liberatory character to this knowledge. 'Disease is not a fall that one has, an attack to which one succumbs, but an original flaw in macromolecular form.'[10] As such, as 'living beings we are the effect of the very laws of the multiplication of life.'[11] But if this liberates us from a model of normativity, it also slams us up hard against the limits of reproductive rights and, crucially, the 'right' to disability. For women's modern reproductive rights, and recent advances in genetic pre-planning, have been developed precisely to diminish or expunge the results of chemical breakdown and biological error. The liberation from biological normativity and the defence of the error, therefore, come, in certain circumstances, with enormous responsibilities and challenges. Do we want a world where disability – or biological error – is forever being made to appear inconvenient?[12]

Now, as is evident in Foucault – certainly the early Foucault of the 'Introduction' – this embodiment-as-error is not so dissimilar to the Heideggerian concept of errancy: humans do not fall into error – as if into a ditch, as Heidegger famously puts it – but, in their practice and thought, start *from* error, in so far as, Foucault says, 'error is at root what makes human thought and its history.'[13] Both reject a purely epistemological or Cartesian understanding of the error, in which error captures the subject, on the basis of the subject's failure to live up to his or her powers of reason. In this respect Foucault's attack on Enlightenment reason is double-edged. That is, on the one hand, there is a history of the error that suppresses the subject (and difference) under the objectivist blindnesses of science, but on the other hand – and this is why he is interested in the determinate, non-subjective character of error in Canguilhem's theory – there is a history of error in which the errancy of the individual subject is constitutive in its intersubjectivity of the historical process itself. In short, error is being's historicalization; and this, in Canguilhem's language, is liberatory, in so far as, in contradistinction to subject-centred error, error is not reduced to a primary state of culpability, a kind of singular and intermittent impediment. In this light Foucault makes an interesting remark in the 'Introduction' regarding the post-Cartesian philosophical status of this conception of error:

If the great Cartesian break posed the question of the relations between truth and subject, the eighteenth century, as far as the reflection of truth and life are concerned, introduced a series of questions of which the *Critique of Judgement* and the *Phenomenology of Spirit* were the first great formulations.[14]

In other words (as Foucault appears to be suggesting), formatively in Kant, but emphatically in Hegel, the subject, truth and error are brought into a non-normative, 'pathological' alignment for the very first time. Indeed in Hegel, in particular, error and truth become interdependent and co-determinate, displacing the theory of the autonomous rational subject from the centre of the operations of reason (what I call in Chapter 1 the de possessive subject). In this sense the implication is that Hegel's critique of the subject and Canguilhem's critique of the subject share the same philosophical target: the Enlightenment's rationally transparent subject; and as such, on this basis, Canguilhem's theory of error is, Foucault argues, philosophically where the modern critique of this subject truly begins as a science of the subject. Now this has a certain appeal, but it is wrong historically and philosophically. Certainly, Hegel systematizes the productiveness of error and as such incorporates the 'pathological' subject into the historical unfolding of truth. This is a break that is also at the core of this book. But this pathological process is no stranger to the Enlightenment itself. Indeed, Hegel is the great *inheritor* of the Enlightenment's questioning of its own promulgations of reason and progress.

In the early French Enlightenment in particular, we see emerge an extraordinary range of critical engagements with error, truth and the subject, belying the Foucauldian notion that the Enlightenment is where the 'monstrous' and 'pathological' are expelled. Between the 1750s and 1790s in France, the concept of error is the subject of an extensive philosophical enquiry, across a large corpus of writing from within the pre-Revolutionary liberal bourgeoisie and the aristocracy, in which, for the first time, the productiveness of the error is given some credence. Denis Diderot (1713–1784), Maquis (Nicolas) de Condorcet (1743–1794), Etienne Bonnot de Condillac (1715–1780), Anne-Robert-Jacques Turgot (Baron de Laune) (1727–1781), Jean-Louis Castilhon (1720–1782) and Jean de Rond d'Alembert (1717–1788) all register a greater tolerance of the error in thought and in practice than hitherto within the liberal bourgeoisie.[15]

For Diderot, pure unmediated knowledge is impossible, and as such the search for knowledge must pass through a disorganized, unpredictable world; for Condorcet, unnecessary deliberation can just as easily cause error and, therefore, to risk error provides the greater reward; for Condillac, in the interests of metaphysical modesty, truth represents a wayward path; for Turgot, error doesn't prevent progress and truth, inactivity does – humans have to pass through a thousand errors before arriving at truth; for Castilhon, likewise, error provides the future conditions for truth; and for d'Alembert, the necessary wandering of knowledge may produce the false lights of error, but also the authentic flash of truth – error precedes truth. In general, therefore, this range of defences of errancy prefigures what is fundamental to the systematic incorporation of the 'pathological' subject in Hegel: errancy in thought and practice is intimately linked to the emergence of new pathways to truth. As a consequence what these early Enlightenment writers produce, at the very moment of reason's conjoining of the rational subject to the natural sciences, is a kind of nascent dialectic of enlightenment in which the Cartesian subject is exposed to a tentative (Kantian and Hegelian) historicization. In fact this defence of errancy even finds its way into the writing of the mathematician and Cartesian Bernard le Bovier de Fontenelle (1657–1757), a contributor to the *Encyclopédie* (1751–1777 with later supplements and revisions in 1772, 1777 and 1780). 'We are not at all permitted to arrive all of a sudden at any reasonable conclusion on any subject – whatsoever; first we are required to wander for a long time, and pass through diverse kinds of errors.'[16] We might say, therefore, that modern dialectics begins here in the notion of truth as a kind of wandering *through error*, as opposed, that is, to the notion of the error as parasitic on truth, as the incorrigible realm of the mistake.

The historical evidence for this nascent dialectic in France is superbly marshalled by David W. Bates in *Enlightenment Aberrations: Error & Revolution in France* (2002), perhaps the best book on the modern formation of the concept of error yet written; and I am indebted above all to his archival, historical work. In this the value of his writing foregrounds what is a persistent problem regarding the historicization of the Enlightenment: its theoretical congregation around its Germanic, Kantian moment of intense rational self-reflection, and the fact that the majority of German intellectual contributors were writing before *and* after the French Revolution, bringing, as a result, a further critical and moral mediation of error to the question of truth and enlightenment. Thus the character of Germanic discussion of error and enlightenment is quite different to that of France. Before the Revolution, discussion of errors remains close to the old Cartesian pathways. For instance Karl Leonhard Reinhold

(1758–1823) talks in the journal *Der Teutsche Merkur* – one of the key forums of the early German Enlightenment – of the need to construct a 'rational culture'[17] in which 'every error [that] deviates from truth limits the capacity of reason, and serves as bulwark of ignorance.'[18] Similarly in the famous debate on enlightenment in the *Berlinische Monatsschrift* in 1784, to which Moses Mendelssohn (1729–1786), Kant, and Ernst Ferdinand Klein (1744–1810), amongst others, contributed, any discussion of the dialectic of error and truth is subordinate to the clear light of public reason. In both instances the enlightened subject is almost 'unblinking' in his or her powers of reflection. This heightened anticipation changes, as it does in France and elsewhere, after the Revolution, when error is now dredged up to be identified with the monstrous failure of *misguided* enlightenment and reason, the enlightenment that goes 'too far', that places reason back in the realm of shadow and darkness. Johan Fichte, no unthinking conservative, is nevertheless quick to reattach this monstrousness to the error after the French revolution. In 1793, in his strange and conflicted address to the Princes of Europe – the quasi-deferential nature of an address to the monarchy being a rhetorical quirk of the German Enlightenment – he declares the French Revolution to be a 'dreadful spectacle'.[19]

> Powerful revolutions are always a daring risk for mankind; if they succeed, the victory that is achieved is well worth the adversity that has been endured; if they fail, they force this way through misery to greater misery. Gradual steps forward are a more certain path to greater enlightenment, and it to the improvement of the political constitution.[20]

It is possible to talk, then, of a distinction between an early dialectical account of error and a post-Revolutionary termination of this dialectic, in which the error is returned to its pure Cartesian otherness, or identified, in the writings of the most conservative detractors of the Revolution, with the sinful fallenness of man. To be clear, here, Fichte is not in this latter camp – his address outstrips Kant in its call to the infinite creativity of free independent human beings, yet he is broadly in the category of those theorists after the Revolution that are quick to dissolve this brief and engaged reflection on the productiveness of error. Bates shows, indeed, how deep this retreat occurred in France and in Europe after 1795. In the writings of the theocratic authoritarians the Abbé Barruel (1741–1820),[21] Joseph-Marie comte de Maistre (1753–1821)[22] and Louis de Bonald (1754–1840)[23], in particular, we see the stark formation of a counter-revolutionary theory of the error, that, of course, feeds into that long-standing and residual post-revolutionary, anti-Enlightenment tradition that numerous conservatives, reactionaries and romantic anti-capitalists have drawn on from the nineteenth and twentieth centuries to the present (Heidegger being one and Carl Schmitt, an admirer of de Maistre, being another).[24] In this counter-revolutionary theory of the error, errancy, as in pre-revolutionary writing, is still the epistemological key to truth, but is now the persistent *source* of human weakness, and as such the thing to be overcome, or stalled or controlled, in a kind of imperious Augustinian separation of the errors of humans from the perfected truth of God. Thus for de Maistre the errancy of humans represents the endless wandering of humans from the straight path of God's will, and therefore political agency is best understood as the constant task of introducing and reintroducing order into this mass of bewildering and barbaric contingencies. Or as Bates puts it: politics for de Maistre is always about 'acting as a force of order in an eternally imperfect and discordant condition.'[25]

We might say, therefore, that the greatness of Hegel in 1807, in *the Phenomenology of Spirit*, rests on his theoretical destruction of this counter-revolutionary theory of error, and the preservation, reconstitution, expansion and subsumption of the early moment of the dialectic of errancy. For Hegel, the error is not the humble sign of human finitude, or, conversely, the outcome of a dangerous theoretical hubris, but rather the gateway to the renewal of truth. Reason, is, in short, impure, rather than pure.[26] In this sense, at one level, Hegel is the heir to Diderot, Turgot and d'Alembert. For Bates, however, this post-Enlightenment Hegelianization of error, far from being a challenge to a counter-revolutionary theory of error, is the point where the dialectic of error succumbs to determinism and the instrumental logic of nineteenth-century science. As he argues:

> Looked at from the perspective of error and truth, the Romantic insight, Hegelian dialectic, positivist sociology, laissez-faire political economy, Darwinian evolutionary biology, statistical analysis, Marxist economics, all were systematic ways of, if not eliminating error and aberration from the world, at least reducing it (epistemologically) to mere appearance.[27]

Bracketing Hegelian dialectic and Marxist economics and positivist sociology and statistical analysis within the same framework is clearly tendentious, and, as such, represents the fundamental weakness of Bates's account (there is an implicit debt to the postmodern perspective that he is keen to distance himself from in his 'alternative narrative of modernity'[28]). Hegel and Marx are, above all else, the redoubtable critics of positivity, and therefore the conflation above severs the emancipatory legacy of the dialectic of error from its negative dialectical continuation in the Hegelian and Marxist tradition. Yet Bates is at least right to insist (within a Foucauldian-Canguilhemian framework) that this continuation has not been a self-conscious theoretical component of the critique of positivity within the Marxist tradition, and in this sense he is on stronger ground; dialectic has tended to subsume the component functions of a dialectic of error under the broader category of negation. But even so, just as there is a hidden, marginal, subordinate dialectic of error in philosophy, the philosophy of science, psychoanalysis and art, there are various, repeated encounters with 'error' in the history of Marxism that reveal, through the influence of Hegel, the persistent presence of the early Enlightenment's reflections on error. And these moments, not surprisingly, exist mainly within the area of political praxis, where the recognition and incorporation of the 'error' and 'mistake' become crucial to thinking through the relations between strategy, struggle and the historical process. Indeed, we can point to how Marxism, in this respect, is no different from the pre-Revoutionary and post-revolutionary theorists of politics and the decision in late eighteenth-century France in turning to the truth–error dialectic at key moments of political blockage, crisis or defeat. Hence a certain pattern emerges in the way Marxism historicizes the defeat or crisis of the workers movement, beginning with Marx's own reflections on the Commune in 1871–72: the errors of praxis become the site where the struggle and the proletariat renew or reaffirm themselves.[29] In periods of organizational crisis and revolutionary failure this move towards truth-in-error occurs again and again, down to the post-Stalinist vicissitudes of today. Thus, in 1904 after years of the hounding of the workers movement in Russia and Poland, Rosa Luxemburg writes: 'Historically, the errors committed by a truly revolutionary movement are infinitely more fruitful than the infallibility of the cleverest Central Committee.'[30] (Luxemburg is attacking Lenin's nascent disciplinary control of Social Democratic Party education, in order to make a wider claim on how Marxism enters into the life and dynamism of the proletariat, and, as such, how the party might best represent this life and dynamism; for Luxemburg, the proletariat is, in this regard, the very crucible of creativity, and therefore, in the spirit of Condorcet, should not fear error and, accordingly, nor should the party.) Similarly, in exile from the USSR in the wake of the defeat of the Republic in Spain, Victor Serge writes his important essay, 'Marxism in Our Time' (1938) on praxis, Marxism and self-reflection: Marxism cannot be anything but a continual process of self-revision, and therefore, it cannot get along without anything but 'hypothesis and error'.[31] And again in 1962 in the wake of the Soviet invasion of Hungary and the deepening crisis of the PCF (Partie Communiste Française), Henri Lefebvre introduces the Socratic concept of *maieutic* (knowledge that arrives after or in spite of the subject's conscious intentions, or 'weak thought') in order to ironize the rituals of faith in orthodox Marxism: 'the path of truth passes through dissimulation and even worse, via defeat.'[32] The revolutionary does not raise himself or herself above the world, but takes strength from this weakness, 'the strength of negation and the negative'.[33] Likewise in 1967, after the retreat of revolutionary forces in Bolivia, Régis Debray, declares in *Revolution in the Revolution?*: 'For a revolutionary, failure is a springboard. As a source of theory it is richer than victory: it accumulates experience and knowledge.'[34] And in response to the defeat and dispersion of the revolutionary forces of May 1968, Raoul Vaneigem, writing at some distance from the party-form of Marxism, but nevertheless in the spirit of Luxemburg, asserts: 'Too bad if the taste for pleasure is a fine source of error. We will never make as many mistakes as the amount of blood spilled by intellectuals of past revolutions testifies to and which is etched on their hearts. I prefer spontaneous mistakes to truth imposed. Rather the creator feeling his way than the coherence of the leader.'[35] These, of course, are a few dissident and marginal voices within Marxism or on its heterodox fringes; and in this sense they do not amount collectively to anything approaching a coherent understanding of error and dialectic. Yet there is a sense that they all share with the writers of the early Enlightenment, and the (late) Hegelian Marx and Engels themselves, that the critique of positivity is embedded in the ironies and opacities of history. As the later Engels says, in a strong Hegelian and prefigurative 'psychoanalytic' vein, in *Ludwig Feuerbach and the End of Classical German Philosophy*:

> The will is determined by passion or deliberation. But the levers which immediately determine passion or deliberation are of very different kinds. They may be partly external objects, partly ideal motives, ambition, 'enthusiasm for truth and

justice,' personal hatred or even purely personal whims of all kinds. But, on the one hand, we have seen that many individual wills active in history for the most part produce results quite other than and often the very opposite of those willed, and that therefore their motives are likewise only of secondary importance in relation to the total result.[36]

That is, there are no transparent wills engaged on transparent projects with transparent outcomes. And therefore, in classic Hegelian mode, the truth-consequences and value of certain actions only become apparent in the light of their passing and disappearance. Indeed, the passing of the event and our subsequent reflection on its outcomes is the very requirement of the emergence and development of its truth-content and the possibility of future practice.[37] This is why Zhou Enlai famously was to say when asked in 1953 what he thought about the significance of the French revolution: 'It is far too early to say.'[38] What we might learn from, and about, the French Revolution as a reflection on praxis is yet to come.

What this incorporation of ironization into praxis allows us to lay claim to on a wider scale is that Marxism may not have a theory of error, but it is has a recurring sense of itself as participating in history as a process where error is produced as truth and truth is intimate with error. That is, the relationship between error and praxis is embedded in the fundamental split between the failure of the proletariat to rationalize its own interests on the basis of the concept of universal emancipation and the failure of the bourgeoisie to realise its own claims to universality on the basis of its own (quasi-scientistic and technocratic) claims to rationality. The status of the proletariat's failure as a universal class remains undecided at present, therefore, precisely because the bourgeoisie is unable to foreclose on its own claims to universality. Because of this, the proletariat and bourgeoisie cannot dissolve into each other. Consequently, in the light of this contradiction, reflection on the error in political praxis – here specifically the 'failures' of revolutionary praxis – is the means by which this contradiction continues to be thought, tested and confronted.[39] In this sense this is the specific social and political terrain on which the dialectic of enlightenment proceeds.

So, does (Hegelian) Marxism need a theory of error, when it has dialectic? In other words is dialectic, or dialectical irony, adequate enough? Well, a number of things need to be addressed here. First, a theory of errors is not the solution to revolutionary praxis or the trauma of history, or a means of improving or smartening up dialectic. Second, and concomitantly, a theory of errors is not what we need in order to slough off the historicism and hubris of the past. This is always an invitation to idealism, and its recent cognate postmodernism, which has drawn extensively from the Nietzschian-Heideggerian coupling to produce an overweening identification of the Enlightenment with science's suppression, control or blindness to difference. Error, or errancy in the Heideggerian sense, is taken as evidence of the delimited space of history as a space of becoming. For Heidegger, 'Dasein's voice remains[s] precisely autistic, a voice that says "nothing", instead indicating the failure of its own self-presence . . . the failure of its own foundation becomes its ultimate moment of self-appropriation.'[40] Yet, nevertheless, in keeping with Foucault and Canguilhem, we need to think the error back into being and history, in order to mark errancy as the space of history and being. And this is why the irony and maieutic in dialectic, albeit central, are not enough; we need a theory of the logic and space of error, in its *knowledge specificity*, across its major disciplinary and theoretical domains: philosophy, philosophy of science, psychoanalysis, political praxis and art. For it is in the disciplinary-specific problems and vicissitudes of these domains that we can begin to offer a dialectical account of error and errancy. To these ends I want to distinguish five principal areas of errors: (1) the *epistemological* (in philosophy); (2) the *veridical* (in the philosophy of science); (3) the *lapsidian* (in psychoanalysis); (4) *the ironic and self-ironizing* (in political praxis); and (5) the *actionist* (in artistic practice). At various points these different orders cross over: the veridical does not escape the epistemological; the epistemological does not escape the lapsidian; and the ironic and self-ironizing do not escape the actionist – or the epistemologial for that matter. Thus these distinctions are not fixed categories, merely ways of drawing out what is distinctive to different orders of errors across different practices and domains of knowledge. Nevertheless, where these categories do overlap and infuse with each other we see where some kinds of error take on shared characteristics at the expense of other characteristics. In this sense what is at stake is not so much the general productiveness of the error – this much is pregiven across these practices and disciplines – but the different registers and dynamics in which the error-truth dialectic unfolds. Thus if the 'error' sustains discourse, sustains communication, sustains political praxis, and sustains art and culture (in the sense described at the beginning of the introduction), will any old errors do?

Are lapses, mistakes, and displays of uncertainty and error, purposeful and productive in all circumstances? Of course, this is implausible, and if taken seriously a major misunderstanding about the premises of this book. Errors of action (failure to realize an intended outcome), errors of judgement (failure to realise the value of things) and errors of cognition (failure to realize the truth of things) function under very different conditions and importantly have very different consequences, given the nature of the practice and issue at hand. In this respect, across these distinctions and across these practices and disciplines there are errors of *direct* import and errors of *indirect* or *delayed* import, and it is this key difference that we need to bear in mind in the following. For example, a surgeon's mistake is highly costly for patient and surgeon alike: death or injury for the patient; being struck off or disciplined for the surgeon. (Indeed the high cost of such errors has become a branch of research all by itself in medical ethics.) Similarly, the goalkeeper who makes one too many unforced errors, losing matches and getting his team relegated, incurs huge financial costs to his club.[41] These are direct errors of high import, and therefore could hardly be said to be productive. On the other hand, the purposeful error of the artist and scientist in the pursuit of the 'unknown' is – possibly – productive, or at least relatively cost-free. In the short term or long term it may lead to the renewal or extension of a given 'research programme' or perhaps to the formation of a new one. In this respect the productive function of the error is not a universalizable condition of all practices; sometimes – contra Hegel's 'damage limitation' approach to error – errors do not necessarily secure a future for thinking and practice at all, but remain unassimilable, unsublatable, and thereby actually prevent and destroy practice and thinking. The error that destroys a career may be assimilated by an other or others, but not by the person who committed it. Accordingly, there is no sense of the virtuous 'error' in the abstract in this book; there are only contingent errors, matched by the contingent conditions of their production, assimilation, eradication and transformation.[42]

But are truths, therefore, simply errors in disguise, mistakes and failures waiting to be exposed in all their banality and elementariness? For the philosophy of science in the twentieth century, this represents a familiar picture of the positive category of the error: the recognition and eradication of errors provides the scientist with the means to 'go on' and inaugurate and possess new forms of knowledge. On this basis errors are a bit like hidden treasures: things that are invisible but are clearly known to be and therefore need to be chased up and hounded into visibility, thereby allowing the scientist to perform the very activity he or she is trained to do: the production of verifiable knowledge. The idea of the error-as-truth-in-disguise, however, is limited as a general model of the error by its overt or covert positivism. That is, errors in the pursuit of truth are more than busy little workers for veridical truth, more than the engine of scientific fallibilism. This is because the eradication of the error in the name of truth implies that errors exist only to be exposed and *eradicated* in the name of truth. Errors, however, also have another kind of life, a veiled and subterranean one, in which the exposure and verification of the error is always *struggling and failing* to enter the realm of knowledge. Indeed, in a paradoxical sense, it is precisely this failure of the error to give itself up to the operations of knowledge that constitutes its truth-value. This is the realm of the error in psychoanalysis, which represents the truth of the divided condition and opacity of the analysand *who cannot be told the truth*, and the analyst who is *unable to tell the truth*, because the truths he or she wants to tell the analysand are unable to freely find their target.

In psychoanalysis there is no bedrock of (or agreed) transparent rationality which analysand and analyst share. If this were so the analysand would be the consistent beneficiary of the knowledge and insights of the analyst. 'You are suffering from x, as a consequence of a and b, and I suggest you do y, in order to change or ameliorate this state of affairs.' But, as psychoanalysis shows us, in the practice of the session this is never the case given the analysand's resistance to his or her submission to the truth of the analyst. The truth of the subject, therefore, has to be discovered in other, 'non-veridical' ways by analyst and analysand. The analyst, in other words, has to forgo the pursuit and elucidation of knowledge-as-evidence in order to 'tell the truth', 'distractedly', at a glance – hence the centrality of the error, mistake, and the lapse as the key unconscious materials of truth in the Freudian and post-Freudian (Lacanian) session. Attention to these materials helps to expose the gap between what the analyst knows and what the analysand believes he or she thinks she knows about herself and the analyst. In this respect the analyst, as someone who knows something that the analysand doesn't know about herself, is not able to communicate this truth until the analysand knows that she 'doesn't know'.

The constitutive force and drama of the error in psychoanalysis brings us, accordingly, to the first psychological 'law' of social praxis: the law of non-contradiction, namely, *I cannot purposely and willingly and in good faith act against my own manifest purposes, beliefs and understanding*. As Plato says through the mouth of Socrates: 'we maintain that it is impossible for anyone not to possess that which he has possession of, and thus it never happens that he does not know something he knows.'[43] In other words, it is impossible to act on, or truly think, what I believe to be false. Thus, it is perfectly feasible for someone to argue for two propositions which are contradictory, but only if they are *not known* to be contradictory. What is not feasible is for someone to argue for two propositions knowing them *to be* contradictory.[44] As Wittgenstein argues, it is impossible – or 'idiotic' as he puts it – to say, 'I have never been on the moon – but I may be mistaken' (outside that is, of mental illness).[45] Similarly, I cannot insist that turning left in my car will lead me to safety and avoid driving off a cliff to my death, when I know turning right will secure this.[46] In other words acting on inconsistency is possible only when the subject is mistaken or lacks 'overall' knowledge. Now, of course, this doesn't exclude those – spies, con artists – who say and do things opposed to their true beliefs, just as we all might err on the side of concerted deception in order to cover our tracks or protect the sensitivities or interests of another. But even the spy doesn't actually *believe* what he or she appears to believe, because belief is a singular state, even if we all resort at times to deceiving others about our beliefs, or remain uncertain about our own beliefs. The law of non-contradiction, therefore, is evidence of how subjects act on beliefs (whether those beliefs are correct or not, or injurious to themselves or not); however, what it cannot answer is *why* people set out to deceive. This is why psychoanalysis is invaluable here: what psychoanalysis superadds to the law of non-contradiction is that error is constitutive of belief and action in a fully ideological fashion. Errors are not just the means whereby subjects actively externalize their own future horizons as knowing-subjects (the domain of learning through error), they are the very ground of subjectivity, belief and judgement. The effects of unconscious error and the consequences of the explicit error, the error of omission, haunt all our actions and judgements. Which brings us back to Engels's reflections on social praxis: social praxis's primary claim to manifest action and practical reason is also the extended realm of the unconscious act.

In this respect the law of non-contradiction lays the ground for a materialist and historical account of the error. Because the truth or untruth of our beliefs and actions cannot be spoken in the first person in the present tense, our recognition and assessment of error is necessarily both retrospective and social; criticism, therefore, is not derivable solely from self-reflection, but from our engagement with the observations, reflections and theories of others. Social theory and historical knowledge, as such, are constructed from the viewpoint and beliefs of the observer, not just from the viewpoint and beliefs of the historical subject;[47] and the viewpoint and beliefs of the observer will, in turn, be transformed by the viewpoint and beliefs of other observers (the depossessive subject).

In this way, political praxis is structured through self-ironization and the aleatory, in so far as the truth of human agency is presupposed by the accidental and the contingent. And this is, precisely, where art and political praxis overlap: art, like political praxis, grasps the potentiality of the moment and the future through a consciousness of truth-as-risk.[48] The decision to act may be based on the prior judgement and assessment of given or possible future conditions, but there is no point where the best outcome of a decision taken can be predicted or guaranteed in advance. This is why the decision-to-act invariably issues in a sense of failure and loss. Thus to act in the objective interests of a given outcome which is not predetermined (the making of an artwork, the making of a revolution) is something that, at the point of the decision taken to follow a particular action, is always premature. Now, this is not to confuse the making of artworks with the making of revolutions. Artworks are made all the time under these uncertain, contingent conditions, revolutions rarely. Yet both operate through a similar understanding of the relationship between reason and failure. To fail in the detail or totality of making an artwork or revolution is not to fail *as such*, and, therefore, to fail in securing the conditions for the future production of artworks and revolutions. On the contrary, failure regrounds the risk-seeking powers of future decisions. This is why, although some failures in art and political praxis necessarily remain failures, other failures provide the means by which future decisions are able to regain their explanatory bearings and cognitive and social settings. *The failure that results from poor judgement and misguided criteria, and that has a detrimental or nullifying effect on practice, is no less productive than the failure which transforms understanding and agency but is defeated in practice.* Consequently, in needing to distinguish between different orders of error we also need to distinguish between errors and different orders of truth and untruth. Thus although errors may lead to failure, we need to keep failure at an important level separate from the epistemological concept of error. This is because the place of failure in the relationship between praxis and desire is, in no strict sense, based on a veridical model of judgement. The failures of a given action, for example, may not be the result of any actual weakness or limitation on the part of an agent or agents, but, on the contrary, the outcome of the inhospitable, unsympathetic, underdetermined, or alienating circumstances or context in which the action is performed or attempted to be performed. This is the difference between the culpable error (the inappropriate action based on inattention or misjudgement) and the error that is derived from incapacity or impairment (lack of available access to knowledge). Thus the failure of an action in these circumstances is taken to be something that was, on the basis of retroactive reflection, beyond the immediate control of the agent or agents; there is, therefore, no *fundamental* error of thinking or judgement at stake. *Circumstances prevented the action succeeding.* Similarly, the failure of a given artistic process or strategy may be the result of a lack of knowledge or competence on the part of the artist, but this does not necessarily result in the artist moving forward on the basis of correcting his or her practice against a preconceived notion of what is competent. Rather, the acknowledgement of failure leads, even encourages, the artist to make something anew from a position athwart his or her perceived failure; and, in a sense, this process of adjustment and correction is potentially endless. In addition there can be no pejorative understanding of failure in psychoanalysis, given the fact that it is precisely failure that allows both analysand and analyst access to a process of free exchange and knowledge that unveils the truth of the speech of the analysand. So epistemological errors and failures of knowledge may be close partners across these disciplines and practices, but they are certainly not interchangeable. The important consideration here is that failure doesn't produce an objective loss to reason, given that nothing is lost to reason absolutely.

Now, in a way this sounds vacuously Hegelian and tautological. 'A lesson can be learned from every mistake.' But, nevertheless, there is something worth holding onto from the logic of Hegel's supersessive practice here. There are many instances where the production or errors are irreconcilable with good practice, but there is no point where the second-order theorization of these errors is extrinsic to practice as such. Errors are productive, then, in so far as they are able to be re-produced theoretically as truth-productive and incorporated into further practice. In these terms the productiveness of the error avoids all the problems associated with a Humean type scepticism, best exemplified by the well-known Clifford-Principle – avoid falsehood at *all* cost. 'It is wrong always, everywhere, and for everyone, to believe anything upon insufficient evidence.' If this vulgar (and violent) principle of evidential truth were applied with any consistency, very few of our beliefs and truth claims would pass muster, and as such little of our daily conversation, social relations and social practice would survive scrutiny. 'If all we are entitled to say we know must be absolutely certain, then of course we have no knowledge of the future, and no knowledge of anything else.'[49] Clifford-the-True, then, has impeccably high standards, higher than Descartes himself; he accepts absolutely nothing.[50]

But doesn't the productiveness of the error bring us back to the hard-line fallibilist or falsificationist concept of error in the post-Kuhnian philosophy of science? That is, back to the notion that the theoretical assimilation of the error produces the conditions for the transformation and expansion of the hard core of a research programme and veridical truth. Not strictly because, unlike in the sciences, social praxis and art's second-order assimilation of the error is not based on an *accumulative* account of the success or failure of a given research programme. The concept of transformation in science, then, is directed towards clarifying and refining the normative conditions of research on the basis of *discarding* error. The creative resources for this process may come from the lost creative byways of research (Paul Feyerabend, Imre Lakatos),[51] rather than from the perceived forefront and centre-stage of an institutionally legitimated research programme, but, nevertheless, research is indebted to the prevailing forms and standards of knowledge and practice in a given field. The actions of the scientist are predetermined precisely by customary, institutionalized practice, until that point when the accepted skills and procedures of various branches of a particular science are challenged and transformed by new research. Risk, in art and revolutionary practice, certainly, assimilates the error in a second-order fashion as the basis for clarifying future practice, but there is no generalizable theory of the error-free practice that might be handed down as a shared body of knowledge to other practitioners or activists. *There is no transferable theory of art, just as there is no transferable theory of revolution.* Rather, each situation and each event requires new kinds of risk-taking based on available experience. In other words, risk and the accumulated knowledge of past risks is a response to emergent and contingent sets of conditions.

Here something general and unifiable begins to emerge. In art and political praxis, because truth claims are necessarily situational, reflection on and incorpation of 'error' into knowledge therefore is subject to a model of truth which is radically discontinuous – even if the risk of action is based on a commitment to historical continuity. In science, in contrast, the situational production of truth claims is rationally contained and deepened by the history of science. That is, truth cannot proceed in a radically discontinuous fashion, in a kind of a Clifford-the-True fashion; it must exhibit a *non-arbitrary* relationship to the progress and development of science and knowledge. As Roy Bhaskar explains:

> in order to demonstrate some mistake some proposition must be asserted (some theory accepted and framework worked within). In order to learn from our mistakes we must *know* that (and when) we are mistaken. Lacking from fallibilism, as from classical empiricism, is the key concept of knowledge necessarily possessing a material cause: antecedently established knowledges; science's means of production. It is not necessary that a scientist works within any particular framework or accepts any particular theory; but it is necessary that he works within (accepts) one.[52]

The alternative is a mere Kuhnian shift and displacement of 'paradigms' in a collapse of science into relativism, pragmatism and the idea of research as a process of creative supersessions in the manner of neo-avant-garde art practice (although for Kuhn, paradoxicially, this discontinuity between paradigms is framed within a model of progress).[53] That is, with the unmooring of a theory of errors from a sense of the continuity of science (the acceptance of induction as justified and nature as uniform) we are unable to access a concept of truth, because clearly, without there being necessary connections between matters of fact, we would not know what errors would look like (as Plato first noted).[54] That is, all errors would look like truths, or rather, claim to be truths, in Nietzsche's sense. Falsificationism in science, therefore, is prior and operative, but, if science is to be an ongoing, social activity, it cannot, as Bhaskar says, *persistently* return negative verdicts. On the contrary, the refutations of fallibilism must, at some point, be *replacements*, and in functioning as replacements claim to deepen our knowledge. This means that for errors to be adjudged to be errors on the basis of the veridical claims of truths, and therefore re-inscribable in second-order fashion as productive, science must place a high emphasis on experimental testing as a continuous theoretical and practical resource (Deborah Mayo).[55]

This substantive methodological boundary between the self-ironizing actions of political praxis and artistic praxis and science forces us to decide, then, how we talk about errors and falsificationism as the motors of practice. Where does the productiveness of the error in science overlap with the productiveness of the error in art, philosophy, political praxis and psychoanalysis, and where does it divide?

Art's relationship to the claims of knowledge may be discontinuous and non-accumulative, but, nevertheless, it shares with science the notion that its judgements about best practice are based on some notion of the explanatory power of its theoretical commitments. Art may not have to subject itself to the inductive *principles* of science, but it still has to locate itself – outside of its own specific disciplinary demands – in relationship to the historical and social-scientific possibilities of collective praxis (even the most asocially exoticised high-modernist art). Art, even in its rejection or denial of the social, is a claim *on* the social and collective. So, even if no single artwork is falsifiable as a form or item of knowledge, its theoretical claims can certainly be evaluated in terms of the work's social coherence or incoherence, critical assiduousness or lack of assiduousness. But there is an important rider to this: whatever judgement about the social content of art might be made, the ironic function of the error in art is not subject to a rationalist, inductive assimilation. And this is where art diverges from both science and political praxis and converges with the lapsidian model of the error in psychoanalysis. That is, at a fundamental level the produc-tion and assimilation of the error in art is also about articulating the *limits* of art itself as a category.

THE ERROR AND THE LIMITS OF ART

In art, like science, the error is what sustains the possibility of practice: of 'going on'. But 'learning from mistakes' is not a shared resource across art's multiple voices and possibilites, something that improves the indi-vidual and collective powers and qualities of art. On the contrary, the error is what allows the artist to do what is *not* expected, and as such challenge the notion that art is improvable or better understood when it is assmilated on the basis of its pre-given conditions of familarity. Thus the production, possession and repossession of the error or mistake in art – that is, art's embodiment of the strategies of anti-art and anti-form, of inchoateness, 'failed speech' and 'failed communication', and all the other means of invoking non-identity, disorder, indeterminacy, and so on – is precisely about dissolving, qualifying, questioning, and undermining those heteronomous processes that bring art into being as a category. Science and political praxis do not assimilate the error (or failure) in this way. Science and political praxis do not voluntarily seek their own destruction or dissolution as categories, or subject themselves to a succession of feints and dodges, on the basis of the critique of their alienated character. This would lead to chronic incoherence and indecision. Ultimately, therefore, the self-ironizing production and assimilation of the error in art – under the supersession of art itself as a category – represents a universal claim on truth, and, as such, on all such other claims to truth. In short, the unwillingness of art to accept the constant pressure to assimilate itself to capitalist exchange and capitalist reason, is a reproach to the failure of science to provide a consistent and substantive critique of its own alienated character. Accordingly, the error in art, art's refusal to do the right thing, the proper thing, might be better seen, not as critique of science as such, but as a critique of the *social relations* of science, and therefore a reflection on what the place of a future non-alienated conception of art might be under a non-alienated conception of science – that is, under the creative transformation of both art and science as forms of collective social and cultural praxis.[56] In this way the error in art (and psychoanalysis) is, under capitalism, able to take on a privileged dialectical role, in contrast to the role of the error in science and political praxis. That is, art's self-ironizing critique and displacement of its own conditions of possibility challenges the reified identity and instrumental functionality and limits of the production of truth in other practices (See Chapter 5).[57]

One should be absolutely clear though here. This is not an argument about the strengths and virtues of non-veridical truths and the limitations of veridical truth. That is, this is not a version of standard Romanticist critiques of scientific reason. But rather that at some point the truth claims of science and political praxis must be convergent with the aleatory and non-consequential effects of the aesthetic, or more precisely 'aesthetic thinking'. By this I mean that what art continues to produce and effect, even under its locked down commodification, is a determinate negation of what is 'proven to be the case', the pre-given pathways of knowlege. It therefore asks questions about its relationship to power, institutions, truth, knowledge, that the veridical claims of science can only partially ask, under the strict law of science's inner development. This is why art and psychoanalysis have come to establish a profound relationship to truth under mature capitalism. This is because both identify the error and failure as a source not just of the development, or improvement, of a research programme, but the constitutive means of *sustaining* praxis-as-truth, of renewing the possibility of truth, against its positivistic enemies. Indeed, in psychoanalysis, the error, as one of the manifestations of the unconscious, has a significant part to play in resisting the constant social and cultural pressure (both inside and outside of psychoanalysis as a discipline) to humanistically re-centre knowledge, truth, the self and the will.[58] The 'error' in psychoanalysis is always testimony to *other* causal chains.

Assimilating the error to truth in the renewal of truth, then, is not the same as drawing a veil over truth. Rather, the purposefulness of the error here derives from the desire *for* truth; the recognition and reflection on errors is that which *renews a compulsion for truth*, and not the dissolution or eradication of truth as such. The error, therefore, in keeping at some level with the epistemological and historical capaciousness of Hegel, is the motor of truth, the thing that keeps truth in the air, in movement, rather than that uninvited, disruptive thing which prevents truth or lies outside of truth. The error is, consequently, constitutive *of* the truth-form; its special intimate.

ONE

ERROR, TRUTH AND THE SUBJECT

THE ERROR AND THE POSSESSING SUBJECT

In *Theaetus*, Plato's famous exposition of Socrates' dialogic method, he examines the formation, conditions, applications and applicability of knowledge. He begins this by first deposing intellectual authority – the philosopher – as the arbiter of knowledge. In this, the philosopher – Socrates – reveals himself to be merely a facilitator, not a fount of 'first principles'. When people come to learn from him, Socrates says, they in fact reveal that how much they know is a result of their own actions and powers of reflection. 'I am not in any sense a wise man; I cannot claim as the child of my own soul any discovery worth the name of wisdom.'[1] In this sense Plato begins the *Theaetus* with a defence of knowledge as self-production, or as an autogenetic process. 'All are wise' may be Plato's motto here. This allows Plato to move the dialogue on knowledge and truth forward in accordance with Socrates' interlocuter, the eponymous Theaetus. As such, in dialogue with Theaetus, Plato is then able to address on what basis do we know. If knowledge is self-production, is it the result simply of direct experience or perception, or the 'creative ideas' of the subject, or is it rather a process of reflection on such experiences and perceptions? Plato argues that knowledge and perception are not convergent and that only a 'process of reasoning'[2] is able to 'grasp being and truth'.[3] But importantly, there is no process of reasoning and reflection without us knowing what we have perceived, that is without us being able to recall the thing we have seen and distinguish it from other (like or unlike) things. Therefore knowledge is a claim to

knowledge *of* things and not the outcome of speculations or supposi-
tions about such things. Consequently, error or the failure to know is not
possible outside of knowledge's basis in our familiarity with (and recall)
of these things. In this, Plato talks about things in the world imprinting
themselves on the senses, and the clearer and more lasting these imprints
are, the better the person is able to 'judge truly'.[4] The production of
error *as* error, therefore, is as a result of our sensuous possession of a
given thing. '[A]t no point does it happen that we do not possess what we
possess, whether we are in error about anything or not.'[5] The upshot of
this is that *we can only be mistaken about something we have knowledge of already*
(and not mere de-contextualized guess-work). The massive significance
of Plato's *Theaetus* lies, therefore, in the fact that knowledge is necessary for error. Or rather, an error is not worth talking about and assess-
ing unless it is grounded in the subject's familarity with – or possession
of, in Plato's language – the thing in question. In the earlier work (*The
Republic*), however, error tended to be identified with ignorance per se.
Failing to know is seen simply as the absence of knowledge. The *Theaetus*,
in contrast, as Bernard Williams says, addresses

> the fundamental point that error is not only different from mere ignorance, but
> in a certain way excludes it. I can only make a mistake about something only if I
> know it, or know something about it, or know enough about it for my false belief
> to be a belief about the thing.[6]

This leads us to ask: what do we need to know in order to make, or recognize, a mistake?

This immanent model of the error grounds Western epistemology, in
so far as this tradition takes as axiomatic that the subject must have knowledge of a thing before it can offer a true or false belief about it. In this
respect the Platonic model seeks to wrest the production and verification of knowledge from mere opinion or doxa. Thus, significantly, Plato
distinguishes error from ignorance in order to stress that the accumulation
of knowledge, and its accomplishments, is a hesitant and extended process. This is why the de-subjectivization of knowledge is simultaneously
accompanied by its embodiment in – to use a modern construct – the
fallible subject: the subject who strives to know, and know more. Hence
the methodological imperative of Socratic dialogue for Plato: knowledge
is worked towards on the basis of the putting to work of the immanent

powers of human reflection. In this respect the error is necessary to, and constitutive of, this process of labour.

But this is not a theory of the productive-error in the modern Hegelian sense, as I mapped out in the introduction. This is because Plato does not accord any special powers to the error; it is not as yet the 'motor' of truth, so to speak. Rather, more prosaically, in discerning truth from error there must be, as Plato rightly insists, subjects who actually seek to embody this truth-seeking process, otherwise truth is simply, and crudely, no more than handed-down 'true judgement'. The possessing subject of truth, then, is what Plato's philosophy passes onto the Enlightenment and its struggle with scepticism and the formation of scientific method: the *subject who labours to know*.

Thus, in Descartes's *Meditations on First Philosophy*, the possessing subject becomes crucial to the very foundation of the subject of truth, the subject who labours to know. 'I' possess truth on the basis of the autonomous powers of my intellect. But here possession is something quite different to that in Plato. Descartes certainly inherits Plato's distrust of the senses, but in the name of 'pure thought' the processual possession of knowledge by the intellect is stripped back to a bare-boned scepticism. For Descartes only two things are certain: his own existence as a thinking being and the existence of God. In fact the former is wholly dependent on the latter. He knows that he possesses the faculty of judgement and intellect, and he knows that these faculties guarantee him the powers of truthful reflection, but only because he knows that everything worthwhile in him is derived from the largesse of God, because everything of worth in the world is derived from this largesse of God's. So, since he cannot believe that God would want to deceive him, 'he surely did not give me the kind of faculty which would ever enable me to go wrong while using it correctly.'[7] But despite this belief in the goodwill of God, Descartes recognizes that the faculty of true judgement is nevertheless subject to many mistakes and inconsistencies. When it comes to turning away from God – turning away from contemplating God's infinite powers – and reflecting on himself, 'I know by experience that I am prone to countless errors.'[8] Thus in the *Meditations on First Philosophy* Descartes sets out to address this gap and pinpoint the source of these errors of judgement as the outcome of the process of 'pure' judgement itself. In doing so he revises the assumption that the perfection of God is in any way coextensive with the gifts the deity bestows on humans, and therefore, the idea that the faculty of judgement could be anything *but* imperfect. '[I]n so far as I am not myself the supreme being and am lacking in countless respects, it is no wonder that I make mistakes. I understand, then, that error as such is not something real which depends on God, but merely a defect.'[9] Conseqently, in contrast to the infinite powers of God, his own nature, is 'very weak and limited'.[10] This essential weakness of his faculties then, is the basis by which Descartes will examine the cause of his errors.

But the weakness of the faculties is not the result of any weakness of intellectual understanding per se, the outcome of any kind of inherent feebleness ('for since my understanding comes from God, everything that I understand I undoubtedly understand correctly.')[11] The problem lies, rather, in the fact that when errors occur, they occur as a result of the intellect having extended itself to matters it doesn't or cannot understand. It is the over-confidence of the intellect, or over-extension of the will, therefore, that is for Descartes the cause of error. Because when the will turns aside from what is amenable to the intellect – what is 'true and good'[12] – the faculty of judgement is unable to 'perceive the truth with sufficient clarity and distinctness.' As a result judgement falls into the sinful clutches of indistinctness and vaguery. In order to avoid error, the answer, Descartes insists, is to withhold judgement on things that one does not know about, or is uncertain about, 'for if, whenever I have to make a judgement, I restrain my will so that it extends to what the intellect clearly and distinctly reveals, and no further, then it is quite impossible for me to go wrong.'[13] Hence it is always preferable for the subject to refrain from making hasty judgments because the production of error is usually the result of ideas prematurely advanced or adhered to. The production of error, therefore, is the outcome of the injudicious use of ideas, and these are injudicious or false precisely because in failing to accurately represent their object (material or otherwise), they open up the subject to mistaking what they take to be true as what is true. So, errors can be avoided if, and only if, the intellect is put into practice in instances where attention is given to those things 'I truly understand'.[14] Errors are prevented only when the subject is overwhelmingly certain that what is being denied or affirmed obtains or does not obtain. In turn, this judicious distillation and application of the understanding confirms God's bestowal of intellect. Once it is recognized and accepted that the intellect is limited – once the indeterminacies of intellectual hubris and immediacy are cast aside – the truth-telling powers of the subject are then able to coincide with those of

God. In essence, when one does perceive clearly it is exemplary evidence of God's largesse at work.

The logic of this argument in this form – I understand with clarity what I understand with clarity – is clearly circular. Yet, Descartes' scepticism about what is received from the senses places his philosophy in tension with any concept of knowledge as 'received' understanding from God or with religious revelation. Although God bestows the light of reason, we are all responsible for our errors, and therefore, we are all responsible for correcting them. Thus it is precisely because we are prone to errors and are able to recognize them, that I am able 'to free myself from preconceived opinions'[15] and knowledge is able to proceed. In this respect, as a number of Cartesian scholars have pointed out, this mediation of the ideal through the imperfect or impure, has its origins in Augustine's cosmology.[16]

In, *On Free Choice of the Will*, Augustine argues that the visible absence of perfection in the universe is the means by which we achieve our perception of its harmonious wholeness.[17] That is, the localized absence of perfection in the universe is how we recognise the perfection of the whole; in the absence of perfection – in the localized manifestation of the corrupt and ugly – perfection is enhanced overall. But how can a universe created by God be both perfect and imperfect simultaneously? This is because, as indivisible, and consequently, as the representation of absolute perfectability, God cannot possibly bestow perfectability on his created forms. This would make all things indivisible with God's perfectability and therefore nullify his exceptionalism. All created things, accordingly, are limited in their perfection, and as such, what 'perfections' living creatures are able to possess are only relative to this absolute perfectability. However, although God is the creator of the universe – of its material diversity and imperfections in living creatures – the internal and external corruption of these bestowed imperfections is not created by God. The corruptibility of nature, therefore, is the means by which God defines his harmonious work through living things, although he is not the author of these forms of corruptibility. That is because the corrupted absence of perfection is not created by God, this allows the larger forces of harmony to prevail and thereby define and enhance God's work of perfection. Descartes argues for something similar in his theo-epistemology. The errors of judgement and perception, although the outcome of imperfect faculties bestowed by God, are not dependent on God. Consequently, the imperfection in human faculties is one of the means whereby living beings are able to be distinguished from the indivisibility of God; otherwise living beings would possess God-like infallibility and possess the kind of unbearable, implausible, super-percipience I describe at the beginnning of the introduction. Thus although Descartes tests and probes the senses in the interests of clarity and truth, he is also quite relieved that the human senses are not the failed or feeble organs of God-like super-percipience. This is where 'error' becomes interesting in a proto-scientific and anti-theistic way in his writing. Because God is not the donor of human error, any errors that derive from the use of our own faculties are the result of our own weaknesses and deficiencies. In this sense, although man is an imperfect creature (in Augustine's sense) his imperfection takes on a more capacious meaning once his finititude as a living creature is recognized. Although man can never know things as God knows them, absolutely, nonetheless as a finite thinker, a creature susceptible to error through free will, he is able in certain circumstances to shed the privations of error, and, as such, contribute to the greater harmony of God's whole. As Cecilia Wee explains:

> Since he cannot inhabit the divine point of view, he cannot understand God's purposes in making him imperfect and prone to error (or even how such error can be freely willed within that order). Thus, Descartes can only evaluate the order of the universe as it relates to himself – that is, from his own finite point of view. From this finite perspective he recognizes error to be the absence of a perfection that he could possess, and should work towards.[18]

Descartes' working towards the removal of the privation of error as a 'pure' reflection on reason is the foundation of seventeenth-century epistemology: If I judge 'without prejudice and clearly I will judge truly'. In this way the Cartesian revolution is a huge challenge to school philosophy with its indebtedness to truth-through-inherited-authority. But in John Locke, the great inheritor of Descartes' mantle, Descartes' emphasis on the conditions of certainty is dimmed, transforming the relations between self, truth and error. Like Descartes, Locke declares the self-rationalizing self as the key nodal point of reason. It is only on the basis of my own powers of reflection that I am able to critique forms of inherited and customary thinking: 'If thou judgest for thyself I know thou wilt judge candidly.'[19] Similarly he declares that the bounds of reason should not overstretch themselves. 'If we can find out how far the understanding can extend its view, how far it has faculties to attain certainty, and in what cases it can only judge and guess, we may learn to content ourselves with what is attainable by us in this state.'[20]

Thus, as in Descartes, he takes a certain distance from the elevated ambitions of pure reason. But here the key phrase is 'we may learn to content ourselves'. Like Descartes, Locke is keen to protect the intellect from 'disputes about things to which our understandings are not suited.'[21] But, in this instance, the rejection of an over-active will is not a just way of allowing us to take cognisance of what *is* true (as an expression of God's beneficence and powers of intellectual bestowal). Rather, for Locke, because we cannot exercise certainty over all things we should actually be *unworried* that some things escape our knowledge. In other words, Descartes' anxiety over certainty and the indulgences of hubristic imagination may be right – the very foundation of knowledge – but they also too easily put in jeopardy the pursuit of forms of knowledge within a narrowly verifiable grasp of reason. This is because Descartes' essential mathematical model of certainty, of the corroboration between truth and God – mathematical truth being the imprint of God's reason – is too indebted to a notion of intellectual innateness: when we define truths we are, in a sense, confirming their prior, hidden existence. Locke, then, asserts, like Descartes, the limits to knowledge (and the sham claims to truth inherent in flights of imagination) but, at the same time, gives a new materialist emphasis to the Platonic notion of possession in the production of knowledge. Thus what distinguishes Locke's epistemology is that reason is not just something refined through the explusion of the errors of perception and logic, but the *learning and development of the logical and perceptual procedures* of 'clear' thinking. Reason has to be *exercised*, moreover, it has to be subject to the individual attainment of a shared process of dispute.[22] In this, the re-affiliation with Plato, is, at another level, also marked by an anti-Platonic rejection of reason exposing its own innateness to the exercise of human powers. Knowledge is not lodged dormant in a singular understanding, but has to be produced through learning and the exercise of the faculty of judgement.

> [M]en are supposed not to be *taught* nor to *learn* anything *de novo*, when, in truth, they are taught and do learn something they were ignorant of before. For, first, it

is evident they have learned the terms and their significance, neither of which was born with them.[23]

A certain decentring of reason, or exchange of the practice-of-reason for pure reason occurs here. Whereas, in Descartes, reason is made the outcome of the vigilant rational subject, in Locke we find the first (Kantian) indications of human reason as a historical and social process:

> human knowledge, under the present circumstances of our beings and constitutions, may be carried much further than it hitherto has been, if men would sincerely and with freedom of mind employ all that industry and labour of thought in improving the means of discovering truth.[24]

In this light Locke is remarkably candid about how little science and philosophy (in the seventeenth century) does know, asserting that knowledge rarely reaches beyond experience. 'I fear the weakness of human understanding'[25] . . . 'Our knowledge being so narrow'.[26] . . . There is a 'huge abyss of ignorance'.[27] '[W]e are utterly incapable of universal and certain knowledge'.[28] *'[W]e have very imperfect ideas of substances.'*[29] As such, Locke places the greater emphasis on what he calls the need for *ideas* (conceptual abstractions), the want of which continues to produce these levels of ignorance and the reduction of thinking to experience. The reign of 'darkness',[30] 'destitute senses',[31] 'disproportionate'[32] knowledge, then drives Locke's Cartesianism, producing an extraordinary and relentless bifurcation of reason: on the one hand the need and requirement to expand the (nascent) sciences and on the other the sheer difficulty of this task. The result is that a very different tone and set of expectations enters philosophy's theorization of the error and mistake. Whereas in Descartes the explusion of error is made to reinforce the splendour of 'pure reason' (disbelieve everything that is not certain and the light of God will illuminate and release your powers of reason), in Locke, knowledge and error are made to get on 'piecemeal' in order to get science moving. This is why *An Essay Concerning Human Understanding* uses the images of the defeat of reason so much and so startlingly. The light of God's reason may shine down on the faculty of judgement, but not at the expense of the human intellect and the production of reason. As a result, for all Locke's fealty to a Cartesian vision of God's bounty, he is militant about not confusing faith with knowledge. 'For *faith* can never convince us of anything that contradicts our knowledge.'[33] Which is to say that assent for any given proposition cannot be derived from any form of revelation, religious or secular. '[W]hatsover truth we come to the clear discovery of from the knowledge and contemplation of our own *ideas*, will always be certainer to us than those which are conveyed to us by *traditional revelation*.'[34] Wild supposition in science is no different from the assertion that belief alone can ground truth. Both substitute speculation for the process of reason – the premature possession of the thing by the idea.

What Immanuel Kant inherits from Locke and Descartes is that philosophical error leads from an overactive imagination, religious or otherwise. Indeed, what tends to produce error is what Spinoza calls a kind of feigning,[35] or a willingness to let the senses take over the necessity of ideas. But if Kant inherits the anti-sense machinery of seventeenth-century epistemology, he does so without unduly preoccupying himself with the discussion of errors and mistakes per se. In this sense, the theorization of the philosophical or rational subject in Kant is not solely an epistemological problem, as in Descartes and Locke, in so far as knowledge and truth are not *organized* around the defensive figure of the fallible subject, who invariably fails to know, or fails to make good on what he claims to know. In this, the ambitions of thinking are set far in advance of what we can confidently claim to understand – with clarity and distinctiveness – through our sensible, empirical intuition. Indeed, this is the great Copernican revolution of Kant: knowledge requires input not just from the senses but from *organizing concepts*. Or rather, empirical intuition and conceptualization are mututally dependent. As he says in the *Prolegomena*: 'Experience . . . can never teach us the nature of things in themselves.'[36] Judgements of experience are not based on the direct cognition of the object, but on pure concepts of understanding which are not dependent on the variabilities of experience. The pure concepts of the understanding, therefore, are *a priori* principles of possible intuitions. Thus, in contrast to Descartes and Locke, experience is not a mere ensemble of empirical experiences. However, the faculty of understanding is not an autonomous category, but rather, the place of conceptual connection of given empirical intuitions. Consequently, when we read Kant, Descartes and Locke seem extraordinarily *pre*-conceptual, in as much as the 'destitution' in knowledge Locke talks about so vividly produces an unmistakeable philosophical tentativeness at the level of philosophical abstraction. Kant shatters this tentativeness by linking reason and the understanding with conceptual thinking. 'The greatest part, of the business of our reason consists in the analyzation of the conceptions which we already possess of objects.'[37] In this respect Kant pushes certainty and error further back in his considerations than its empirical justification in Descartes and Locke by reflecting on how it is we know what we claim to know. How does experience of the world acquire certainty, he says, when our experience and empirical knowledge is itself fragmented and fortuitous? It acquires certainty, or claims for certainty, through the application and use of cognitions – *a priori* cognitions which lie above the sphere of daily experience and which humans possess as an immanent mechanism and achievement of consciousness. These *a priori* cognitions as the materiality of consciousness, in other words, organize how and under what conditions thinking takes place, allowing us to conceive of objects and causal processes beyond the limits of our sensible, empirical intuition. Accordingly, Kant introduces into the vagaries of human reason, a bridge between the two traditions I have briefly mapped out: a classical and Platonic philosophy of ideas and a Cartesian critical empiricism. Plato released thinking from the inhibitions of the senses, but in the process abandoned understanding to the 'void space of the pure intellect';[38] Descartes and Locke challenged the anti-empirical recklessness of Scholasticism, but in turn they were unable to reflect on the conditions of the possibility of thinking itself (without falling, as in Descartes' case, into theism).

> Thought is certainly not a product of the senses, and in so far is not limited by them, but it does therefore follow that it may be employed purely and without the intervention of sensibility, for it would then be without reference to an object.[39]

In this sense, the driving force of Kant's philosophy is the demotion of scepticism from the forefront of philosophy, and as such is part of a general raising of philosophy's conceptual tone.[40] Kant's overall schema is perhaps best understood, paradoxically, as a *re-classicizing* of philosophical modernity as philosophy emerges from its pre-modern conditions. That is, Plato may have led philosophy into the indivisibilities of the void, but following Plato, above all else, humans' capacity for understanding has a much 'higher vocation than that of merely spelling out phenomena according to synthetical unity.'[41] As a result, Descartes and Locke's empirical preoccupation with the perils and pitfalls of the error looks like a distraction, a way of delimiting philosophy and actually lowering its tone, or at least failing to raise it. Thus, in one of the few sections in the *Critique of Pure Reason* where Kant talks directly about errors, the section on the Transcendental Dialectic, he sets out to abandon any notion that the senses or empirical intuition in fact err or make mistakes at all. This is because the senses, in fact, do not *judge* and therefore are not in a position to make mistakes.

> It is therefore quite correct to say that the senses do not err, not because they always judge correctly, but because *they do not* judge at all. Hence truth and error, consequently also, illusory appearance as the cause of error, are only to be found in a judgement, that is, in the relation of an object to our understanding. In a cognition, which completely harmonizes with the laws of the understanding, no error can exist. In a representation of the senses – as not containing any judgement – there is also no error.[42]

In other words, errors do not derive from the failure or weakness of our faculties but from a breakdown or weakness in our understanding and knowledge. Therefore, a reversal of Cartesian priorities takes place here. Errors do not pre-exist the understanding, something the understanding comes along to sort out later after the truthful exercise of our perceptions, but are coterminuous with its operations. In these terms there is a significant decentring of the empirical, Cartesian philosophical subject. Subjects make errors, certainly, and they make them with their given faculties, of course, but the production of errors is not the result of the faculties' subjection to an overactive and excessive will. On the contrary, because the will (here the act of conceptualization) is the very motor of understanding, the subject is thereby not caught up in a sceptical and self-scrutinizing resistance to its excesses. The theological premise upon which Descartes' pure reason is organized – the *self*-rationalizing self that knows what the senses bestow truly through God because he abjures distraction – is discarded, to be replaced by the cognitive and historical mechanisms of reason. 'Reason sets out from the idea of totality'[43] – that is from the historical and ontological structures in which humans find themselves. This means that the Cartesian *fallibility* of the thinking subject – the notion that it is humans who are responsible for their errors – is no longer expressed in terms of the fraught gap between the tremulous self-scrutinizing subject and the world (between the knowledge of God's perfection and the active incarnation of human imperfection), but, as the temporal basis of understanding.

For, as Kant puts it, our internal intuition of the world is only possible mediately, through external experiences and our temporal conditioning. We cannot escape a critical account of reason, then, simply by advancing 'the limited nature of our faculties'.[44] The outcome is that errors are no longer the thing that our God-given faculties help us to avoid in a state of 'suspended' purity, but the very material of reason, 'the permanent condition of all actions of the human will.'[45]

But if Kant downplays the philosophical priority given to the error within the empirical realm of the faculties – as the thing that supposedly stymies our thinking and reason – he opens it up in another direction. In his attack on Cartesian critical empiricism as a 'pretended science'[46] he argues that it is impossible for the subject to develop an empirical understanding of their own psychology, of 'internal sense'. This is because the subject cannot present itself as a self as an object of its own thought processes. Descartes' pure, rational thinking 'I', therefore, is the thing *to be* explained, and not the thing to be assumed, because 'I am' can never be a predicate to thought. I 'do not represent myself in thought either as I am, or as I appear to myself; I merely cogitate myself as an object in general, of the mode of intuiting which I make abstraction.'[47] In other words, I cannot explain my own thought processes to myself because reflection on the fact 'I am thinking', or 'I'm thinking this', is purely speculative. I can certainly say 'I am' refers to a subject, myself, here and now, but this proposition does not contain any empirical knowledge of what it is to be a subject, myself, here and now. As Freud and Lacan and others have noted, this gap between self-consciousness and self-knowledge is one of the key entry points of psychoanalysis. In critiquing Descartes' pure reason, Kant presents the subject of truth as divided against itself. This means that error – as Hegel and Lacan were later to acknowledge – is situated *in* the operations of truth and reason itself, and therefore not something that can be isolated and excluded on the basis of reason. Because what we know of ourselves cannot be identical with the truth of ourselves, self-knowledge is what others bring to the understanding of ourselves and our understanding of others. Which is another way of saying, contra Descartes, that, as Georges Dicker puts it, we 'derive even knowledge of our inner states from knowledge of things outside us.'[48]

However, to turn Kant into a precursor of psychoanalysis, is not to turn Kant into a theorist of the irreconciled or divided subject.[49] Thus, if Kant dissociates the error from the operation of the faculties, in order to locate it in the operations of historical, knowledge-producing subjects, it would be wrong to assume that, as the 'inventor' of the subject, to quote Étienne Balibar,[50] Kant has a formalized psychological interest in error as a discrete category of knowledge. On the contrary, the error is still the thing to be challenged and expunged in the interests of reason. With the development of new fields of scientific knowledge, the subject-of-knowledge is at pains, first and foremost to resist the deceptions and 'illusions' of the mind, and as such the 'evil consequences of error.'[51]

> [W]here reason is not held in a plain track by the influence or of pure intuition [mathematics], that is, when it is employed in the transcendental sphere of pure conceptions, it stands in great need of discipline, to restrain its propensity to overstep the limits of possible experience, and to keep it wandering into error.[52]

Thus, at one level, this is still the language of Descartes here. Yet, in breaking away from the classic position of the Logos as the fixed site of reason, Kant is the first philosopher to theorize reason as a dynamic and historical process. Thus, although Kant is preoccupied, in the *Critique of Pure Reason*, with the development of transcendental forms of reason – with the subject's powers of abstract reasoning – these are constituted and transformed by a rational subject, who is in turn, transformed by these transformations. In this, Kant *historicizes* reason; reason is linked to the practical and theoretical operations of the thinking subject. As Yirmiyahu Yovel argues:

> No set of universal norms is rational in itself, except as it is constituted by the subject and can be recognized by him as such. And correspondingly, we become rational not by complying with a system of preestablished norms, but by setting up the norms with with which we comply.[53]

In these terms it is possible to see the function of the error in Kant as split between, on the one hand, the contingent operations of historical reason, and on the other, the transcendental drive to raise the conceptual or scientific tone of philosophy. By this I mean that the error takes on an explicit dualistic character: for the knowledge producing subject, the error is the thing that *limits* reason as self-knowledge, yet on the other hand, it is the thing that scientific ambitions of philosophy must *dispel* at all costs. Indeed science's capitulation either to occasional or to systematic error is 'reprehensible'.[54] This, of course, is an expression of a deeper antinomy in Kant's philosophy: the absence of any dialectical bridge between the rationalizing subject and empirical history. Kant may open up the operations of reason to history, and he may in turn decentre knowledge from the Cartesian certainties of 'I am' or 'I believe', but this finitude of reason is placed in unyielding tension with an overarching rational teleology. History is the process by which humans realize their powers of reason, in defiance, so to speak, of their actual limits as reasoning beings. Indeed it is precisely this gap between the finititude of human reason and the ideal ends of reason that drives history towards the development of freedom and the highest good. The subject, in a sense, strives towards this ideal horizon. But bridging this gap, therefore, places inordinate pressures on the finite rational subject to meet the requirement demanded of these ends. Human reason as historical reason needs moral education and sustained enlightenment and, therefore, is an accumulative process.

Consequently, after the publication of the *Critique of Pure Reason*, much of Kant's philosophy is taken up with bringing the finititude of reason into alignment with the demands of practical action, or practical reason, in which reason is sustained and developed within an expanding ethical community. We have to 'examine reason not in relation to objects, but in relation to [the] will and its causality.'[55] It is not surprising then, that the rational subjects who are best placed to sustain this community – those with time and leisure to reflect on reason's educative demands – are the aristocracy and the emerging bourgeoisie. Indeed, as the facilitator and fount of enlightened ideas, the higher classes realize reason's universal interests, thereby putting in place the conditions for the abolition of unreason (exploitation, superstition, ignorance). Kant's historicization of reason, therefore, is confined to where reason – in the eighteenth century – is believed to best find itself: that fraction of the bourgeoisie and aristocracy that endorsed and participated in the Enlightenment's scientific self-reflection.[56] What it is unable to do, for fear of reason's dissolution, however, is embed itself in the experience of all social classes, and therefore in those spheres of action and reflection where reason would not seem to operate, or only provisionally. Kant then, fails to fully historicize the development of the powers of reason, in so far as the operations of reason do not transcend its privileged 'transcendental' sphere; reason is embedded in those practices and forms which appear rational, from the perspective of the enlightened bourgeoisie and aristocracy. In other words, rationality is seen to be absent from those lower forms of culture and politics that are unable to meet Kant's transcendental criteria. This makes it impossible for Kant to think of the error as the actual *site* of reason. Indeed, what Kant provides for a productive theory of the error, with one hand – the gap between self-consciousness and self-knowledge – he takes away with the other: the confinement of the historical development of reason to where it is most 'conspicuously' transcendently embedded.

ERROR AND THE DEPOSSESSIVE SUBJECT

It is Hegel, then, who will accomplish what Kant's failed to do: unite empirical history with the operations of reason. And as such, Hegel, can be seen as the first theorist of error as the site of knowledge, enlightenment and emancipation. This is made strikingly apparent in Hegel's first major work, the *Phenomenology of Spirit*, in particular, the well-known preface on philosophy and scientific methodology.[57] In the preface Hegel pushes the Kantian antinomy between the rational subject and empirical experience, reason and history, to breaking point. The rational subject is no longer, as in its residual Cartesian form in Kant, constituted as a point of preconstitutive reflection on reality, but is actually, materially, sensuously constituted by its (fragmentary and conflicted) engagement in the world. Consequently Hegel's principal line of attack is a critique of the notion that the development of reason is determined by the autonomous, self-stabilizing application of formal processes of thought to external objects. The subjective pure 'I' of Kant – that which secures the ground of understanding through its unifying powers of consciousness – is not directly self-positing, but, on the contrary, the outcome of a self-reconstituting process; the self negates its identity, returning to itself as a positive, actualized identity, that in turn, is subject to further negation and further positivisation. '[T]his self-reflection in being-other – and not some original unity as such, or an immediate thing as such – is the true.'[58] Accordingly, 'certainty' has merely a provisional or notional status for Hegel. Claims on truth are not the ready-made outcome of a given methodology or formal process, but are subject to the mediations of the self's non-identity with itself, and the subject's mediation with the non-identity of other selves. '[T]ruth is not a minted coin which can be pocketed as such, finished and ready.'[59] This places the operations of truth in conflict with the idea of certainty *tout court*, in so far as truth emerges as a consequence of a processual unfolding and mutuality. And this is why immediate sense-certainty – as a primary example of the failure of truth – begins the *Phenomenology* and *truth-as-process* emerges at the end.

In this sense, although Hegel inherits the Cartesian/Kantian 'I' as the necessary starting point of knowledge, he subjects it to a thorough going historicization, in which truth is the interdependent and supercessive movement of itself within itself. *Truth is historical or it is nothing.* The overarching significance of this is paramount, in so far as the conflation of truth with certainty is dissolved. That is, in opposition to Kantian abstract rationality and all hitherto metaphysics, the object of truth does not stand solely to be refuted and demolished, and therefore to be discarded, but to be sublated as a weak or failed part of a larger and unfolding truth process. In this the self-negating subject demands or necessitates a methodological transformation in understanding. The process of negation does not stand above what it speaks of, but incorporates it in a positive manner, into new forms, which contribute in their particularity, to an emerging (non-teleological) 'whole'. As such, claims on truth are subject to two interrelated outcomes: no single proposition or sentence can speak for the truth, and as such exists as a partial and contingent truth-form ('the finitude of the partial categories of understanding');[60] and truth claims are continually transformed in the light of their immanent critique and sublation, forming an unfolding whole ('the whole evolution is what constitutes the content and the interest').[61] In this sense, the negation of the object of truth is a self-nourishing process; the re-possession of the object is formed from its inadequacies and failures, which in turn are opened up to further negation and re-possession. The implications for a productive theory of error are both obvious and profound here. The recognition and possession of truth is predicated on an emergent and immanent process of conceptualization, rather than being imposed formally on objects, and therefore, internally and externally driven by the contradictions and inadequacies of its objects of understanding. As such, error is not the the thing to be abhorred at all costs, the thing that reason must drive out of science, but is constitutive of the wider and unfolding movement of knowledge and truth. 'Error or other-being, when superseded, is still a necessary dynamic element of truth: for truth can only be where it makes itself its own result.'[62] The profundity of this statement lies in Hegel's refusal to follow Kant in assuming that contradictions and inadequacies are *sufficient* enough for the object of understanding to be discarded. On the contrary, what is discarded contributes through its inadequacies or contradictions to the historical labour of reason.

This is what Hegel means by the error being the dynamic element of truth. For although, in the Cartesian-Lockean-Kantian sense, errors are still very much things to be eradicated from the science of philosophy for Hegel, through their supersession they provide the means by which new forms of knowledge emerge. Consequently, in forthright opposition to Kant, Hegel places a greater emphasis on the *preservation* of the superseded object as a source of knowledge, thereby giving the epistemological function of the error a wholly new status – or at least a new status which is at odds with the logic of Cartesian-Kantian 'abstract' rationality. The error in its negation and supersession establishes an *explicit positivity*. In this we might talk of a 'new life' of the error in Hegel, then, in as much as the teleology of reason is given another kind of trajectory. Truth is no longer the possession of the pure rational subject (and by extension that of Kant's ideal community: the bourgeois and aristocratic intelligentsia, who think 'from above', so to speak) and therefore takes back from the object of knowledge a reflection of its own desire for purity and clarity – but a consequence of the subject who in the recognition of his or her own powers of self-negation, finds truth *in* the contingencies and contradictions of his or her own subjectivity, and in the contingencies and contradictions of the world. Now, this is not to say that this sets up an irrevocable break with the legacy of Kant; it is easy to overstate the distance between Kant's 'pure' subject and Hegel's 'impure' subject. Kant's model subject of rationality is itself subject at various points to an 'impure' understanding of subjectivity and agency as a consequence of its defence of the law of non-contradiction. In recognizing that rational self-knowledge is built upon the reflections that others bring to the formation of the self, and therefore, that the subject can never be identifiable with itself on the basis of its own powers of self-reflection, Kant also recognizes the capacity of practical reason to promote actions *at odds* with an agent's own intentions and self-descriptions. The claims of political progress are subject to outcomes not anticipated by its participants; just as political progress is not simply the work of the temperate moral will, but also of gouging ambition, systematic violence and cruel exploitation – out of destructiveness and calumny is brought forth its other. In this sense we might talk of Kant here as a precursor to Hegel's 'cunning of reason',[63] and as such acknowledge a continuity running between Kant's rationally embedded subject and Hegel's critically *embodied* subject. Yet, in Kant, recognition of the self-contradiction of the 'I' is limited to the unconscious effects of the non-reflective ego. This never develops into a theory of negation in which the subject truly confronts the other in its relationality. Hegel's theory of negation not only removes the barrier between self and other, but between reflection and the development of reason as historical consciousness. This is why Kant's notion of error, despite the anti-Cartesian break it makes with a pre-conceptualized account of the faculties and its historicization of reason, is still locked into the cognitive constraints of the autonomous subject. In Hegel, by contrast, the error becomes truly desubjectivized, so to speak, in so far as the gap between intention and outcome, conscious decision and unconscious desire, empirical immediacy and truth, is removed from the auspices of the autonomous rational subject, to be placed in the realm of history proper. This is not to say that the subject disappears from Hegel's system, but rather, that it is no longer morally and cognitively so narrowly conceived, as in Kant. (The principal rationality we have in Kant is a self-critical one). This is why we might talk about Hegel as bringing a theory of truth and error under the ironic sway of historical consciousness. The gap between intention and outcome, conscious decision and unconscious desire, empirical immediacy and truth, establishes the law of non-contradiction as the foundation of dialectical reason: we can struggle for truth and speak to truth, but we cannot *know* truth on the basis of our own experience.[64] As Hegel says in the *Phenomenology*, the subject 'cannot know what he [really] is until he has made himself a reality through action'[65] (that is through the consciousness and actions of others). As a consequence there is a fundamental shift 'downwards' in Hegel from where truth speaks. If truth is historical, and thereby 'after the event', those who invariably speak for truth – the powerful – are by definition deposed from the place of their own confidence and self-justification. This is why the error takes on a very different character in Hegel. Because reason, as subscribed to by the powerful, cannot escape the vicissitudes of error, Kant's rational teleology is divested of the link it makes between its overt moral presumptions, the self-interests of the aristocracy and the emerging bourgeoisie and universalism. History is not just made from the exercise of the rational will under the rule of bourgeois law, but from the messy and conflicted embodiment of subjects in the collective byways, retreats, reversals and cul-de-sacs of politics and culture. Indeed, it is the production of reason out of, and in response to, these deflections and failures of historical development and progress, that constitute the material ground of historical truth (what Hegel famously called Spirit).

Now, this is not to say that this Spirit is cognate with the interests of the lower classes and the proletariat – this is to read Marx's critique of Hegel back too easily and simplistically into Hegel – but rather, that in exchanging Kant's embedded rational will for an embodied rational will, Hegel establishes a view of the development of reason as grounded in the *working through* and *overcoming* of those lower forms of culture and politics that block or inhibit universal human freedom (or the absolute meaning of being). Effectively then, reason looks for the manifestations and signs of this freedom (the Absolute) in the concrete, contingent objects and relations of everyday life, across all classes. And of course this is where subject and object, theory and practice cohere in Hegel: *historical subjects make their reason from their material and intellectual engagement with, and transformation of, and failure to transform, the world.* Or more precisely, as a socialized subject, the 'I' is both determined by, and the creator of, the world he or she inhabits. This means, for Hegel, therefore, that the universal ends of reason cannot be imposed on recalcitrant objects, but must be produced – as a historical process – through the actual failure of this universality to find its realization in the world. Consequently, it is precisely in the ironic gap between intention and outcome, conscious decision and unconscious desire, empirical immediacy and truth, that reason is given this temporal form. Errors, therefore, as the constitutive materials of progress, of the work of the unconscious, and the 'cunning of reason', are no longer the enemies of truth, but their medium and mediator. Truth and error become intimates and dialectical partners. This is why, in the language of Descartes, the pursuit of knowledge may represent the realm of uncertainty and falsity, but it is also the means by which truth emerges. In this sense, to return to my earlier remarks about Kant and the error, by entering this new temporal order, the error in Hegel generates a different *positional* or *spatial* sense for a theory of truth. If truth 'is the movement of itself within itself'[66] this means that the critique, dissolution and supersession of the error is never just a matter of the cut that leaves no remainder on its way to the future. On the contrary, under the logic of Hegel's *Aufhebung*, no error is ever forgotten or lost to the historical process; for in its failure to realize reason, or in its dereliction of truth, it not only provides the sustenance for the continued realization of reason and truth, but it offers the means to reimagine and reconceptalize what truth was in the pursuit of further enquiries into truth. Thus every negation is an immanent determination, in which its negated content is preserved in the memory of all previous negations. Hence, *to* negate involves a two-way movement: a move away and 'above' the thing negated and a move back to the thing negated in order to prepare the ground for the possible re-possession of the thing negated and for further negations. This move back and forth, then, presupposes that the viability of any system of truth must be based on the interiorization and recovery of its own unfolding and conditionality. For truth to emerge, and continue to emerge, it must be able to represent itself back to itself as a coherent conceptual and developmental process. And this is what Hegel means precisely by truth as the movement of itself within itself: negation is the 'self-movement of the Concept.'[67] Or as Adorno defines it in his *Hegel: Three Studies*: the self-movement or labour of the concept, 'is both labor inherent in thought, which is by nature dialectical and the labor inherent in following an object that is by nature dialectical. Thought imitates the dialectical nonidentity of reality, in which the subject participates.'[68]

This concept of truth as self-movement, however, is not one focused on, or constitutive *of* the subject – certainly not in the sense that Kant understood the subject. This is something we need to be clear about. When Hegel talks about the subject, and the participation of the subject in the self-movement of the concept he is not referring in Kant's sense to a singular interiority, defined by its autonomous capacity for synthesizing representations. This is merely the husk of subjectivity. On the contrary, because the subject is never transparent to itself or all to itself, the synthesis of representations is always in a state of dissolution or preparation for dissolution. As Hans-Georg Gadamer outlines:

> the structural identity between the processes of what lives and [Hegelian] self-consciousness demonstrates that self-consciousness is not at all the individualized point of 'I=I,' but rather, as Hegel says, 'the I which is we and the we which is I', which is to say, spirit.[69]

What is 'alive' – in movement – is in the species or the collective and not in the individual alone. This is the meaning of what I call the desubjectivization of the subject in Hegel's system. For negation to produce the self-movement of the Concept, clearly there must be such things as subjects

– intersubjectively grounded in the lives of other subjects – but all this subject can know as truth is in a constant state of flux and dissolution in the process that is 'we, which is I'. The coming or interjection of the other is the becoming of the self. However, interjection is not *introjection*. The subject is not thereby reduced to the other, 'any more than it finds itself in the other', as Jean-Luc Nancy argues. '[T]he subject rather becomes becoming itself, to the extent that becoming must be understood, not as a becoming-this-or-that, this one or that one, but as negativity itself.'[70] Thus, in these terms, despite Kant's philosophy possessessing a quasi-Hegelian sense of the historicization of reason, for Hegel the subject theorized by the history of philosophy is actually very different to that of Kant. Whereas Kant's subject confronts external reality face-on, in all its self-possessive autonomy, Hegel submits and dissolves this rationality into an explicit developmental process of subject/object self-mediation, thereby attacking Kant's history of philosophy as a moral teleology. (For Hegel, Kant's moral will is a mere 'moral ought' stranded from world history).[71] Thus, whereas Kant's possessive subject seeks to establish a link between rationality and moral will, and as such the possible intimacy between moral subjectivity and moral history, Hegel's depossessive subject transcends the realm of individual morality by placing the subject, in its negative dissolution, directly within world history. The subject doesn't make history through the force of its moral will, but is, in its self-movement as socialized singularity, historical through and through. Hegel rejects Kant's realm of individual self-consciousness and moral scrutiny, therefore, by making self-consciousness historical and collective. As a consequence an important question arises: can a subjectively depossessed subject, such as Hegel's, take responsibility for his or her own truth claims and errors? And, if so, in what ways?

The emergence of the Western philosophical subject (and by extension of philosophical idealism) is formed, essentially, out of the self's encounter with the frailty of reason and truth, and the underlying and rebarbative exposure of the subject to the powers of error. This, essentially, has been the theme of our philosophical narrative so far. This places certain pressures in the way of philosophers within this tradition. First, to arrest the value and significance of these errors (Plato, Descartes, Locke); and second, later, to incorporate them into the philosophical tradition, but as things to be suppressed and excluded whereever possible (Kant). This is the difference between Descartes and high-Cartesianism and its

adaptation and amendment in Kant and post-Kantian philosophy generally. In Descartes, for the subject to countenance error is for the subject to
lose connection with reason and thereby reason's intimacy with God. In
Kant, for the subject to countenance error is to put in jeopardy the moral
teleology of reason. In Hegel, however, Western philosophical idealism,
as it culminates in German Idealism, decisively weakens this (idealized)
subject of truth. If Kant opens up a tentative space of critique of subjective self-transparency, Hegel systematizes it, dissolving the subject, not as
one might expect into the general flow of subjectivity, but into a system
of structured interdependence between subject and object, subject and
subject. Certain losses and gains are produced as a result of this.

In order to release the productiveness of the error from its moral/rational
stranglehold for world Spirit, Hegel has, in a sense, to disconnect the
subject – so to speak – from its fear of, and responsibilty for, its own
errors within the domains of action, judgement and cognition. For, it is
precisely the generation of these feelings of culpability – certainly in their
original theological forms – that prevents the emergence of the subject of
knowledge as a conscious collective and unfolding subject, returning the
self, as a consequence, to the anxious subject of the 'feeble' senses and
weak moral will. (The Kantian 'I' of pure moral rationality forever sees its
failures in action and cognition in the world as evidence of the need for
moral *self*-improvement, and therefore, narcissistically and anxiously craves
the return of approval or love from the world, through the moral refinement or reinforcement of the self). Hegel, rather, through his depossessive theory of the subject, introduces a fundamental 'point of indifference' in the self's moral and cognitive relation to the world. In intuiting
himself or herself in every other being as a moral being and intellect – 'the
I which is we, the we, which is I' – the subject's moral consciousness and
actions are made a necessary condition of socialization, rather than the
self-possessive fulfillment of a moral law.[72] This 'point of indifference' is
not *moral* indifference to the other, but, rather, the rejection of the subject
as a thing, or singular substance. Thus, if the subject is not identical with
itself in these terms – that is, exists as something which is permanently
distinguishable from itself as self – the *subject-as-subject* does not actually
exist at all. Which is not to say that Hegel does not think of the self as a
subject, but rather, that the rejection of the subject-as-subject dispenses
with the notion that the subject-of-truth is that which remains external to

its object of perception. As such, Hegel rejects another important element of Kant's philosophical subject: the notion that concepts are external to reality and imposed on reality by humans. As Yovel explains:

> This 'subjective' idealism, as Hegel calls it, gives priority to the subject over the object, and makes reality a function of knowledge. By contrast, Hegel claims that the Concept – in his sense – does not reside in our knowledge alone, but is implicitly at work in the *object* of our knowledge, that is, within reality. And as reality evolves towards its Concept, it enables knowledge, too, to evolve more clearly and to consciously explicate that implicit Concept.[73]

Hegel's refusal to countenance the notion of the subject-*as*-subject, therefore, rests on the priority he gives to the unification of the self with the immanent truth of the object (as a process of self-actualization). And, explicit in this convergence of subject and object, of course, is a sense that reason needs to engage its other – the intractabilities of daily existence, suffering, failure and error – as the means through which its rational essence – universal emancipation – is realised. 'The rational essence must become other-than-itself in order to be able to eventually return to itself on a higher level.'[74] Consequently, the demolition of Kant's pure subject in terms of the depossession of the subject – the subjection of the subject in its otherness to error, failure, suffering – is the process through which reason has to pass in order for reason to actualize itself and the liberatory force of negation.

> [I]n his inner most core Hegel sensed that the nature and destiny of human beings can be realised only through what is estranged, only through the world's domination, as it were, of human beings. Human beings must appropriate even the powers that are hostile to them; they must insinuate themselves into them, so to speak. Hegel introduced the cunning of reason into the philosophy of history in order to provide a plausible demonstration of the way objective reason, the realisation of freedom, succeeds by means of the blind, irrational passion of historical individuals.[75]

The outcome of this exercise of reason – as becoming itself – is not one that the subject has any ideal control over, but is thrown into, and is thrown by. Hence the depossessive subject for Hegel cannot be a stable subject of representation at all – of self-positing identity and knowledge

– but, in its self-negation, the outcome of relentless appropriation and self-dissolution. The individual subject in Hegel's philosophy is therefore at all times relieved of the responsibilty of making authorial claims to knowledge because, whether true or false, such authorial claims to knowledge are fundamentally divergent from any truth claims the subject might legitimately make in the here and now (that is, they cannot be assessed and warranted historically by the subject) and, therefore, become extendable beyond the life of the individual subject. The subject, in its finite actualization, can only ever be the mere bearer of knowledge, one small part of the realized truth of the whole. This means that an important aspect of a theory of the productiveness of the error is diminished in Hegel: the subject's necessary *culpability* for his or her mistakes (precisely that part of the possessive, Cartesian tradition of theorization of errors that renders the error as something with existential, not just, cognitive consequences). Hegel's 'point of indifference' may release the subject from the perturbations of the moral law, 'releasing' the self into history, but at the same time it weakens the link between *self*-knowledge and action (the principal assertion of Kant's philosophy).

Thus a certain loss arises from Hegel's progressive detachment of the error from the moral will in its attempt to dissociate it from the (narcissistic) failures of Kant's moral subject. Because it is precisely the culpability of the subject for his or her errors – his or her responsibility for them in Descartes' sense – that acts as the creative part of the sublative function of the historical process. The development of self-knowledge, then, cannot but contribute to (even if it doesn't decide) the quality of the sublative process undertaken. To recognize an error as one's own error, in order to derive scientific or critical meaning from the recognition and scrutiny of error, is, in a sense, to make a value-claim through the possession or repossession of the error. This is absolutely necessary if desire is to shape knowledge and praxis. In contrast, to pass an error on and abandon it as a source of knowledge, as a consequence of one's recognition of the small intersubjective part one is able to play in a collective process and its historical transformation-as-truth, is, in a sense, to 'let it go', and as such lose its meaning as the basis for future intervention into practice.

Thus, if the subject's involvement in the self-movement of the Concept, as Hegel asserts, is not a fixed process of representation but continuously posited – if what is negated and sublated always returns to the emergence of Spirit – in what specific ways, and in what specific forms, does the movement through, and sublation of, error produce truth? What is produced and returns to self-movement of the Concept through the process of historical sublation, and how might this be recognized and used as the unfolding of the whole? The methodological possession and uses of the error in science and art, is something we don't learn from Hegel, and, as such, there is a lack of specificity to Hegel's general understanding of the productiveness of the error. There is no breakdown of the error across practices and disciplines in Hegel, no sense of it functioning in different registers with different demands across philosophy, science and art. This is why, in the discipline where the discussion of errors has assumed a heightened level of epistemological clarity – the philosophy of science – Hegel has been the *persona non grata*. And this, correspondingly, is why Adorno, could say, paradoxically, in his partisan defence of Hegel against his scientistic critics, that Hegelian philosophy 'has been rendered obsolete by science and scholarship'.[76]

It is no surprise, then, that Hegel's notion of the productiveness of the error has been written out of the Popperian and Lakatosian versions of the philosophy of science, and indeed out of most philosophies of science. Hegel is identified with the sins of historicist vaguery and worse. But it is precisely the limitations of the theory of error in Popper and Lakatos that rests on their resistance to, and distance from, Hegel and the dialectical tradition. For a theory of error never gets off the ground in their philosophies of negation, so to speak, given Popper's and Lakatos's relentless fallibilism. That is, the life of errors and mistakes in science (and human praxis) are never allowed, or rarely allowed, to have positive and progressive content *as* errors. Popper for instance, says little about errors, other than that deductive falsificationism is successful at removing them.[77] One philosopher of science, however, who has resisted this view of errors – though she is no Hegelian herself – is Deborah Mayo.

> If we just ask ourselves about the specific types of mistakes we can and do make, and how we discover and avoid them – in short, how we learn from error – we would find that we have already taken several steps beyond the models of both Popper and Lakatos.[78]

'The aim of science is not avoiding anomaly and error but being able to learn from anomaly and error.'[79] This places her work in an intriguing position in my narrative: on the one hand her critique of Popper and Lakatos operates in the spirit of Hegel and dialectic – to release the productiveness of error fully into the demands of scientific progress – but on the other, like Popper and Lakatos, she is unwilling or disinclined to make any larger social claims about error or the development of knowledge in science (admittedly, like most other philosophers of science), and as such renders it philosophically corrigible. In the next chapter, therefore, I want to look at how the productiveness of the error in the philosophy of science, both breaks with Hegel (in certain ways for good reason), but is nevertheless compelled to return to Hegel's clutches (for equally good reasons) in order to think science's own past, present, and possible future. In this respect we are obliged to return – or better, renew – our philosophical understanding of the possessive subject, in order to assess the costs and strengths of the desubjectivization of the subject. In doing so, we can further develop our understanding of the subject of truth as produced in Hegel and the Western philosophical tradition and analyze in what ways it is useful for a theory of error across various practices.

TWO

ERROR, SCIENTIFIC PROGRESS AND VERIDICAL TRUTH

STRAIGHT TO ITS AIM

The formation of the rational subject in the Western philosophical tradition intersects with the emergence of the natural sciences. Indeed, Western philosophy saw itself as a nascent science, philosophy *as* science: Descartes, Locke, Spinoza, Kant and Hegel were all indebted to the slow advance of the natural sciences, and so saw philosophy, at one level, as an underlabourer for its empirical truths. But Kant and Hegel also discerned in the natural sciences and mathematics an inherent anti-historicism and static relationship between knowledge and truth. If philosophy was an underlabourer for the natural sciences and mathematics it also needed to be their redoubtable critic. In Kant, mathematics, in particular – as a non-conditional form of truth – is attacked for its self-evidentiality, the fact that under this model of truth reason pursues its path *straight to its aim*.[1] 'In mathematics definition belongs *ad esse*, in philosophy *ad melius esse*.'[2] Thus although Kant talks about this self-evidentiality as the strength of the mathematical sciences, he nevertheless sees this strength as representing a partial or limited form of reason. In this way he views mathematics, along with the inherent anti-philosophical methodologies of scepticism and empiricism, as ultimately all failing to capture what philosophy promises *in fine*: the Metaphysical being of the rational subject. In other words mathematics and physics provide only a knowledge of 'appearances' (something Hegel also emphasizes); philosophy, on the other hand, allows room for faith, passion and desire.

Kant sees philosophy, essentially, as a spontaneous activity contingent upon the creativity of the reasoning subject and not the application of a given set of norms, or reason in search of a method. This is because it is philosophy's job not to reveal the pre-established harmony of nature, but to actually produce it in thought. Claims to reason, therefore, have to be constituted by the subject himself or herself, in the act of reasoning. Accordingly, reason sets itself immanent goals through the actual privations and the lack inherent to the subject, and consequently, makes the amelioration or eradication of these privations and lacks a condition of the pursuit of reason. The place of the natural sciences in Kant, therefore, runs aground on the teleological content of this self-reasoning subject: namely, the fact that reason is not based on the explication of a fixed or universal method but on the temporal and self-transforming gap *between* the rational subject's latent and ideal aims and their actual application. As a result the natural sciences may operate as the ground of reason, but the natural sciences, in and of themselves, cannot supply the practical ends of science and of reason; this is the task of philosophy. This is why, as the first philosopher of *historical* reason, Kant sees reason as realized in history and not in abstract universal norms.

SCIENCE AS SYSTEM

This rejection of universal norms, and scepticism about the self-evidentiality of mathematics and the natural sciences, is directly inherited by Hegel. In fact, Hegel forces even more light between his philosophy and the mathematical rationalism of the Enlightenment than Kant, compromising further the tentative alliance between philosophy and the natural sciences. Fundamental to the *Phenomenology of Spirit*, for example, is the distinction between Understanding (*Verstand*) and Reason (*Vernunft*). The Understanding – the realm of mathematics, physics and the natural sciences generally – belongs to the surface dimensions of reality, to pure externality; Reason, in contrast, provides an inner reflection of the content of reality. The reason of philosophy, therefore, is not that which simply observes, or is containable within the demonstration of propositions. This is the death of reason, and paradoxically utterly subjective in its empirical truth claims, because it is constrained by the perceptual self-limitations of the (Cartesian) subject. However, if Hegel is critical of mathematics and the natural sciences for their static relationship to truth, nevertheless he does not dismiss the scientific validity of these approaches. Rather, he insists, such approaches should recognize the non-dialectical limitations of their truth claims and, as such, refrain from devising a transcendental method that should serve as a model for philosophy. This is because the non-dialectical sciences are unable to make good their claims to truth, given that they cannot establish a coherent relationship to the uses to which knowledge in the sciences are put. In other words science can't *think* its relationship between knowledge and a conception of the whole; only philosophy can do this, in as much as philosophical thought doesn't *end* with the singular proposition, but, in a sense, begins with it. (There is direct link here to Heidegger's notion that science can't *think*, that is can't think its relationship to the whole). This is why dialectical philosophy necessarily, for Hegel, has a privileged relationship to the whole. Because philosophy transcends every finite possibility of knowledge through making every possibility of knowledge historically relative, the whole is not something that science can know in a transparent, empirical fashion. Dialectical philosophy, then, exposes science to the historical and transitive demands of the whole by rejecting outright any link, or symmetry, between truth and the singular proposition. In this respect Science, as opposed to 'the sciences', has a particular content that needs to be acknowledged in Hegel's and Kant's systems.

In the eighteenth and nineteenth centuries, Science is not the name for particular disciplines, such as mathematics or physics, but the attainment of a certain epistemic ambition – that of complete or absolute knowledge. As a consequence, for Kant and Hegel Science and System are identical. This means that if philosophy is to attain the status of Science, it must achieve formal integrity and a certain intellectual scale as a system of thought. But, as I have stressed, for Hegel philosophy cannot borrow this systematization wholesale from the sciences, given the fact that the putative systematizations of empirical science are built upon the conjunction of (dead) singular propositions. Or, as Adorno puts it in his Hegelian voice: 'Unlike science philosophy knows no fixed sequence of question and answer.'[3] Systematization must account for something more than the accumulation of scientific facts, of external links of inference; rather, it must account for the very character and dynamic of systematization itself; that is, reflect on systematic knowledge's own conditions of possibility and transformation. The whole must include its own generation as part of the system's explication of its truth claims. For Hegel, therefore, systematization constitutes a *journey-to-truth*, in which philosophy turns back to correct and expand its previous claims, as a gradual self-explication of reason. This journey-to-truth has its self-reflective origins in Kant's 'Transcendental Doctrine of Method' in the *Critique of Pure Reason*, but for Hegel, Kant's concept of self-reflection lacks internal and external movement and, therefore, fatally weakens Kant's claims to systematization and the status of his philosophy as a Science. By listing the categories in a self-defining fashion, Kant loses the dynamic structure of the categories' mutual negation and their non-identical emergence and transformation.

This struggle in Hegel over the scientific status of philosophy and the philosophical status of science, of system and absence of system, in an important sense marks the last ditch defence of philosophy against the sciences. The rise of the natural sciences in the seventeenth and eighteenth centuries had placed a huge pressure on philosophy to collapse itself into the empirical verificationism of the new sciences. Indeed, after Locke, philosophy was in a radically transformed situation: the idea that philosophy was the quintessential framework for all human knowledge was implausible. This is why Hegel's bid for a new kind of systematization in philosophy was so bold, and so against the grain. He negates science, in order to regenerate philosophy on the same systematic level as science. But, this re-systematization is not an attack on science as such, as if in a backward glance to, or in Romantic homage to, pre-scientific metaphysics. Rather, he negates what we might call the rising hubristic impatience of science in order to subject science to the same process of historicization as philosophy itself. Thus science and philosophy meet under a new model of dialectical systematization: the diachronic sublation of knowledge, in which the history of knowledge is preserved and transformed. Science is sublated within the re-systematization of philosophy as history. Thus, on the basis of this sublation, Hegel reclaims philosophy's status as the fount of all possible knowledge – as the *regina scientiarum* – but on a qualitatively new basis: philosophy and science emerge and converge under the sign of interchange, integration and reconciliation. Systematization as sublation means something quite specific, then: truth becomes the consciousness of, participation in, the *all*.

This is where Hegel's concept of systematization is profoundly different from Kant's, and from the whole history of the formation of the rational subject and scientific practice: rationality and knowledge is not simply a matter of our self-consciousness, or the mastery of our senses, of refined inwardness, so to speak, but also of our 'forgetfulness' as subjects; that is, our (reflective) openness to what lies outside of ourselves, and as such our recognition of our limited capacities as singular thinking beings in the pursuit of knowledge. In this Hegel echoes the divinization of consciousness in Greek philosophy: the highest form of self-consciousness is that which lies beyond the forms of individual consciousness in the submission of individual consciousness to the supraconsciousness of divine being (supraconsciousness here being translated by Hegel into collective praxis and consciousness).[4] This notion of a supraconsciousness is something that Hegel believed had been lost to philosophy after Descartes, and his narrow pursuit of self-reflection; Hegel insisted that, overall, individual self-consciousness plays little part on its own in the pursuit and development of knowledge and practice.

Unsurprisingly, therefore, Hegel is the *persona non grata* in the philosophy of science. Knowledge as consciousness of, and participation in, the All, is precisely what the new sciences, in their race away from metaphysics between the 1880s and 1960s, have taken a virulent objection to. Indeed, as Gadamer says, when we ask what caused Hegelian philosophy's rapid decline in the eyes of philosophers and scientists alike during this period, the answer is simple:

> The mounting up of modern research in all fields of science has discredited the claim . . . raised and defended for the last time by Hegel of prescribing for the sciences of nature . . . of integrating them with [an] a priori system of thought.[5]

In other words, the empirical demands of scientific investigation have made the collective dynamic of consciousness and the critique of science as a system subordinate to the professional development of the scientific subject, and his or her claims to be the master of his or her senses and intellect. From Pierre Duhem on to Rudolf Carnap and Popper, the philosophy of science has assigned a singular importance to the individual scientific subject, who in his or her assiduous attention to observational protocol and technical procedures moves science along by the careful and self-scrutinizing control over the experimental process. The weight of theoretical endeavour in most philosophy of science has been the insistence, therefore, on science less as a collective and social endeavour, than on the Cartesian refinement of the (scientific) subject as an 'unmediated' or pure intelligence, or what is commonly known as methodological individualism. Hegel's dialectical theory of sublation is considered too weak in accounting for the exclusion and *removal* of error in scientific research. In this sense the philosophy of science in its modern inception and development repossesses the Cartesian tradition in order to repossess the (rational) subject of error – the subject who is culpable for his or her errors, and in seeking to dispel them, *passes knowledge on*. There is something wider at stake, then, in the modern philosophy of science's dismissal of metaphysics: the precise role and function of the error in accounting for truth and progress. In order to trace this issue, let us first look at the modern rise of the scientific subject and the philosophy of science's critique (and adaptation) of Hegelian dialectics.

THE UNITY OF SCIENCE AS METHOD

One of the founding texts of the modern philosophy of science and logical positivism is Rudolf Carnap's *The Unity of Science* (1932). Unbending in its claims for science's autonomy, it represents the final divergence between science and philosophy, after Hegel's attempt to hold them together through the first half of the nineteenth century. Scientists do not pursue science to better understand Truth or effect a better place for science in the world, Carnap argues, but on the contrary, in order to empirically verify physical descriptions of the material world on the basis of successful experiment. In this it is precisely logical analysis and logical analysis alone (rather than logical analysis in conjunction with philosophical supposition) that is able to provide the conditions for this process of verification. And, thus, it is the historical intrusion of the problems of philosophy into the philosophy of science that has undermined the nature of what scientists do, in so far as philosophers ask questions of science that are subjectivist and irrelevant (culturally and socially determined) and as such unwarrantable. Although Hegel is not named in *The Unity of Science*, there is an implicit critique of Hegel and all his later (Marxian) works, on the grounds that Truth, History, the Real (as opposed to the actual), are empirically unverifiable and therefore have no place in science; science verifies specific knowledge claims, it does not presume to talk of Truth.[6]

All statements belonging to Metaphysics, regulative Ethics, and (metaphysical) Epistemology have this defect [the absence of logical relations] and are in fact unverifiable and, therefore, unscientific. In the Viennese Circle, we are accustomed to describe such statements as nonsense.[7]

The disdain for metaphysics here is partly a response to the mess Isaac Newton and other scientific-religionists got into regarding the 'true causes' of experimental knowledge. For Newton it was the job of the scientist to pass on verifiable mathematical knowledge; the ultimate arbitrator on the causes of such knowledge, however, was the work of religion. Carnap and the positivists drop the latter as an unnecessary embarrassment: science has no need to explain the ultimate cause of anything, particularly via the claims of religion; passing on verifiable knowledge is itself what guarantees meaning, everything else is hot air. And the basis for this is that scientific methodology, unlike philosophy, has a shared validity for all those who participate in it. For Carnap this takes the form of a general convergence between what he calls different 'protocol statements' (the various first-person statements in which scientific descriptions are initially articulated and framed) and the physical states under scrutiny. Thus every statement in the protocol language, despite its subjective inflections and origins, can be translated into a physical statement that describes the state of a given physical entity. Hence various protocol statements may emphasize the distribution of parts of a given physical entity in different ways, but they at least recognize that a body is in a given state, and therefore are able to 'predict that what other states of this body may be expected to occur.'[8] In this, science becomes, essentially, physics, in so far as every scientific fact can be translated into a 'determinate property of a spatio temporal position (or as a complex of such properties).'[9] Thus, it is possible to reduce all languages used in science to this basic or universal physical language in so far as it is possible to find a physical equivalent (physical coordinates) for all scientific facts. Science develops on the basis of an incremental increase in the 'observational stock' of previous experiments, in conjunction with the employment of a set of logical principles to determine which hypotheses are best placed to confirm the observations of a given experiment or experiments.[10]

THE SUBJECT-WHO-IS-NOT-A-SUBJECT

Carnap, then, offers an influential model of the scientific subject that will come to shape the philosophy of science in the twentieth century: what I shall call here *the scientific-subject-who-is-not-a-subject*. That is, the psychological make-up and emotional predilections of the scientific subject have absolutely no bearing whatsoever on the outcome of scientific experiment and knowledge. Indeed, the job of the scientific subject is to find and confirm inferential connections between the protocol statements and physical descriptions as a condition of the intersubjective truth of these statements. In this light the scientific subject-who-is-not-a-subject takes on a quasi-utopian character as the bearer of the ideal of scientific Unity: only the quality of logical inference based on the quality of empirical observation can guarantee the generation and passage of knowledge.

This kind of positivism was soon open to attack by those who had earlier declared themselves in allegiance with logical positivism, such as Karl Popper. In *The Logic of Scientific Discovery* (1935), published shortly after *The Unity of Science*, Popper attacks Carnap's form of Physicalist positivism on three major grounds: that there is no given logical method particular to science, and, therefore, that there is no transparent logical reconstructive path leading to the physical laws of nature; that the translation of scientific facts into physicalist descriptions cannot account for the (messy) progress of knowledge; and that there is no inference to theories from singular statements which are verifiable by experience. Thus the protocol statements that represent the basis of Carnap's theory of inductive logic are essentially arbitrary, in so far as intersubjective coherence is no guarantee of knowledge. The latter, of course, is the core of Popper's famous attack on verificationism in *The Logic of Scientific Discovery*: scientific statements are never fully verifiable, only testable, and as such must be subject to a process of falsificationism, in which statements are criticized on the grounds of their relative probability. The probability of a statement increases with diminished degrees of falsifiability. But the diminishment of falsifiability is not thereby a signal to accept the given statement with any degree of finality; falsified statements, with a high degree of probability, in turn, require, in the light of future inquiry, further appraisal. Appraisal follows appraisal, as Popper puts it. The rigour and exactitude of testing, therefore, is crucial to Popper's understanding of the scientific subject, and the (relative) distance he takes from positivism's scientific subject-who-is-not-a-subject. For rigorous testing requires a scientific subject that does not protect itself from the instabilities of verification, and therefore from the would-be neutrality of logical method. The rigours of falsifiability require a different kind of logical methodology, in which the subject accepts his or her hesitant and uncertain immersion in the scientific process. In these terms, in the 1959 introduction to *The Logic of Scientific Discovery*, he tracks this subject in the following way: 'every discovery contains "an irrational element", or a "creative intuition"'.[11]

> I am inclined to think that scientific discovery is impossible without faith in ideas which are of a purely speculative kind, and sometimes even quite lazy; a faith which is completely unwarranted from the point of view of science, and which, to that extent, is 'metaphysical'.[12]

And:

> We frequently work with statements which although actually false, nevertheless yield results, which are adequate for certain purposes.[13]

Now, this is not evidence of Popper slipping into a psychologistic mode: *The Logic of Scientific Discovery* is a weighty attack on subjectivist approaches to scientific probability – no amount of rational 'feeling' or intuition can ever *justify* or explain a scientific statement. However, there is a discernable shift here, which brings the scientific subject into alignment with Kant and Hegel's critique of science's putative transcendental method; the scientific subject is not always in the place that he thinks he or she is, and is therefore not always in control of the processes of discovery and explanation that logic thinks fit to validate. Essentially, then, his model of falsifiability places a greater emphasis on the self-contradictory and unstable space of 'the logic of scientific discovery', opening up this logic, in a tentative way, to dialectic. By critiquing empiricist induction through a process of rigorous falsifiability, creativity in the production and testing of theories becomes open to a greater attention to the search for truth-in-error, in theories: 'it is always the theory and not the experiment, always the idea and not the observation, which opens up the way to knowledge.'[14] Consequently, the scientific subject is a subject who is 'creatively irrational', 'intuitive' and 'productively false' *within* theory; there is no straight path between observational statements, theory production and inductive logic. It is unsurprising then that Paul Feyerabend and Imre Lakatos later pick up on these early reflections of Popper's, advocating what is largely an explicit rejection of the scientific subject-who-is-not-a-subject. In Feyerabend this, of course, is famously a scientific subject who *is* a subject, the scientific subject who brings the messiness of interiority to the laboratory as a necessary corollary of 'creative irrationalism' in theory.[15] Similarly, in *The Methodology of Scientific Research Programmes* (1978), Lakatos argues that the direction and quality of scientific research programmes is 'determined primarily by human creative imagination and not by the universe of facts which surround us.'[16] But Popper never seems happy with these kinds of reflection on the scientific subject, because although they provide the basis for the justification of a theory of falsificationism, and for science as a theory of theories, they also threaten the possibility of scientific realism. That is, the scientific subject who *is* a subject is too close to the Bayesian notion of the scientist as someone who 'believes that', who accepts a statement on the basis that one set of beliefs, advocated by its defenders, seems more coherent or plausible than another. This is the death of science for Popper given that it fails to make an affirmative distinction between what is actually 'false' and what is actually 'true'. This places Popper fully in the Tarskian formalist-realist camp, certainly after the publication of *The Logic of Scientific Discovery*. After fully accepting Tarski's formal view of subject-less truth in the late 1930s – 'it is not that *I* know that snow is white, snow *is* white'[17] – Popper seeks to extract himself from the subject–object dialectic he opens up in *The Logic of Scientific Discovery*. In this sense this shift is marked by an increasing anti-Hegelianism, which by then had become standard fare in the philosophy of science across all schools. The function of Tarski's formal account of truth for Popper, therefore, is to mark out a space, in a classical realist sense, between truth *and* the subject (that is, establish the idea of there being a correspondence of scientific statements to facts as a kind of regulative idea of truth). But for all attempts to extricate his methodology from any taint of dialectic it continues to determine his frame of reference. This contradiction is foregrounded in his later theoretical formalisation of the scientific subject, 'Epistemology Without a Knowing Subject'.[18]

This is not a return to a universalist Carnapian logical method for science. It does, however, represent a consolidation, in the spirit of

Carnap's scientific *subject-who-is-not-a-subject*, of what the scientific subject is ideally assumed to be. For idealist forms of epistemology, be they inscribed in Descartes or Kant, or in Bayesian theories of science, knowledge is pursued and studied in a subject-sense: 'I know', 'I am thinking', 'I believe as such'. In science, however, knowledge is not knowledge in this subject-sense. Although scientific *subjects* produce knowledge, scientific knowledge belongs to an objective domain of problems and arguments free of the determinations of subjective belief and advocacy. 'Knowledge in [this] objective sense is *knowledge without a knower*.'[19] By this Popper means that the scientific subject is beholden to the external requirements of the accumulative 'logic of scientific discovery', and not to the force and suasiveness of the subject's scientific beliefs.[20] Yet, because the direction and content of this domain of objective questions and problems is not self-evident, the scientific subject – and this is where Popper continues to distinguish himself from classical logical positivism – cannot assume that objective criteria produce consistently objective results. Even though a research programme may have been planned and sustained with great care and assiduousness, producing high levels of falsifiability, 'it will as a rule turn out partly in unexpected ways.'[21] In other words, research programmes invariably produce new possibilities, new aims and new problems. Every step of the way 'will create new unintended facts' and 'new refutations'.[22] But, although these new possibilities and problems arise as a result of the creative activity of the scientific subject, these new possibilities and problems are not in themselves created by the scientific subject. On the contrary, 'they emerge autonomously from the field of new relationships which cannot help bringing into existence [such things] with every action, however little.'[23] Something revealing seems to be happening here, then, that is symptomatic of the philosophy of science's broken or troubled relationship with philosophy and dialectic. Popper, in critiquing the 'pathological' subject of Hegel – the subject who is unable to truly know what he or she knows – as a subject who is too close to the Bayesian scientific subject, immediately falls back into a pathological 'Hegelian' frame of reference in order to register the creativity of the scientific subject: the scientific subject's creativity is the outcome of an uncertain, indeterminate process. This indicates not only an ambivalent reading of Hegel on Popper's part – or rather a shaky sense of where he thinks he stands in relation to the Hegelian tradition – but, as a consequence, demonstrates a strange interplay between the possessive Cartesian subject and Hegel's depossessive subject. Let's try and break this down. First, though, let's look at what he has to say on Hegel himself, as Popper is keen (ironically), in *Objective Knowledge: An Evolutionary Approach*, to resolve what he asserts is a possible confusion between his position and that of Hegel's;[24] then, in the light of this discussion, let's unpack his theory of the scientific subject further, and its relationship to a theory of error.

For Popper, Hegel is the great determinist, the great theorist of the subject subsumed by the historical process of World Spirit: 'individuals . . . are instruments, instruments of the Spirit of the Epoch, and their work, their "substantial business" is prepared and appointed independently of them.'[25] Moreover, Popper adds, Hegel is a crude scientific relativist. He is not interested in eliminating contradictions, because he believes contradictions propel history forward. 'Thus rational criticism plays no part in the Hegelian automatism, no more than does human creativity.'[26] This is a standard caricature of Hegel, even on the Left: automatist, determinist, and anti-rational; and as such Hegel becomes a kind of straw man for Popper in order to attack what he sees as the baleful influence of historicism on science, the notion – perhaps best represented by Pierre Duhem – that scientific knowledge develops bit by bit (in a slow accretive way) towards a theoretical completion of the whole. For Popper, Hegel is a kind of historical puppet-master, for whom history is merely the medium through which the contingent subject passes on its way to the Absolute. But, this crude inversion of Hegel is precisely why Popper needs to keep his distance from Hegel, because, ironically, it is this objectivist history that remains closest to his own version of the scientific subject-who-is-not-a-subject. That is, Popper's scientific subject-who-is-not-a-subject exists in a world of scientific problems that 'exists to a large extent autonomously' and 'vastly exceeds the impact which any of us can make upon it.'[27] This leaves the scientific subject, as it were, in a position comparable to that of the position of the subject in Popper's caricature of Hegel – as a subject without a convincingly dialectical relationship to its object of mediation. The result is that the primary emphasis Popper places on the deductive rejection of theories, at the expense of the slow build-up of inductive support in the production of knowledge, produces a scientific subject that is unable to meet the demands of its own purported (hesitant) 'creativity activity' and the unintended consequences of research.[28] In other words, fallibilism leaves the scientific subject at a distance from the contingencies of the scientific process in exactly the same way that Popper's caricature of Hegel's subject is taken to be 'outside' of history, as its mute passenger (for Popper, Hegel's notion of supraconsciousness is simply a super-monad and not a multiple and transformative space of singularities). And this, in turn, is the result, essentially, of Popper's theory of error and specifically the role of error-elimination in Popper's deductive method.

ERROR ELIMINATION

Error elimination is the very core of Popper's fallibilism and the deductive rejection of theories, and as such is what distinguishes his fallibilistic scientific subject from Duhem's scientific progressivist subject, Bayesianism, Hegel and all other forms of would-be historicism. For, it is precisely the radical and continuous *expunging* of error that 'leads to the objective growth of our knowledge – of knowledge in the objective sense. It leads to the growth of objective verisimilitude: it makes possible the approximation of (absolute) truth.'[29] As a consequence, the 'creative activity' of the scientific subject-who-is-not-a-subject takes on a particular kind of objectivist identity through this process of error elimination. In subordinating itself to the exosomatic demands of an autonomous realm of scientific problems, the scientific subject-who-is-not-a-subject becomes the vigilant *identifier and producer* of error.[30] The upshot of this is that the deductive powers of the scientific subject are given a newly possessive Cartesian identity: the job of the scientific subject is not simply to problem-solve, but to capture error as a result of severe and strenuous forms of eliminative logic and testing. Popper's Cartesianism here is directed towards a particular end: to make it impossible for the scientific statement to hide anomalous or inconvenient facts, despite the statement having the appearance of knowledge. Yet, if the elimination of error drives the growth of knowledge, the error is never a source of reflection in any explicit fashion, and in a way that would make it compatible with Popper's recognition of the significance of 'creative irrationalism'. Popper says very little about the positive knowledge that might be acquired through the recognition of errors themselves. At one level, of course, this is a symptom of Popper's anti-Hegelianism: to openly recognize the productiveness of errors is to openly recognize the productiveness of contradictions; and, with this, science is on the rocky road to relativism. But on another level it reveals in what way the error holds up as a placeholder for knowledge in his deductive methodology. Errors for Popper are broadly the *extruded detritus* of the scientific process, and as such need, unambiguously, to be left behind as the mere husks of knowledge. Thus, in this sense, errors are placed in problematic and constricted position as a consequence of Popper's falsificationism: on the one hand, it is evident that we learn about the world in the face of errors, but on the other hand, it is not clear how and under what conditions this process of learning takes place. What errors do, and how they do it, tends to disappear as a problem for science as soon as fallibilism kicks in. In *Error and the Growth of Experimental Knowledge*, Deborah Mayo outlines what is at stake:

> The view that we learn from error, while commonplace, has been little explored in philosophy of science. When philosophers of science do speak of learning from error – most notably in the work of Popper – they generally mean simply that when a hypothesis is put to the test of experiment and fails we reject it and attempt to replace it with another. Little is said about what the different types of errors are, what specifically is learned when an error is recognized, how we locate precisely what is at fault, how our ability to detect and connect errors grows, and how this growth is related to the growth of scientific knowledge.[31]

Thus a number of key points are raised here: (1) What are the different forms of error subscribed to by the logic of scientific discovery? (2) How are these errors actually recognized and processed?; and (3) How, and in what way, does the knowledge generated by the recognition and processing of errors contribute to the growth of knowledge? As such, Mayo lays down a certain kind of epistemological challenge to Popperian and post-Popperian (Kuhnian) philosophy of science: there is no point saying science learns from errors, without producing, methodologically, why this is the case. For Mayo, therefore, this involves nothing less than a recalibration and re-theorization of inductive thinking in scientific method, as a challenge to the loss of focus of the function of the error, as a consequence of Popper's deductive approach, of bold conjectures. Errors need error theory, or rather, *better* error theory. Before, we discuss the strengths and vicissitudes of Mayo's error theory, then, it is important that we clarify the problems of induction and deduction.

INDUCTION, DEDUCTION, ERROR AND METHOD

One of the abiding epistemological problems for the philosophy of science is perhaps science's oldest methodological problem: if scientific knowledge was obtainable simply through reference to the principles of logic there would be no need to test and justify the results of our experiments. Our understanding would be presupposed by these principles. Thus, for instance, in respect of the 'rigours' of inductive logic, in our inference from observational evidence to general laws, it is impossible to say with any certainty that the truth of the laws follows from the truth of the evidence –that is, all sheep appear to be white, until we meet our first black sheep. As such, inductive truths tend to be presented on the weakest (inclusive) of bases: all sheep are white *and* black. In this way, inductivism is scientifically non-contentious and banal if restricted to locally testable domains, but highly contentious when it stands in for universal law-like states. When this occurs it becomes identifiable with a disastrous perspectivalism, leading to a reduction of the real to the manifest and self-evident and the very destruction of the possibility of science as such: the identification of the real with the making visible of determinate structures and the necessary stratifications of reality. Deductivist logic, in contrast, rejects outright the notion that scientific statements are built from the bottom up from observational data. Rather, observations from data are themselves the result of theoretical claims, and therefore theories have to be experimentally tested against (observational) theories. This places a greater emphasis on the need to disprove theories on the basis that no theory can claim a positivistic identity with the data. This, of course, represents Popper's post-positivist contribution to the philosophy of science: scientific truth is not a consequence of theories matching facts, but of theoretical labour on (observational) theories. Scientific truth is the result of what is successfully falsified, and in turn what is successfully falsified needs (in the light of further theoretical endeavour) to be tested again. The outcome is that deductivism can never stop testing, for to do so is to betray the possibility that the successful test hides further anomalies and problems that have to be theoretically probed. This means that deductivism operates in a perpetual state of epistemological postponement, in which the results of experiment can never be complete, and therefore never applied with any conviction. As a result, Popperian deductivism produces a particular kind of scientific subject-who-is-not-a-subject, a subject who, in his or her subordination to a given set of exosomatic problems, is driven by the permanent demands of falsification. Critics of Popper's deductivism, such as Imre Lakatos, have tended, then, to emphasize its tendency towards theoretical accelerationism; that is, its rapid rejection of defective theories at the expense of their residual strengths or powers. As Lakatos argues: 'For Popper, progress consists of an incessant, ruthless, evolutionary confrontation of bold speculative theories and respectful observations, and of the subsequent fast elimination of the defective theories.'[32] The key word here is 'fast'. Popper's theoretical accelerationism weakens the multi-temporal space of scientific discovery, the fact that the materials of scientific progress may also lie in the margins and cul de sacs of past and would-be falsified theories, and therefore rely on the recovery of ideas and questions seemingly long superseded.[33] This is why Lakatos develops his notion of the 'research programme' as key to the developmental logic of scientific progress and the position of the scientific subject-who-is-not-a-subject. For under the explicitly collective nature and alinear direction of the research programme, the basic unit of scientific investigation and truth is not the isolated theory or statement per se, but the capacity of scientific investigation to maturely *outgrow* those defects, anomalies and inconsistencies that would normally – under the auspices of Popper's falsificationism – put the whole investigation in jeopardy. Lakatos's research programme gives a kind of formal content and ideological boost to Popper's early critique of scientific method: it is *precisely* anomalies and inconsistencies themselves that allow scientific investigation to breathe and progress to take place.

As a consequence, Popper's accelerationism has a crucial impact on the recognition and eradication of errors as the key determinate of the logic of scientific discovery. In his epistemological impatience and intolerance towards keeping a theory afloat despite the theory's only (marginal) inconsistencies, the error's role in experimentation suffers a retreat and diminution of its content. For once the error is the thing to be expunged with the defective theory it is no longer a possible source of other research work within a given research programme. This is the central concern of Mayo's *Error and the Growth of Experimental Knowledge*. For Mayo, Popper's attack on the classic inductivist principle that experimental data are essentially unproblematic produces an irreal or unrealizable form of experimentation. Scientific discovery not only lives with (or has to live with) anomalies and contradictions, but, in its halting pathways through anomalies and contradictions, it actually at some point or points produces verifiable confirmations. Hence unless we have some inductivist warrant that allows us at some point to argue from particular instances to general statements, 'nothing can be justified, shown to be mistaken or called into doubt.'[34] Thus the problem with Popper's falsificationism is that its accelerationism makes it difficult to make errors speak with any consistency because the process of learning from errors is itself considered to be too much at risk from its own instabilities and uncertainties. Consequently, as Mayo insists, we have to be greater inquisitors of errors. We need to:

> Interact with, simulate them (with models and computers), amplify them: we have to learn to make them talk. A genuine account of learning from error shows where and how to justify Popper's 'risky decisions.' The result, let me be clear, is not a filling-in of the Popperian (or the Lakatosian) framework, but a wholly different picture of learning from error.[35]

How then, precisely, does the scientific subject learn from errors in ways that don't short-change, and as such improve, the experimental process? Mayo divides her response into eight different categories; and ideally these work in conjunction with each other: (1) after-time checking or self-correction: rigorously checking the data or evidence to be used in a hypothesis; (2) before-trial planning: the assimilation into the planning and design of a trial of the accumulation of, and reflection on, past mistakes; and as an extension of (2), (3) the systematic collection and correlation of known and anticipated errors; (4) evaluating the effects of mistakes: by developing knowledge of the effect of mistakes, scientists are able to rule out certain errors as responsible for given effects (consequently knowledge of the effects of mistakes is used to 'subtract out' their influence after the trial); (5) simulating errors: it is important, in order to gain information, to stage what would happen – if possible – if a certain error were committed; (6) amplifying and 'listening' to error patterns: a significant way of learning from errors is to amplify or exaggerate their known effects in order to detect them; (7) counterintuitive robustness: the deliberate varying of assumptions in order to see whether the result or initial hypothesis is still adequate; and (8) the repeated severe probing of errors: the further assiduous development and use of testing after previous testing procedures have proven successful. This represents a testing procedure, then, with a particularly 'good chance of revealing the presence of a specific error, if it exists – but not otherwise'.[36]

As is evident from the above, Mayo, like Popper, begins from the demand for severe criticism; that is, from a position of vigorously trying to find errors in hypotheses. It is the job of the scientist to push and push again – and then push a bit further – in their experimental enquiries. But this is not a more strenuous version of Popper's theoretical accelerationism, for Mayo's insistence on what we might call the need for an increased monitoring of errors is not an invitation to scientists to ratchet up the refutations willy-nilly. The passing of a hypothesis after severe testing is potentially a *constructive* moment in the testing process. At this point the testing produces a good claim to reliable knowledge. Which is not to say in turn – in keeping with Popper's criticism – that this encourages the scientist thereby to automatically assign a degree of *probability* to the hypothesis – but rather that the hypothesis's successful resistance to the test enables the scientist to infer the hypothesis's reliability. Hence without this constructive moment it is unclear why 'passing severe tests counts in favor of a hypothesis'.[37] The best Popper can say on this score is 'that it did better in passing the test the previous hypothesis failed' and that 'it will also have to be regarded as possibly true, since at the time t it has not been shown to be false.'[38] Mayo, therefore, in rejecting the claims of probability, does not exclude the possibility of experimental testing generating reliable knowledge. This means a certain kind of epistemological shift from Popper's understanding of the error as the extruded detritus of the experimental process to a notion of the error as *productively internal* to this process. For Mayo, the job of scientists is still, of course, to avoid errors, but, significantly, learning and progress takes places *despite errors, in the presence of errors*. Yet this assiduousness is not a refinement of deductive thinking, of Popper's bold conjectures, within the experimental process. As much as Mayo rejects a justificationist or verificationist approach to knowledge – as in Carnap's problematic notion of science being built on good, solid, empirical foundations – she is also critical of the part theorizing actually plays in the experimental process. Rather, her concern is to improve the *methods* and *strategies* – and therefore the scientist's powers of inductive analysis – of the experimental process. The burden of knowledge falls above all else on the framework, quality and perspicacity of the experimental test. In this way the eight categories of error testing outlined above are designed to provide the interrelated means for the severe exposure and examination of what we might call the five primary categories of errors scientists invariably face in the laboratory: mistaking the effects of an experimental apparatus for real effects; mistaking chance effects for real correlations; accepting mistakes as genuine in the measurement of a value, quantity or boundary; mistaking as genuine a misunderstood causal factor; and mistaking the assumptions of experimental data on the basis of laboratory or discipline (Bayesian) peer pressure. Now these thresholds for error are not just anomalies that scientists are adept at keeping at bay with 'scientific reason', but deeply embedded in the experimental process itself and, therefore, shed some actual, and much needed, methodological light on Lakatos's notion of the scientific research programme as a space for living *with* anomalies and contradictions. On this basis, the parameters of the experimental process, and the dynamism of a research programme can both be said to be defined, for scientific investigation, by the permanence of these error thresholds. Consequently, for Mayo – contra Popper – the refinement of scientific method – the improvement of the capacities and powers of testing – rests on how theoretical hypotheses and experimental techniques challenge each other's outcomes and expectations.

This, in turn, has an important contribution to make in the critique of the deeply problematic distinction Thomas Kuhn makes – and which dominated the philosophy of science in the 1960s, 1970s and 1980s – between 'normal' science and 'revolutionary' science.[39] Kuhn's position changed on this distinction – as did his views on many things[40] – but suffice to say, in his initial and influential formulation, 'normal' science, is the routine laboratory work of qualifying and adjusting what is taken to be knowledge in a given discipline – 'mopping up operations'[41] – and 'revolutionary' science is the good, vital, 'experimental' stuff that transforms the discipline and what is taken to be scientific truth. These changes are grouped, as is well known, under the heading of a paradigm shift, which Kuhn describes tendentiously as a displacement of the governing or majoritarian conceptual framework 'through which scientists view the world'.[42] The formulation and reception of this new paradigm establishes not just a new scientific language for understanding the world, but, essentially, a 'new world'. Not many philosophers of science had an encouraging word for this distinction in the 1960s and 1970s, and quite rightly so. Kuhn's neo-Kantianism was criticized overwhelmingly by Popper, Feyerabend, Stephen Toumlin[43] and Kurt Hübner,[44] amongst others, for its discontinuism, relativism and subjectivism, and, certainly in Feyerabend and Lakatos, the two major philosophers of science with a modicum of understanding of science's social base, for its undialectical sense of historical transmission and transformation. As Feyerabend was to argue, Kuhn's history of science is driven by a monolithic counterposing of theories, with little sense of internal struggle within and across competing scientific communities. 'If normal science is *de facto* monolithic as Kuhn makes it out to be, then where do the competing theories come from?'[45] In other words the idea that normal science trundles along without incident, mending here and amending there, then, is suddenly refuted, is a mystification, leaving 'revolutionary' science as the work of a scientific *deus-ex-machina*. Rather, 'inventing goes on all the time',[46] and as such normal science reflects the continuous ground of competing theoretical frameworks. Moments of qualitative transformation in scientific understanding are the emergent result of a continuous process of struggle and counter-struggle within the domains of 'normal science'. As Popper was to add, in this respect, the actual history of science does not support a model of the paradigm in which a dominant theory in a given disciplinary field is superseded by another dominant theory, precisely because scientists don't give up a central or prevailing theory within their scientific field without there being a discernible increase in content in the new theory over the prevailing theory. To do otherwise is to assume that scientists have no investment in a notion of science as a system of refinement or advancement of general scientific truths and are prepared to take on theories that merely serve their own research interests; this is the 'logic of *historical relativism*.'[47] Indeed it is, and as such Kuhn demonstrates little detailed interest, despite his commitment to an ostensibly social model of scientific development, in either the ideological and social struggles inherent to the institutional/ social formation of 'research programmes' or in the scientist as scientific subject. This means that his model of change in science produces a highly skewed understanding of how scientific knowledge grows and the position of the scientific subject as experimental subject (as an inventor of experimental techniques) within this process. And this is why Mayo has little sympathy for the inflation of deductive approaches in science after Popper and Kuhn. For although she follows Popper and Lakatos and others in criticizing Kuhn for placing a disproportionate emphasis on the incommensurability between scientific theories as the motor of scientific change, this is not because she is overly concerned with the fact that Kuhn has a poor understanding of science as a field of continuous theoretical struggle. On the contrary, what grounds scientific continuity and scientific growth (and therefore 'normal' science) is a relatively stable tradition of testing, or what she calls standard testing, a tradition that for Kuhn, Lakatos and Popper alike is wholly questionable on empirical grounds. Yet it is precisely a stable tradition of testing for Mayo that is best placed to undermine the discontinuism of the paradigm model of scientific change (and in my view allows us to focus on some of the problems of the subject-who-is-not-a-subject within the deductive tradition, as I discuss below). The creativity of the scientific subject lies not simply within the speculative moment of theory, but in the opportunities for experimental knowledge that arise from the testing of hypotheses. The growth of knowledge is not secured by the falsification or amendment of a well-supported theory, but by the maintenance, refinement and development of standard testing.

> For post-Kuhnian holists, observations are paradigm laden or theory laden and testing hypotheses does not occur apart from testing larger units . . . The lesson I take from post-Kuhnian philosophy of science is that we need to go smaller, not bigger – to the local tests of 'normal science'.[48]

This would seem to place Mayo in the category of the New Experimentalists of the 1980s (in particular Ronald Giere, Ian Hacking, Peter Galison and Nancy Cartwright), who in their rejection of Kuhnian conventionalism and hard-nosed Popperian falsificationism attempted to develop a refined epistemological account of the scientific experiment. However, for Mayo the good intentions of this post-conventionalism either got waylaid or diluted in a kind of empiricist *revanchment*. Thus much of this thinking followed Hacking in the early 1980s in arguing that what the scientific subject learned from experiments did not need to rely on the testing of a theory.[49] Likewise, Galison proposed theory-independent criteria for experiments on the grounds that experiments have a 'life of their own'.[50] Mayo is not a 'new experimentalist' of this stripe, and as such is concerned to draw a line under the post-Kuhnian 'empiricist' turn, steering, as she puts it, a path between the old logical empiricism and the old conventionalism. Yet, nevertheless, in line with the New Experimentalists, she is concerned first and foremost to defend the claim that the production data within the experimental process is able to act as an adjudicator and force of constraint in matters of scientific judgement. And this is why an explicit theory of error becomes crucial to this process (and for our wider understanding of the dialectics of error). Because it is the function of the error that brings the fundamental question of the New Experimentalism into sharp relief: *in what ways and to what ends* do scientific experimentalists actually reason?

If the Popperian, Kuhnian and post-Kuhnian philosophy of science largely gives up on this question, New Experimentalists highlight it as a problem only to narrow its scope by stressing the significance of experimental activities at the expense of precisely why the testing of the outcomes of experimental activities may or may not lead to objective knowledge. Thus Mayo is perhaps closer to some of Ronald Giere's writing here than the other New Experimentalists, in so far as Giere has at least stressed that experimental knowledge grows through the interrelationship between the development of the instrumentation and tools for data acquisition, and theoretical production.[51] But in Mayo, importantly, *nothing* is given in this relationship, neither data *nor* hypotheses:

> An adequate account of experimental testing must not begin at the point where data and hypotheses are given, but rather must explicitly incorporate the intermediate theories of data, instruments, and experiment that are required to obtain experimental evidence in the first place.[52]

In this way the experimental process is built up from a series of mediations between three interconnected models of enquiry: a primary model of primary scientific hypotheses, models of data generation and models of experiment that link the two other models via the development and finessing of test procedures. Thus, the experimental model sits in the middle of the chain, so to speak, mediating the questions formulated by the primary hypothesis, as they pass through the data recovery model and back through the experimental model as a reflection on the primary hypothesis. The production of data in this process is mediated by how it has performed in the experimental model as a basis for revising or challenging the primary hypothesis. How does the production of data satisfy the theoretical assumptions of the experimental model? In the sense of the experimental model within this loop, data has a two-way function: on the one hand to establish analytical techniques for linking data produced as a result of the experimental model of enquiry, and on the other hand connecting the primary hypothesis to the experimental data. This feedback model, then, avoids the tendency within deductive models of enquiry to begin from the primary hypothesis and then pass directly on to the data for confirmation or disconfirmation. By allowing the primary hypothesis to pass through an experimental model, which then, in turn, establishes the experimental conditions for the production of data, the data is able to generate viable questions that further develop the testing of the validity of the primary hypothesis. But what about the abiding problem of underdetermination, the issue that Popper, Feyerabend, Lakatos and W. V. Quine, and others, have stressed as being the fundamental weakness of the role of data within the inductive process? If data cannot pick out the validity of a given hypothesis with any surety then evidence for hypotheses *at all points* within the experimental process will be underdetermined; one hypothesis will have as much status as another. It is this epistemological gap that has tended to undergird the anti-realist Bayesian tenor of much post-Kuhnian philosophy of science: the claims of test results are, in the end, indistinguishable from the beliefs of scientists who promulgate them, and as a result even the most resolute New Experimentalists end up as Bayesians.

How, then, does Mayo deal with the problem of underdetermination? By, in short, casting her experimental model as a means of increasing the possibility of *learning* from error data and thereby increasing the probability of objective knowledge. The significance of the interrelated nature of the experimental process rests, therefore, on the increased capacity it generates for error recognition and learning from error as a way of raising the bar for accurate and vigilant testing. Learning from error on this basis allows for a greater attention to the distribution of errors within the various pathways and nooks and crannies of the experimental process. 'Experimental learning is learning about the probabilities (relative frequencies) of specified outcomes in some actual or hypothetical series of experiments – it is learning about an *experimental distribution*.'[53] The feedback process allows the scientific subject to break down the component parts of the experimental process in order to test those areas, boundaries, gaps, points of transition, that become lost or fuzzy from a broader or larger-segmented perspective. Severity of testing, then, is a result of tightly controlled *piecemeal* moves. 'When enough is learned from piecemeal studies severe tests of higher-level theories are possible ... The accumulated results from piecemeal studies allow us at some point to say that several related hypotheses are correct and that a theory solves a set of experimental problems correctly.'[54] But how do these 'accumulated results' from piecemeal testing actually secure knowledge from the testing for error and avoid the problem of underdetermination?

For Mayo, Popperian, Kuhnian and post-Kuhnian falsificationism and conventionalism, and the downplaying of inductive knowledge and error theory go hand in hand with a cursory commitment to statistical science, or one particular branch of statistics: error probability statistics. Error probability statistics focus, above all, on the *procedures and techniques generating the evidence*. In this way this form of probability statistics develops strategies for testing data from an examination and laying out for scrutiny all aspects of the experimental process (the hypotheses, sample size, experimental procedures, tools and equipment, and so on) before the experiment begins. This is in order to secure the experiment some protection from the assumption that all that is called for in a successful experiment is a logical fit between evidence and hypothesis, as ascribed to by Carnap and Popper. On the contrary, a good test is good precisely because it puts in place a multiple number of checks and counter-checks across all parts and aspects of the process. Probability statistics monitor how well the experimental process 'discriminates between alternative hypotheses and how well it facilitates learning from error.'[55] Importantly, what this attentiveness to the detail of experimentation puts in place – as a routine matter of procedure – is that for statistical knowledge to be useful it needs to be radically anti-conditionalist. That is, scientists committed to learning from error need to keep thinking that the outcomes of tests are not the *only* possible outcomes, irrespective of how good the testing and results appear to be (in the light of a favoured hypothesis). For 'reasoning from the result that did arise *is* crucially dependent upon how often it would arise.'[56] A good test, therefore, has to build this expectancy for other outcomes into its procedures. This captures two significant procedures for error probability theory that meet the requirements of experimental severity: it is short-sighted to declare an error absent if the current evidence based on current levels of experimental technique leads us to believe it to be so; and, conversely, if a good test is shown to have a chance of detecting an error that leads the scientist to assert that a hypothesis is probably false, then the continued probing for further errors has a good chance of showing that the hypothesis *is* false. In this sense, error probability theory works to deepen the detection of errors that are presently undetectable as the inductive basis for further hypothesis testing. Where experimental tests are unable to guarantee these anti-conditionalist conditions – where the conditions for mounting severe tests are inoperative or poor – inductive knowledge is unable to prevail, and suffers from all the problems of underdetermination already described. Thus the primary function of error probability statistics for Mayo is that they are able to play an exacting role in *modelling* the process of scientific induction. Without close modelling in this respect, without sharpening up *how* the data is arrived at, inductive science – as its Popperian and Kuhnian critics rightly assert – is utterly elastic. Scientific progress, for Mayo, therefore, is impossible without the special intimacy between learning from error and the modelling of induction that a feedback-driven experimental process is able to provide. The growth of knowledge is inconceivable without a certain stability of testing across theoretical domains as the basis for argumentation from learning from error.

Mayo's model of error learning is distinctively small-scale in the moves it makes. The error for Mayo is largely what is hidden in the overlooked and hidden gaps and interstices of the experimental process, and in this sense it provides a valuable corrective to hard-core deductivism. The failure of Popperian, Kuhnian and post-Kuhnian philosophy of science is that it has been unwilling to go small enough in these terms, leaving the falsification of theories at the mercy of hidden extraneous factors, and as such subject to the vicissitudes of Bayesianism. But in going small what kind of error theory does Mayo, in fact, provide, and how, as a result, does it sit within a dialectical (post-Kuhnian) conception of science?

Mayo's attack on Bayesianism and all the ills of subjectivism in science places her firmly in the realist camp. Error theory, for Mayo, is important precisely because it *improves* on science's commitment to the possibility of objective knowledge, her theory straddles both the demands of realism and the critique of logical method in science (the delimited place of creative experimental practice in post-Popperian philosophy of science). Thus, on the one hand, she lines up with Lakatos's and Feyerabend's extension of Popper's underdeveloped critique of logical method and Carnapian logical omniscience, but, on the other, she is opposed to the relativist implications of deductive and theoretical creativity in science as a whole. Accordingly, she recognizes, along with Lakatos and others, that scientific progress is not secured solely through a logical fit between data and hypothesis. Rather, knowledge is produced out of a series of questions asked of experimental data as a result of what is learned from errors generated earlier in the experimental process. And in this sense her work places inductive reason back at the centre of realism. But this theoretical reconsideration of scientific methodology does not translate into any systematic account of the scientific subject and the social production of science itself. In this respect her 'small scale' move is accompanied by a narrowing of the social implications of her critique of Popper and deductivism. This leads to a general indifference to the epistemological and ontological implications of the error, which places her work surprisingly in the ruling anti-Hegelian camp within the philosophy of science, and in her 'piecemeal' analyses closer to Carnap's anti-metaphysics than she would no doubt be prepared to accept. Indeed, although the error is foregrounded as the site of productivity, the function and role of this productivity in science is not examined. Hence we learn little from Mayo about why an improved (materialist) theory of error is important for a post-Popperian and post-Kuhnian philosophy of science, beyond that, it challenges how deductivism and falsificationism tend to produce a theory of science that operates at a distance from the actual day-to-day procedures and challenges of the laboratory. If Bayesian subjectivism is the enemy of objective knowledge in science, what kind of a scientific subject *is* the subject who learns creatively from errors? How is the scientific subject-who-is-not-a-subject developed and transformed by a theory of error and the critique of deductivism?

SCIENCE AND THE TEMPORALITY OF THE ERROR

What is required is not just an improved theory of errors in science – a commitment to living with errors in order to discover what truths they might generate, as against their elimination as experimental detritus – but a dialectical account of the philosophy of science in which errors provide a *determinate role*. This means bringing what we have learned from the post-Popperian critique of deductivism and the need for a theory of error within the experimental process into closer theoretical alignment with a dialectical theory of realism. For if it is has been necessary, following Mayo, to 'go small' in order to recover the dynamics of experimental truth, it is now important to reverse the process and insist on the social totality of science as a system, relinking the concept of error with Hegel (and Hegel's critique of science) and his realist critics.

The history of the philosophy of science after Duhem (Popper, Kuhn, Lakatos and Feyerabend), for all its emphasis on science as a social activity (irrespective of whether it is committed to some version of realism or not), has tended to focus simply on the 'intersubjective' conditions of this process of socialization. In this respect, the scientific subject-who-is-not-a-subject, whether it be the classic Cartesian subject of Carnap, the quasi-Cartesian subject of Popper and Lakatos, or the post-Cartesian subject of Kuhn and Feyerabend, is, despite its various levels of institutional articulation across this body of writing, cast as an autonomous agent amongst other autonomous agents. The critical cost of this for a dialectical theory of realism (and errors) is a fundamental confusion about where the scientific subject stands in relation to the objective production of knowledge and the real. Modern idealist philosophies of science (Popper, Kuhn et al.) have addressed only one side of science's social question – what are the scientific-institutional conditions of the possibility of individual scientific experience and practice? – and not the other part of the question: What are the conditions of possibility for science *as a social and critical activity as such*?[57] The latter question implies a very different kind of scientific subject-who-is-not-a-subject than hitherto. Science is not concerned simply with the continuous accumulation and falsification of data, nor, in fact, with the discipline-specific growth of knowledge, but with understanding and verifying the mind-independent mechanisms involved in the generation of phenomena in nature and as the basis for deepening our understanding of the stratifications of nature. On this basis, science as an institutional practice – as the production, development and intellectual discipline of subjects-who-are-not-subjects – is produced and articulated in two related, but essentially separate, dimensions, what Roy Bhaskar has called the transitive and the intransitive. The transitive dimension is the socially produced knowledge of the natural world – what here we have been referring to as the experimental processes of science – and the intransitive dimension is the realm of causal mechanisms and generative structures which exist and act independently of these processes and of all human consciousness. 'Science as a process is always intrinsic to "thought". However, by perception and access to objects, viz. things and causal structures, existing independently of thought may be obtained.'[58]

This ontological gap between the transitive and intransitive realms establishes two conditions: first, scientists, in producing science, do not 'find' themselves in, or express themselves through, nature; and, secondly, as a consequence of this, there is a shift of onus in scientific discovery and practice away from the creativity of the singular scientific subject and a given set of experiments as the transformation of scientific tradition, to the notion of science as a social activity that pre-exists the 'normal' or revolutionary individual contributions of scientists. Science is an ongoing social activity that is irreducible to the consciousness of particular scientists engaged on particular experiments, in so far as scientific knowledge is irreducible to the individual thinking and judgements of particular scientists themselves. Science, in other words, is a collective and ongoing system of knowledge production (of the analysis of structures and events independent of human consciousness), in which at no point is this system of knowledge to be taken as the outcome of individual sense experiences and activity. This is not to say simply that knowledge is larger than any contribution a single scientist may produce, but, rather, that the generation of scientific knowledge is itself a social product and, therefore, cannot be conceived as, and passed on as, an individual acquisition. 'For any cognitive act to be possible there must be a material cause; some knowledge established, given to us, already produced. No sum of individual cognitive acts can yield knowledge.'[59] In these terms there is another and better name for the scientific subject-who-is-not-a-subject: namely Hegel's 'forgetful' subject, the subject who is conscious of himself or herself as part of a supraconsciousness; that is, something that is the product of the activity of humans, but is irreducible to the individual contributions of those humans. The advantage of this model – in contrast to the subjective inertness of Carnap's and Popper's subject – is that the scientific subject-who-is-not-a-subject consciously reflects the discontinuity between the subject and claims to objective knowledge, without suppressing or discarding the fact that it is precisely subjects who make, advance and defend these claims.

This Hegelian and post-Cartesian notion of the scientific subject as an effect of distributed intelligence has recently become a concern of the growing interface between the philosophy of science and the cognitive sciences. Edwin Hutchins, Andy Clark, Karin Knorr Cetina and Ronald Giere have all addressed the notion of 'collective cognition' as a way out of the methodological individualism of the post-Popperian and post-Kuhnian philosophy of science.[60] Hutchins and Clark argue that mind is a category that now increasingly extends beyond its location in the physical body through the mnemotechnical resources of computers and digital technology. Cetina – perhaps the strongest advocate of a *post*-subjectivist (and latter day Carnapian) position for the scientist – argues that under laboratory conditions the epistemic identity of the scientific subject is erased, and replaced by the functions of the experimental process itself. This is because very little of the detail and workings of the experimental process takes place in any individual scientist's head, being distributed across the activities and cognitions of a number of individuals directly or indirectly involved in the experimental process. Most experimental situations cannot be carried out or assessed by any one individual. Giere, similarly, sees the problem of a stable scientific subject – the singular scientific subject armed with logic – as a phantasm. As such this growing literature on the edges of the philosophy of science brings the philosophy of science foursquare into the orbit of the critique of the subject, particularly in the area of the recent cognitive sciences themselves. If Hutchins and Clark, and others, weaken the distinction between consciousness and its prosthetic extension in external technologies, W. Teed Rockwell, following Cetina, sets out to destroy the last vestiges of mind/body dualism from within the philosophy of mind and neurosciences. Rockwell, however, defends a model of distributed theory of consciousness from *within* the body itself. Following recent work in the neurosciences, Rockwell argues that consciousness exists in the entire nervous system and not just in the head, and is, therefore, the outcome of chemical exchange and communication throughout the *whole* body. Thus, following the standard anti-Cartesian precept of recent work in the philosophy of consciousness – there is no single place in which consciousness 'sits', no theatre of the subject as Daniel Dennett puts it – Rockwell goes even further to argue that parts of the body may be 'partial embodiments of the mind.'[61]

> If consciousness is an emergent property of the brain-body, there is no need for information to be carried back to the brain for the self to be aware of something. Any appropriate physiological event in principle could embody a mental event no matter where it took place.[62]

This means, according to Rockwell, that less neuronal communication occurs at the synaptic level than we care to imagine. To declare that one feels a certain emotion does not mean that one is in a particular *brain state*, but rather that 'the cells distributed throughout one's body had received the particular dosage of ligands that was responsible for that emotion.'[63]

Physiological and neurological evidence for distributed corporeal consciousness is presently sketchy, however there is enough evidence to suggest that the vectors of consciousness are not just contained within discrete brain states. This leads, however, to a crucial epistemological problem that all other theories of distributed consciousness face in their critique of methodological individualism: if our concepts of consciousness are no longer stable, and as such scientific logic is a consequence of a prosthetic and collective process of intelligence, what is left of the scientific subject of judgement and intention? Where exactly *is* the scientific subject-who-is-not-a-subject armed with an improved theory of errors and an improved assessment of inductive thinking? Is this scientific subject just another phantasm? As Rockwell himself observes: with the putative displacement of consciousness from brain-states, and the acceptance that the self is socially and culturally embedded, 'it is not obvious how we can account for the existence of errors.'[64] That is, in the realm of the post-Cartesian subject, it is not obvious how we can account truthfully for the existence of errors on the basis of individual judgement. (For Descartes, let us recall, the elimination or suppression of error is based on the quality of judgement – its contemplative attentiveness – derived from the subject's individual powers of reason). Judgement, in these terms, as such is *not* there in any subject-sense, or culpable sense, as I outlined in Chapter 1; it is perpetually deferred by the cognitive limitations of the subject, or held to be an outcome or effect of the collective.[65] Is this model of distributive intelligence another, and scientifically 'reputable', name for scientific scepticism, and the Nietzschean collapse of truth into error? Ronald Giere thinks as much. Such an epistemology, he willingly admits – in line here with Rockwell – clearly provides a necessary corrective to a fundamentalist, central-state materialist Cartesianism and its idealist cognates. But problems arise – indeed these are the problems that Mayo indirectly addresses via her inductivist theory of errors – when the notion of extended or distributed consciousness makes it impossible for the scientific subject to take *individual responsibility* for learning from error as a part of a given experimental process or research programme in order to pass this data on. In other words, science as a socialized and pre-given activity is always the space where scientists are compelled to *define and live with errors*; the distributed experimental process as a convocation of subjectivities cannot in and of itself do this kind of work. Giere's solution, though, is equally problematic. In his criticisms of the distributive model, he is too eager, in his talk of 'our ordinary concept of individual human agents',[66] to re-establish a modified methodological individualist model of the subject. For Geire, the standard (humanist) concept may be compromised and idealized, but it provides, at one level, he suggests, a sufficiently robust understanding of how knowledge is actually produced to make it worth defending. This immediately strips out what is definitional and challenging about the notion of 'distributed knowledge'. Despite the failings of post-subjectivist models of the scientific subject in their abandoning the subject of error, the distributed character of knowledge does at least have the virtue of displacing the very thing that remains largely unexamined in post-Popperian and post-Kuhnian philosophy of science: the epistemological identity of the scientist himself or herself. Geire offers complacency by comparison.

In this respect, a sharp choice faces socialized models of the scientific subject-who-is-not-a-subject. Between, on the one hand, a kind of pragmatist post-subjectivist model of distributed cognition (a model which is becoming increasingly 'common-sense' at the interface between the cognitive sciences and the philosophy of science), and on the other hand, a critical and dialectical model of the scientific subject, in which distributed intelligence becomes an extension of dialectical realism. Thus Hegel's depossessive subject is able to provide a strong defence of the latter, in so far as, despite its understanding of the delimited function and dispersed character of the subject, it remains in its powers of distribution a *subject of truth*. The dialectical scientific subject-who-is-not-a-subject possesses scientific subjectivity precisely because it operates (collectively) as a bridging point between the transitive and intransitive realms, between the claims of knowledge production and a stratified world of causal mechanisms and structures independent of thought. On this basis the subject-who-is-not-a-subject generates a necessary kind of realist paradox: *he or she defends a particular proposition or hypothesis as a claim on our deepening understanding of a mind-independent world, but without assuming these claims to be subjectively derived from their individual judgements.* The scientific subject-who-is-not-a-subject (in his or her depossessive identity and distributed function) remains at the point of their defence of a particular proposition or hypothesis, the possessor of the *possibility of truth*. In the Platonic sense I outlined in Chapter 1, in order for truth to distinguish itself from untruth, subjects must become actual possessors of the procedures of truth-production and therefore of their own errors. Or, as Bhaskar puts it in a related Platonic fashion, 'In order to learn from our mistakes we must *know* that (and when) we are mistaken.'[67] That is, *we* must lay claim to errors in order to make errors speak to the truth-operations of science. Without this, truth is either the abstract distributed function of the experimental process (as in Cetina), or the hearsay of others – the thing Locke and Kant rightly criticized about School philosophy. Hence a theory of errors is indivisible from the scientific truth claims of specific subjects, irrespective of the distributed or post-subjectivist nature of scientific knowledge. A dialectical theory of errors and a dialectical theory of science, converge, then, precisely on the grounds that the scientific subject-who-is-not-a-subject is both subject and *not* a subject.

HEGEL, 'NEW DIALECTIC' AND ERROR THEORY

As such, in order to elaborate and defend a dialectical theory of errors that captures inductive practice as the basis of scientific truth and the error as the basis of transformative practice, it is necessary to defend, not just a dialectical theory of science – which many anti-realist philosophies of science would acknowledge in principle – but a dialectical concept of the scientific subject, for it is precisely the latter that obviates the false objectivism of pure deductivism and falsificationism and Carnapian 'scientific method'. In order to do this successfully, therefore, we need, first and foremost, a philosophy of science that has interiorized Hegel and dialectic in order to be able to reflect back on Hegel and dialectic and the philosophy of science itself. But, as I have stressed, the social theorists of the philosophy of science since Kuhn have not been terribly adroit at this, or even interested in this possibility, given their tendency to adopt some version of methodological individualism, weakening what science might learn from Hegel, and what science might offer by way of productive critique (after Marx) of Hegelian dialectic.

The recent major exception to the prevailing idealism and methodological individualism has been Bhaskar's scientific realism, a clear advance on the social and epistemological incoherence of Kuhn's philosophy. Bhaskar's, *The Realist Theory of Science* (1974) was the first systematic philosophy of science to theorize the scientific enterprise not simply as an institution-governed practice of intersubjectively given norms, but as a fully socialized one, in which scientists were agents engaged in a collective, self-transformative and progressive activity. However, for all its assiduous critique of deductivism, Popperian falsificationism, and the idealism of post-Kuhnian philosophy generally, Bhaskar's transcendental realism was neither dialectical nor very Hegelian. Indeed, Bhaskar's division of science between a transitive and intransitive domain was in sharp need of a concept of change and transformation at the level of knowledge production and truth. This problem was addressed in the later *Dialectic: The Pulse of Freedom* (1992), an ambitious attempt – at one level – to bring a realist philosophy of science into explicit alignment with dialectical theory. Bhaskar's considerable achievement in *Dialectic* was to finally demolish the speculative discontinuism that so seemed to plague the post-Kuhnian division of the philosophy of science into 'normal' and 'revolutionary' science. For Bhaskar, there is only *one* science, so to speak, but one that is internally riven and unstable, given its open-ended, historically conditioned and non-predictive character. A defence of the open-ended character of science had of course played its part in Popperian and post-Popperian falsificationism, but this defence of openness had always been compromised by these theories' overstrenuous critique of inductivism and a sceptical view of scientific progress. Bhaskar's dialectical realism, in contrast, provides a non-sceptical and transformative account of open-endedness by insisting on the dialectic of inconsistency and incompleteness at the very heart of scientific practice and social praxis (and scientific progress). Because the world is fundamentally open, transformative scientific activity generates further incompleteness, on the basis that the absenting of one absence generates the theoretical conditions for the absenting of other absences. 'In an open world neither inconsistency nor incompleteness are ineliminable; and the possibility of both are transcendentally necessary conditions for science.'[68] Bhaskar's defence of open-endedness, in this respect, is based on a primary commitment to science's position within, more broadly, a theory of negation – what he calls the 'ontological priority of the negative.'[69] That is, negation is the name given to two primary and interdependent transformative functions of science, the first of which we have already met: (1) the deepening and extension of our knowledge of nature on the basis of the removing of constraints to this knowledge (through experimental activity and theoretical production); and (2) the absenting of absence as leading to an absenting of *ills, blockages and contradictions*. In *The Realist Philosophy of Science*, this link between knowledge production and the absenting of absence was certainly attenuated, leaving Bhaskar's social conception of science in a delimited transformative relationship to nature and the social world; in *Dialectic* this link becomes the defining characteristic of science's transitive domain and progress, and as such provides the would-be missing connection between knowledge, science and emancipatory praxis. Indeed, the concept of the absenting of absence allows Bhaskar to connect realist method in science to a concept of negation as the very motor of emancipatory thinking and practice. Negation is not simply the means by which the provisional character of truth is secured within the transitive domain of science, but is the very ground of science's embeddedness in the movement of knowledge to truth. Thus absence and negation are *ontologically prior* to presence and positivity on the grounds that absence and negation always outreach and overstretch presence and positivity. To assume otherwise is to fix science and praxis in the image of received truth and inherited knowledge: 'in making we cannot simply replicate the conditions of our making, we must negate or absent.'[70]

This has important implications for our dialectical theory of errors: the eradication of, and learning from, errors represents the ontological ground of the renewal of truth. By prioritizing negation, the absenting of absence and ontological incompleteness, science and praxis are released from the stultifications of Popperian falsification and post-Kuhnian scepticism, in which 'negation' is severed from any wider emancipatory horizons. And in this sense Bhaskar, here, echoes the point at the very beginning of my introduction: the passage of truth through error *sustains* the possibility of truth; that is, truth cannot *think itself* positively, and therefore must continually mediate its failure to achieve its own self-reconciliation. But, if Bhaskar's notion of the absenting of absence is able to contribute to a dialectical theory of error and the philosophy of science, it nevertheless is diminished overall by its dissociation of a theory of negation from Hegel: 'I want to show that it is possible to think and act dialectically without necessarily being a Hegelian.'[71] This is a mistake. In a strange kind of replication of the anti-Hegelianism of the early twentieth-century philosophy of science and nineteenth-century and contemporary critics of Hegel, Bhaskar condemns Hegel to a metaphysical shadow life, in which the Hegel of his realist critique is not much different from the Hegel of bourgeois caricature. Hegel is a philosopher of the dialectic of reconciliation; a philosopher of realized history, and, therefore, fundamentally a theorist of positivity over negation. Accordingly, his philosophy suffers from 'onto-logic' stasis and congealment[72] in which 'negation is lost in a pacific sea of positivity';[73] his thinking 'panlogicize[s] being',[74] and hypostatizes thought;[75] he produces a history which is 'smooth, continuous, unilinear and closed',[76] generating a dialectic that moves towards a 'final glaciating repose',[77] and, therefore, he 'lends his whole effort to the transfiguration of an actuality that has already been defined in bourgeois individualist, that is to say, analytical and empirical realist terms';[78] as such, Hegel is the supreme 'non-dialectical dialectician'.[79] 'Hegelian freedom is the fate of the Stoic; his logicism that of positivity; his reason that of the rationalization of the actually existing order of things.'[80]

Not only is this critique historically incorrect, politically baleful, and philosophically incorrigible (for a philosopher of some power, such as Bhaskar), it is also hard to recognize how it might, at any constructive level, be identifiable with a concept of dialectic worth defending, certainly for a theory of errors. But this is not surprising, for, despite Bhaskar's would-be dialectical 'deepening' of the realist philosophy of science, such a critique ends up not only distancing Marx from Hegel, but distancing dialectic from Marx and the Marxist legacy, based on the fact that Bhaskar replicates a commonplace misreading of Hegel as an idealist, a position, of course, that Marx himself unfortunately contributed to – via his early sympathy for Feuerbach. The consequence of this history of misreading is that Bhaskar appears to be doing the right thing – as with many others who have taken this path – in critiquing 'historicism', 'endism' and 'positivism' in the name of Marx's 'critique' of Hegel's idealism, but in fact ends up diminishing Marx and the Marxist tradition as such. This critique inevitably results in positioning non-Hegelian dialectic at some distance *politically* from Marx and the Marxist tradition, weakening what is epistemologically preferable about Hegelian dialectic to non-Hegelian dialectic: its essentially unfolding, sublatary function. Thus we might say that not only have nineteenth-century liberals, and twentieth-century methodological individualists (Popper) and neo-liberals (Friedrich August von Hayek), invariably got in the way of reading Hegel – of reading Hegel closely – but also numerous Marxists and neo-Marxists, by their willingness to accept Marx's own poor (Oedipal) reading of his own philosophical and political mentor.[81] In this respect there is a strange complicity between the nineteenth-century liberal critics of Hegel such as Rudolf Haym and Alexander de Tocqueville, twentieth-century logical positivists such as Carnap, and neo-liberals such as Hayek, and the post-Marxist theorists and 'dialecticians' of the new capitalist Restoration (Norberto Bobbio, Bhaskar and Alain Badiou) – that is, they all attack Hegelian dialectic on the grounds of Hegel's would-be dialectical exultancy and historicism. Now this is not to say that Bhaskar and Badiou in particular are straight-forwardly *anti*-Hegelians (in the sense that Hayek and Bobbio might be described as such),[82] or that their anti-historicist critique of Hegel cannot provide necessary and valuable insights into dialectic (which I will come to below), or provide a renewed understanding of the connection between negation and emancipation (which is where, as I have stressed, a theory of errors rises or falls), but that their attack on Hegel, politically and epis-temologically, shares a covert framework with the attacks on Hegel by his reactionary and counter-revolutionary critics: the weakness of Hegel's thinking on history and freedom lies in its essential processual function (and as such its fundamental statist-positivistic character).

A defence of Hegel as a materialist, and a defence of Marx's profound debt to Hegel, represents, therefore, more than a philosophical adjust-ment to a corrupted and self-corrupting philosophical tradition; it marks a major point of defence for Marxist dialectic and the Enlightenment legacy, and here the emancipatory dialectic of error and dialectical defence of the philosophy of science. Without Hegel, we lose a certain revolution-ary dialogue and continuity between science, dialectic and error that allows contingency to *override* historical process (one of the problems with the Foucauldian-Canguilheimian axis and its modification in David W. Bates). Thus, those twentieth-century writers on Hegel who have resisted the idealist line politically (V. I. Lenin, Antonio Gramsci, Raya Dunayevska, Daniel Bensaïd, Domenico Losurdo, Sean Sayers, David MacGregor, Yirmiyahu Yovel, Jean-Luc Nancy) as against those Hegelians who have compromised with it (Theodor Adorno – to a certain extent – Charles Taylor) have all insisted on two significant things: the continuities between Hegel and Marx, and the essentially anti-positivistic and non-determinate character of Hegel's philosophy. This latter is crucial in contesting what has become the major dividing line between the 'new dialectic' and Hegel: the fundamental openness of the former, as opposed to the closed nature of the latter.

Let us look more closely, then, at Hegel, and some of the misunder-standings that surround his legacy, before we return to our discussion of the philosophy of science and error theory. First, Hegel's purported ideal-ism. Hegel's insistence that thought is identical with its objects does not entail a belief in the convergence of thought with reality. The categories of thought may be identical with the real, but this does not mean that thought and external reality are the same, and therefore that reality is reducible to thought. This, essentially, is what Marx inherits from Hegel: human consciousness is active and truth-producing of the external world, but thought is itself irreducible to the world. Moreover, through these truth-producing capacities, thought also transforms itself in transforming the world. As Marx says in *Capital* Vol. 1: 'Man not only effects a change in the materials of nature; he also realizes . . . his own purpose in those materials.'[83] In Hegel this process is called 'ideality'– the intersection of theoretical and practical human activity – in Marx, explicitly 'revolutionary praxis'. Ideality and revolutionary praxis, therefore, share a common transformative language. For Hegel, absolute ideality or Idea – 'the identity of the theoretical and practical idea'[84] – is the result of freely conceived human sensuous activity, and as such is represented by Hegel as the outcome of a double and interconnected emancipatory process: the simultaneous gaining of freedom by humans *from* and *within* nature and *from* and *within* society. Marx calls his version of this dialectical logic communist consciousness and praxis: the freely determined exercise of human powers within a society of freely determined producers. Thus for both Hegel and Marx the long-term struggles of theory and praxis bring about the possibility of a higher level of social objectivity: the socialized individual in his material and intellectual labour becomes the actual subject-object of history; that is, simply, individuals are determined *by*, and the producers *of*, the society in which they find themselves. And, for Hegel as much as Marx, these socially produced powers of self-actualization are driven by the negation of those forces and ills that prevent the universal realization of these powers. As such, 'reason in history' – the principle, of course, by which Hegel is usually condemned – is not the work of an immanent and unfolding abstract intellect, or supraintellect, but of reason's definition, development and defence 'from below'. As David MacGregor declares, in Hegel: 'The rational principle underlying the movement of history is carried forward precisely by those oppressed groups and classes (and their allies) who stand to benefit most from its realization.'[85] In this way, as MacGregor rightly observes, 'there is no "mystificatory side" to the Hegelian dialectic.'[86] On the contrary, Marx and Hegel share similar commitments based on the self-actualizing and transformative capacity of human beings. Consequently, those who believe it is possible to wrestle

Marx from Hegel in order to install Marx in the 'normality of modern science' (to quote Daniel Bensaïd) understand nothing of Marx, and, as such, flagrantly distort Marx's reliance on Hegel: there is no Marxist critique of positivistic science without Hegelian dialectic.[87] In this light, as Domenico Losurdo insists, the 'idealisation' of Hegel produces, at a deeper level, not only a fundamental misrepresentation of key concepts, but the essential depoliticization of these concepts' positional role within his philosophy and the political and philosophic culture of his time.[88] For instance, the central concepts of the actual and the Absolute are rendered mute or opaque by their reification as positivistic or illicit metaphysical categories, in writers who, carelessly or willingly, fail to understand the specific conditions of their theoretical production. Let us take these two important concepts in turn.

The actual: Hegel's elision of the actual with the rational is invariably condemned as evidence of Hegel's fundamental irrationality, servilism and conservatism: 'what is, is what is real' is the usual tag – a criticism recently reasserted, in separate ways, by both Bhaskar and Badiou. However, for Hegel, the actual=rational has quite a different meaning. Far from being the name Hegel gives to empirical immediacy and its day-to-day masters, the actual is a strategic or immanent content that is latent in, or emergent from, everyday appearances. Thus when Hegel talks about the actual and the rational being *one*, he is not talking about the conflation of appearance with truth, but, on the contrary, with how appearances are in their internally divided content, the driving force of change and emancipation. In short, appearances contain the rational kernel or seed of other forces, countervailing forces; and as such the actual is the name of those emancipatory tendencies that emerge and coalesce in collective action over a given period, which, in turn, contest and challenge prevailing powers in order to redirect the historical process. Thus for long historical periods the actual as the subsumption-of-the-rational remains spectral or dormant, until under pressure from below the prevailing powers are no longer able to control or subsume those countervailing forces and rule in the same way to the same ends. The active mode of the actual, then, for Hegel – negation – is not just the outcome of the subject's non-identity with itself, but is immanent *to* social objectivity itself. Large-scale socio-political transformation is not, in fact, the direct outcome of subjective agency at all (although the coalescence of such subjectivities is the prerequisite of such change), but, rather, the socially produced subjective outcome of the unresolved conflicts of social objectivity (the conflict between the emergent forces of the actual-as-rational and the prevailing powers and interests of a given period). As Losurdo puts it:

> Socio-political transformations are not the result of a merely subjective project: the 'change' (*Veränderung*) – we are told in the *Philosophical Propaedeutic* – 'is marked by the disparity between one and itself', that is, the actual; it is therefore 'the negation of the negative that the something (*Etwas*) has in itself' [*Werke in zwanzig Bänden*, IV, 14]. This is how the dynamism of the French revolution is explained . . . the 'negative tendency' as assured by the Enlightenment did nothing but 'destroy what was already destroyed by itself, [*Werke in zwanzig Bänden*, XX, 295–96]. The assertion of the rationality of the actual is not therefore the negation of the change, but its anchor to the objective dialectic of the actual.[89]

The notion of the actual-as-the-rational, then, for Hegel, represents a profoundly materialist understanding of the gap between the empirical and the emergent, appearance and truth, and as such is identifiable socially and politically, above all else, with reflection on and the critique of determinate conditions of a given state of affairs. This is why Hegel was always a formidable critic of unrealizable ideals, and as such a strong and principled defender of where and when freedom and the forces of emancipation needed defending in concrete, transformative ways. Thus Hegel's concept of the actual serves two functions: on the one hand, to obviate the political and epistemological investment in ungroundable and unsustainable forces and powers by insisting on the essential opacity of the real; and on the other, a recognition that this opacity is internally inconsistent and riven by contradiction, and therefore the site of its own transformation and dissolution. This is why Lenin and Gramsci read Hegel as the great theorist of the conjuncture, indeed the supreme thinker of the dialectical interrelation of particular and universal within a given concrete socio-political context. Yet this conjunctural mode, based on the notion of the actual-as-rational, has confused and dismayed many on the Left. Indeed, if the opacity of the actual frustrated the Romantic urgings and idealist flights of fantasy of Hegel's liberal critics – Hegel as the bastion of statist intervention, assimilation and control – on the Left it has been seen, ultimately, as an endorsement of a concept of change internal to bourgeois appearances and logic. These latter criticisms have of course centred mainly on *The Philosophy of Right* and its seeming abandonment of the popular democracy of the French Revolution for a bourgeois-statist, and top-down, conception. Two interrelated issues need to be addressed, however, in any adequate reading of this text. First, the largely reactionary anti-statist character of the counter-revolutionary writing on politics of the period, in which the implementation of the rule of law during the French Revolution, inhibiting the 'freedom' of the aristocracy, inhibits the freedom of all; and second, the rise on the Left, (but also, freely borrowed and developed in part by the anti-statist liberals themselves) of a Rousseauian, post-Jacobin conception of Natural Law, in which freedom is identified with the freedom from all social ties and conventions. The latter is invariably framed in the language of the inalienable rights of man, and has a static or 'primitivist' conception of freedom: the rights of man can only truly be secured in the very face of modernity and progress. In this the defenders of Natural Law, in the spirit of Rousseau, advocate a pastoralized model of development, in which the institutionalization of law is the very antithesis of freely derived human exchange. Accordingly, the counter-revolutionary Restorationists had little sympathy with a model of development that would imagine sweeping away all relations of power. The virtues of Natural Law, on this basis, therefore, are treated highly selectively by the Restorationists: they function principally as a version of pre-modern pastoralism, in which the hierarchies of the 'natural' social order are to be re-stabilized, the stronger replacing the weaker. Now, Hegel, in the language of Rousseau (his great mentor, along with Diderot), speaks of the inalienable rights of man, but at no point in his philosophy is their defence ever framed within a model of Natural Law. This is because the rights of nature, for Hegel, are no more than the right to be subject to the forces of arbitrary will and indiscriminate violence: nature 'red in tooth and claw'. Consequently, we need to see the 'statism' of *The Philosophy of Right*, as a response to those counter-revolutionaries and bourgeois thinkers – the majority – who adopted some version of Natural Law in order to argue for the restoration of the *ancien regime* and defend existing property relations. *The Philosophy of Right*, is a vivid example of the actual-as-rational in operation: freedom is not to be defined by its abstract form under existing social, political and economic relations, or derived from some metaphysical principle, but as the hard-won outcome of a long process of struggle and development. Losurdo again:

Freedom is indeed a natural, inalienable right, but of a historical nature, a 'second nature.' Freedom and inalienable rights do not precede progress, but are the result of it. The result of man's complex and contradictory struggle to build a world in which he can recognize and actualize himself. And it is in this 'second nature' that man gains 'awareness of his freedom and subjectivity' [*Die Vernunft in der Geschichte*, 256–57][90]

The accusation of statism and servilism, then, needs to be placed in its concrete socio-political setting: namely, that in the 1820s and 1830s those who advocated some version of Natural Law or stressed that freedom could be achieved outside of the mediations of a political community guaranteed by the State (in conditions where the working class and independent artisans had little or no protection from those in power) were the out-and-out reactionaries. Hegel – almost alone in his condemnation of Natural Law in the 1820s – resisted this, because, in his defence of the French Revolution, he was aware that the democratic struggles of the plebeian classes were not secured simply by freedom from the arbitrary edicts of the aristocracy, but by the implementation and institutionalization of equality in law. The bourgeois State, then, for all its oppression of the plebeian classes, was also the place where concrete freedoms and advances were to be won and defended. Yet Hegel was not thereby a 'reformist' in modern parlance, nor had he any illusions about the bourgeois state. The freedoms won by the plebeian classes were shaped by the merely formal content of freedom under bourgeois law (a principle, of course, that Marx made his own). This is why Hegel's defence of Absolute monarchy, on occasions, as against elected monarchies, was based on the fact that, with the rise of the power of the big landowners under the new elected monarchies, it was harder to defend the interests of the peasantry against the increasingly arbitrary dictates of these baronial landowners in the countryside, just as he has no compunction in calling for a 'revolution from above' if it means the smashing of the remnants of feudal privilege. The point at stake here, then, is that the promise of the actual for Hegel is also to be determined by the given case at hand. In addition he was always conscious of the formal democratic content of would-be republics themselves, real or imagined. The idea of a Republic was not in itself coextensive with freedom (a prevailing illusion of the Rousseauian Left). Indeed, the 'glory' of ancient Sparta and Rome was based on expropriation and counter-revolution.[91] Thus, what separates Hegel from the anti-statist liberal tradition and from Rousseauian Jacobinism is precisely this attention to concreteness, the very thing that his critics attack him for neglecting, and which paves the way to Marx.

But you wouldn't know this from reading Bhaskar and Badiou's critique, particularly; ironically, given that they are both indebted to a version of Hegel's divergence of the empirical and the real, and as such to a notion of the actual-as-immanent-tendency, or force. Thus for Bhaskar the separation of the empirical, or what he calls the actual, from the real is formulated on the basis that the real remains hidden, undisclosed, latent, unactualized at some level. Yet if the concept of the 'actual' shifts position here, its content remains largely the same. In Hegel the actual – as the name of the real – is immanent to the empirical; in Bhaskar, it is the real, rather, that is immanent to the actual. Thus, whether it is named as the actual or the real, for Bhaskar and Hegel such negative content exceeds the positivity of appearances. Similarly, in Badiou, dialectic is driven by the gap between the 'what of the thing' (identity) and 'what-it-is-not' (non-identity). For Hegel, he says, 'Reality is in effect the moment of the unity of being-in-itself and being-other.'[92] That is, dialectic is marked by the divergence of a Third Term that supplements the existence of the two (the empirical and the real).[93] Truth, therefore, in the spirit of Hegel, is secured in the gap between the insubstantiality of the empirical and the ontological reality of the real. But, if this divergence between the empirical and the real is accepted as a basic principle of dialectic and science, here the comparison with Hegel ends. This is because both Bhaskar and Badiou attack Hegel for not carrying through the negative implications of this logic to its 'proper' emancipatory conclusions. For Bhaskar, Hegel's dialectic is stalled, or rendered inert, because of its subsumption and incorporation of the not-one under a system which is essentially additive, accumulative, inclusive and englobing, in which each moment, each development or set of developments, is the self-stabilizing outcome of a previous less developed phase. As a result, 'nothing except absence is lost.'[94] 'Positivity and self-(identity), the very characteristics of the understanding, are always, restored at the end of reason.'[95] Consequently, inconsistency, contradiction and error can never rise to a point where unactualized negation can truly challenge (bourgeois) appearances, or the 'actual' in Bhaskar's sense of the term:

> in an Hegelian *Aufhebung*, is not error . . . lost? Hegel will perhaps want to say the erroneous has been retained as a partial aspect of the truth, but either the error

has been cancelled in the coming-to-be or fruition of the end or nothing has been cancelled and *Aufgehoben* loses its threefold meaning – to annul, preserve and sublimate – and the whole Hegelian project is without point or rationale, for at the very least, a lack of reconciliation to actuality must be lost. In fact in any genuine (materialist) *Aufhebung* it is clear that something has to be lost, even if it is only time.[96]

Inconsistency, contradiction and error, then, are always, according to Bhaskar, demoted and ultimately dissolved through Hegel's additive and englobalising conception of *Aufhebung*, unable to release their disjunctive and system-threatening content, and more precisely their scientific content. This is also Badiou's point in both *Being and Event* and *The Logics of Worlds*. Hegel's concept of the actual subordinates identity, the what-is-not, to the 'absoluteness of the Whole, which is each thing governs its change and raises it up to the concept.'[97] Hence negation in Hegel, for Badiou, is, so to speak, put on the back foot. Negation may be at the very origin of appearances, since negation precedes and determines all appearances, but nevertheless this 'cannot satisfy us'.[98] This is due to the fact that, for Badiou, Hegel's negation of the negation always retains the mark of its own emergent identity. And for Badiou, in an echo of Bhaskar, this means that the supplementary Third Meaning produced in the gap between the one and the not-one is subject to two convergent and delimiting forces: the negation of appearing as a negation of *bourgeois* appearing, and the mediation of the concept, or Notion (freedom). In this 'generative ontology',[99] therefore, nothing ever fails to appear as the conceptual mediation of the Notion and the Whole and as such nothing exists – in its unactualized actuality – as a 'non-appearing' exception to 'the local laws of appearing.'[100] In other words, in Hegel no negation of the negation is ever allowed, in its subtractive identity, to break the terrible momentum of the present as the servant of the past. The present, thereby, becomes the already pre-given, sublated outcome of the past. For Badiou, this logic is the logic of a historical 'appeasement' in which the present is never actually *created*; that is, is always subordinate to the self-stablizing moment of its arrival. In this sense, for Badiou, Hegelian dialectic parallels bourgeois historicization: 'history' is fetishized, whilst the present is barred from the unsublatable truths of the past. To break with the present bourgeois (and Leftist) cult of genealogy, therefore, means more than invoking unactualized actuality; it means actually 'restoring the past as the amplitude of the present'[101] Thus if politics is to truly exist, History as sublatatory process cannot; it has to negate itself. Badiou is straightforwardly unambiguous on this matter: 'History does not exist.'[102] Whatever progressive genealogies and narratives it might throw up, the present is not the cohesive and accumulative outcome of a promissory process. On the contrary, 'there are only disparate presents whose radiance is measured by their power to unfold a past worthy of their own.'[103] The promise of the actual, then, is founded on a succession of discontinuous singularities, linking or montaging one given situation to another across history and space, past and present. This in brief outline is Badiou's notorious concept of Event: truth and historicity exist only as exceptions within a given historical situation, and are given universal form in the present through the incorporation of the (radical, emancipatory, subtractive) *consequences* of the traces of the historical Event in the present. 'We would say that a [historical] subject is an operative disposition of the traces of the event and of what they deploy in a world.'[104] In *Logics of Worlds* this 'post-historical' dialectics is given an increasingly telescopic and rarefied form in which truth, in its movement from past to present and present to past, is identified as both generic and infinite. He gives the example of the prehistoric painterly representation of horses in the caves of Chauvet-Pont-d'Arc and Picasso's painting of horses from the 1920s. Although these painterly forms exist in separate historical worlds, they both attest to the invariance of the Idea: here, the veridical claim that 'this is a horse'. No matter, therefore, what we might bring to the table in order to distinguish the historical character of these forms of picturing, there is a generic truth–procedure in these modes of representations that extracts itself from those historical communities (primitive communism, early modernism) that produced these forms of picturing. Hence in Badiou there is a fundamental displacement of the actual, a 'leap over' the actual, shifting the focus of the unactualized from its temporal and continuous realization in the moment to a kind of alinear conjunction of past, present and future (what Badiou designates as the eternal or trans-temporal conditions of truth). In a similar fashion Bhaskar rejects what he calls Hegel's process of 'dialectical suction'[105] in favour of a form of dialectical spatio-temporalization that emphasizes constellationality over sublation. Dialectic is not simply about historical change; it is also concerned with

> presence and the co-presence of the absent and the present (with constitutive sedimentation, dislocation and lag – in the senses of both decay and delay) and of

the absent-in-the-present, and vice versa – and with alterity, sheer difference and much else besides.[106]

We can see, therefore, in these two writers here, a certain ahistorical logic appearing, what Badiou himself refers to as a different 'temporal arc'[107] for a post-Hegelian dialectic: namely, a radical anti-historicism, in which constellationality displaces totality, discontinuity displaces continuity, alinearity displaces linearity, historical telescoping and compression displace causality, and conjunction displaces process. In these terms, anti-historicism has proven to be a powerful critic of nineteenth-century evolutionary, linear and organicist schemas in the theory and philosophy of history, and their adaptation by their Stalinist and social democratic heirs. And, consequently, Hegel's overwhelmingly sublatory dialectic does not escape some of Badiou and Bhaskar's criticisms of the limitations of his theory of the actual, as outlined above. Hegel has an underdeveloped sense of the past – futures past – as *unactualized actuality* across space and time. As a result, the error is caught between competing temporal forces. On the one hand, the actual is the productive site of the error, in so far as the destiny of humans must pass through what is most estranged from them. But, on the other hand, error is either what lies unassimilated and unstructured, and therefore something to be brought under control, or it is lost altogether in its passage through the sublatary process. Bhaskar and Badiou are right, then, in identifying in Hegel's writing a dissolution, or narrowing, of the historical exception, of futures past rendered mute by the negation of the negation (although, let it be said, Hegel was no leveller of the past in the name of the future; his concept of the actual as countervailing force is designed precisely to think the relationship between appearance and change in non-historicist, anti-linear fashion).

Bhaskar and Badiou's constellationality and discontinuism, respectively, continue an anti-historicist philosophical programme that has its recent origins in Benjamin's recovery of a necessary, messianic, 'ahistorical' moment in dialectic and the theory of revolution. The present is not simply the gateway to the future through an unactualized *present*, but the redemption of futures past, in a historical compression of futures past, present and prefigured. Benjamin, as much as Badiou and Bhaskar, however, is writing in a period of massive historical retreat for the Left, in which historicization is now subject to mnemotechnics of defeat that Hegel was not party to, or was only at the beginning of. In this, Hegel had no need

– as, to a certain extent, Marx had no need – to build a dialectical redemption of the exception into his sublatary programme. The struggle, as for Marx, was to clear a path for modernity. But, even so, for Hegel this is no 'straight path'. Hegel was no social evolutionist or historical organicist. On the contrary, Hegel always contrasts his methodology to that of conservative organicists and social evolutionists. Organicism, he declares, 'takes place in a direct, unopposed, unhindered manner', in contrast to his dialectics, in which 'Spirit is at war with itself.' Thus, if organic development presupposes a peaceable or unfolding growth of reason or prosperity or democracy, his dialectic demonstrates history as a 'stern, reluctant working against itself' that involves 'a severe and mighty conflict with itself.'[108] This is why Hegel's development of a sublatary dialectic in the *Phenemonology of Spirit* derives from the experience of defeat – the defeat of popular democracy in the French Revolution. This, of course, does not obviate the criticisms of Hegel's failure to derive a historical dialectics from the conjunction of unactualized past and present, but it at least draws a line under the idea that Hegel's sublatary method – World Spirit – derives from an *unilinear* developmental model. There was no 'true path' to freedom for Hegel, only a splintered, deflected, pathologized and self-pathologizing one; history proceeds by its fallen and shadow side. Yet if Hegel was not an unthinking historicist, he was, first and foremost, a radical developmentalist, something quite different. Thus his sublatary programme was designed to do one thing above all else: to reveal and defend the notion that human development carries within it a non-regressive dynamic that makes it impossible for the productive, material and cultural advances of modernity to be forgotten or dissolved in the name of the status quo ante. The global historical process is certainly subject to political retreats, to socially destructive implosions and deflections, to the emptying out and reification of emancipatory technique and forms, but there are no historical 'returns', this side, that is, of global catastrophe and the absolute wiping away of all accumulated productive and technical capacity, human knowledge and skill. This is what distinguishes Marx and Hegel from their peers and their contemporary critics: that the global development of the productive forces and the cultural and political enfranchisement of millions of people constitute an advance in socially objective technique that benefits the millions who follow in its wake. And this remains a non-regressive dynamic, despite the (temporary) advance, or consolidation, of reactionary or counter-revolutionary forces and the unyielding violence and divisions internal to the rise of capitalism. The proletarian class struggle for Marx, and the emancipation of labour for Hegel, therefore, is built not just upon the resistance of workers to these forces politically, but on the fact that workers – given their objective position in the division of labour – participate in a continuous process of engagement with, and transformation of, these inherited techniques as a universal struggle for workers' autonomy. Workers' labour, therefore, is the accumulated memory of the struggle for labour's emancipation, even in conditions where workers have lost all contact with this memory. Now, this is not blithe optimism (something that Hegel was hardly noted for), or a Promethean faith in the ingenuity and will of workers (something that Marx has been unfairly chastised for), or even a confusion of the advance of technology and science under capitalism with enlightenment, but a dialectical commitment to the notion that the struggle and efforts of human beings to release themselves and the present from various ills, constraints, wants, oppressions and ideological imprisonments – taken previously to be natural or a question of fate – function as a standing reserve that cannot be undone – even if the struggles themselves, at given moments, might be forgotten or suppressed, or rendered mute or retarded. This is progress not as a uniform, ascending, rational development (Progress as Universal Enlightenment), but as the increasing participation of the many in the development and transmission of general social technique and general intellect. For both Hegel and Marx, the mark of modernity's progress over feudalism and Absolutism is precisely capitalism's expansion of the division of labour, and, as a result, its increase in the social determinancy of labour as a general liberatory and democratizing force.

It is not surprising that this non-regressive developmental dynamic has come to be identified with what is seen as the most terrifying and instrumental outcome of this logic: the Absolute. Hegel's concept of the Absolute is invariably identified as the imagined end-point of this process of development, a place of resolution and the dissolution of antagonism, contradiction and difference. Indeed, if Progress is the secular creed of World Spirit, the Absolute in this language is its apotheosis. Similarly – particularly in the classic anti-progressivist arguments of Horkheimer and Adorno – such a faith in the transformative function of labour under capitalist modernity fails to register the instrumental burden and discipline of such abstract labour: its uncontrollable domination of productive and unproductive labour and destruction of nature in the name of technical development and increasing specialization, represented by a globally permanent arms economy and the present and deepening ecological crisis. As Adorno argues in *Hegel: Three Studies*, Hegel's principle of becoming – the negation of the negation – is fundamentally identitary, and therefore the Absolute as the end-state of this process represents the teleological outcome of a 'closed system of thought', in which development is no more than a rationalization of capitalist 'progress'.[109] Adorno identifies what he sees as a homology between Hegel's subsumption of the non-identical under the self-movement of the concept (freedom), and the self-expanding logic of abstract labour. 'In Hegel, abstract labor takes on magical form . . . The self-forgetfulness of production, the insatiable and destructive expansive principle of the exchange society is reflected in Hegelian metaphysics. It describes the way the world actually is.'[110] That is, such a process confirms the way the world actually is. For Adorno, the subsumption of the non-identical into the self-movement of the concept evokes, in a way similar to the criticisms of Bhaskar and Badiou, a totalizing subject–object dialectic that swallows up the actual; and, accordingly, the Absolute provides nothing more than a metaphysical gloss on a self-identical, self-expanding system. There are two misunderstandings that need to be addressed here. First, the identification between the negation of the negation and the expansion of abstract labour. For Hegel, the negation of the negation is not the symmetrical expression of self-expanding capital, but its immanent critique, in so far as, for Hegel, there is no freely independent place outside of capital's logic. Second, the Absolute is not an *end*-state, but a qualitative extension and break with the past, an absenting of the fundamental absence of bourgeois culture: the divorce of theory (Idea: freedom) from practice. In this respect the Absolute is the moment of practice and theory's, or practice-as-theory and theory-as-practice's, mutual exchange, what Hegel calls second negation or absolute negativity. 'The Absolute Idea is, in the first place, and thus at the same time, the unity of life with the idea of cognition.'[111] And implicit in this outcome, therefore, is the resistance to any simple conflation between capitalist 'progress' and progress as such. Thus we need to keep separate here a crucial distinction between a notion of the historical break and historical summation. At one level the Absolute is the raising up and break with bourgeois relations in the name of a set of new human relations. As such we can legitimately talk about this as a full human liberation: the Absolute means 'finding a world presupposed before us, generating a world as our own creation, and gaining freedom from it and in it.'[112] But this full liberation is not a *completed* liberation or the termination of the historical process. As Jean Luc-Nancy says: 'Hegel neither begins not ends; he is the first philosopher for whom there is, explicitly, neither beginning nor end, but only the full and complete actuality of the infinite that traverses, works and transforms the finite.'[113] Thus letting the Absolute install itself in history is, precisely, putting praxis-as-thought to work as freedom: freedom from private property, freedom from bourgeois rights, and freedom from the despotic ego. Therefore we need two kinds of historical critique. On the one hand, rightly along with Bhaskar and Badiou, we need a defence of the open-endedness of the historical process (that is, on this matter, a theory of history in alignment *with* and not at the expense of Hegel). As Bhaskar correctly says, in an open world inconsistency, incompleteness and errors are ineliminable. But, on the other hand, we also need a critique of open-endedness in the spirit of second negation and the Absolute. For there is a world of difference between assuming that the Absolute represents the end of meaning, change and negation, and that it represents a qualitative transformation in human relations. There is a world of difference between an 'ending' and 'the end'. Badiou, Bhaskar, Adorno and others lose the necessary moment of positivity in Hegel's concept of the Absolute, of the negation of the negation, the fact that on the basis of a developmental logic not being able to continue in the same way to the same ends, the emergence of the unactualized in praxis brings such a process to an end. The loss of this positivity in Bhaskar's dialectic is particularly ironic given his explicit commitment to such a moment in his critique of the 'endless' negation of Popper's falsificationism in *A Realist Theory of Science*. Yet this is one with the increasing fetishization of negation in *Dialectic*: the unactualized *overwhelms* the positivity of what exists, of the actual – which is quite different from saying, with Nancy, that negation exceeds the positivity of what exists, and is qualitatively transformed by this positivity through its unfolding. '[T]he unrest that *we are* . . . is where the proximity of the absolute finds, or happens upon, itself: neither possession, nor incorporation, but proximity as such.'[114] Thus we might say that the concept of negation after second negation is itself changed, not that second negation dissolves negativity *tout court*. The political consequences of this fetishization of negation are all too familiar: without sublation or *Aufhebung* and a notion of (deflected) progress, negation easily leads to Chiliasm, nihilism or abstract transcendentalism – positions all too visible in their various ways in Bhaskar's 'spiritual' writing after *Dialectic*, the Badiou of *Logics of Worlds*, and many of Adorno's critical theoretical heirs. Negation easily ends up in subtractive or transcendental flight from the 'positive', into the infinite, ineffable, the inexistent, or the past as the future.[115] As Badiou puts it symptomatically in this light: 'the phenomenological world does not "raise itself" to any realm whatsoever.'[116] To defend Hegel, therefore, is to do more than defend his philosophical achievements, it is to defend his place politically in a tradition of emancipatory Enlightenment thought 'from below' shaped by the (conflicted) idea of development that Marx continued.

HEGEL'S CRITIQUE OF SCIENCE AND THE DIALECTICS OF ERROR

Hegel's commitment to the transformation of the implicit rationality of bourgeois society is based above all else on a dual dialectic move: the simultaneous theorization *and* critique of totality, thereby cutting across any of idea of organic, evolutionist and unilinear developmental progress. If there is no thinking and practice without a conception of totality, there is no thinking and practice without the critique of totality. Hence the importance of Hegel's critique of natural science in his defence of philosophical method. Hegel is not anti-science, but he is certainly highly critical of the idea of scientific methodology speaking for truth, and certainly for a truth of the whole. Thus he absolutely rejects the notion of scientific progress as the peaceable and steady accumulation of facts, and science as the queen of knowledge. From this perspective he brings to the philosophy of science an additional, and missing, aspect to our defence of a dialectical scientific realism: a critique of science-as-social-practice. Despite the global advances of natural science (evident in Hegel's day with the emergence of the factory system), the principles and methodology of natural science produce an alienated and fragmented consciousness. There is a fundamental separation, enshrined in scientific methodology, therefore, between the claims of scientific truth and the social relations in which they are embedded. That is to say, scientific methodology as an accumulation of facts confirms the self-given: the facts are the facts; no amount of explanation about the social conditions of scientific development can change that. The result is that science continually dissociates itself from its social effects in the name of truth. And this finds its repeated expression in what Lacan once called the social platitudes of scientists and philosophers of science[117] – their failure, in matters of politics and philosophy, to be equal to the symbolic and conflictual demands of the social. Lacan is referring principally to Einstein (who was actually better and more astute than most other scientists), but it can be said as a general principle that outside of their specialist domains of thought, scientists and philosophers of science tend to be afflicted by various social atavisms, idealist or utopic vagaries and primitivist doggerel (Richard Feynman, Alan Sokal and Stephen Hawking being the most familiar, if not the worst, offenders). Let us also not forget that Chomsky once called Lacan a 'charlatan', the standard name-calling of beetle-browed positivists. Now Bhaskar is clearly at one with Hegel in his critique of this form of scientific positivism – indeed he argues that even those philosophers of science who reject this kind of thinking (such as Popper) fall into this trap, allowing scientific self-criticism and self-negation to exist in an autonomous realm of activity and knowledge. But, unlike Hegel, Bhaskar does not have anything like a critique of science as system, despite having a theory of the social production of science.[118] This is because his anti-Kuhnian realism overcompensates for the ruling relativism in 1970s philosophy of science and the rise of post-Frankfurt-school anti-scientism: science is incoherent without a sense of itself as an accumulative or incremental process. In this respect, his realist philosophy of science steps in, and in a sense compensates for both the actual heteronomous capitalist practices of science and the blockages of emancipatory social praxis. Now, science *is* incoherent without a sense of progress, and as such a commitment to the deepening of our knowledge about an intransitive realm of mind-independent processes and structures is singularly important. Adorno's critique of positivism never really addresses this, leaving science wholly at the mercy of its social-capital logic and the anti-science relativists. Science on this basis is no more than an extension of oppressive capitalist statecraft. But if Adorno and Horkheimer's view of science is overdetermined by the collapse of science into actual and unactualized industrial-state violence (fascism, the nuclear bomb and the post-war arms race), this does not obviate the importance of their Hegelian critique of science as an intellectual system – this is one of the most significant aspects of their critique. What is *lost to the world* at the moment of scientific truth? That is, what does science veil or impede in its claims to solve all the world's empirical problems? This is an old question, of course, one that philosophy has posed to science since the seventeenth century, but under modernity and the forces of capital accumulation it takes on a new immediacy and pathos, as science and scientific methodology become increasingly reified as the only trustworthy and calculable sources of knowledge. There are two separate points here. If Adorno and Horkeimer lose sight of the social contradictions of science as science is brought under the sway of capital accumulation – in so far as scientists cannot be held to ransom for the socially constrained and coerced outcomes of their research – nevertheless, scientists, individually and collectively, are capable of reflecting on science as a social practice as part of their day-to-day practice, something that Hegel was particularly concerned with. That many – the majority – of scientists don't engage in these forms of reflection, under the cover of a Carnapian-type scientific methodology, is one of the reasons late twentieth-century philosophy of science exists in the form that it does: to critically expose and redress the socially impoverished account of scientific methodology and thereby give theoretical scope and clarity to scientific creativity. As I have explained, this critique has itself suffered from its own impoverishments, given its unwillingness to develop a dialectical realist account of science as a system. Even the best of these critiques, such as Bhaskar's, has tended to attack relativism and methodological individualism, without attacking science's submission to capital and Scientific Truth. This leaves an ontology of negation, the absenting of absence, in something of a quandary in Bhaskar's model: for there is no critique of capital – and the removing of its ills – without a critique of science – in its socially capitalized form – and of technology. Hegel's defence of philosophical truth as against a scientific positivism of the Whole, therefore, is a good place to start, in so far as it renders the story of science vulnerable to other sources of value, which science inevitably leaves behind: emancipation is not gauged principally by what scientific advance allows us to do, but by how it contributes to our freely determined place in the world, a habitable, sustainable place. This in turn has additional implications for our theory of error.

Let us recap the position developed here: science is socially produced production, in which knowledge is collectively produced and distributed, albeit through the individual efforts of particular scientists and technicians. Thus the scientific subject-who-is-not-a-subject, in the objectivist language of positivism, is both a subject and not a subject. This allows us to avoid the pitfalls of post-subjectivist critiques of methodological individualism: the scientific subject is not simply an effect of an exosomatic scientific process or distributed process of knowledge, but is a subject *of* truth, in so far as he or she stands in possession of the errors he or she recovers and discovers as part of the experimental process. As Gaston Bachelard declares in the spirit of this subject of truth: 'What a deep joy there is in making confessions of *objective* errors! To admit that one has erred is to pay the most single homage to the perspicacity of one's mind. By doing so we re-live our education, intensify it . . .'[119] The epistemological possession of the error is of particular importance, therefore, given that the labour of the scientific subject is placed, following Mayo, inductively inside the experimental process (at the interface between experiment and hypothesis), rather than deductively in the realm of bold conjecture and falsificationism. In this way the eradication of the error within the experimental process changes its function here, in keeping with Hegel's sublatory thinking. The error is not that which is simply expunged and left behind as detritus, but that which enables other work to continue and be recovered at different times and in different contexts. In this respect, science proceeds progressively in an alinear fashion and asymmetrically *through* the error. But nevertheless the function and the role of error in Hegel is not itself unproblematic. As the theorists of the 'new dialectics' have shown, the sublatory character of Hegel's dialectic tends to dissolve the content of the error – on its way to a 'greater' identity. The emphasis on the experimental process and 'going' small in recent philosophy of science has been a way of obviating this philosophical and scientific problem (which Popper unconsciously reproduces). The singularity of the error as part of the experimental-specific labour of the scientific process restores at some level the scientific subject-who-is-not-a-subject as a subject of truth. This is important in maintaining a realist commitment to scientific advance and to scientific knowledge as knowledge of a mind-independent world. But going small experimentally replicates some of the older problems of logical positivism: scientific methodology and the error are rendered in the language of technical proficiency – probability theory – separate from any philosophical account of 'progress', 'growth' and 'experiment'. The part a theory of errors might play in the critique of deductivism is rendered socially anodyne. The result is that the importance of the error as a way of modelling epistemology and our relationship to the world becomes critically opaque, given the excruciatingly high levels of technical scrutiny and monitoring involved in successful experimentation[120] This leaves a crucial question unanswered: what is at stake critically in defending the productiveness of errors, beyond what it contributes technically to an improved theory and practice of experimentation? And this is why Hegel's philosophical critique of scientific positivism as the language and practice of *unreflective totality* remains vital to answering this. By bringing the error into alignment with an understanding of science as a system, *Hegel at no point allows scientific truth and advance to stand in for truth and progress as a whole.* Science's progress is not the progress of the world. And this is why he continues to remain so suspect to those who believe that 'all human problems are fundamentally resolvable with the progress of science.'[121] This means that any deepening of our understanding of the structures and processes of nature, as evidence of the open and transitive condition of knowledge, cannot be separated from the critique of science as constitutive of this open-endedness; scientists may be able to 'control' the experimental process, but not science as a social system.

Consequently, we need a four-plane subject–object schema of critique of the error in our dialectical realist theory of science: (1) a scientific-subject-who-is-not-a-subject (a distributed subject) who possesses, who 'owns', the experimental process, and as such the production and productiveness of errors; (2) an experimental process that, in its feedback loops, supports this process, and as such allows the scientific subject to live (in theory) with the errors and anomalies it detects; (3) a theory of scientific growth that allows such errors and anomalies to function as a standing reserve for the development of a given research programme, thus avoiding the accelerationist falsification of hypotheses in Popper; and (4) the broader subjection of 'growth', 'advance' and 'progress' to the notion of science as an alienated and partial system of knowledge (in this sense no different from all other claims to knowledge). On this basis, the 'error' faces four ways simultaneously: first, it signifies what the business of science has to define and control in order to render itself coherent as a workable account of the world (the removal of error); second, it has to recognize that this process of eradication is not methodologically transparent and, therefore, that science has to accede to the fact such errors are highly difficult to detect; third, as a consequence, scientific advance takes place not at the expense of errors but in their permanent company, which means that errors are not simply the annoying backdrop to experimental science, but its material content and dynamic; learning from error, then, is about learning how errors might speak, or continue to speak, within a given research programme; and fourth, the unintended and unimagined outcomes of successful experimentation as errors-of-practice in the world have to be folded back into a critical account of science as system. Without this, in particular, the error remains epistemologically confined solely to the success or failure of the experimental process. It is the implications of the latter, then, that most science ignores, as Hegel understood, and that psychoanalysis, of course, has made its own: truth as the unintended breakdown or failure of knowledge. For if science is called on to recognize the unintended consequences of errors-of-practice outside of the laboratory, this is not to say it is happy doing so.

THREE

ERROR, TRUTH AND PSYCHOANALYSIS

If the error is the *onto-theoretical* basis of the subject and the growth of knowledge, what is the relationship between the error, consciousness, and being? Specifically, how is the error constituted in the theory of the subject and subjectivity proposed by psychoanalysis? This is the principal concern of this chapter. But, if the philosophy of science presents us with a theory of the error that is largely at odds with post-Kuhnian deductivism, psychoanalysis meets the error full on, so to speak, meaning that the implicative and culpable language of errors is internal to the very dynamic of psychoanalytic theory and practice itself. However, we shouldn't be too expectant and self-satisfied here. Again, in keeping with the emergence of the Western philosophical subject, and the development of the philosophy of science in the twentieth century, a theory of errors here is to be reconstructed from a fragmented and heterogeneous theoretical base. Freud wrote very little directly on errors;[1] Lacan, admittedly, wrote more and with far greater acumen and, as such, was particularly attuned to the role of the error in analysis, but, overall, he is unconcerned with producing a theory *of* errors that a post-Freudian psychoanalysis might adhere to.[2] Nevertheless, despite these omissions and discontinuities, it is in psychoanalysis that we meet an epistemological subject who is ontologically grounded in reflection on the error and the mistake, and therefore a subject not at odds with the constraints and limits of transcendental reason. Indeed, psychoanalysis is where our scientific subject-who-is-not-subject is given a more capacious identity, in so far as the tension between the depossessive and distributed subject and the posssessive subject is made explicit as a matter of practice and thought. Or, rather, more precisely, the issue of how the error is identified and possessed in theory, and therefore in which ways it might generate knowledge and truth, is central to the psychoanalytical session and to psychoanalytic ethics.

Let us remind ourselves: psychoanalysis is not simply a theory of, and therapeutic response to, the conflicts of subjective life, but more concretely, of how the subject attempts to master and fails to master his or her powers of reason. Accordingly, within the Freudian and Lacanian traditions (privileged here), subjectivity has a singular relationship to the operations of critical reason: human subjectivity is possible precisely because of the incapacity of the subject to render himself or herself intellectually transparent to himself or herself. Subjectivity is the actual outcome of the subject's representation of – or failure to represent and stabilize – the process of division and non-identity constitutive of selfhood. Rather than the subject being subject *to* a process of splitting, therefore – as if the subject exists as a uniform entity prior to this splitting – the subject is the processual *outcome* of this scission. As we discussed in Chapter 1, Kant's subject of reason takes a notional account of this splitting, in so far as Kant is acutely aware of the immanent crisis of consciousness that haunts transcendental reason: the subject speaks 'reason', speaks in the language of reason, aspires to reason, but is undone by the gap between consciousness and knowledge, knowledge and truth. Yet if transcendental reason is unable to secure the self-identity of the subject, nevertheless the gap between consciousness and identity/knowledge forms for Kant the dialectical basis of reason. It is precisely because the subject is 'not All' that the transcendental agency of the subject is, in fact, possible, because it is precisely through the gap between consciousness and self-knowledge that reason, desire and the will are able to emerge. This is the radical advance of Kant's philosophy. The whole of psychoanalysis, then, might be said to be an extended reflection on this Kantian gap between consciousness and knowledge; and, as such, it is understandable why Kant's subject of reason would seem to have so much in common with the subject theorized by psychoanalysis. Both Kant's subject and the subject of psychoanalysis actualize reason through a *failure* of reason. But, of course, these two subjects are far from similar in their understanding of this failure. Kant has no theory of the unconscious, and therefore the actualization of reason through the failure of reason is merely a formal acknowledgement of the effects of subjective dereliction; despite Kant's insights into this process these effects rarely trouble the coherence of Kant's subject. In psychoanalysis, however, the unconscious is the explicit and radical name given to this process of dereliction, and, as such, it transposes the actualization of reason through the failure of reason into a systematic encounter with the gap between consciousness and self-knowledge. Hence this is why Hegel is such a 'psychoanalytic' figure for psychoanalysis (certainly for Lacan): his disinterest in, indeed antagonism to, the transcendental philosophical subject of reason places the actions and thinking of the subject outside of the subject's immediate or direct control. Reason is not a set of attributes or skills that the subject commands and exercises at will, but is the name for the subjectively dispossessed space which the subject inhabits and struggles in, and ultimately has little control over.

The agency and will of the psychoanalytic subject is built, therefore, from a greater, or more explicit, sense of dereliction and internal division than Kant, enabling the subject as other to himself or herself to emerge as a coherent philosophical concept. Armed first and foremost with a theory of the unconscious, psychoanalysis, therefore, is what happens to the subject of philosophical reason when the still-birth of Kantian philosophical reason is brought into conflict and dialogue with the 'unreason' of subjective life. It is no surprise, accordingly, that psychoanalysis is the domain where the error, the mistake, the lapse, have flourished as explicitly productive concepts, for in a direct reversal of the status of the error in Western metaphysics and the philosophy of science it is no longer the detritus to be expunged, the object to be cornered and hunted down, but the thing to be cherished, noted, and embraced. This means that we enter the debate on the error in psychoanalysis from a quite different place than in the Western philosophical tradition and the philosophy of science. The error is something that the analyst – and ideally the analysand – is *wholly* attentive too. Now this is not to say that the Western philosophical tradition and the philosophy of science have been inattentive as regards the function and status of the error – as I have stressed in the opening chapters, the persistence of the error as a philosophical problem grounds the formation of the philosophical subject and the idea of scientific progress in the philosophy of science, despite the error's shadow existence as a critical concept, and despite philosophy and the philosophy of science's de-registration of its productive effects. Moreover, in recent post-Popperian philosophy of science – specifically Deborah Mayo – in response to the need to think of errors as productive, the epistemological ideal of science is held to be best represented by a *slowing down* of the falsificationist drive inherent in a given research programme – hence the importance of the recalibrated place of induction in Mayo's re-theorization of the experimental process. In this respect recent philosophy of science and psychoanalysis both, equally, recognize the importance of *living with errors*. But, if they both share a formal cognizance of the importance of living with errors, the knowledge produced from such attentitiveness in psychoanalysis has very different outcomes and implications, and as such a different processual shape. If in the philosophy of science living with errors is always a consequence of the need to exceed the error with theoretical conviction and surety – that is, science has at all times to work hard to provide a coherent basis to its truth claims, because to be uncertain in matters of truth fundamentally retards the possibility of reason – in psychoanalysis living with errors represents the ever present realization that the knowledge of the analyst is dependent upon the contingencies and singularity of the transference process, which in a sense is *always* 'retarded', always subject to veiling, misunderstanding and delay. Delay is *properly constitutive* of psychoanalytic method. Which is not to say that the analyst and analysand never arrive at knowledge and truth, but that the production of truth has to be modelled on a case-by-case basis.

Thus, as both Freud (and the early Lacan) insisted on, the truth claims of psychoanalysis have the character more precisely of an art, a form of Aristotelian *technê*, rather than a straightforwardly deductive method. As Freud declares: 'the most successful cases are those in which one proceeds, as it were, without any purpose in view, allows oneself to be taken by any new turn in them.'[3] In this regard *technê* is similar to the intuitive skills involved in the uncertain and discontinuous production of an artistic object; the development of the work is based not on rules followed, but on what is learnt from the specific and unique problems encountered. Thus the intepretations of the analyst have to be developed on a contingent basis. Yet, if the association between artistic *technê* and psychoanalytic *technê* is apposite, the interpretations of analysts are not crafted *like* artworks. The analysand's responses are not materials to be moulded and unified by the analyst into a freestanding intervention. For it is not the omniscient interpretative creativity of the analyst that enables truth to prevail, but the analysand's *response* to the analyst's interpretations, which means that the analyst's role is always subordinate to the resistances involved in the analysand's responses, and, therefore, is creatively *decentred*. As Giovanni Vassalli explains – an author who has written extensively on the Aristotelian origins of technique in Freud – the shift in Freud's mature writing, from the early 'scientism' to an artisanal practice, defines psychoanalytic method as an art which is subject to a particular kind of discipline. *Technê* does not privilege the psychoanalyist as 'artist' as such, but as a kind of skilled craft technician for whom interpretation is linked to deduction in order to create a flexible form of *conjectural reason* – hence the central supposition that psychoanalytic technique, in its constitutive delayedness, is above all else a processual involvement in the conflictual 'materials' of the session. The analyst and analysand are engaged in the maintenance of an open-ended process that might capture the unpredictable and unexpected.[4] In this regard there is something of Charles Sanders Peirce's conception of knowledge-by-abduction in Freud's account – developed around the same time as Freud's notion of conjunctural reason – abduction being the name Peirce gives to the formation of an explanatory hypothesis. Abduction 'starts' a question, or puts in place a suggestive hypothesis in order to explain a unanticipated observation, and is therefore as a result, Peirce claims, the only logical operation which actually *introduces* a new idea into scientific practice.[5] In a psychic realm where the things under scrutiny are constantly blurred and lack definition, a special kind of technique needs to be employed in order to generate knowledge.

It is perhaps understandable, therefore, as Vassalli notes, that we frequently encounter in Freud's writing the word *Erraten* in relation to the open-endedness of psychoanalytic technique. *Erraten* means 'guess', a word of course that is clearly ammunition for all those Popperians and positivists who have denounced Freud's *technê* as relativistic and anti-scientific, and, as such, a word that tended to get dropped in the early-English transla-tions for fear of reinforcing this impression. In translating Freud his early-English interpreters were keen to defend psychoanalysis as an extension of the natural sciences in order to avoid these kind of detractions. Yet, this word captures quite succinctly what Freud's notion of psychoanalysis as a conjunctural and conjectural craft implies: namely, the capacity of the analysand to constantly move beyond the 'given' and the 'givens' that lie beneath such a 'given' and other 'givens', as a precursor to construction work, and, accordingly, enable the analysand to think as a detective might think when faced with a collection of seemingly self-evident clues and circumstantial evidence that does not add up. As Freud argues, in the case of both detective work and psychoanalysis we are concerned with a secret.

> In the case of the criminal it is a secret which he knows and hides from you, whereas in the case of the hysteric it is a secret which he himself does not know either, which is hidden even from himself. . . . In this one respect, therefore, the difference between the criminal and the hysteric is fundamental. The task of the therapist, however, is the same of that of the examining magistrate. We have to uncover the hidden psychic material; and in order to do this we have invented a number of detective devices.[6]

Lacan extends and deepens this notion of psychoanalysis as an 'art' or craft in two interrelated and substantive ways: by subjecting the role of the analyst to an increased scrutiny, and by focusing on the ethics of the analytic situation as a problem of language and signification. As he insists in *Freud's Papers on Technique 1953–54* (1988), there is a need to, 'Submit[. . .] analysis to an examination which itself is analytic.'[7] That is, Lacan certainly follows Freud in accepting that analysis 'is an experience of the particular',[8] and as such follows Freud in abrogating a stable 'method', but at the same time he recognizes that the ways in which the analyst might practice this knowledge of singularity in analysis – with what means and from what position – is not something that Freud explored in any systematic way, and, therefore, was in need of further elaboration if the *radical implications* of Freud's technique were not to be diluted against the ego-psychologist revisionists. For certainly in Lacan's early seminars it is precisely *how* Freud practiced that separates Freud's achievements from all the attempts after the Second World War to reassimilate psychoanalysis into the natural sciences and, hence, into conformity with some notion of scientific positivism. Thus Lacan's reflections on technique are concerned first and foremost to develop and strengthen those ethical characteristics of the analyst's role that distinguish psychoanalysis as conversational praxis from the idea of psychoanalysis as a medicalized cure. Of particular significance in this respect is the actual speech or linguistic role of the analyst in the transference process.

Freud of course is extremely conscious of the dangers involved in the interpretation arrived at too quickly, and the interpretation that is based too confidently on the ego of the analyst himself or herself. This self-scrutiny is the very basis of Freud's analytic craft. But, nevertheless, for Lacan this

self-scrutiny remains theoretically underdeveloped as actual intersubjective speech acts. Thus what preoccupies the early Lacan is precisely how
the analyst and analysand speak to each other, and, as consequence, what
kind of decentred role the analyst *should* best take, and, therefore, what
scientific identity the psychoanalyst and psychoanalysis should properly
possess. He sees in Freud a residual forcing at work on the part of the
analyst, given Freud's long-standing commitment to a depth model of
analysis in which the analyst slowly moves through the resistances of the
analysand to that which is 'hidden'. Freud admittedly was fully aware of
the limitations of his own depth model, on the basis that there was something operative in the unconscious that repeatedly caused the analysand
to 'not want to know'. But the implications of 'not wanting to know' are
not expressly reintegrated into his reflections on technique, leaving the
analyst exposed to his or her own desire to complete the analysis through
the repressed truth of the past. For Lacan, however, there are no 'hidden
depths' to be redeemed because the analysand's resistance *is all the way
down*, meaning that the analyst has to be conscious always of the analysand 'not wanting to know' as a condition of the transference process
itself. Yet the analysand 'doesn't want to know' not simply because of
what is repressed, but because he or she is continuously exposed to the
desire of the analyst's drive *to* 'know', which confronts the confines of
the ego: namely, that which always presumes that it knows, even when it
releases itself from the hold of a given neurosis. Resistance, therefore, is
not due to a fear of exposure on the part of the analysand, but a fear on
the part of the analysand exposed to the analyst's drive to know, of the
truth arriving in the wrong form, that is, too early, too late, too forcefully,
or too ambiguously. Indeed, the foundational struggle between truth arriving too early or too late is one of the constant pressure points of each
and every psychoanalytic session, exacerbated by the specific condition of
each analysand. Thus for some neurotic patients fear lies in the possibility of the analyst releasing her from her desire, as an analysand, to know,
and therefore initiating the completion of the analysis, whereas in the case
of other neurotic patients, 'not wanting to know' is driven, in fact, by the
reverse: the incessant demands of the analysand *to know*, to be told the
truth, here and now, immediately, with dramatic gusto, forcing the analyst
to find ways of 'slowing' the analysis down. So, the transference process
effects a particular dynamic of knowledge production and dissemination:
the analyst must resist the constant demand on the part of the analysand

to 'know' immediately (simply another, if more assertive, example of 'not wanting to know'), and also the strategies and ruses of the ego's 'not wanting to know', by ensuring that the refusal to answer in some instances, or answering judiciously in others, allows the transference process to continue. This is why Lacan's preoccupation in *Freud's Papers on Technique 1953–54* and *The Ego in Freud's Theory and in the Technique of Psychoanalysis 1954–1955* on the premature or forced interpretation produces a decisive shift in the Freudian identity of the analyst who 'knows'. The hesitant and deliberative tenor of Freud's understanding of psychoanalytic technique as decentred craft, becomes, expressly for Lacan, that of *the craft of the critique of mastery itself*. Hence, for the speech of the analyst to succeed in analysis the analyst must constantly depose himself or herself from the functional attributes of the subject 'who knows', for without this deposition the ego of the analyst is prey to the pressures 'to know' that the analysand necessarily brings to the session. This deposition, however, is not because the analyst shouldn't know for fear of imposing his or her knowledge, but because the refusal of a preconditional mastery enables a productive ignorance to prevail. 'I ask you once again to risk yourselves in the unknown, in the zone of ignorance, which we must never forget in the analytic experience, for it is the position we automatically adopt.'[9] In this sense ignorance is the term Lacan introduces to conjoin the condition of the analyst and analysand as those who 'do not know' to their respective desires to know. But this is not a shared dialogue, as if analyst and analysand were equally ignorant, or ignorant in the same ways. On the contrary, ignorance – or wise ignorance – is also designed to facilitate what is ultimately the essential disparity between analyst and analysand: the fact that it is the job of the analyst to *understand* the analysand, albeit in time, and with extreme caution and hesitancy. Ignorance is psychoanalytic craft by stealth, allowing the analyst to work through each case in relation to its profound singularity.[10] 'There is no possible way into analysis without this point of reference.'[11] Ignorance, then, for Lacan is the watchful praxis of the transference process: by withdrawing, or shifting critical focus when necessary, the analyst maneouvres the analysand into a space whereby they are able to dis-identify from the analyst, and at the same time displace the desire of the other, leading in turn to the analysand's eventual avowal of the essential emptiness of the other's desire. In an important sense the praxis of transference runs precisely counter to the ideal of intersubjective dialogue as a harmonious exchange between partners, so familiar from Plato, Carnap's scientific positivism and pragmatic language theory. For the transference process is cognate with, or far closer to, a lover's discourse, with all its affective bonds, than it is an exchange of information or a pedagogic lesson. The desire of the analyst to know is embedded, essentially, in the fantasy of the analysand: the fact that the analyst's beloved or hated status as the person 'who knows' has little or nothing to do with what the lover really lacks or wants.

Following from this, there may be a notional correspondence between the psychoanalytic session and the scientific experiement and scientific research programme on the grounds that both scientific experiement and psychoanalytic session are exploratory in an extended temporal sense, but the analyst's 'scientific' relationship to the object of exploration – the analysand – is embedded and entangled in the veilings and misapprehensions inherent to the transference process. Hence, unlike in the setting of the scientific experiement, the notion of living with errors – of the subject waiting to fulfill their objective role as the person who knows (or is obligated to know), of waiting as a result of the patient extension of the scientific process – the psychoanalytic session is determined by, and is the outcome of, the exchange between analyst and analysand. As Robert Caper explains:

> Psychoanalysis resembles the experimental sciences in that it forms hypotheses that are tested against evidence on their way to becoming established (or not) as theories. But while theories in the experimental sciences are established by the construction of controlled experiments, psychoanalytic theories are established by the absorption of the uncontrollable experience of the analytic session.[12]

This is why in the psychoanalytic encounter there are expressly two processes of error production, rather than the singular one we encounter in the process of scientific experimentation: first, the processes that pertain to the reconstructive work of the analyst as he or she formulates his or her 'hunches', and second, those processes that pertain to the evasions, inversions, misrecognitions, illusions, convictions constitutive of the speech of the analysand, which the analyst notes, recovers and interprets. In fact these two processes are determinate upon each other, or more precisely interpolate each other. As Dany Nobus argues in his extended account of transference in Freud and Lacan: 'if the transference always integrates an object in the present, analysts cannot escape their being made into the object of their analysands' transference, through which they not only elicit but also crucially shape their patients' reactions.'[13] The errors of the analyst are therefore not just based on the usual indeterminacies and missteps involved in interpretation and deductive work. Rather, the errors-in-interpretation of the analyst *actually produce and configure the content of the errors* he or she receives back from the analysand. Thus, the interpretations of the analyst are derived from the errors-in-translation of the analysand's words, which are a previous mistranslation of the analyst's speech. Consequently analyst and analysand are involved in a mutually compounding chain of mistranslation. In this sense the *erraten* of the psychoanlytic encounter is another way of talking about the repeated failures or blindnesses of the transference process; that is, between the failure of the analyst to locate where precisely the truth of the analysand's speech lies, and, accordingly, the resistance on the part of the analysand to the speculative truth of these probings. There is never a stable, continuous place from which the analyst launches his or her analysis. The labour of *erraten*, then, is the process whereby the failure of reason in the transference process becomes the reason *of* (productive) error, and, as a consequence, remains a good covering description for what is required in response to the misrecognitions constitutive of the relationship between subject (the analyst) and object-as-subject (analysand).

This is why a discourse of error is prominent in Lacan's writing on transference, the session and the ethics of psychoanalysis, for it allows this process of misrecognition to prevail at an explicit theoretical level. If technique must depose mastery, error must in turn impose its rightful claims on knowledge. As Lacan declares, it is only by calling for a retreat from mastery and 'method' that 'genuine speech joins up [productively] once again with the discourse of error' in psychoanalysis.[14] This is reflected in the very different conceptual status given to the error in Lacan in comparison to that of Freud. Errors feature only intermittently in Freud's writing, and when they do, as in the short chapter 'Errors' in *The Psychopathology of Everyday Life* (1901), they remain the sole possession of an epistemology of repression, and not the material praxis of the transference process, or of the knowing-subject as such. 'What I wanted to suppress often succeeded against my will in gaining access to what I had chosen to relate, and appeared in it in the form of an error that I failed to notice.'[15] In short, the concept remains undertheorized. In Lacan, however, it becomes the explicit corrollary, or motor, of psychoanalytic truth, on the basis of what Freud's discovery of the unconscious announces as the Copernican revolution of psychoanalysis: that the subject in speaking or not speaking *always says more, far more, than he or she means to say*. Hence the error becomes the medium of that which speaks more than it does. In this sense we need to clarify why the error is crucially important to Lacan and to post-Freudian psychoanalysis generally, and how it and psychoanalysis stand more broadly in relation to the practices of science and our scientific subject-who-is-not-a-subject.

LACAN'S 'FERTILE ERRORS'

Lacan's discussion of errors appears primarily in the seminar 'Truth Emerges from the Mistake' in *Freud's Papers on Technique 1953–54, The Ego in Freud's Theory and in the Technique of Psychoanalysis 1954–55,* and in the *Ethics of Psychoanalysis 1959–1960*. In these three texts the inculcation of 'wise ignorance' is accompanied by a discouse on 'fertile error'.[16] By fertile error Lacan means the production of knowledge immanent to analysis, given the analyst and analysand's subjection to the delays, veilings, misapprehensions and misrecognitions of the transference process. For at no point is the truth of the subject sustainable outside of this 'closed' process. In other words, access to the truth of the speech of the analysand is only available to the analyst in the dimension of deception and untruth. In this Lacan provides an explicit link between psychoanalytic technique and what we have already noted in Chapter 1 as Hegel's pathological encounter between the subject and truth: error signifies not that which truth extrudes, but that which in its processual unfolding sustains truth. As such he extends the new positional and spatial logic of the error introduced by Hegel. .

> It is clear that error is only definable in terms of the truth. But the point is not that there would be no error if there were no truth, as there would be no white if there were no black. There is more to it than that – there is no error which does not not present and promulgate itself as truth. In short, error is the habitual incarnation of the truth.[17]

In this respect the psychoanalytic paths of truth are wayward, in so far as error speaks the truth and truth speaks of error: 'the paths of truth are in essence the paths of error.'[18] So, what distinguishes psychoanalysis from other forms of knowledge, Lacan avers, is that truth unfolds 'within the order of error'[19] Error catches or produces truth when a mistake in the speech of the analysand speaks of more than the analysand believes that he or she is speaking. 'In analysis, truth emerges in the most clear cut representative of the mistake – the slip, the action, which one improperly calls *manquée* [missed, failed, abortive].'[20] Consequently Lacan is keen to distinguish truth immanent to errors from the mere breakdown in syntax, the glitches of computer programmes, or the malfunctioning of machines. Whereas the latter are simply accidents of machinic logic or formal laws, and as such infer the breakdown or omission of pre-given actions or units of information, the former generate another knowledge: that is, the signification of the error lies in yet another meaning or meanings in the 'symbolic function which is manifested through' the evidence of errancy.[21] This is why the error for Lacan is the close intimate of language and speech and the transference process. For the significance of mistakes of logic and the malfunction of machines fall, as he puts it, by the wayside as outcomes that are only 'true' for the actual processes in question. In psychoanalysis, and the analysis of speech, in contrast, the error maps a complex world of causation and desire. Accordingly the distinction Lacan makes between logic and machinic processes and the errors immanent to the speech of the subject becomes a fundamental description of human subjectivity: errors are precisely the domain of subjects *who talk and reflect on how they talk*, and, therefore, of creatures who are able productively to take possession of their mistakes and the mistakes of others. At one level there are superficial echoes here of Heidegger's concept of error: Lacan talks of being 'thrown into'[22] the errancies of subjectivity, but on another level he extends what I have called the discourse of culpable possession of the error in Descartes, Locke and Kant into the realm of the unconscious proper: 'There isn't one philosopher who hasn't insisted, and rightly so, on the fact that the very possibility of error is tied to the existence of language.'[23] Thus the error, certainly in Lacan's early writings – where the influence of Hegel is at its most explicit – becomes central to marking out where psychoanalysis borders, overlaps and distinguishes itself from science and other practices; the error for Lacan is what determines the subject in his or her otherness and relationality. On this basis, the error functions on two Hegelian levels in Lacan: on the one hand it is the constitutive form of human subjectivity, and on the other it is the specific material conditions of intersubjective exchange (here, of speech analysis and the transference process). Let us take the former point first, which might be best described as the ontological principle of the subjective dereliction governing what we have so far described as the onto-theoretical basis of the error.

Lacan follows Hegel in arguing that the subject is a subject in so far as it is not a subject, meaning that if the subject could stabilize itself as thing or fixed substrate it would cease to be a subject. For the non-subjectifiable identity of the subject is precisely the condition of the subject's possibility, what we have referred to above, in our discussion of Kant, as the gap between consciousness and self-knowledge. Subjects, then, are subjects in so far as they are not things, but self-directed, desiring agents. But if subjects becomes subjects by acting, the subject risks objectifying itself *as* a thing in the process of realising its subject-status. This is because in acting the subject traverses its subjective good intentions: that is, the subject always realizes something other to that which he or she intended, leaving the subject disconnected or alienated from its plunge into actuality – Hegel's famous dictum about the Owl of Minerva always flying at dusk. In this sense Lacan follows Hegel in asserting that in completing a goal, the subject realizes and interiorizes the incompletion of that goal, producing a flight back into subjectivity, starting the process of subjectivization-desubjectivization again. As Mladen Dolar argues: 'The Hegelian act is thus, like the act in psychoanalysis, by its very nature a failed act, and its failure brings forth the dimension of the subject's truth.'[24] This 'failure' of the act, is in some sense, then, the correlate of Lacan's conception of error here (although errors need to be kept quite distinct from failures, as I discuss in detail in the next chapter, and, therefore, are far from being synonymous with error theory). For what Lacan introduces via the Hegelian notion of the 'failed' act into the discourse on error is that the idea that the subject's dereliction resides in the realm, not simply of ideological misrecognition, of ideological falsehood, but of limited or partial understanding and agency. The error then is productive of subjectivity.

This represents a crucial difference for our narrative, because it concretises the distinction I have already drawn out between the Cartesian and Lockean explusion of the error as untruth, and the critical advance Hegel makes in terms of the assimilation of error as truth-in-process. This is why Lacan (after Freud) designates a specific theoretical identity for psychoanalysis, quite different from science and philosophy – which takes us to our second point: error's relationship to the materiality of the analytic process itself. Psychoanalysis is the assimilation of the error-as-truth distinct from – if nevertheless epistemologically connected to – the mistake as a falsehood. In analysis the analysand may profess all kinds of falsehoods, he or she, indeed, may litter his or her conversation in analysis with all kinds of conscious mistakes, but these do not necessarily tell the truth of his or her speech (and its relations to the other). On the contrary, these falsehoods and mistakes may be utterly irrelevant to the truth of this speech. As such, in Lacan, the error-as-truth in psychoanalysis is of a different order to that of the epistemological equation of the error and mistake in philosophy and science. This is because under the concept of the error-as-truth the subject's derelection and ideological self-deception is rendered in its appearance *as* an indirect source of truth; a truth in disunity, if you like. That is, truth must of necessity pass through error (reflection in and on error), because in the order of the subject, truth is only accessible through the analysis of failed or misunderstood intention. So, the important point here is that the movement through error – through the misrecognitions, misapprehensions, veilings, and self-deceptions of the transference process – *enables* truth to appear.[25] And this, of course, is Hegelian, precisely in as much as the error-as-truth presupposes a subject 'who knows' or seeks 'to know' in a way that is very different from experimental science and the transcendental reason of the traditional philosophical subject.

From this perspective there is something larger at stake philosophically and politically in Lacan's psychoanalysis: in what way should the psychoanalytic subject *speak* to science? Or more precisely in what sense does the conception of error-in-truth allow an expressly post-Hegelian subject to prevail as a radical opening into scientific thought and praxis? For, if Lacan is indebted to Hegel's critique of scientific truth, armed with the Freudian unconscious, he establishes a confrontation with scientific method and philosophical idealism that draws a line underneath the truth-in-error of psychoanalysis quite distinct from the non-identitary function of consciousness in Hegel. 'Hegel didn't abandon the central function of consciousness, although he does allow us to free ourselves from it.'[26] As such, how does the subject-who-is-not-a-subject of psychoanalysis, in its difference from the subject-who-is-not-a-subject of science, challenge the scientific subject of science? Let us look then more closely at the relationship between psychoanalysis, science and the error.

PSYCHOANALYSIS, SCIENCE AND ERROR

As outlined in our discusssion above, the particularities of the transference process challenges the very notion of the scientific subject-who-is-
not-a-subject as someone who is waiting to 'know', in as much as the
decentred craft of the analyst is the practice of a subject-who-is-not-a-
subject *without* its customary recourse to the positivistic ideal of science.
In these terms Lacan does not believe in this (received) ideal of science
for psychoanalysis. This is as a result of the fact that the analyst cannot
adopt a convincing observer role that builds on accumulated knowledge
as a transmittable method, and therefore allows a stable progression from
specific instances to general laws. The work of the unconscious – of
both the analyst and analysand – prevents this. Yet this does not mean
that this undermines the work of psychoanalysis as science as such, as if
this subjectively breaches all proper scientific endeavour. As Jean Claude
Milner argues, 'there is effectively a theory of science in Lacan's work'[27]
– the science of the Real that is introduced as a result of the anti-positivistic scientific axiom introduced by Freud into psychology: because
self-conciousness is *not* constitutive of the subject, the subject-*as*-subject
cannot be constitutive of scientific method. Thus the scientific claims
of psychonanalysis lie precisely in the epistemological and methodological shift they introduce into the objects and procedures of experimental
science: psychoanalysis is *the science of a speech that does not know itself,* and as
such reflects on objects that are unknown (and can not be fully known)
to the analysand. Hence, with 'an unparalled precision [psychoanalysis]
separates two entities: in one, self-consciousness can be supposed to be
non-essential without contradiction; and in the other, self-consciousness
cannot be supposed to be non-essential without contradiction.'[28] In other
words, the subject-who-is-not-a-subject of science is effectively removed
in psychoanalysis from its objectivist role within the positivist tradition,
in so far as psychonanalysis brings to consciousness, as the very praxis
of analysis, the limitations of the subject who knows. But at the same
time this is not quite the depossessive subject specific to the distributed
scientific subject-who-is-not-subject of the new cognitive sciences. The
subject-who-is-not-a-subject of psychoanalysis is not the outcome of a
collective labour or shared knowledge (although, of course, the accumulation of psychoanalytic knowledge forms a corpus of exemplary psychoanalytic practices for the profession). On the contrary, without the singular

intersubjective exhange of analyst to analysand through the transference process, psychoanalysis does not exist. Does this mean that the scientific subject-who-is-not-a-subject, then, in Lacan is nothing more than a supra-Bayesian? – there are only the free-ranging interpretations of individual analysts; in the end, only good stories. (The history of Lacan's reception as an idealist within Anglo-American poststructuralism would suggest something like this.) But if Lacan insists on the interpretative skill of the analyst, for this to have meaning interpretations have to be *correct*; that is, they have to have the force of a truth. Thus, when the symptom is correctly interpreted, the analysand and analyst share the recognition of a certain requirement specific to their encounter: the need for the analysand to give up his demand for love in the session (that is, his demand to be affirmed as a lover or negated as unworthy of being a love object) in exchange for a commitment to his or her own authentic desire. In this respect psychoanalysis remains attached, paradoxically, to the possessive Cartesian logic of objectivist science: for without the role of the analyst and the subject 'who knows' – who will eventually present a convincing interpretation in the light of given evidence, albeit in a oblique way – the resolution of the transference process is unable to take place. If the desire of the experimentor in science plays no determinate role, this is 'not so in psychoanalysis, where the transmission of the analysis is marked by the analyst who transmits it.'[29] (Genevieve Morel). This is because the truth-fulness of the intrepetation has to be delivered and registered as the result of a *perceptible struggle and risk for truth*, in which both analyst and analysand have shared.

Successful interpretation, then, is the outcome of a process in which the analyst not only possesses the symptom of the analysand – as any scientist might possess the materials of an experiment – but is correspondingly also possessed affectively by the life and history of the symptom itself. This is why the error becomes so crucial for Lacan: because to be possessed by something is to succumb to all its messy alterity and contingencies – although, to qualify this, to possess the symptom is not thereby to *succumb* to it. Whereas the possession of the error in scientific experimentation sutures the scientific-subject-who-is-not-a-subject to the experimental process, the possession of the error in psychoanalysis exposes this suturing process to constant reflection and amendment. Thus it is the struggle to know the symptom on the part of the analyst, and at the same time to resist the symptom (that is, the analyst's resistance to taking pleasure from the analysand's symptom, as a pervert might), that constitutes the truth of the transference process. This makes Lacanian psychoanalysis's relationship to knowledge in itself a singularly divided one: in the struggle to live within, and break out of, the 'lover's embrace' of the transference process, the relationship between analysand and analyst is essentially agonistic. *Analysand and analyst contest the truth of the analysand's speech.* Yet the speech of the analyst cannot itself be explicitly agonistic. The correct interpretation has to be spoken sideways, or in a strongly inferential way, never directly.

This hailing of another science, or another voice for science, points to the very heart of the politics of psychoanalysis over the last sixty years. For when Lacan asks, in his critique of scientific positivism, how might the psychoanalytic subject-who-is-not-a-subject speak to science? he by definition links his critique of objectivism in scientific method to Hegel's critique of science as a system. Thus it is no surprise that those who have accepted this call are on the 'other side of scientific positivism': namely Marxism, and various theoretical, artistic and literary discourses indebted to Marxism and critical theory, precisely those, then, who are best positioned outside of psychoanalysis to listen to the dialogue that psychoanalysis has initiated inside psychoanalysis with science. Marxism and psychoanalysis before the Second World War, of course, saw in each other, at times, a friendly advocate. But this advocacy was invariably based on a mismatch of aims; Freud had little or no sympathy for the language of progressivism, even if his thinking was deeply attached to a defence of Enlightenment and secular values; and, therefore, it was perfectly understandable, if nonetheless problematic, that Marxism before and after the Second World War kept confusing psychoanalysis with 'ideology critique'. But it is after the 1960s that Marxism becomes psychoanalysis's ideal interlocuter, or an interlocuter better suited to psychoanalysis's theory of the subject. Because it is precisely at this point that Marxism begins seriously to theorize its own crisis and political defeat in line with a critique of the humanism and positivism that had propped up its orthodox and reactionary adherents, and therefore was more than willing to place itself in the interlocutory position of analysand. What Marxism lacked – a philosophically robust theory of the subject-as-not-a-subject – became the terrain on which Marxism responded positively to Lacan's radical disinvesment in scientific positivism, as a response to its own inherited positivisms. Hence the key Marxist interlocuters of psychoanalysis during the sixties and after – Louis Althusser, Etienne Balibar, Alain Badiou, down to Ernesto Laclau and Slavoj Žižek today – all share one thing at least: that over the last forty years Lacan and Marxism have been inseperable, in so far as they both share what Žižek has correctly called an 'engaged notion of truth'.[30] 'They are both struggling theories, not only theories about struggle.'[31] Or conflictual sciences, as Althusser once put it.[32] Thus we might say that over this period Lacan's writing has been at the very centre *of* Marxism, so to speak, even if few Marxists would claim a direct allegiance to Lacan's writing, or would recognize psychoanalysis as an ally of emancipatory politics.[33] This is because the subject-language of psychoanalysis – the destitution, deposition and desubjectivization of the subject – is the means by which the subject as an agonistic political signifier becomes both credible and operable when the conditions of its own erasure and failure become visible, a reflection of what, at one level, Althusser called 'the objective (politico-theoretical) task of clearly settling accounts with Lacan.'[34] Another way of saying this is that Lacan's meeting of Freud and Hegel introduces a subject-who-is-not-a-subject into Marxism that is able to theorize the limits of the subject's intelligibility as a political being, of its rupture, failure, and, as such, its constitutive and productive capacity *for errors*. Yet if Marxism has 'assimilated' Lacan this does not mean that Marxism and psychoanalysis have been travelling on the same train after the 1960s, and therefore that Marxism and psychoanalysis share the same political horizons, or that the error theory of Lacan has made its way in any productive sense into historical materialism – far from it. This is why Žižek's comments, for all their diagnostic truth, fail to render how difficult this dialogue has been. Althusser, Balibar and Badiou all, in a sense, gave up on Lacan, and in so doing drew attention to the political limits of his psychoanalysis. Similarly, those who have assimilated Lacan to a new (antiutopian) politics (Laclau and his followers) end up weakening what is truly revolutionary in Lacan and psychoanalysis and disabling an emancipatory politics in the process.[35] As such the centrality of Lacan to the 'working relationship' of psychoanalysis to Marxism is not fixed, and as such is crucial to how the subject-language of destitution, desubjectivization and deposition is theorized and politicized. For neither Althusser nor Badiou has a theory of the error, which ultimately affects how they interiorize Lacan's critique of the subject and the psychoanalytic subject as such. In the next section, then, I want to look at how Althusser's and Badiou's critiques of Lacan fail Lacan's intervention into scientific positivism, by their tendency to stress the second condition of the analyst–analysand encounter: the analyst's hesitancy and withdrawal in the transference process, or the submission of the analyst to the analysand's neurotic repetitions. This will allow us to put a little flesh on the response to Lacan's call to how psychoanalysis might speak to science, or speak at all, and also bring our error theory into better alignment with a realist understanding of the political subject *after* psychoanalysis (the implicit theme of the next chapter). A good place to start this discussion, therefore, is Althusser's extraordinary on-off correspondence with Lacan, in so far as it reveals what Marxism, in its first flush of post-humanist love, wanted from psychoanalysis in the 1960s, but in the end realized psychoanalysis was unwilling to deliver, leaving Althusser bereft (and Althusser's historical materialism holed below the water line). Afterwards we will look at Badiou's use of Lacan in his *Theory of the Subject* (1982), which touches on similar questions to that of Althusser, but with very different conclusions.

LACAN'S SILENCE

As is well known, Althusser wrote various eulogies to Lacan in the late fifties and early sixties, outlining the affinities between his own emergent anti-humanist Marxism and what he saw as the decentred account of the subject in Lacan's psychoanalysis. What is less well known is the correspondence Althusser conducted with Lacan in which he 'chases' Lacan down, courts and love-bombs him in order to affirm their mutual interests. The correspondence, then, tends to be terribly one-sided, with Althusser explaining himself to Lacan, and Lacan offering in return a few lines of encouragement, or a few pleasantries.[36] This results in a kind of risible desperation on Althusser's part, as he does his best to explain the importance of Lacan's psychoanalysis and the significance of Lacan's thinking in relation to his own position. After outlining, in eight long pages, questions of psychoanalytic technique and 'theoretical pedagogy'[37] on 4 December 1963, and not receiving a reply, he writes again on 10 December in a ten-page letter: 'Your silence has great value for me: I expected it.'[38] In other words: I am honoured to receive the silence of the master, which is I know bestowed lovingly. He continues: 'You have all the art and talent needed to settle a question with a word, to chase off flies, bores and gossips.'[39] Or, rather: I'm not a bore, gossip or parasite, because I'm your devoted student, who knows the true meaning and value of your silence. And again:

'Your silence is priceless',[40] and again: 'Thank God I am writing to you; so you have remained silent . . . Your silence: it was that in you a discourse other than the howl of indignation and bitterness continued, alive, giving to the man you are the reason, and the courage of that silence.'[41] That is: you are silent, so I may speak, I thank you. The similarity here between this exchange with a silent partner and the withdrawl of the analysand from the bond of love in the transference process hardly needs mentioning. Indeed, it is so close that one might suspect that Lacan's silence was enacted precisely to place Althusser in the position of analysand. Yet mention it we must in these terms, because the actuality and spectre of silence and the failed encounter continues to inflect their exchanges and long-term relationship until 1981 when Lacan died. Whatever friendship is disclosed between these two men, in this selection of letters from the early 1960s, it is not based on an actual exchange of ideas, as if Lacan was eager to find out how Marxism's engagement with psychoanalysis might speak the language of science 'on the other side of scientific positivism'. This is because we might say Lacan is betrothed at the time to another, silent and seemingly more attractive, partner, Heidegger, whose needs (his death drive) are greater and more consuming. In this respect, Lacan's silence is not the silence of a master, exactly, but the response of someone who in hailing Althusser (Marxism), and finding that he is now an object of love, does not want to appear betrothed to his love object's other love object: Marxism. So in order to be a little surer of our footing, let us also remind ourselves of the psychoanalytic context in which these exchanges took place.

During this period both Lacan and Althusser are primarily concerned, respectively, with the false and seductive overtures inflicted on psychoanalysis and Marxism. For Lacan it is the humanist dregs of ego-psychology with its drive to submit psychoanalysis to some normative account of human behaviour, and for Althusser it is the subjectivist, humans-make-history in their own creative image, softening of Marxism in response to Khrushchev's revelations in 1956 and the oppressive and philosophically bankrupt legacy of Stalinism. As Lacan was to say in 1957 on the general state of psychoanalysis: psychoanalysis should not allow itself to be taken, 'advantage of [by] some false identity.'[42] And so, of course, neither should Marxism, as Althusser might have added promptly. Thus Lacan at the time was preoccupied, above all else, with to whom psychoanalysis might be properly addressed. What worried him was not that it should find, as a result, only one, monogamous interlocuter 'on the other side of scientific positivism', but that it should not fall into the wrong hands altogether, hands that might strangle its singularity and *love it to death*. Perhaps, then, Lacan had intimations, despite Althusser's vigorous defence of his work, that Althusser's Marxism could only paralyze it, turn it into a new version of 'ideology critique' or a super-articulated theory of the subject on its way to be being subsumed by historical materialism. This is speculation, but nevertheless again and again Lacan's words *never arrive*. Thus in a letter to Althusser on 1 June 1964 he says: 'I preferred not to run the risks of the Italian mail . . . for my wishes to reach you',[43] so these few fleeting greetings will have to do. And the poignant and beautifully suggestive letter of 19 October 1965: 'I did not have time that day to knock on your door. I would like to be sure that someday, doing so, I would not be disturbing you.'[44] *I would not be disturbing you*. Rather, is not the opposite implied here. If we were to meet as collaborators, as intellectual confidants, you would be disturbing me in me disturbing you, disturbing the delicate equlibrium of psychoanalysis as it fends off its false friends and foes alike. Moreover, there is an added threat here: let us both not forget it is psychoanalysis that is *truly* disturbing for it carries within it its own delirium. 'The point is not to know whether I speak of myself in a way that conforms to what I am, but rather to know whether, when I speak myself, I am the same as the self of whom I speak.'[45] So do you really want to be disturbed, more than I already have disturbed you? For psychonalysis is what disturbs, unforgiveably so. And finally a letter from Althusser to Lacan on 11th November 1966, one of the last from this period, and before their relationship becomes more distant and sours: 'You are not alone.'[46] Because I know what it is to be alone, because my letters arrive and yours don't. Ten years later, however, the line has gone completely cold, and Althusser has reversed many of his judgements about his former mentor and ally, as if he is now deaf to what carried his materialist opening up to psychoanalysis forward. As he argues in 'The Tbilisi Affair' (1976), 'instead of offering a scientific theory of the unconscious [Lacan] gave an astonished world a philosophy of psychoanalysis.'[47] Where philosophical systematizing was the thing Althusser singled out for praise in the early letters, here he criticizes Lacan for removing psychoanalysis from the natural sciences, the destinal home of all true sciences he declares, as indeed both Freud and Marx, he argues, asserted, and as such were fundamentally committed to. 'I recall that Marx says that historical materialism ought to be considered for what it is, a "natural science" for history is part of nature.'[48] And in a letter to Elisabeth Roudinesco, the future biographer of Lacan, he accuses Lacan's techniques and concepts of creating 'confusion' and ultimately being 'sterile'.[49] Yet despite his reversal of opinion, and disinclination to speak of his early attachment to Lacan, in 1980 he returns again to the question of Lacan's 'silence', in response to Lacan's dissolution of the Ecole Freudienne de Paris (EFP). Present at the infamous meeting of the EFP at the Hotel PLM Saint Jacques in Paris, the first thing he notices and objects to is how disconnected Lacan seems from his audience, mumbling and muttering his presentation. The old loved one, who hasn't talked, hasn't talked enough, is *still* not talking, even though the professional status of psychoanalysis is being shaken to its roots! Althusser sits back and reads *Le Monde*. Then after Lacan concludes he is struck by how passive and silent the audience is, as if the significance of Lacan's words had completely bypassed them: '"But what are you waiting for?" There was no answer except for an incomprehensible evasion. "But would you be afraid? Of what? Of Lacan? Of yourselves? Of the idea of being an analyst?" And so on. Total silence.'[50] This was a 'surprising silence', he adds later.[51] And then he realizes the silence is not fear or indifference, but the false imposition of the 'analytic act'[52] onto what was first and foremost a political situation: 'hoping no doubt from the silence in which you maintain yourselves and from the words emanating from the mouth of our holy man (or from [his] silence) for the wherewithal to understand what you are doing and what [you] want.'[53] But this is 'rubbish'.[54] It is utterly mystifying to assume that 'doing politics'[55] is no different from the psychoanalytic act, or might substitute for politics. The audience's 'silence' is no more and no less than the misplaced internalization of the analyst's 'ignorance'. So, here is the dénoument for Althusser in his reflections on Lacan's silence: the silence extracted by Lacan from his audience reveals the secret shame of psychoanalysis: its fundamental depoliticizing logic and energy *at key moments of crisis, when silence is evasive and inappropriate*. Althusser, then, back in the realm of silence with Lacan, speaks one last time in Lacan's defence, to pull back the silence, to make psychoanalysis speak 'otherwise', speak directly in the language of emancipation. But the letter never arrives – as Althusser might have suspected all along. As he was to say, in 'The Tbilisi Affair' – as it turns out, very much as a valediction to Lacan before the EFP meeting – Lacan famously says 'a letter always arrives at its destination.'[56] 'I will oppose the materialist thesis: "it happens that a letter does not arrive at its destination."'[57] Here, then, is the disappointed Marxist interlocuter who hears the call for a science beyond the confines of scientific postivism – a science of conflict – but who retreats and falls back into the comforts of an older psychoanalysis, even an older Marxism: *Why can't psychoanalysis be a 'proper' science, and let us receive what we ask for?* This is a compelling question, and one that has repeatedly been asked by Marxism. But, for all its reasonableness, it falls short. For what Althusser fails to see is that silence is not always the line of least resistance, the customary passive-aggressive mode of the angry and put-upon, the language of the politically non-plussed. It is also the space of contestation, of tactical adjustment, of lying low as the renewal of speech. Isn't the intrusiveness of Lacan's silence also contestary in this sense? Isn't silence also agonistic? I say this because in calling for the reunification of psychoanalysis with the natural sciences, Althusser gives up his decentred Lacanian subject to a formal account of Marxism as a 'science of conflict'. For, without a commitment to this refusal to speak in the language one is called on to speak in, that one is expected to speak in, the destitution of the subject as a source of resistance to its own interpellation as a subject – the Subject Who Knows – is rendered inert and incomprehensible. Thus, silence might be said to be the preparatory subjective space of resistance and politics, and therefore encloses a content not available *for immediate transmission*. And in a contemporary world where everything is ready for immediate transmission, this has its additional virtues. Althusser, then, doesn't just fail Lacan on this point, he fails the core function of the error in Lacan's theory of the subject. For pertinently, here, the productiveness of the error in Lacan allows us to avoid this question of disappointment, so destructive historically to the relationship between Marxism and psychoanalysis. The error, in so far as it is *the daily language of that which fails to arrive*, prepares us for what, authentically, does arrive. This means that that which does arrive may take much longer than we imagine, and indeed may arrive in a form that is quite unexpected. So, why is there a need to be disappointed by psychoanalysis, when psychoanalysis actually arms us and strengthens us for disappointment?

BADIOU'S REPETITION

Another disappointed, if less personally affected, interlocutor of Lacan is Alain Badiou. Badiou's writing on Lacan and the subject, however, represents the post-Althusserian expulsion of this hankering after the stabilization of psychoanalysis as a natural science. In this, Badiou is both the fierce defender of Lacan's philosophy *of* psychoanalysis, in so far as he is a strong adversary of Althusser on this issue, but also Lacan's sharper and more insightful political critic. Like Althusser, Badiou returns to what stops or weakens politics or the political act in psychoanalysis. As with Althusser, he touches on the technique of psychoanalysis as the work of subjective deference towards the analysand. Or rather, the cost of psychoanalytic technique – of the *erraten*, the hunch and indirect speech – is that the analyst, despite the idea that he puts 'himself in the position of representing, through being the agent, the cause of desire' (Lacan),[58] encourages the analysand in his or her neurotic repetition. Indeed, this is the other secret shame of psychoanalysis: in the end, the extreme moderation of the psychoanalytic cure. 'The truth is that the psychoanalytic cure has no real aim other than that of readjustment to its own repetition. Hence Lacan shows extreme moderation in relation to his own power as an analyst.'[59] At a fundamental level psychoanalysis abdicates a certain responsibility for political *re-education*. Re-education here being not so much a case of pull-yourself-together and get out and organize, but a recognition of the need for a *direct and destabilizing confrontation* with the fragile fictiveness (ideological effervescence) of the symptom, in order to expose the symptom's class origins. 'A radical toppling of one's subjective position, that is, the interruption of the repetitions induced by the subject's previous (class) position.'[60] In this light, 'political re-education' deserves, as Badiou suggests, all the charges humanism throws at it – 'brain-washing', the 'destruction of individuality' – for it avows that one subjectivity must die for another to emerge. This Maoist-type critique of psychoanalysis is of course dubious and Badiou soon admits it, for his real target is less psychoanalysis as such than bourgeois culture's anti-political investment in the psychoanalytic cure: psychoanalysis's dependence on, and management of, lack. If political re-education can easily throw the analysand into a state of psychosis – in so far as truth and the real achieve a forced and premature synthesis – psychoanalysis's political timidity in the face of lack draws an unwarranted reactionary strength from the neurotic repetitions of the subject. 'Look at the reverse side' of political re-education, Badiou declares, it is 'nothing but a plea for the eternal ignorance of the loss that constitutes the I. [It is] a mere defence of the right to repetition.'[61] So, it is in this sense that Badiou and Althusser share a problem: the tendency, or implication, in psychoanalysis, for the truth of the subject to reside in the mastery of a lack that proceeds unambiguously from the 'epistemological mistrust' of the transference process.[62] But if Althusser is defeated by this – that is, is unable to see how Lacan's silence might contain and prepare an agonistic politics – Badiou is less doleful. Thus in opposition to the assimilation of psychoanalysis into the natural sciences, or the reactionary dismissal of Lacan as an obscurantist, Badiou remains loyal to Lacan's psychoanalytic philosophy: truth is implacably and necessarily founded on scission. In this Lacan 'is ahead of the current state of Marxism'.[63] Hence what is at stake is not how the truth of subjective lack and repetition constrains political re-education, but how the subject is always *more* than the mastery of loss. Marxism has always told us this, but so distant has this truth been from the destitution of the subject that it has always sounded like humanist 'good cheer'. On this score we might say that all Marxist humanists of 'good cheer' should be encouraged at least once a year to read and inwardly digest Schopenhauer's 'On the Suffering of the World'.[64] And this is what Badiou means by Lacan being ahead of the current state of Marxism (certainly in the early 1980s, that is). For there is no pretence that the subject who exceeds the mastery of loss is also a subject who is mastered by loss. Badiou, consequently, offers a different emphasis: each subject for Badiou emerges at a place of crossing *between*, 'a lack of being and a destruction, a repetition and an interruption, a placement and an excess.'[65] But this involves more than a dialectical balancing act between lack and excess, repetition and interruption, in so far as it is the subject's very placement as the product of the law of lack that forces and enables the excess. The subject is, precisely, in its 'return' to the world – in Hegel's sense – the very excrescence of its determinate subjectivity. Hence the subject's excess emerges constitutively from repetition and lack – although this process of emergence is not thereby a *re*-centring of the subject as the result of this excess. Badiou argues that the ruling tragederian account of this lack and repetition in Lacan – derived largely from Freud's 'Beyond the Pleasure Principle' – is epistemologically inadequate in shaping a theory of the subject that is worthy of this (decentred) excess and forcing. Badiou, then, in making a move against Lacan's tragederian subject, seeks a different classical and mythic pairing to stand in for the law of lack: Aeschylus and Orestes (a figure of struggle), rather than Sophocles and Oedipus (a figure of mortification). However, before we discuss this and its implications for a theory of error and the subject, let us recall what Lacan means by repetition in his reading of Freud's 'Beyond the Pleasure Principle' (1920).

Almost from the beginning of his Seminars, Lacan places the utmost importance on Freud's 'Beyond the Pleasure Principle'. Indeed, he sees it as the key to psychoanalysis in the modern period, after psychoanalysis's first rush of natural scientific and medicalized optimism at the end of the nineteenth century. This is because it is where Freud recognizes, as a matter of ontology, that there is something at work in the unconscious, in human subjectivity, that doesn't satisfy the immediate need for the balance and maintenance of the psychic system. Something gets stuck in this drive to equilibrium that continually threatens the homeostatic balance of the system, what, up to this point, Freud had referred to as the 'pleasure principle'. As Freud says:

> The manifestations of a compulsion to repeat (which we have described as occurring in the early activities of infantile mental life as well as among the events of psychoanalytic treatment) exhibit to a high degree an instinctual character and, when they act in opposition to the pleasure principle, give the appearance of some 'daemonic' force at work.[66]

In fact this 'daemonic' drive to repetition, far from being opposed to the pleasure principle, is another manifestation of it, in so far as the drive to restore what has passed is intensely comforting and satisfying: 'the re-experiencing of something identifiable, is clearly in itself a source of pleasure.'[67] This is the origin, famously, of the death drive: repetition is no more, no less, the protection of the organism from disruptive external influences, enabling it to preserve itself and die in its own fashion, repetition representing a conservative diminishment of external stimuli and excitation in the interests of self-preservation. The death drive, therefore, *serves* (or perhaps appropriates is a better word here) the pleasure principle, given the unobtrusive way in which this diminuition of external stimuli undergirds the homeostatic balance of the organism. The pleasure of contraction (of repetition) is conjoined to the pleasures of constancy. But in the end this drive to self-preservation carries with it what Freud calls a quiescent return to a state of the 'inorganic'[68] and what Lacan calls the very 'cessation of pleasure',[69] for, ultimately, the pleasures of contraction become a search for unpleasure. The carrying back of the present into the past becomes a self-aggressive block on the vitality of homeostatic balance. For Lacan, this search for the pleasure of unpleasure through repetition is ultimately what confronts the analyst in the session, and as such transforms the would-be vitalist energy of Freud's early psychoanalysis into the realm of death-in-life. Jean Laplanche, in his exploration of this theme, explains this very well in *Life and Death in Psychoanalysis* (1970):

> It is as though there were in Freud the more or less obscure perception of a necessity to rebuke every vitalistic interpretation to shatter life in its very foundations, with its consistency, its adaptation, and in a word, its instinctuality – concerning which we have noted how problematic it is in the case of humans.[70]

So, repetition according to Lacan is the law of the death drive, and the thing that shadows the transference process at every turn, in so far as its carrying back of the present into the past is in cahoots with the ego: 'The ego experiences reality not only in so far as it lives it, but in so far as it neutralises it as much as possible.'[71] Thus not only does repetition structure the world of objects, it structures the transference process itself. If, for Badiou, the subject is divided between repetition and interruption, placement and excess, repetition is irreducible to an act of pure substitution; that is, repetition enacts, or provides, the conditions for its its own breakdown, and the possibility of the non-repeatable. Repetition, as a contraction of the present into the past, is susceptible to interruption and transformation. This emergence of the non-repeatable, of course, is key to what Lacan understands as being constitutive of an authentic psychoanalytic cure; the psychoanalytic cure is what *escapes* repetition. But, nevertheless, Lacan does not claim that this actually exceeds the law of the lack. And it is this that Badiou rejects. For Badiou, ultimately, the mastery of the lack is inevitably directed at recreating a retroactive dependence on the cause of the symptom. But if Badiou conceives of repetition as susceptible to transformative breakdown, interestingly, his theory of the non-repeatable is opposed to the role of error within this process, or within a dialectics of the subject generally. As he argues, it is precisely the role of errors in the transference process that actually produces the process of psychoanalytic deference in the first place. Avowing that error, mistake and failure 'holds' in the analyst and analysand, encouraging the analyst not to push too far; to challenge the analysand openly, to confront and work on the symptom directly, is to exacerbate the symptom, and cause the analysand to shut up shop or 'run away'. In this respect, Badiou attacks Lacan for suturing lack to repetition. It is the encouragement and parsing of the error in the interpretation of the symptom that defines the privileges of psychoanalytic ignorance. Indeed, far from truth propagating itself in the form of 'errors' (as Lacan avows, following Hegel), for Badiou errors are the suspect detritus of poor judgement, and the lingua franca of capitalist 'common sense'. 'Should it be such a cause for joy that error is the commercial agent of truth? Let us beware of those people who are all too hasty to consent to the noon-day of the half-said. They cowardly lean to the wrong side.'[72] The error, then, is returned, with a kind of partisan fervour, to its old Cartesian moorings, to its non-productive side. Yet a few pages later he insists: 'Let us argue to call dogmatism any Marxism that pretends to restore the line without anything aleatory, right in front of us.'[73] This ambiguity is certainly confusing, and confusing in relation to any examination of the different orders of error, but admittedly perfectly understandable. Firstly, because of Badiou's anti-Hegelianism (which we have already discussed), and, secondly, because of his insistence on anti-tragederian metaphorization of the law of lack, that doesn't subject an ontology of lack and repetition to deathly finititude. Errors, *as the daily language of that which doesn't arrive*, would seem for Badiou, then, to be far too weak a description for the interruptive and forceful work of desire. This is why, for Badiou, Marxism as a *politics* is fundamentally opposed to the practice of psychoanalysis, for the analysand's possession of the error in the transference process is, ultimately, of a different order of consequence than in politics. In psychoanalysis there is no *avoidance* of errors as a matter of mastery over life and death. Whereas, in revolutionary politics avoidance is a strict priority; that is, there are no productive errors, only forthright or weak decisions that enable 'correct practice' or 'incorrect practice', retreat or advance. Hence revolutionary politics – as conceived by Badiou, here under the mantle of Maoism – is a constant process of vigilance *against* unnecessary errors, and, therefore, is unable to relax in the face of errancy. Thus if Lacan's subject is the subject *of* Marxism for Badiou – that is, the subject is a consistent repetition which exceeds or ex-sists this process of repetition – the practice of revolutionary politics is opposed to the practice *of* psychoanalysis. As such, Badiou echoes Althusser's reservations about the 'silence' at the heart of the psychoanalytic cure; in the end, as Althusser declares, 'Freud's object is not Marx's object.'[74]

This is why Aeschylus and Orestes are key to Badiou's re-metaphorization of the truth of the subject. For what distinguishes Aeschylus's heroes as opposed to Sophocles' heroes, he asserts, is that they do not think and act under the unthinkable and unimaginable – the law of repetition as the substitution of the same. 'His excellence assuredly is on the side of the thinkable. It consists in *turning away from any return*.'[75] Or rather, in returning to the place where he begins his endeavours, the courage of the hero who has removed himself from this anterior place provides the possibility of another place. 'Even though we have to return – and it's this return that makes the subject – there can arise an enlightened overcoming of what no longer entails any return.'[76] Whereas Oedipus returns without remainder to his former place, Orestes' courageous call for justice in the face of the law allows his inevitable return to divide or break the return to the same. In this sense the link between insurrection and death in classical tragedy is split, in so far as the law of repetition is unable to fulfil itself in doom-laden destiny: 'It is one sided to declare the subject tragic; nevertheless tragedy exists.'[77] Exactly. But if Badiou splits the theory of the subject from the imposture of the tragic, his substitution of courage as the language of forcing produces another kind of imposture: forcing as a voluntarist heroicization of subjectivity. This removes the breakdown of the law of repetition from what I shall call the *sublative law* of the error – the challenges of tactical wisdom, comedic invention and the science of the contingent – as the daily mediatory logic of resistance and struggle. Thus, I would stress that we need a third classical pairing in order to make the re-dialecticalization of the subject after psychoanalysis 'work', a missing pairing that is implied in Lacan's productive understanding of the error, but to my knowledge is not discussed at all by Lacan: Aristophanes and Praxagora, a character from Aristophanes' later play *Assembly of Women* (*Ecclesiazusae*).[78] In other words, we need a theory of the subject after psychoanalysis that speaks the language of lack and repetition in the mode of ironic and comedic sublation. For in the subject's return to the same we also need the decentring strategies of deflation and self-deprecation.

ARISTOPHANES' LITOTES

Aristophanes is not a playwright in whose work a given decision or missed action shatters the continuity of history. Nevertheless he is a highly politicized writer in whose plays the mockery of power and of inflated ideals places the characters and his audience members in a position of complicit subversion. But this subversion of power is not the work of cynical displacement, a return to the same through the fleeting and fissiparous high of comedic disruption. Aristophanes' characters may spend most of their time mocking the pretensions of tragic heroes and the tragic playwrights – indeed the writers of tragedies, such as Euripides, appear frequently in his writing – but much of his work is tied to a critical inversion or displacement of hierarchy and the same. Thus many of his characters speak 'out of place', or 'out of turn'. Now of course the social conventions and institutions of classical Greek theatre tended to encourage this. Only men performed on stage, and therefore men took all the roles of women, and it was predominantly men (and rarely slaves) that attended productions, allowing a strong social inclusiveness, and closed playfulness. The complicit subversion of Aristophanes' plays was partly a result of these closed, male exchanges. Yet despite these conditions Aristophanes' characters do not speak as they should, that is they speak contrary to their social roles, or in conflict with the expectations of their social roles – even slaves – in ways that belie the cosiness of these arrangements. At the beginning of *Wasps*, for example, the very first lines are spoken by two slaves, Sosias and Xanthias, who are discussing their dreams, having just woken up guarding their master (Bdelycleon), outside his father's house (Philocleon). Xanthias's dream concerns a group of sheep 'with little cloaks' he has imagined seated at the Pynx (the Athenian Assembly on a hill inside the city wall west of the Acropolis) listening to a 'rant by a rapacious-looking creature with a figure like a whale and a voice like a scalded cow.'[79] This rapacious-looking creature is none other than the leader of Athens, Cleon, a pro-war despot who came to power in Athens after a period of radical democracy under Pericles (462–461 BC), and whose disparaging description would have been instantly recognizable to the audience (flagged up also by the names of the two leading characters), if not wholly acceptable – Cleon was fairly popular for having taken on Sparta militarily. The play is concerned with one particular aspect of Cleon's aggressive destabilization of Athenian democracy: his corruption of the Assembly jury system by increasing attendance payment to Assembly members from one to three obols, encouraging members to vote for the prosecution. Cleon died in 421 BC and the play was first performed in 422 BC, so Cleon's legacy was certainly a current and contentious issue. That Aristophanes opens the play, then, by having a slave directly abuse Cleon is tendentious enough (albeit that these criticisms are couched in the recollection of a dream, the necessary form of social criticism of all voices 'from below' from Ancient Greece to William Langland's *Piers the Ploughman*). But the slave then addresses the audience as if he is a tribune. That is, he takes the audience into his confidence, explaining with surety and humour what will follow, as if he is the playwright's surrogate. Now the surety of the slave's voice is not the playwright speaking in the language of the slave's emancipation. There was *no* discourse of slave emancipation in Ancient Greece (although slaves were of course manumissioned), and Aristophanes' two slaves soon return to their servile and invisible role. Yet something interesting happens here, as elsewhere in Aristophanes' writing: *something is spoken in truth, which no one strictly believes because of the form in which it is spoken, yet it remains as truth after the truth has been assimilated as an error.* Which is not to say that many people in the audience when the slaves spoke did not believe that Cleon was a rapacious fool, but that the attack on his rapacious foolery is able to stand, because being spoken by a slave it had no real political consequences. It is error, therefore, that carries or contains the truth content here. Or rather, it is that which is perceived as error, in the lapsidian spirit of Hegel, that actually enables truth to appear. This is why Aristophanes is also a master of the principal trope of inverted speech or literary error, the litote: an affirmation by negation of the contrary, for example 'I really hate you' as an assertion of love. We see this to great effect in the *Assembly of Women* (circa 392 BC).

The *Assembly of Women* is also concerned with the future and legacy of Athenian democracy, but here Aristophanes directs his ironical gaze towards the rise of a 'leftwards' turn in Athenian politics: 'common goods' communism, the egalitarian sharing of all production and services (partly derived from the political legacy of Sparta). The defenders and agitators for this politics in the play are group of radical women led by Praxagora, the wife of leading Assembly member Blepyrus, who are not only distrustful of the male leadership of the Assembly, but partisan opponents of the hierarchies and oppression that the male politicians bring to Athenian politics as a whole. As Praxagora argues in conversation with Blepyrus and a passing citizen, Chremes: 'I assert that it is necessary for everyone to share and have everything in common and to live the same, and not for one to be rich while another is miserable.'[80] Objections to this are immediate from Blepyrus, but become particularly strident when Praxagora also argues for the common availability of women's bodies. Blepyrus mocks this on the grounds that no one will want to have sex with the old and ugly and, therefore, the supposed egalitarianism of 'free love' is self-defeating, and consequently a good indication of the limits of 'common goods' communism overall: people want the collective benefits of communism, but are not prepared to submit themselves to its individual discipline. The rest of the play is taken up with this egalitarian sexual 'folly'. It has been said that Aristophanes' voice is that of Blepyrus – or something close to it – and that the play is a sardonic critique of communism as an ideal.[81] Well, it is certainly a mockery of the narrow and instrumental version of the communism argued for, at times, by Praxagora, a communism of goods that is surprisingly similar to the one that Marx always disparaged for its crudeness and vulgarity. But whether Blepyrus is the voice of Aristophanes or not, his voice is one of the weakest and most unconvincing in the play, whereas Praxagora's voice – which, remember, issues from a man voicing a woman as a critique of men's political power – is the strongest and most vivid. Here then is the litotic at its most compelling in Aristophanes: what is presented as absurd in its manifest heroic truthfulness, in its deflation and defeat, retains its truthfulness. Now this is not to say that *Assembly of Women* has a hidden utopian content; this would be absurdly anachronistic and destructive of the political singularity of the play. But rather, and more convincingly, what is distinctive about Aristophanes' use of the litote is that we may see that the political subject or hero may return to the same place – and of course there is no other place to return to – yet at the same time, in following the return, we are witness to a journey in which things speak otherwise, and as such cannot be trusted to speak in the language ascribed to them. The subject may return to the same place, but this return is shaped by all kinds of meanderings, reversals, switchings and cunning sideways moves, which drain the returning subject of any purblind and inflexible fidelity to a given ideal. Even the superegoic identity of the classical Gods is mocked in Aristophanes. In *Frogs*, for instance, Dionysus descends into Hades wearing a yellow nightdress, buskins (high-laced boots favoured by tragic actors), a lion skin over his shoulders and carrying a heavy club: an Athenian Fred Flintstone, no less. Consequently, if the returning subject fails to arrive in another discernable place, nevertheless it does not arrive stripped of all subjectivity, or with a subjectivity stripped raw by uncomprehending struggle. So, in this respect what we encounter in Aristophanes, above all else, is the incorporation of political speech into a language of error that is profoundly at home with the actual and the contingent. That this accomodation of the actual might easily be interpreted as comedic cynicism – as it has been by generations of classicists – does not alter the fact, however, that Aristophanes' writing speaks to an anti-heroic (and Hegelian) modernity: it is not the moral heroism of the priveleged individual that moves the political process forward, but the strength of collective action, which, in turn, finds its conditions of possibility (and heroism) from its own (limited) endeavours.

The issue here for our purposes is not that the self-ironizing subject of Aristophanic comedy allows us to helpfully triangulate the psychoanalytic subject as a subject of lack and repetition. By introducing Aristophanes alongside Aeschylus and Sophocles (both of whom, incidently, Aristophanes had the highest regard for)[82] we are not concerned to provide a more 'rounded' picture of the subject as divided between lack, excess and contingency; an acceptable figure of finitude for our times. On the contrary, what the return of the subject in the speech of error in Aristophanes enables in our reflections on the psychoanalytic subject generally, is to develop a theory of the subject in which the supplementary return-to-the-same is not just the expression of a continuing fidelity to excess-as-struggle, but a commitment to struggle as a process of inversions, meanderings, and cunning sideways moves. The breakdown of the law of repetition is also the law of ironic reversal and transformation, as Hegel understood. This would appear, at one level, to chime with Badiou's advocacy of Orestes' refusal of deathly finitude, as an expression of the need in Marxism to defend a certain kind of historical patience and weakness. 'To defend Marxism today means to defend a weakness. We must *practise* Marxism.'[83] Indeed, this is hard not to disagree with. It would be churlish, therefore, despite Badiou's political explusion of the error, not to see the possible connection here between the productive function of the error and the possession of weakness as a critical notion. But there is 'weak thought' and 'weak thought'.[84] What is precisely problematic about Badiou's Orestian subject is its *re*-heroicizing occupancy of a 'vacant' historical process. By identifying the subject with a courageous fidelity to the excess of a forcing, the subject and the 'return to the same' are ultimately placed at odds. This is because fidelity to the excess of a forcing is designed in Badiou principally to stand in for the absence of collective historical agency, and as a result courage is opposed, essentially, to the actual. And this is why Badiou has such an antipathy to the error: for truth-in-error presupposes continuinity and adaptation, and therefore a subject *embedded in the progress and retreats of the historical process*. Revealingly, on this score, Badiou argues that 'to fail means nothing . . . [failure] always happens.'[85] But if failure means nothing then the subject has no place by which to define and ground and reflect on its courageousness as a condition of collective praxis, and as such makes it impossible for the truth-in-error to do its mediatory historical work. Lacan's Hegelianism serves a important function here. Despite his Sophoclean dramatization of the law of the lack as tragic and mortifying, Lacan has the utmost respect for the ironic and deflationary speech of the slave in Hegel's master–slave dialectic in the *Phenomenology of Spirit*, a speech that in speaking 'otherwise' owes something to the litotic inversions of Aristophanes' slaves. This is due to the fact that the identity of the slave – always in error for the master – cannot but expose the truth of the master: that is, the truth of the master – his belief that it is his benificence alone that bestows life on the slave – is in fact the alienated outcome of the slave's labour, and as such is as much constrained by his relationship to this labour as is the slave. But in so far as the slave labours he is able to produce values and meaning and therefore transform himself in relation to the world. Whereas in so far as the master 'labours' solely on controlling his relationship to the slave and other slaves, he produces nothing and learns nothing.

> Hegel finds a way to show that what results from [history] is that in the end it is the slave who, through his work, produces the master's truth, by pushing him down underneath. By virtue of this forced labor ... the slave ends up, at the end of history, at this point called absolute knowledge.[86]

Therefore, the inequality of the relationship is inverted. It is the errant condition of the slave that is ultimately world-transforming. Lacan's commitment to truth-in-error as a matter of psychoanalytic technique, then, brings to light the ironic and comedic value of this sublatory logic in Hegel. As Lacan says with insight, if with extreme exaggeration, '*The Phenomenology of Spirit* is hysterically funny.'[87] Irony and truth-in-error prevails over self-identity as a condition of historical consciousnes and the dissolution of the bourgeois ego. Accordingly, Hegel's own antipathy to the pathos of heroic individualism is a seriously funny business, because the subject who does not think of himself or herself as a subject-who-is-not-a-subject (that is the person who thinks of themselves as a master of his or her own circumstances, and of knowledge) is, indeed, extremely funny, even when pursuing the most glorious ideals or inflicting the most terrible pain and destruction. That Aristophanes wants to keep his gods in yellow nightdresses is not fortuitous.

SKIRTING PSYCHOANALYSIS: ERROR, LANGUAGE
AND THE POST-KANTIAN SUBJECT

In this final section I want to draw up some points of connection between this self-ironizing subject-who-is-not-a-subject and various responses in language theory and analytical philosophy to the post-psychoanalytic condition of the subject. This is because at this stage we've only begun to address the question of error, language and agency (one of the concerns of the next chapter) and, therefore, barely discussed the agonistic implications of Lacan's reflections on language and psychoanalytic technique. How does psychoanalysis as a 'science' of the failure of the mastery of reason bear upon political agency? So in prepration for the next chapter on history, political praxis and error, and in order to stake a broader claim on truth-in-error, I believe it is important to point to a number of conjunctions between the psychoanalytic subject, error theory and a revised, post-Kantian philosophical subject, particularly in the light of Badiou's political disconnect between psychoanalysis and politics. These conjunctions are useful, in particular, because the critique of 'transcendental reason' and the ego has found its way into recent analytical language philosophy, analytical political philosophy, and the philosophy of language, as a problem focused on the limits of cognitive, intersubjective and discursive reason. In this sense the failure to master reason in psychoanalysis is a way of reconnecting error theory to the inherent crisis of the philosophy of the subject. Thus, I want to address three specific issues that I feel have a crucial bearing on this, and on what we have so far discussed: in what ways might it be *rational* to cause oneself to act irrationally, or in error? Conversely, in what ways might it be irrational, or errant, to act rationally? And in what sense is the actual fear of committing an error a condition of ideological legitimation, and, as such, a means of constraining thought and action, particularly political action?

The last point is a precondition of the second point: the fear of error produces forms of rationalization that may produce detrimental or irrational effects. Just as the first point – acting rationally through error, or accepting the risk of error – is an explicit critique of the last point. As such the notion of error-in-truth outside of the immediate confines of psychoanalysis provides scope for a discussion about belief and agency that challenges the usual extensionalist definition of intentionality in the philosophy of the subject or philosophy of mind: namely, that psychological invariance is normatively essential if actions are to be congruent with beliefs – a notion that analytical language philosophy historically has made its own. To defend the concept of extensionality is to accept that 'inner conflict' or self-division is irrelevant to the execution of actions.

Now, recalling our earlier discussion of non-contradiction it is impossible to conveive of the subject of thinking and saying what he believes to be the case, as false, in the first person. It is logically impossible for me to say: 'I mistakenly believe this.' Yet obviously this does exclude that possibility that the avowal of a given statement may not be avowed with complete surety or certainty, in so far as the failure of the subject to master his own powers of reason invariably produces a subject who is able to override logic, risk aversion, utility and the integralness of belief (those things that the philosophy of the subject tell us are inviolable). Indeed, it is impossible to square the defence of extensionality – the insistence that 'internal' and 'external' forms of persuasion are largely irrelevant to the execution of actions – from the actual life of actions themselves. For extensionalists, in the light of the law of non-contradiction, there is no such thing as 'weak will'.[88] But if we cannot rightly claim misbelief for our beliefs, a decision taken is not necessarily the most wanted, or the most appropriate. It may be impossible for people not to do what they think they ought to, but this does not prevent inconsistency. As Roy Edgley insists: 'there is no logical impossibility in being inconsistent, either in belief or action.'[89] Let us look at the three points above then, in turn.

First, the question of acting rationally in error. In *Ambiguity and Logic* (2003), the logician Frederic Schick recalls a fascinating story told by George Orwell.[90] Fighting in the Spanish Civil War Orwell is confronted by a fascist in the distance, half-dressed and pulling up his trousers. Orwell raises his gun but doesn't shoot, feeling a sudden rush of empathy for his fellow soldier. What up until then had been clear and focused – the need to kill fascists in order to defend the Republic – suddenly became fuzzy. 'Before the soldier appeared Orwell had a reason to shoot. He thought that shooting would kill a fascist, he wanted to kill a fascist, and he saw his shooting as killing a fascist. But facing the man holding up his pants, he no longer saw it so, and his reason came apart.'[91] What produced this moment of grace, Schick asks? A change of 'seeing' or ideological disinvestment? Whereas up to that moment fascists were legitimate political targets, this fascist was now a 'fellow' human being, as preoccupied with the minutiae and routines of everyday life as anyone else. Schick is not saying that Orwell experiences a conversion to humanitarianism or pacificism, exactly, but that at this moment his reasons for being in Spain and fighting are overridden by a different 'picture' of things that puts his reasons for shooting fascists in jeopardy. In seeing the situation this way Orwell 'disambiguated'[92] the scene, accomodated it. Under what conditions he disambiguated it, however, Schick does not care to venture a judgement. For clearly the shift to seeing the fascist as a 'fellow' human being may be as much an outcome of a certain political intransigence – that is, given his sympathy for the revolutionary and anti-Stalinist group POUM (Partido Obrero Unificación Marxista), Orwell's refusal here to see this particular fascist as a barbarian becomes, possibly, a covert form of anti-Stalinism – as it is an eruption of humanitarianism. Indeed, one may be indexed to the other, and, therefore, represent an expressly *political* choice: 'I will spare this fascist, because I can – fuck Stalin.' Similarly, in a place of seclusion and relative safety Orwell is clearly in a position to make this silent choice. In the heat of close combat such an option diminishes.[93] Seclusion produces reflection. Nevertheless, if we cannot be sure about the specific conditions governing this shift in 'seeing', it is hard to equate this act of grace with the exercise of rationality, given Orwell's failure to maximize the utility of his role as a soldier and killer of fascists. The sparing of fascists cannot be a consistent choice if he wants to remain in Spain and fight for the Republic. Yet, if we think of rationality in terms of the consistent maximization of what is in our 'best interests', 'most people aren't rational.'[94] As the law of repetition tells us, the death drive forces asunder the maximalization of such interests. The analytical philosopher Hartry Field has also explored this question of the inconsistency of belief states. Like Schick, Field asks: if relations between belief and the world are predicated solely upon what is logically feasible, how can the inconsistency or failure of beliefs be adequately represented within such a schema? For once the picture of rational action is undercut by inconsistency and failure, the ascription of the rules of logical reasoning to belief states is weakened. Indeed, Field goes as far to say that this failure of logical omniscience – in an undeclared concession to psychoanalysis – is commonplace: 'even in quite normal and optimal conditions our beliefs are unreliable'[95] – or, rather, not wholly consistent.

But if Orwell's action is thereby 'irrational', in so far as he is prepared to pursue it consistently (that is, pursue it this side of Orwell converting to pacificism or fascism), nevertheless, in its inconsistency his action possesses 'another rationality'. By not killing the fascist – by making a manifest political error – Orwell opens up a space for a reflection on the political consequences of combat, a space that all soldiers experience. In war and revolution, killing is always accompanied by the interdiction: *Who shall I not kill?* For in 'not killing' when I can kill, or should kill, as a soldier, I recover my autonomy, my capacity for grace, as a human being; and this is particularly acute for revolutionary or radical soldiers, where grace is never far away from the demands of revolutionary consciousness. I am reminded in connection with this point of a story I was once told by a documentary filmmaker about the war in Nicaragua in the 1980s. An American journalist had accompanied a Sandinista company into the countryside, where the company ambushed and killed a group of Contras. The journalist and the female commandant then walked through the dead bodies, the journalist revelling, perhaps more out of relief than triumphalism, in the fact that all the Contras had been killed so quickly and so efficiently. The female commandant turned around, and said, severly: 'Don't gloat, they are also our brothers.'

So, what Schick's example points to is how choices that don't maximize the utility of actions – acts of grace, actions that are ostensibly in errancy – can act counter-rationally in rational ways. This is one of the functions of the error as evidence of the breakdown of the will: the error prepares or enacts the death of an ungiving and unworkable rationality, and the birth of a new rationality.

Second, the question of the irrationality of the rational. I want to take as my example from the philosophical literature, here, Derek Parfit's reflections on *rational irrationality* in *Reasons and Persons* (1984).[96] What is interesting about Parfit's reflections on this question of the irrationalization of the rational is that the irrationalization of the rational may become, or has to become, a form of explicit risk-taking. Thus in contrast to Orwell's weakening of his political will at the point of its enactment, here the recourse to the irrational as the rational, or counter-rational, is performed deliberately *as* an irrational act. This is what we might call an example of the *radical and explicit reversal of rational self-interests*, and as such represents the ironic exposure of action as a maximilization of utility. Parfit takes the situation of a violent burglary. A man and his children are threatened with death during a burglary. The father says, promptly, with a gun at his head, 'Go ahead and kill me and my children, I don't mind.' The burglar is thrown by this, psychologically deposed from the position of someone who supposedly has absolute control over the fate of his victims, and consequently feels indecisive about what he threatens to do. As a result he decides to withdraw and run, without attacking the man or his children, rationalizing that if the man is that crazy, he would not be a reliable witness anyway or someone who is likely to call the police; in other words the burglar feels he can get away without committing violence and with his self-respect intact. As Parfit argues: the father reasons quickly that he has little to lose in making himself irrational for there is an outside chance that in making himself irrational he may disturb the equilibrium of the attacker's own irrationality by confronting it on its own ground. Hence if he and his children are possibly to die, making himself irrational is neither here nor there with respect to the fate of himself and that of his children. Parfit's example here of inverted self-interest is a kind of bravura performance that few under aggressive attack would have the courage or ability to 'rationally' pursue. Yet it points to an interesting resolution of the problem of rational actions in certain conflictual situations, traumatic or otherwise. In such an instance, majority opinion would advise that what is best for the victim is to 'talk down' the aggression and potential violence of the burglar; indeed, to try and persuade him of his vested interests, to encourage him to get away with the minimum of inconvenience and the maximum of rewards. But being rational in this way – that is discursively interpellating the burglar as someone who might freely discuss their own irrationality – would appear to be an impossibility after the death threat. The father reckons that such rationality would infuriate the burgular, and drive him to the atrocities that he threatens. So 'rationality' as non-contradictory reason has to be jettisoned here, throwing to the wind all pretence of rational action as the maximilization of utility: stay calm and trust in the 'good will' of the attacker. What works, on the contrary, is precisely the *projection of irrationality*.[97] And so, 'since it was rational for [the father] to cause [himself] to be like this, this is a case of *rational* irrationality.'[98] In this respect the weakening of rationality as a weakening of the maximilization of utility is a direct subversion of the adherence to rationality as a kind of transparent speech. So, where is the truth-in-error here? How does rational irrationality further clarify our understanding of the subject as that which fails to master its own reason as the outcome of an indefatigible will?

The action of Parfit's imaginary father is not as a result of ideological uncertainty, as is Orwell's decision not to kill the fascist; his rational irrationality, therefore, is not the consequence of an ideological shift in these terms (although he may have assessed very quickly that the police/ social services consensus on talking the aggressor down was dangerous in this instance). However, a shift of sorts does occur: the father realizes that the only conversation worth having with his aggressor is not one of fair exchange – that is, based on an appeal to the aggressor's rationality – but one that submits, in an act of unequal exchange and powerlessness, to the aggressor's ultimate demand: to die at his hands. This then completely subverts the usual conditions of an 'ideal speech situation' commonly advanced within the philosophy of language and analytic linguistic philosophy. In refusing the normative demand of language-as-communication (in Jürgen Habermas and Paul Grice, for example: exchange as rationally motivated agreement),[99] the father uses language as an instrument of force. His reckless evacuation of self-interest is so disturbing as to break the spell of the burglar's own aggressive demands, and as such his words have more in common with the agonistic exchanges of the psychoanalytic session than they do with a notion of shared 'communicative action'. Jean-Jacques Lecercle's language theory, borrowing as it does from Lacan, takes this notion of language-as-force as axiomatic.

> The nature of human language is to be agonistic; we do not speak in order to co-operate by means of peaceful exchange of information, but in order to fight, to dominate the opponent, to claim a place in the field, which is evidently a battle-field. Rather than a co-operative ethics of discussion, we have a primitive situation in which speakers represent a threat to one another.[100]

There is an air of rhetorical exaggeration here, as if all speech acts consisted in combative struggle at the expense of rationally motivated agreement. But nonetheless, Leclercle is right to assume that speech acts are also contestatory acts, and therefore do not sit easily within a language model and a model of social action that proclaims communication as the maximilization of shared interests. Words, as Lacan insists, at all points of the transference process, are the traces of ideological struggles, the symptomatic remnants of anterior causes, and therefore are distressing, disturbing and destablizing. This is because language is not the externalization of an interiority, but the internalization of an exteriority (the Symbolic), with all the historical and familial retinue that this carries. In this respect, Lacan begins from an important premise, which analytic language philosophy invariably fails to address in its construction of language as an ideal system or stable form of correspondence or equivalence with the world: language is neither the result of a process of becalmed intersubjective interpellation, nor the syntactical mechanics of information, but the outcome of a struggle between bodies and their affects, what Lecercle calls the 'violence of language'.

What is useful about Lecercle's psychoanalytically derived agonistic language theory is that it is wholly opposed to the restoration of a formal model of truth – truth *without* a subject – in recent analytical linguistic philosophy. In this mimimalist or deflationary account of truth, truth is no more than that which is explained by the standard equivalence schema: namely, 'that *snow is white* is true if snow is white'. This is because, as Paul Horwich argues, the capacity for this proposition to be true 'is guaranteed regardless of how it comes about that an utterance expresses the particular proposition it does.'[101] Thus on this basis, 'truth is not strictly attributable to utterances, or to linguistic or mental acts' at all.[102] The minimalist or deflationary theory of truth, therefore, goes one step further than Tarski's use of the equivalence schema: *not only do we not need a subject for a theory of truth, we actually don't need a definition of truth*. The equivalence schema is sufficient enough for this job, in so far as it provides a use-independent notion of truth that is adequate to how the majority of speakers of the English language actually experience and apply their use of English sentences in the world. Clearly, though, we do need to establish the uses of truth, for otherwise language languishes in a wholly formalistic and artificial relationship to its ordinary uses. '[T]he most serious worry about deflationism is that it can't make sense of the explanatory role of truth conditions: e.g. their role in explaining behaviour, or their role in explaining the extent to which behaviour is successful.'[103] Quite. Deflationism's 'scientistic' deposition of the speaking subject from the truth-operations of language produces an account of language and truth that reduces truth to what is most non-metaphysically robust: truth as a simple and transparent notion of equivalence. Horwich and others defend this reduction because they do not want a concept of truth in which propositions may be 'more or less true'. In this, deflationism's 'realism' makes its point well. But a sense of what is true may not fit the equivalence schema (or T-biconditional) and at the same time not be 'more or less true'. This is as a consequence of the fact that the standards of truth demanded by deflationism operate in contradiction to the actual truth-conditional realities of everyday speech acts. Because minimalism or deflationism distinguishes the concept of truth sharply from speech acts and their truth-conditions, it is utterly indifferent to how truth actually makes its way in the world. 'Minimalism involves the contention that truth has a certain purity – that our understanding of it is fairly independent of other ideas.'[104] 'Fairly independent' is, of course, seriously question-begging, but the point is clear enough: the concept of truth here has nothing to do with how we actually use language to gain knowledge of the world – namely from the inconsistent, error-filled speech acts of others – and therefore how we employ our conceptions of what is true on this basis. Thus in defending what *is* true solely as equivalence, deflationism is reduced in its resistance to truth as a metaphysical problem, to produce a formal and emptily sequential account of truth. By defining truth at the micro-propositional level, truth is confinded to the infinite presentation of this propositional form: 'the sun is hot only if the sun is hot', 'Paris is the capital of France only if Paris is the capital of France', etcetera, etcetera. But a significant number of generalizations – the generalizations that philosophy mostly operates with – that are true, are true precisely because they operate in a way opposed to this, for example the generalization, 'all men are mortal'.[105] This expresses a truth about all men without us having to detail all instances of men's mortality: Mr A. Runymede, of 52 Railway Sidings, Chipping Norton is mortal; Mr B. Valance, of 133 Beech Avenue, Throgmorton is mortal; Mr . . . etcetera, etcetera. Thus deflationism represents the purity of truth from the position of a false closure in the interests of an improbable, temporal outcome. But, crucially, the deflationist concept of truth is a narrowing of truth because it believes a concept of truth can exist without a definition of truth; in short, without the subject of language having to ask that old and tedious philosophical question: what *is* truth? It deposes truth, therefore, from the subject of language use, because it believes truth to be *no more* than this steady state equivalence. Truth and true-belief have no explanatory role.[106] The equivalence schema is 'a priori and conceptually basic'.[107] Admittedly, this is a minority position in contemporary analytical linguistic philosophy. But its rational formalism, either of a realist or idealist character, is certainly not: the technical diminution of metaphysics, as an expression of 'common sense'.

Consequently, the relationship between language and truth, as evidenced in the example from Parfit above, is expressly not one of rational equivalence between speakers or between a correct proposition and the world, for in order for the subject to *be* rational, his or her speech acts invade and disturb without the pretence of communication. This gap, then, between speech acts and the maximilization of utility as an expression of an integral will, is what links such thinking on language to the decentred subject in psychoanalysis. The subject in language is agonistic as a result precisely *of* its decentredness – 'the linguistic and the psychic are so intermingled as to be almost identical'.[108] And this is perhaps a stronger route across the political divide between psychoanalysis and Marxism than Badiou is prepared to take. Like Badiou, Lecercle's subject-who-is-not-a-subject is subjected to a language that he or she makes their own, and fails to make their own, but for Lerercle this is *a continuous and immersive struggle*. The subject is always on the 'edge' of language, so to speak, always in struggle with it and against it – as my two examples have attempted to show. The threatened father wins the argument not by the judiciousness and cogency of his argument, but by its spontaneous, unpredictable and affective force. In this sense the prospect of error, the arrival of error, of speech acts that betray the 'stability' of language as correspondence, as grammatical and syntactical system, and communication, is something, therefore, that is indivisible from language as a trace of ideological struggles and affective force. Hence error-in-truth is a crucial part of the speech acts and agency of this continuous struggle.

What Lacan does not provide, however, is any clear sense that these traces of ideological struggles, this embodied speech, this 'violence' of exchange, this error-in-truth, is also attached to the subject's *overall position* within the sociality of speech acts; that is, the place from which the subject speaks as someone who is already spoken by the language he or she speaks. This is something that Lecercle is particularly valuable on, and as such enables our subject-who-is-not-a-subject as a subject of error to gain a certain critical leverage. Before language can make any claim to communication, creativity, correspondence or equivalence with the world, its operations and exchanges represent a 'system of places, sites of struggles and power relations, but also a process of subjectivation through the assignment of places.'[109] Speakers emerge from 'interlocution from the linguistic agon that unites and opposes them.'[110]

This sense of language as agon is also made clear from a slightly different position in my final example: speech as the fear of error, or the fear of 'not knowing'. Here I want to look at Trevor Pateman's reflections on the lapsidian in *Language, Truth & Politics* (1975), a text that represents one of the first political interventions into Anglo-American language philosophy's comfort zones. If my example from Derek Parfit pinpoints the affective force of language as a kind of risk strategy, Pateman's reflection on the error in *Language, Truth & Politics* takes an opposite position on the question of risk: why is it the case that the speech acts of those who are called on to 'know' defer to the master's voice (or conversely reject the voice of the master altogether), and, as such, avoid at all costs the threat of error? For those who believe themselves to be without knowledge, and without the possibilty of achieving it, the social shame of 'error' is mortifying: 'strategies of *evasion* [regarding knowledge claims], are most often and most importantly, it seems to me, strategies for avoiding the penalties, which generally attach to being an *unsuccessful* inquiring man [sic]. And I would suggest that the social penalties meted out to those who simply don't inquire are less severe than those suffered by those who try, but unsuccessfully.'[111] These 'penalties', therefore, are not incurred by those who avoid the possibility of error, but by those who risk error in the pursuit of knowledge. In this way 'not wanting to know' – as a rejection of the pursuit or validity of some claim to knowledge – has echoes of the transference process in psychoanalysis: not speaking on what you are called on to speak, as a means of self-protection. But in daily conversation, of course, the penalties incurred by making an error are far more exacting than in the psychoanalytic session. In the session the analysand is given the space and permission at all times to make errors, and as such there are no social penalties in this sense – that is, there is no public shame attached to them – although persistent avoidance of the consequences of the discussion of errors obviously delays the dynamics and successfulness of the cure. Thus what Pateman's analysis touches on is the place of the subject within the intellectual division of labour as an expression, in Lecercle's sense, of *subjectivication*: the assignment of the speech acts of the subject to a pre-given place, and therefore to pre-given competences. The rejection of knowledge here curtails the number and character of speech acts the subject is willing to make. And this is why Pateman was, in many ways, on the ground floor as regards the political and social account of the productiveness of errors. His critique of the intellectual division of labour is framed in such a way as to give maximum space to the subject who in committing himself or herself to new knowledge embraces error *without fear of reproval*. In other words, an emancipated subject *is one who invites error*. 'If it was insisted that one should not claim to know anything except where it was impossible that one should be in error, then one would never (or almost never . . .) be able to make a claim to empirical knowledge.'[112] As such there is an explicit class dimension to Pateman's analysis: making errors in the pursuit of knowledge is in the direct interests of those who fear the cost of errors the most: the powerless. The resistance to error in speech, then, tends to be most pronounced in those who have the most to lose from being exposed to the social costs of such errancy: the working class and the dominated. As a result, Pateman lifts the debate on error and language out of its traditional subject-centred, philosophical orbit into post-Kantian alignment with the depossessive social function of the error in Hegel: 'error is not an individual but a social problem, and that the reduction of error require's social change.'[113] Following Hegel, Pateman recognises that the error is dynamically constitutive of truth and of social transformation. The second half of the quotation above, however, is problematic.

Pateman's error theory is weakly attached to an epistemological account of emancipation: with the unblocking of the class obstacles to knowledge, he asserts, the subjectivication of the working class as a class resistant to the social cost of errors, and their submission to their inhibiting, ideological function, will dissolve. As Lecercle shows convincingly, this over-privileges 'knowledge' as a set of emancipatory speech acts external to the subjectivication (and subjection) of the subject. That is, although emancipation is necessarily tied to the release of speech acts from their prevailing conditions of class constraint, it is impossible to imagine emancipation as directly tied to the release of speech acts *from the process of subjectivication as such* – as if there was an emancipatory speech waiting on the other side of this process of subjectivication. On the contrary, the undoing of the language of place (in Badiou's formulation) and the place of language is immanent *to* language use; the interpellation of the subject in his or her place produces its own process of counter-interpellation as a condition of language use itself. 'I counter-interpellate the language that interpellates me into what I am. I play with it, I exploit its virtualities of meaning, I reclaim the names by which it pins me down or excludes me.'[114] There are two important political implications here. First, more generally: emancipation is a condition of the subject's exposure to error as a condition of the renewal of truth, and not just to its reduction or eradication (to reiterate our Hegelian point in the last chapter: humans must pass through what is most estranged from themselves in order to liberate themselves from what is most estranged from themselves); and second, and more specifically: the 'epistemological' fear of error in conversation fails to make sense of the extraordinary capacity of the working class and the powerless *to* resist the inhibitory mechanisms of the error and failure in collective action. The illiterate or poorly literate, or politically 'uninformed', do not fear the making of mistakes or a lack of knowledge in order to act collectively in their own interests, or make a revolution. On the contrary – as in the case of the *sans-culottes* of the French Revolution or the workers and peasantry of the Russian Revolution – they fully expose themselves to its vicissitudes. This makes the fear of error in daily conversation dissolve under the dynamic and demands of class struggle.

What conclusions might we draw, then, from these reflections on the psychoanalytic subject-who-is-not-a-subject and error theory, and post-Kantian reflections on the subject in language theory and analytical philosophy? First of all we need to pay close attention to what explicitly links psychoanalytic error theory (Lacan) to the risk of confronting, exploiting or assmilating the error. As I have argued, the political resistance to error (Badiou) is not a secure pathway to knowledge and emancipation. On the contrary, by avoiding error one invites or sustains powerlessness (Pateman), or neurotic repetition (Lacan). Second, therefore, we need to pay attention to how the overcoming of this resistance to errors registers its effects inside and outside of psychoanalysis. Inside psychoanalysis this overcoming of the resistance to errors is the work of an indirect forcing or prompting within the transference process. Outside of the realm of psychoanalysis it is the work of a direct forcing, or a kind of political confidence in speech and action (Lecercle and Pateman). Both acts of forcing, though, are predicated on a certain kind of risk: the subject risks the costs of errors in order to risk the possibility of truth and emancipation. Which leads us to my third point: the connection between this submission to risk and the agonistic condition of speech acts. As in my example of the rational irrational act (Parfit), it is precisely the absence of rationally motivated agreement, and, as such, the reliance on the affective powers of language, that 'wins' the argument. Hence, in certain situations, if what we take to be rational is allowed to prevail, rationality is undermined, producing a form of rationality that threatens the successful outcome of an action. The situation needs the agonistic 'force' of irrationality to restore a productive rationality. This understanding of the immanent rationality of irrationality, therefore, puts us in better shape to analyze the social risks and costs of error in the next chapter on error, history and political praxis. For it is here that we are confronted explicitly with the necessary risks and social costs of the error, far removed from the production of truth in the psychoanalytic session and the transmission of knowledge in the experimental scientific process.

FOUR

ERROR, HISTORY AND POLITICAL PRAXIS

HISTORY AND THE 'UNCONSCIOUS'

When Frederick Engels argued, in *Ludwig Feuerbach and the End of Classical German Philosophy*, that 'many wills active in history for the most part produce results quite other than and often the very opposite of those willed'[1] he obviously had Hegel in mind, for Hegel, above all else, is the master of the historical accident and the fortuitous after-effect, and as such, in his writing, he is not just attentive to the gap between self-consciousness and self-identity, action and outcome, but more generally between historical event and historical meaning. This is why for Hegel the meaning of a historical event is never self-identical with the intentions of its participants and their imagined view of its outcome. As Hegel declares in *The Science of Logic*, because actuality is precisely the unity of necessity and contingency, we cannot know actuality, immediately, through its direct possession.[2] The meaning and significance of the event, therefore, is precisely a retroactive construction, given that there is no stable correspondence between the representations historical actors give of their intentions and the outcomes of their actions. Historical meaning operates in this gap between intention and involuntary outcome and, as such, between the impact, or lack of impact, of this involuntary outcome on the intentions and plans of future actors. The meaning and significance of a historical event, thereby, is not fixed by its manifest outcomes or by the imputed intentions of its dominant or subordinate historical actors, but is the 'work' of history itself. The implications of the unfinished or thwarted aims of historical actors, and the unresolved consequences of an event, will be determined in the light of the outcomes of future events, and the questions they then, of necessity, pose to the interpretation of this past event, and the past generally.

But if in *Ludwig Feuerbach* Engels's reflection on the unwilled here touches on what appears to us as the 'psychoanalytic' content of Hegel's thinking on experience and knowledge, Hegel's 'unconscious' – his Owl of Minerva – is not the unconscious of Freud and Lacan, or of psychoanalysis as such. Rather, Engels and Hegel's unconscious is no more and no less than what was commonly identified in the nineteenth century as the generally unbidden effects of human action: those unpredictable and unexpected outcomes that the subject had little or no control over, and, therefore, whose meaning can only be disclosed after their passing. In this sense there are two notions of the 'unconscious' at play here: a pre-psychoanalytic one, in which the immediacy of knowledge is always being betrayed by the temporal demands of reflection and further reflection, and a properly psychoanalytic one, in which the impossibility of the immediacy of knowledge grounds the reflective powers of the knowing subject as such. It is the former, then, that functions pre-psychoanalytically in Kant, Hegel, Engels and Marx's critique of historical immediacy, and that will mainly preoccupy us here in our discussion of politics, history and the error. For what psychoanalysis makes clear is that it is only the *individual* subject that has an *unconscious*, and, therefore, that the unconscious proper is only available for analysis in the intersubjective encounter of the transference process itself. History – as the unfolding struggles of collective wills and classes – may exhibit aleatory effects and involuntary outcomes – indeed is inseparable from these effects and outcomes – and, accordingly, is necessarily subject to various unconscious pressures and determinations, but it cannot as a developmental process be subject *to* psychoanalytic reflection; collective subjects cannot be psychoanalyzed. To try to do so is to enter that highly dubious and reactionary realm of the 'collective unconscious' and, in turn, to pass into the equally dubious realm of the History of Ideas (*Weltanschauung, Zeitgeist*). Indeed, this approach is to confuse the historical encounter with the subject in analysis, with the process of historical reconstruction as such. Psychoanalysis is not just a historical hermeneutics, but an existential and affective intervention into a given life and a biography as a means of transforming that life and biography. Despite its significant hermeneutic potential, psychoanalysis is first and foremost an *active encounter with living subjects*. Yet this is not to say there have been no historians who have tried to produce a psychoanalytic history or tried to psychoanalyze historical figures, but overall the results have been largely adventitious, or conservative, or both.[3]

Hegel and Engels, therefore, necessarily *think* the 'unconscious' in a pre-psychoanalytic mode, even if Engels's approach 'touches' here on psychoanalytic method and understanding. Thus, when they speak of the unwilled, and of History as a realm where historical actors are condemned to speak outside of the place where they believe themselves to be, Hegel and Engels are speaking from a specific *historiographical* position on the unconscious, not a psychological one, namely that Universal History – or, precisely, bourgeois evolutionary history – is never identical with its own claims for progress. In this respect, the emphasis on the unconscious here is tied specifically to the role and identity of the bourgeoisie itself. The rise of the bourgeoisie as a hegemonic class has never been a straightforward matter of the self-conscious expression of its interests; that is, its internal contradictions make its rise to a position of hegemony fraught with all the problems of misrecognition that stem from the suppression or veiling of such contradictions. As the bourgeoisie begins to think of itself as a newly emergent universal class, it begins to identify its historical mission with historical necessity itself, in turn naturalizing this mission. Consequently, whatever involuntary and unwilled outcomes might disturb this mission, these disturbances, it asserts, cannot challenge the overall direction of its aim: rational progress. It is unsurprising, therefore, that, in the period of the bourgeoisie's Enlightenment ascendancy, the involuntary and the unwilled take on heightened ramifications for the critics of this hubris. For the gap between the intentions of historical actors and their outcomes becomes the site of a permanent *ideological hiatus* between the vicissitudes of historical development and the bourgeoisie's vision of progress. In these terms it is possible to talk about the bourgeoisie in this period as actually producing the 'involuntary' and 'unwilled' as distinct historical and political categories, in so far as the rise of the power of the bourgeoisie and its confidence in its historical mission develops in inverse proportion to its default as a class on this mission. For instance, the French revolutionary bourgeoisie of its Enlightenment origins is certainly by 1815 the bourgeoisie of imperial reaction, having quite literally decapitated, or exiled, its radical founders. As Arno J. Mayer describes the situation: in the legislative elections in France of 14–22 August 1815: 'Of the 380 deputies in the new chamber, close to 90 percent were royalists, nearly 50 percent nobles, and 20 percent ex-emigrés.'[4] Thus, if the image of progress still pays fealty to the 'rights of man', it is the rights of markets that now prevail as capitalist industry develops.

This conflicted nature of the bourgeoisie as the agent of capitalist progress is actually reflected in the peculiarly divided status of the bourgeoisie as a class-for-itself in the period of the bourgeois revolutions themselves. That is, at the very beginning of the French Revolution the (industrial) bourgeoisie plays a secondary or subordinate role to that of the revolutionary bourgeoisie and petit-bourgeois (provincial lawyers, state officials, and journalists) who are the main authors of the new constitution and democratic politics.[5] It is this petit-bourgeois fraction and its non-capitalist middle-class and aristocratic allies that provides the initial ideological thrust and moral bearings of the revolution. Few industrialists and their spokesmen participate in the political shaping of the revolutionary process in France, and few contribute to its intellectul milieu. It is not clear, then, how a bourgeois revolution might be made without the central participation of these class interests in whose name the revolution is ultimately fought.[6] But this lack of self-consciousness on the part of the industrial bourgeoisie between 1788 and 1793 – or rather the disconnection between its vanguard status as a class fraction and the political process – is less perplexing, and as such presents less of a problem for historical materialism, once we consider the bourgeoisie as a class that is invariably 'missing' as a unified entity within the revolutionary process. Because bourgeois revolutions are political transformations which arise precisely to facilitate the passage from feudalism (or the remnants of feudalism in the case of the French Revolution) to a capitalist mode of production, lasting power lies with that fraction of the bourgeoisie that can unite the class as a whole behind capitalist development. Thermidor (1794–95), therefore, was essentially the point where the interests of the industrial bourgeoisie expressly aligned themselves with the right-wing majority of the Assembly, in the name of political stability (although the capitalist development of the forces of production doesn't really get going in France for another fifteen years). Hence there is a fundamental difference between the dominant class fraction of the bourgeoisie and its aristocratic allies who make the bourgeois revolution and those forces which actually benefit from it. The great losers of the French Revolution, therefore, were those class agents who actually made the revolution and expected most from it as its radical tribunes: the bourgeois democrats (Robespierre), the *san-culottes*, and the workers (or *bras nus* as Daniel Guérin has called them).[7] As a result, these historical actors are forced aside by the capitalist requirements of what has been *put in motion* by the democratic revolution. Consequently, it matters little whether the bourgeois revolution actively channels the direct participation of the industrial bourgeoisie – whether this fraction self-consciously leads the revolution or not – because bourgeois revolutions in the end are capitalist revolutions first, and popular, democratic revolutions second; and as such, the democratic leadership of the revolutionary fraction of the bourgeoisie acts, ultimately, as the 'vanishing mediator' of capitalist development. In the light of this, Marx and Engels soon recognized that, as a class which is internally riven in this respect, the revolutionary function of the bourgeoisie is fleeting and limited. Its historical work – or the work done by others unconsciously in its name – is soon done, closing, on the one hand, those aspects of the legacy of bourgeois Enlightenment that are inconvenient to capitalist development, and, on the other, opening a path for the bourgeoisie to make peace with those aspects of counter-revolution and reaction that are conducive to its power (social hierarchy, slavery, the monarchy, state religion, free trade).

The heightened emphasis on the involuntary, unwilled and unconscious in Engels is designed first and foremost to explain this 'ghost-like' and fleeting revolutionary status of the bourgeoisie as a class: namely, the fact that as a class it doesn't necessarily need to make a revolution in its own image in order to benefit from the bourgeois/petit-bourgeois democratic revolutionary process more generally (that is, in the early stage of the revolution the industrial bourgeoisie is parasitic on its revolutionary democratic wing and the popular upsurge from below), and that, in power, it appropriates the Enlightenment language of progress in the most instrumental and anti-democratic fashion. Essentially, then, the unwilled and involuntary are used by Engels to point not just to the Hegelian gap between action and outcome, but to the specific ideological character this takes when the bourgeoisie assumes the leadership of humanity and industrial development. The bourgeoisie after Thermidor speaks in the counterfeit language of counter-revolutionary progress; a false universalism, built on conceit, deceit and hubristic ambition. Marx's fury at the counter-revolutionary character of the bourgeoisie after Thermidor is one of the driving forces of his forensic attacks on its personnel and apologists in his political journalism.

Thus in the 1870s, after thirty years of study and critique by Marx and Engels of the bourgeoisie's post-Thermidor condition and development,

Engels's emphasis on the involuntary and unwilled outcome functions precisely, therefore, as a corrective to the bourgeois model of progress: the notion that somehow progress is measurable according to the development of the productive forces and of technological advance. This critique is crucial for Engels in the 1870s, because of the way in which the unthinking progressivist assumptions of bourgeois history after 1848 were beginning to enter the values of the nascent workers' movement. Workers representatives were beginning to talk as if the proletariat could develop in partnership with bourgeois 'progress'. But as Engels argues in *Anti-Dühring* (1878) – following Rousseau – with each advance in civilization there is also an advance in *inequality*, or the generation of new forms of inequality, and consequently progress cannot be measured by a sense of a stable and unfolding continuity from one period to another, but in relation to the underlying conflicts and contradictions of a given mode of production.[8] As such the proletariat can only make a revolution in its *own name*, because its specific interests – self-emancipation – are inconsistent with the system as a whole. The agency of the proletariat, therefore, is quite different from that of the bourgeoisie in this respect: the proletariat cannot appropriate the agency of another class or class fraction to do its historical work for it, for its work is precisely that of the dissolution of classes as such; and, consequently, whereas the petit-bourgeois and the aristocracy were the (eventual) willing partners of the revolutionary bourgeoisie, knowing that their class interests would be best protected under the transition to capitalism, no other class would willingly contribute to its own dissolution as part of a proletarian revolution. In other words there is no measure of progress outside of the outcomes of class struggle itself, for it is precisely the proletariat's irrealization of its own emancipation inside the bounds of capitalist progress that is the true measure by which the intentions of historical actors are to be assessed and judged in the realization of 'historical development'.

COUNTER-REVOLUTION AND ERROR

And this is why Hegel's earlier *Phenomenology of Spirit* is so important to the critique of bourgeois Universal History, despite the constant misidentification by his detractors with its claims. For in Hegel, similarly, there is nothing inevitable and predetermined about bourgeois progress, and therefore historical development is not to be identified with any pre-given

Enlightenment script. This is why the counter-revolutionary dissolution of the French Revolution, and the spread of reaction through Europe in the late 1790s, is fundamental to the meaning and aims of the *Phenomenology* (1807). One of the first major defences of the spirit of the French Revolution in the period of counter-revolution, Hegel's *Phenomenology* tasks itself to think the irreducible world-historical importance of the Revolution *within* and in *conflict with* the space of its attenuation and defeat. The counter-revolution may have dissolved and blocked the popular democratic impetus of the Revolution, but the emancipatory transformations and effects of the Revolution, in the long term, are irreversible, and will survive their temporary destruction. A philosophy of agency – of Spirit, in Hegel's language – must resist the temptation, therefore, to think of progress as an unfolding journey *of* Enlightenment; on the contrary, it is a struggle of endless reversal, inversion and unwilled consequence. Thus Hegel's concern in the *Phenomenology* is to develop a philosophical language that can model such reversals, inversions and unwilled consequences, as a constitutive part of historical transformation; and it is this that Marx, and particularly Engels, inherits – hence the importance of my earlier insistence that the *Phenomenology* is an attack on the pejorative place of the error within counter-revolutionary discourse during this period. Hegel's critical assimilation of truth-in-error – inherited, as I have already insisted, from the pre-revolutionary array of Enlightenment thinkers – is one of the crucial manifestations of this new dialectic. Indeed the error, as an expression of the unwilled consequences of history, reaches a new level of heightened political self-consciousness in the *Phenomenology*, in response to the rise of the discourse of revolutionary and counter-revolutionary error.

The vicious and *ad hominem* attacks on the Revolution by counter-revolutionary exiles and reactionary foreign critics after 1794 invariably focus on the Revolution as a monstrous 'error' of nature, and of reason *tout court*. As David A. Bates has stressed in *Enlightenment Aberrations: Error & Revolution in France*, these counter-revolutionary discourses of the error take over and reverse the largely productive account of the error within the work of pre-revolutionary liberal bourgeois writers, who mostly were keen to link the emancipatory challenges of the Enlightenment with a notion of the waywardness and missteps of progress.[9] In fact, in this corpus of writing the error is associated less with the mistaken judgements of enfeebled reason than with creative wandering. In counter-revolutionary discourse, in contrast, the error is startlingly *unproductive*, the deleterious outcome of an unnatural separation of reason from the predetermined and harmonious divisions and hierarchies of political and religious tradition. For example, in Abbé Barruel's *History of Jacobinism*, published in London in 1798, the author produces a veritable compendium of errors perpetrated by the leaders of the Revolution and their Enlightenment sympathisers. 'Philosophism . . . is the error of every man who denies the possibility of any mystery beyond the limits of reason';[10] those who believe that the *philosophes* and Encyclopaedists are innocent and pure disseminators of knowledge, commit an even graver error: they deny that the revolution was a premeditated conspiracy. 'This error is the favourite error of the Jacobin *missionaries*.'[11] Similarly, in Joseph-Marie comte de Maistre's *Considérations sur la France* (1796)[12] the real errors of the Revolution are those committed by the people themselves, for assuming that they could break with the hierarchies and exclusions of nature. Indeed, such vaunting popular ambition represents a gross impertinence on the part of the governed, because it is based on the false assumption that all men and women, without exception, are worthy of equality and freedom. Here then de Maistre borrows directly from Edmund Burke's widely disseminated *Reflections on the Revolution in France* (1790),[13] the 'breviary of the Western counter-revoution', as Jacques Godechot has described it:[14] equality is contrary to nature, precisely because nature offers no sustainable evidence for it. In this respect, the fundamental error of the Revolution, for Burke, is above all else its raising of political abstractions – specifically the 'rights of man' – over and above the steady and natural course of history and the precedents and particularities of tradition. But if de Maistre identifies errancy with the hubris of Enlightenment, he none the less reserves a special place for the *true* error. The people may have fallen into monstrous errors of reason, but they are also the harbingers of the authentic errors of faith: that is, their enduring capacity to submit themselves to the authority of altar and throne. The sublimity of the people lies in their absolute trust in authority, no matter what mistakes authority makes, and what brutalities it commits in the name of the people. The outcome is what de Maistre envisages positively as a virtuous circle of ignorance: the people of necessity need to live in error (that is, live in error ignorantly of what it means to live in error), in order to sustain their capacity for faith. Hence, the unrealistic abstractions of the 'rights of man': in subverting the very capacity for truth, they destroy the *true and authentic errors* of faith. And it is in this sense that the errors of the people are sublime.[15]

The link between true and authentic error and truth is also a concern of the other significant French counter-revolutionary theorist of the period, Louis de Bonald. In his writing, errancy is brought back into a pre-modern Augustinian mode, providing an ontological grounding for de Maistre and Burke's theocratic authoritarianism. Because humans are of necessity imperfect, the attempt to render humans 'perfectible' through the struggle for equality and freedom for all mocks and challenges the absolute perfection of God. It is precisely because of the imperfection and finitude of humans – the gap between God and his sinful subjects – that humans are able to possess the attributes of faith and submit to the redemptive love of God. Submission through faith also possesses the attributes for a political ontology: in so far as man is sinful, the government cannot represent the people, and therefore the people must be *governed*. It is only one kind of mastery, therefore – in the person of the King – that secures social stability, and prevents men and women from destroying each other. For without the stabilizing 'absence' of the people from the organization of society, anarchy and the realm of the inauthentic error would reign – as proven by the French Revolution. So, it is only when the people submit themselves to altar and throne that they are truly free; that is, truly free from the monstrous errors of reason.[16] Now, such counter-revolutionary discourse is not politically homogeneous. Although Barruel, Burke, de Maistre and Bonald are authoritarian restorationists, they are not authoritarians of the same ilk. Bonald, Burke and de Maistre were not defenders of an unblinking despotism: the French Revolution had at least implanted one thing in their querulous thinking: that the subjection of the people through the charisma of the monarchy was to be administered by a layer of ministers, to balance royal decree. And, in this sense, counter-revolutionary theory from 1790, politically, is a many and varied response to the massive haemorrhaging of aristocratic and royal power.[17] In no leading counter-revolutionary thinker is restorationism a call for Absolutism, *status quo ante* – to the letter, that is – even if the rage against reason and Enlightenment compels them and others to move in that direction. But where they are united is in their exit from history and their abandonment of human agency. This leaves the historical process open to a different set of verities for these writers: religious providence, national destiny, and patriotic and godly duty. As Godechot puts it, for providential thinkers such as de Maistre, the 'counter-revolution will be accomplished at the hour willed by God.'[18]

One of the aims of Hegel's *Phenemonology*, consequently, is to reinstate the productiveness of the error as the contingent presence of human agency in the face of this counter-revolutionary turn to predestination and providential action (what France suffered was, in fact, willed by God! to paraphrase de Maistre), and the extreme counterintuitive account of error-as-support-to-faith. In this respect, Hegel not only restores that earlier Enlightenment commitment to error as 'creative wandering', but mediates the expressly political identity of the error in the Revolution as the struggle for truth. This is why the stakes of errancy are increased politically in Hegel in the period of the error's revolutionary and counter-revolutionary articulation: the Enlightenment commitment to truth-in-error moves into the realm of political struggle, *as a reflection and assimilation of defeat and failure.* The pre-Revolutionary Enlightenment thinkers, of course, took cognisance of the fluctuations and opacities of intellectual progress. But at a significant level the French Revolution destroyed the liberal bourgeois doctrine of human perfectibility in its dominant philosophical form: the notion of the Ideologues (Helvetius, Condorcet, Condillac, D'Alembert, D'Holbach, Raynel) that inequality derives principally from differences in education, and as such can be overcome by education:[19] 'men are all endowed with the same basic physical organization and that inequality among men is attributable, not to inherent differences in the capacity for learning and feeling, but rather to artificial differences in environment, which could be levelled away by legislation and education.'[20] The language of unwilled consequences and of unconscious outcomes – of the flight of the Owl of Minerva at dusk – then, is as much a mediation of the shattered ideals of this model of Enlightenment progress, and the destruction of popular or plebeian democracy, as it is a defence of the irreducibility of the French Revolution as a world historical event. Or, rather, we might put it another way: what the Revolution teaches Hegel is that Enlightenment is not won by peaceable and educative means, but by the violent destruction of continuity. For Hegel, then, the Revolution produces a different temporal order of change that philosophy is compelled not just to represent (as an act of cognitive assimilation), but to enter and possess. This is why Hegel's divorce of the error from its epistemological legacy in Cartesianism, Kant and latterly in the Ideologues, is not a philosophical decision, a decision of abstract reason, so to speak, but a political intervention, for it represents in its passage through the fires of revolution and counter-revolution the very movement of history itself. Hegel tries to think the Revolution as a moment of defeated promise, that thereby lives on in its defeat. This is why, practically alone amongst his peers, Hegel defends the Revolution at the high point of its democratic ascendancy (Robespierre) and subsequent failure, without any capitulation to the critique of the counter-revolutionary errancy of popular action and belief. He makes no concession to the idea that the revolutionary is an aberration because it was defeated, or that its accomplishment was illicit because it enforced its popular will through violence.[21]

ERRANCY, JUSTICE AND THE FRENCH REVOLUTION

This, I believe, places the error in a new political space in this period, in line with what I have argued earlier about the transformed positional logic of the error in Hegel's philosophy. For if Hegel makes the unwilled consequence of historical development, and, as such, the pathologies of progress, the mediating context of human agency and desire, in turn, the error moves from its discrete scientific and moral-religious base to the very centre of historical praxis. And this is only conceivable as a result of the way in which the bourgeois democratic revolution in France forced the error as a matter of political and ethical culpability (and progress) onto the historical stage. By this I don't mean that the French Revolution 'invented' the error in political discourse. But, rather, as the first expressly modern revolution, the French Revolution made the failure to adhere to a programme, a set of principles, an ideal, a vision, a democratic and collective reality for those committed to or supportive of the revolutionary process. To err, to fall into errancy, was not only to betray, deceive, or weaken this programme and set of principles, but to threaten the lives of others, and the life of the Revolution itself. With this, the French Revolution introduces onto the world historical stage the culpable language of error that has been a determining factor of all revolutions since: to fail or to betray the revolution is to err in the face of the revolution's demands and responsibilities. The counter-revolutionary attack on the popular violence of the Revolution, therefore, is a fundamental disavowal of the culpability and errancy at the heart of any revolutionary process: historical actors invariably betray the revolutionary process, or disguise their antipathy to it, or, as future apostates, openly contest it, leaving their actions open to the necessity of defensive or offensive violence. There is, then, no revolution without severe judgements on errancy, given the intimate connection of errancy to matters of life or death.

It is no surprise, therefore, that the concept of error plays such a dramatic political and ethical role in the speeches, pamphlets and articles of the period, because if the mechanics and dynamics of modern revolution are being made for the first time, so is the political response to the Revolution's internal and external enemies. In Robespierre's speeches between 1792–1794, for example, there is a heightened attention to what produces errancy and what makes those who are ostensibly part of the revolutionary process fall into error, for revolutions not only speed up the need for informed response to events, but invariably leave people behind, even those who see themselves as part of the revolutionary process. One pertinent example of this is the career of Emmanuel Joseph Sieyès (1748–1836). In November 1788 he writes the wonderful pamphlet 'An Essay on Privileges'.[22] 'All privileges, then, from the very nature of things, are unjust, odious, and contrary to the supreme end of every political society.'[23] But by 1791 – two years before the Constitution[24] – in his debate with Tom Paine, he writes without irony: 'We need not . . . lose Monarchy, since there will always remain what is its essence, an individual decision.'[25] Not surprisingly – having miraculously survived the Terror – he later plays a leading part in the *coup d'etat* of 18 Brumaire of the Year VIII (9 November 1799) that brings Napoleon Bonaparte to power. As Robespierre declares, in the light of such a (familiar) shift, revolutionary ardour is easily converted into counter-revolutionary accommodation, and, as such, the revolution is obligated as a matter of its daily survival to scrutinize, test and expose the would-be friends and allies of the revolution, 'those false patriots that persecute the people'.[26] Indeed, the revolution is never far from the internal pressures of counter-revolution, because, 'It is much easier to don the mask of patriotism and disfigure the sublime drama of the revolution with insolent parodies, to compromise the cause of liberty with hypocritical moderation or studied nonsense.'[27] Yet if this heightens the need for vigilance, it also heightens the need to distinguish false errancy – counter-revolutionary deceit – from the authentic and necessary errors of the people itself. For if the Revolution demands absolute vigilance against errancy from the defenders of the Revolution, it also demands vigilance against those counter-revolutionaries and short-sighted zealots who falsely accuse, or prematurely accuse, the people of counter-revolutionary errors: 'woe to those who would dare to turn against the people the terror which ought to be felt only by its enemies. Woe to those who, confusing the inevitable errors of civic conduct with the calculated errors of perfidy, or with conspirators criminal attempts, leave the danger-ous schemer to pursue the peaceful citizen!'[28] Clearly what this reveals is less a picture of Robespierre as an incorrigible judge of the perfidious errors of others, than as someone concerned to protect another kind of true errancy against false errancy: errors made conscionably in the name of the Revolution and the general will. And this tone is at times reflected in the reports written by agents of the Ministry of the Interior between August 1793 and April 1794 at the height of the Terror,[29] as in the report filed by 'Pourvoyeur', 19 Pluviose, Year II (7 February 1794) on allegations made against the 'moderate' revolutionary Camille Desmoulins.

> They said he had always been a patriot from the beginning of the revolution; that he had proven himself well, above all at the stormiest moments; that people talk about him as much as about even Marat; that if he has made mistakes it was only an error of the moment, not made through lack of patriotism and that it would be really unjust to forget what he has done since and for the revolution.[30]

But if Robespierre opens up a space for the defence of a productive popu-lar errancy at the heart of the Revolution, he is unable to offer any reliable or secure means of discriminating between such true and false errors. He tends to fall back on the commonsensical notion that the honesty and pure hearts of the accused will prevail, and therefore enable the judges to see without prejudice. How is it possible to 'distinguish dupes from accom-plices, and error from crime . . .?' he asks, in the last of his speeches, on 8 Thermidor 11 (26 July 1794). 'Good sense and justice will make it.'[31] Yet if the judgement of true errancy is far from persuasive here, nevertheless, Robespierre's positioning of error as a space in which the popular will is able to fail, or fall out of line, in *good faith*, carries over the Enlightenment notion of error as wayward truth into the realms of revolutionary political praxis. And this is what Hegel certainly inherits in the *Phenomenology*: the error, as a knowledge 'from below', is essentially the agency and vector of emancipation and truth.

But nonetheless the *Phenomenology* is not a secret homage to Robespierre, nor of course is it an actual examination of the Revolution. In fact, Hegel's concern with error as the surplus of truth does not stretch at any point in his writing to a discussion of the empirical errors of Robespierre, and the revolutionary bourgeois itself, beyond his (passing) criticism of the excesses of the Terror in the *Philosophy of History*.[32] This leaves the world-historical importance of the Revolution, as the highest manifestation of Spirit, in empirical limbo. That is, if Robespierre in 1794 represents the high point of the bourgeois democratic revolution for Hegel – Robespierre 'carried out universally admired *facta*'[33] – there is no corresponding analysis of why the errors of Robespierre and the Montagnards take the form that they do, and as such no basis for a critique that would clarify why the Revolution was unable to proceed beyond this high point and, in turn, fail to prevent the worst aspects of the counter-revolution (Thermidor). Although Hegel allows the errors-as-truth of the popular insurgence of the Revolution to be carried forward historically as Spirit – and this, as I have argued, constitutes the singular importance of his defence of the Revolution – it will take another political tradition, the Marxist tradition, to explain why the errors of Robespierre and the revolutionary bourgeois contribute to the Revolution's demise, and as a consequence why these errors, therefore, define the ways in which the failure of the Revolution *actually* promises an emancipatory politics. In this sense, Hegel's assimilation of the Revolution into his philosophy of Spirit is ultimately indifferent to distinguishing between errancy as the motor of historical agency and the culpability of specific political errors themselves, and, as a result, why the errors of Robespierre and the revolutionary bourgeoisie are ultimately an expression of the historical limitations of this class and the revolution. For if Hegel recognises, in the *Philosophy of History*, that the Revolution had by 1794 run its course, this is not because he has lost ultimate faith in the bourgeoisie as a revolutionary class. This is because Hegel is concerned with the rise of the bourgeoisie and the historical passage of the revolution into the global reach of world history, rather than with attaching meaning to a given set of political errors that might thereby explain the revolution's defeat. In attaching culpability in this way he would have had to break with the revolutionary bourgeois in the name of the democratic Left of the Revolution, a move Hegel was clearly not in a position to make, not because he had little sympathy with the *sans culotttes*, or didn't see the importance of their role in the revolution, but because defending this defeated cohort of the Revolution was marginal to his sense of the world-historical impact of the Revolution as a whole. The specific meaning of the revolutionary bourgeoisie's defeat is not something that Hegel is able to develop, therefore, because the errors of

Robespierre, in alliance with errors of the *sans culottes*, do not exist for him as an emergent opportunity for a new politics. Hegel, consequently, may mourn the defeat of the *san culottes*, but only as the defeated vanguard of *bourgeois* politics. This is why, if Hegel assimilates the political arrival of (revolutionary) error-as-truth on the world stage, it will take Marxism to explain why the link between the unintended consequences of the errors of the revolutionary bourgeoisie and the defeat of the revolution open up at the very heart of this defeat a different political space for the error: the vicissitudes, unwilled consequences, and reversals of proletarian agency itself.

The important question, therefore, that hangs over the revolutionary bourgeoisie's singular and defining error in 1794 – Robespierre's unwillingness after his arrest to mobilize the *san culottes* against a weakened Convention – becomes, for Marxism, less an expression of a missed opportunity for the development of popular democracy than the defining moment of the historical limitations of the bourgeoisie as a revolutionary class. That is, this moment is only definable as a lost opportunity – an error of omission – if we assume that Robespierre and the Montagnards would have managed to retain power, particularly in the face of the growing anti-Jacobin reaction. More than likely the Montagnards would at some point have moved against the continuing popular pressure from below, as they had done throughout the high point of the Revolution; in other words, the 'forward' movement of the Revolution might have lasted another year or more before Robespierre would have moved to finally crush the *sans culottes* in the face of these pressures. But even if the Revolution had been given a stay of execution, the *sans culottes* were not in a position to assume power. With or without Robespierre, the *sans culottes* had no material base to assume power. This is why the leadership of the *san culottes*' withdrawal of support for the Robespierre faction before and during Robespierre's arrest was based on a false assumption: that the Revolution would continue or revive without Robespierre. So, although the impetus of the revolutionary is curtailed by the restorationist pressures internal to the revolutionary bourgeoisie, this restorationist pressure is facilitated by the material weakness of the *sans culottes*, making, in this sense, the 'errors' of the *sans culottes* and the 'errors' of Robespierre the outcome of a historical deadlock that neither could grasp.

Thus Marxism explains the defining error of Robespierre in the latter days of the Revolution not as a lost opportunity for democracy, but as an indication of the in-built contradictions of the bourgeois revolutionary processes itself, as it crashes up against its historical limitations: the fact that *at no point* could *its* democracy guarantee the democracy of *san culottes* and *bras nus* alike, just as at no point could the *sans culottes* and *bras nus* take power in the name of a plebeian democracy. And thus Robespierre's finicky constitutionalism, his reluctance to move against the Convention, the seat of his beloved 'democracy', is a perfect expression of this: namely that, in sitting it out, he hoped the law would resolve these tensions for the bourgeoisie. For Marxism, then, Robespierre's error of omission looks two ways simultaneously. By removing himself from the historical stage, and as such signing the final defeat of the *sans culottes*, he seals the fate of the revolution, but at the same time this closure, in its very finality, defines the emergence of another place for politics, a place beyond formal bourgeois democracy. Now, Hegel's theory of error-as-truth in the *Phenomenology*, in its sweeping, capacious way, allows us to assimilate the truth of the latter in a generic sense: the unintended consequence of Robespierre's defining error is that, in the defeat of the *san culottes* and the *bras nus*, the conditions for a new politics are born. But it is Marxism that is able to see this, shape it and theorize this process in its class specificity, for in its looking back in hindsight to the French Revolution, it is able to precisely define what is released by the defeat of the *sans culottes* and *bras nus* and revolutionary bourgeoisie alike. After Thermidor, Hegel's politicization of the error exits the revolutionary space of bourgeois politics to find a home in the promissory revolutionary politics of the proletariat. As a result, questions of culpability, of failure, of truth-in-defeat, now become directly attached to the historical destiny (and recurring crisis) of working-class politics. But after Thermidor this process signifies more than a shift of the political identity of the error into proletarian mode, for it also represents a qualitative transformation in position, function and content. By this I mean that the would-be monstrous errors of political democracy, of politics from below – in the imaginary of Barruel, Bonald and de Maistre – and which are defended by Hegel, are now the outcome of, are constituted by, the hegemony of counter-revolution. The errors of strategy, position, ideas, as a consequence of the struggles of the proletariat, are locked into the counter-revolutionary defeat of the class. So, at the point where the proletariat emerges as an independent political force in the wake of Thermidor, it emerges into the *permanent counter-revolutionary space of its own defeat*. And in this sense this is the historical condition of Marxism since 1848: it is a theory of proletarian emancipation that is shaped by a permanent state of counter-revolutionary defeat, from Bonaparte, to Thiers, to Stalin, to neo-liberalism today. This is why, interior to Marxism in the nineteenth and twentieth centuries, there is a consistent revolutionary thread of engagement with errors that in some sense defines the class's subordinate political character: with the errors that betray the revolution, the errors that betray the class interests of the proletariat, and, crucially to our investigations, those errors, in the spirit of Hegel, that *sustain* the creativity of the proletariat at the heart of the political process. To echo Lacan's thoughts on psychoanalytic practice, proletarian praxis in these terms, 'unfolds in the space of the error'. Marxism, then, as the reflexive product of its own political history, is, we might say, by definition a post-Thermidorian theory, and, accordingly, at one level, necessarily a theory of revolution grounded in a theory of revolutionary defeat *as* praxis. It is no surprise, therefore, that the French Revolution is the place where Marxism continually returns to understand the origins of this history of defeat and the post-Thermidorian condition of the error and politics. As Daniel Guérin puts it, in his reflections on the lessons of the French Revolution in *Class Struggles in the First French Republic*, written in 1943: 'No defeat is fruitless. It is in defeat that revolutionaries educate themselves, and the revolution comes to a greater self-awareness.'[34] 'Defeat is just the end of a cycle. Until events have fully developed and mistakes have produced their final consequences, it is too early to draw conclusions.'[35] Similarly, as Frank Jellinek stresses, in like mood, in his *The Paris Commune of 1871* (1937): 'The Commune made grave revolutionary errors. Those errors have actually been more fertile for future revolutionaries than the Communards' limited success. For the analyst such as Marx it is the errors that are interesting, not the causes of the errors.'[36] These three quotations are particularly pertinent, then, to our understanding herein of what error theory becomes within certain pockets of the Marxist tradition after Hegel and Thermidor: defeat – and, as such, error – is what provides the basis for the renewal of revolutionary praxis and thought.

AFTER THERMIDOR: MARXISM, COUNTER-REVOLUTION AND ERROR

In this sense, in so far as I have been concerned in the opening chapters to bring Hegel closer to Marx than many may think wise or acceptable, it is now important to open up that gap again, not in deference to scientific orthodoxy, but rather as a necessary requirement of the need to theorize the political specificity of the error within the Marxist tradition in the light of the above. For, if after Therimidor the errors of the ascendant bourgeoisie are of little consequence for a revolutionary politics, the revolutionary meaning of error – the issues of culpability, unwilled outcomes and unintended consequences – passes over as political and existential realities to that of the proletariat. This is why Marxist politics – separate from the Marxist critique of political economy, or Marxist cultural theory, which have quite separate lives in the tradition of Marxist writing – remains at key points a discourse on the error and failure as a renewal of its truth-conditions. In this section, then, I want to look at three important contributions to error theory within the Marxist *political* tradition, in the period of capitalism's 'second counter-revolution', Stalin's victory in the USSR: the writing of Victor Serge, in particular his correspondence and debate with Trotsky in 1936–37, Henri Lefebvre's writing on praxis, failure and irony in the wake of the Hungarian revolution of 1956, and Daniel Bensaïd's reflections on Marxism and defeat in response to the new Restorationist conditions of capitalism during the 1980s. For these contributions prompt us, more generally, to define a specifically Marxist account of error in the twentieth century that provides the coordinates for a political theorization of the error today.[37] In this it also means reconnecting our analysis of error to irony, negation, and the comedic.

THE COMMUNE, IRONY AND MARX'S 'THIRD VOICE'

However, before we examine these three contributions, it is necessary to return to Marx himself. For it is possible to divide Marx's political writing between the early and mid-period writings that are defined by the high expectations of the new industrial workers' struggles, and the later writings that are more qualified, and insistent on the possible extended duration of these struggles. In this respect, the 'Marxism' of Marx, between the revolution of 1848 and the Commune of 1871, may be a theory of bourgeois crisis and the intractabilities of proletarian struggle, but it is certainly not as yet a theory of revolution steeled in the exigencies of revolutionary defeat. The Thermidorian condition of revolutionary politics in the 1850s and 1860s is the very spur for Marx's historical expectations for a proletarian breakthrough, and a new kind of political modernity. Each of the bourgeois regimes Marx examines in his political writing during this period appears to be creaking and shuddering under the growing spectre of working-class politics. But, in response to the defeat of the Commune in 1871, something new enters this world of expectation, as a result of what he calls the 'first revolution in which the working class was openly acknowledged as the only class capable of social initiative.'[38] And this something new is a shift in tone in Marx's writing that the Jellinek quote above touches on: it is precisely the errors inherent to the revolutionary process, the errors that shape defeat, and that shape a politics in the making, that will come to play a part in defining the character and struggles of the class in the future. As Marx insists: the proletariat knows that, 'in order to work out their own emancipation, and along with it that higher form to which present society is irresistibly tending by its own economical agencies, they will have to pass through long struggles, through a series of historical processes, transforming circumstances and men.'[39] Thus, what Marx previously tended to think of as the largely predetermined shape of proletarian struggle – the collective withdrawal of labour of the factory-based industrial working class, and the uprising of the class as a bloc – is challenged and qualified by the experience of the Commune. First, the industrial working class plays a relatively small part in the insurrection, although the flag of the Commune is raised, so to speak, in its name; and second, and importantly, the revolutionary process, at one level, seems to bypass the notion of the proletarian's *accession* to power. That is, the Commune functions as a proto-proletarian experiment in anti-statist collective mobilization, in which the critique of all forms of hierarchy and the implementation of direct democracy are a political priority. As Marx notes, the Commune's anti-statism functions without any of the language of coercion and repressive discipline that had hitherto defined the bourgeoisie's accession to power. The Commune was a 'thoroughly expansive political form.'[40]

In defending the Commune, in discerning its unprecedented character, then, Marx tends to search for language that emphasizes its speculative, hesitant and heuristic qualities: 'the Commune did not pretend to infallibility, the invariable attribute of all governments of the old stamp. It published its doings and sayings, it initiated the public into all its shortcomings.'[41] As a result, Marx sees the failure of the Commune from two perspectives: the errors of its strategy – its failure to take the struggle to Versailles and Thiers' government, its unwillingness to seize the Bank of France, and the instances of Jacobin recklessness – are, ultimately, the consequence of its isolation and political immaturity, but the speculative content of its unprecedented democracy represents the immanent creativity of workers and their allies in struggle. Thus Marx gets a glimpse of what this demo-cratic mobilization of workers prefigures: the destruction of the *political* subordination of the working class. Consequently, Marx's Marx*ism* after the Commune introduces a new critical inflection: how the passage through defeat and the creativity of error are the very means by which workers in their long struggles will 'work out their own emancipation'. Accordingly, Marx gives short shrift to those bourgeois allies of the proletariat who speak in 'the oracular tone of scientific infallibility'.[42] With this discern-able change in tone we see the explicit reintroduction of irony into Marx's writing. But this is not the bitter irony of the 1850s, when, in the *Eighteenth Brumaire*, he mocks the reactionary parody of Louis Napoleon's celebration of the cult of Napoleon I in order to attack the pretensions and unin-tended consequences of bourgeois progress.[43] Here, in the face of violent suppression of the emerging workers, movement, the disruptions and deflations of irony become immanent to the history of workers' struggle itself. The vicissitudes of workers' self-emancipation are reintegrated into the ironies, reversals and opacities of history as such. This introduces an unprecedented rhetorical voice into Marx's revolutionary discourse at this point, which transforms the way in which Marx sees historical materialism as a specifically historical practice: whereas, in the earlier and mid-period writing, the development of scientific knowledge feeds off an ebullient sarcasm and sardonism, producing a powerful sense of history moving forward, here the creative expectations of workers' struggle are mediated by a mixture of loss and mourning. This is why Marx is explicit about working-class self-emancipation as a long creative struggle. Kristin Ross calls this a 'third phase' in Marx's writing – neither expressly scientific in tone and ambition, nor jubilantly sardonic.[44] But if she is right to insist on this shift as a response to this process of historical attenuation, she doesn't specify in what ways this 'third voice' is precisely a shift in ironic enuncia-tion, and as such what this shift in enunciation advances theoretically. In this respect, Marx's recovery of irony, post the Commune, is I believe the voice of someone who thinks of struggle *as* irony, if struggle is to be equal to the contingencies and involuntary outcomes of history. The Marx of the writing on the Commune, therefore, doesn't just employ irony as critique (as in the early writings), but presupposes that knowledge and struggle are themselves forms of ironical enquiry.

It is not unexpected, therefore, that this writing on the Commune figures as a point of contrast in the Marxist tradition when the creativity of workers is threatened, diminished or suppressed, or indeed when the expectations of workers' struggle outweigh the contingencies of history. Marx's 'third voice' is no less the voice of workers' creative praxis. Between 1904 and 1912, for example, during the period of Rosa Luxemburg's repeated attacks on Lenin and the Russian Bolsheviks, she invokes, in the spirit of this 'third voice', the image of the productive 'errors'[45] of workers against Lenin's 'organisation centralism'.[46] The Russian Social Democrats under Lenin are wrapping 'the party up entirely mechanically in the swaddling of a spiritual dictatorship of the central executive'.[47] Now, this perhaps justifiable critique of Lenin between 1904 and 1912 – in a period when, within the Social Democratic party, a perilous clandestinity went hand in hand with a bureaucratic discipline – is less persuasive when Lenin himself undergoes his own ironic and Hegelian education, after the massive reversal of the workers' movement in the wake of the European workers' parties support of the First World War. For if there is a pre-Hegelian Lenin and a post-Hegelian Lenin in this period, it is precisely Lenin's access to Hegel's ironized history in the *Logic* that enables him to think through this crisis – the biggest crisis of the workers' movement since the defeat of the Commune – *creatively*. First, Lenin tears up any residual commitment to the notion that the industrial power and confidence of the European workers' movement constitutes any kind of guarantee of workers' progress; and second, as the war unfolds, he sees this absence as a means of actually freeing up workers from these reformist allegiances: successful workers' struggle depends less on the accumulation of experience and tradition ripened for revolution by the contradictions of capitalism than the opportunities or prospective gaps thrown up by a crisis of a given political conjuncture. Whereas the former tells workers to wait in good faith for the maturation of the necessary objective conditions for revolution, the latter insists on the objectivity of conditions for revolution as the moment when an inexorable crisis invites workers to act, and *carry the historical process before them*. Thus, if the fortunes of the European workers' movement are reversed with the advent of the First World War, the war's weakening of the world system at its borders in Russia – its weakest link – at the apex of interimperialist destruction, produces its own reversal: with the increased revolutionary consciousness of returning Russian soldiers and war-weary workers and peasants in Russia, the attack on the illegitimacy of the Tsarist regime is given mass support, whose immediate demands require a decisive revolutionary solution. So, the First World War teaches Lenin an unimpeachable Hegelian lesson: what seems to be put into indefatigable reverse is in turn reversible. In this respect, the Lenin that successfully leads the Russian Revolution out of the ruins of the war's reversal is a quite different Lenin to the one that Luxemburg attacks for sectarianism and bureaucraticism between 1904 and 1912. In fact, compare Marx's writing on the Commune to Lenin's 'Lessons on the Commune' in 1908, which, despite the fact that it was originally delivered as a speech, presents a blustery defence of the Commune in order to rally the 'troops' of Social Democracy: there is no 'third voice' here.[48] 'The sacrifices of the Commune, heavy as they were, are made up for by its significance for the general struggle of the proletariat: it stirred the socialist movement throughout Europe, it demonstrated the strength of civil war, it dispelled patriotic illusions, and destroyed the naïve belief in any efforts of the bourgeoisie for common national aims. The Commune taught the European proletariat to pose the task of the socialist revolution.'[49] By 1918, however, the 'lessons of history' are mediated by something closer to Marx's 'third voice' and the Hegelianism of the war years. Let us take, for example, Lenin's well-known reflections on what he calls the zigzags of history:

> ... what occasional zigzags we may have to contend with (there will be many of them – we have seen from experience what gigantic turns the history of the revolution has made, and so far it is only in our country; matters will be much more complicated and proceed much more rapidly, the rate of development will be more furious and the turns will be more intricate when the revolution becomes a European revolution) – in order not to lose our way in these zigzags, these sharp turns in history in order to retain the general perspective; to be able to see the scarlet thread that joins up the entire development of capitalism and the entire road to socialism, the road we naturally imagine as straight, and which we must imagine as straight in order to see the beginning, the continuation and the end – in real life it will never be straight . . .[50]

That Lenin seems to be writing himself out of an ironic tangle here, nevertheless, does not detract from the fact that Lenin's voice, armed with two years of revolutionary struggle, is highly circumspect and judicious. Indeed, 'in real life it will never be straight' has precise methodological and historical implications: the detours, displacements, reversals and unwilled outcomes of history are the very materials of proletarian struggle, in so far as the possibilities of proletarian self-emancipation can only exist in relation to the dynamics and intractable forces of world history. At the very point, therefore, where Lenin and the Party recognise that the workers' revolution has – in the spirit of the French Revolution – transformed the very meaning and direction of world history, the future success of the revolution – its destabilization of world capitalism – is now subject to forces that it is unable to control. And, as such, the revolution's capacity to makes its way through these uncontrollable forces, to negotiate with them, is therefore as important, and in fact more important, than the very making of the revolution itself.

Thus, if we are to look for the moment when 'error theory' enters Marxist discourse, it is possible to see its ironic and Hegelian outlines in Marx's writing on the Commune, and his insistence on the *longue durée* of workers' self-emancipation. Effectively his writing on the Commune offers a kind of watershed moment, for unbeknownst to Marx it establishes what was to become the voice of a subordinated proletarian emancipation from within the continuous space of counter-revolution. For with the exceptions of the years 1789–1794, and 1917–1927, counter-revolutionary politics, in its various ideological and state forms, has overwhelmingly shaped the politics of the nineteenth and twentieth centuries, to the point, of course, where its very identity as a category has become invisible – particularly today – and as such subject to all manner of denial. As Arno J. Mayer has stressed, counter-revolution, 'tends not to be recognized and theorized as such.'[51] Indeed, in these terms there *is* no counter-revolution, no long-standing Thermidorian deflections or destructions: the revolutionary irruptions of 1789, 1917 and, briefly, 1968 are minor scarrings, or at most violent moments of self-correction on the smooth continuum of a self-stabilizing liberal succession. It is no surprise, therefore, that during the period of 'second Thermidor' (1927–1973) Marxist politics becomes entirely shaped by this counter-revolutionary framework: 'first Thermidor' either explicitly or implicitly mediating 'second Thermidor'. For if revolution and counter-revolution need to be conceived in relation to each other, then the irruptions of counter-revolutionary terror (as the regressive aftermath of revolution, as in Stalinism and the Nazi's anti-Bolshevism) also need to be analyzed in relation to the continuity of counter-revolutionary forces as such. In Herbert Marcuse's *A Study on*

Authority (1936), Trotsky's *Revolution Betrayed* (1937) and Benjamin's *Theses on the Philosophy of History* (1940), for example, there is a sense in which counter-revolution is the determinate historical space in which the agency and language of proletarian emancipation are now forged (even if Trotsky uses all his rhetorical skills to present the counter-revolution as a hiatus). In fact Marcuse is explicit about this counter-revolutionary continuity, by being one of the first Marxists in the period to present the rise of fascism and Stalinism reaction in relation to a discussion of Burke, de Maistre, de Bonald and one of the authors of a counter-revolutionary constitutionalism in Germany in the 1840s, Friedrich Julius Stahl (1802–1861).[52] Now why is Marcuse explicit about using the concept of counter-revolution in this context, separate from notions such as the 'rise of authoritarianism' or 'conservative reaction'? Because what is at stake are not simply the minor revolts of the reactionary fraction of the bourgeoisie, or the self-interested petit-bourgeois materialism of the new Soviet bureaucracy, but the fundamental capitulation to what Marcuse calls the inherent 'national reason' of counter-revolutionary politics; that is, the submission of all political judgements and decisions to the ultimate court of national and patriotic sovereignity – the very forces that blocked and retarded the democracy of the revolutionary bourgeoisie. Clearly the specific forms this national politics of reaction takes are very different in Nazi Germany and Soviet Russia, but nevertheless what brings both the fascist and the Stalinst counter-revolution into the space of counter-revolution generally is the freezing up of working-class politics inside national and patriotic borders. There are two consequences from this for Marxist political writing in the period immediately after second Thermidor: revolutionary history is defined in terms of the historical *exception* (rather than the sustained, if broken, thread of international struggle and solidarity) and revolutionary praxis necessarily become a discourse of revision, instability and self-reflexiveness. And it is in this sense, then, that I want to discuss the writings of Serge, Lefebvre and Bensaïd. For Serge is, perhaps, the first and most perceptive 'error theorist' within the Marxist tradition. In fact, Serge allows us to see how the formation of the error within political discourse in the French revolution plays out, with quite different implications, in relation to the fortunes of the Russian Revolution and its own counter-revolution.

Victor Serge's major writings – the political theory, political history and novels – exist largely as a post-Thermidorian corpus of work: *Year One of the Russian Revolution* (1930), *From Lenin to Stalin* (1937), the correspondence with Trotsky (1934–1939), 'Marxism in Our Time' (1938) and the fiction *Birth of Our Power* (1930), *The Case of Comrade Tulayev* (written in 1940–42, published in 1950) and *Unforgiving Years* (written in 1946, published in 1971). In this respect, Serge's writing is the first body of writing in theory and in fiction to explore and assess the conditions of Stalin's 'second Therimidor'. But unlike many other Left revolutionaries, who survived the camps or escaped the USSR, or outwitted Stalin's GPU agents, his work remains committed to explaining the Stalinist counter-revolution, and, as such, the disastrous turn that befalls the communist movement, from within the space of Marxism and dialectic. Accordingly, his writing from the late 1920s is notionally attached to Trotsky and the Left Opposition. Yet if his work overall represents one of the most ardent defences of the revolution, he is no unthinking defender of the oppositional politics that rushes in to fill the revolutionary vacuum in the 1930s. As such, if he defends the revolutionary legacy of Lenin (1917–23), and to a certain extent Trotsky, he is also critical of the conversion of such politics into a set of defensive mechanisms that mix egregious optimism and orthodoxy with a logics of betrayal, in short the politics of *Trotskyism*, or *Bolshevik-Leninism*. The forging of a distinction between Marx and Marxism, Lenin and Leninism, Trotsky and Trotskyism, has of course played a discernible part in the recovery or extension of the 'real revolutionary tradition' from inside or outside of the legacy of the Left Opposition since the late 1920s. But this is not Serge's concern, as if he was trying to protect the purity or authenticity of the authors of this legacy. The notion of a protected purity or authenticity is the very antithesis of his politics in the 1930s. For Serge is really the first Marxist thinker to run with Marx's ironic 'third voice', not as a kind of residuum within revolutionary politics and history, but as its pathologized, heterodox ground, or substrate. This is because the political and philosophical deformations of Stalinism produce, for Serge, a fundamental reorientation of the revolutionary tradition in the period of 'second Thermidor' – a shift that Marxism must necessarily confront. And this is, namely, a reactive overcompensation for the failures of the Left Opposition in the USSR, in the form of a sectarian anti-Stalinist righteousness and workerist investment in the vanguard leadership role of the party. That Serge is writing before the exacerbation of these sectarian tendencies after 1945 – fuelled as they were, partly, by Trotsky's misdiagnoses of the impending crisis of both Stalinism and capitalism: both emerged in 1945 greatly strengthened, of course – does not weaken Serge's perceptive critique of Trotskyism as an exile-politics built on moral affect and pedagogic instruction (and a renewed Social Democratic clandestinity), rather than on collective and shared work within the working class – despite Trotsky's own hopes. As one recent sympathetic commentator on the post-war legacy has argued: 'Trotskyism signally failed to establish itself as a revolutionary alternative to Stalinism . . . and one of the deepest reasons [for this] was its growing similarity to the movement it came into being to oppose.'[53] That Serge sees that the Marxism of the Left's opposition in the 1930s is producing precisely these effects is a testament, then, to his commitment to thinking through – creatively, and not at all successfully at times, it has to be said – the very limits of proletarian politics at this Thermidorian juncture. Serge, in this sense – as is reflected more openly in the marvellous late novels – is writing for a moment when the revolutionary tradition can be redeemed and extended, without the distorting heroism of individual and righteous fidelity to the monuments of the past, as if in these monuments lies the untainted truth. It is no coincidence, therefore, that a Hegelian matrix underscores and shapes his narrativization of Stalinism and Marxism: revolutionary history is the realm of the unintended outcome, unwilled consequence and – most insistently on his part – the error. One of the results of this is that he takes little sustenance from the reassertion of orthodox Marxism from the early Bolshevik days, which Trotskyism and a renewed Bolshevik-Leninism both draw on in this period for their moral identity. It is also not surprising, then, that this willingness to test the would-be political authority of the pre-Stalinist Bolshevik tradition ultimately sours his relationship with Trotsky. Trotsky continually admonishes him – and admittedly, at times, for good reason – for being too soft on the centrist tendencies of the emerging European revolutionary movement. As Trotsky says, centrism in revolutionary situations costs lives, or, rather, *more* lives. 'Revolution abhors centrism. Revolution exposes and annihilates centrism. In passing, the revolution discredits the friends and attorneys of centrism.'[54] But if Serge tests the tradition that forms him at the moment of its most exacting crisis, he doesn't run away from the demands of the revolutionary tradition as such. This makes his reflections on the unwilled outcome and on 'error' particularly valuable. Because, in his correspondence with Trotsky and his political articles, his critique of Bolshevik orthodoxy has a prescience far beyond its immediate political context.

Across Serge's post-Thermidorian writing, the concept of the error is ever present, as if this was the secret revolutionary code that Serge discovers in his two decades of intense revolutionary struggle. First, of course, there are the specific errors of Stalinism and its agents, but second, there are also the errors the befall those with the best intentions, and consequently the necessary errors that the historical process subjects all historical agents to and that must be acknowledged and assimilated. In this respect, for Serge, the experience of and resistance to the former is bound up with the negotiation with the latter. Consequently, Marxism in the period of its high Thermidorian ruin (1937–38) is faced with two profoundly historical questions: how is it possible that what appears to be the vanguard of the workers' movement (the Bolshevik party) is actively able to reinforce the national and conservative dynamic of bourgeois counter-revolution? And, as such, under what conditions is it possible to theorize the continuing creativity of the working class's self-emancipation, when the catastrophic errors of the Party (its incompetent and lazy sectarianism in Germany in response to the rise of the Nazis; its corrupt and venal offensive against the Left in the Spanish Civil War), have destroyed independent working-class action? Now, of course, these are also two of Trotsky's key questions in the correspondence and the *Revolution Betrayed*.[55] But running through Serge's correspondence and debate with Trotsky – in an echo of Marx's 'third voice' – is a very different sense, historically and politically, of how these two questions might pan out. Essentially, Serge sees these two questions as internally related to the issue of party-form in both its 'authentic' pre-Stalinist incarnation and its Stalinist one. That is, one of the conditions of the intellectual and political degeneration of Bolshevism (between 1923–27) and its explicit counter-revolutionary function from 1928 to 1938, is, he insists, the continuing fear, or unwillingness, of the Party to give space to its members to act in creative concord with workers, which Trotskyism in its exiled domains defensively reproduces. This is why Serge is particularly sensitive, in the correspondence with Trotsky and in *Year One of the Russian Revolution*,[56] to the discipline–creativity tension inherited from Luxemburg's pre-war criticisms of Lenin. As he argues in his letter to Trotsky of 27 July 1936: the aim is to work 'towards a party ideologically firm and disciplined in action, but unsectarian and without a personality cult in its leadership, genuinely demotic and comradely in its manner, in which people will feel free to be wrong.'[57] Now, 'free to be wrong' is something of a motto for Serge here and elsewhere – but a motto that is clearly hostage to fortune. And, naturally, Trotsky is quick to point this out. In their debates on party discipline in relation to Bolshevik conduct during the sailor mutiny at Kronstadt, and the role of the revolutionary Left during the Spanish Civil War, Trotsky is hard on what he sees as Serge's indulgence towards those Leftist demands that appear to be progressive and principled, but in fact in the end concede a valuable ideological and practical space and initiative to the counterrevolutionary enemy (the influence of the Whites on the revolutionary sailors at Kronstadt, and the GPU in Spain).[58] He is harshest about Serge's 'forgetful' indulgence towards the POUM, whose support for the Popular Front government in 1937, and, as a result, their willingness to disarm as a kind of 'security' for this, enabled the GPU to murder their leader, Andres Nin, and the majority of their cadres. Serge's illusions in the POUM as a new 'post-Trotskyist' political force on the revolutionary Left in Spain – and possibly elsewhere – is, if not naïve, lacking in Serge's usually adept realism on the Thermidorian reaction. But the ideological position that Trotsky would like to place Serge in as a consequence of this misjudgement – 'ethical', suspiciously centrist – is not identifiable with the Marxist of this correspondence, let alone the Marxist of *Year One*, or the later work overall. In *Year One*, he is above all the hardest critic of those who confuse revolutionary practice with humanitarian gestures or centrist good faith. Rather, Serge's increasing emphasis on mass revolutionary creativity – for all its vagueness as a notion – actually represents the pinpointing of a *real problem* (what might the new party – mass party – be like?) and, as a consequence, addresses how might such a new party organize or assist the creativity of the workers inside and outside of its disciplinary borders? This places a greater epistemological emphasis in his writings not just on the 'errors' of Stalinism, but on the 'errors' of pre-Stalinist Bolshevism, and their continuation in the orthodox 'errors' of the Trotskyist opposition during the high Thermidorian period, as a means of openly mediating this possibility, and as such providing the *speculative and critical conditions for surviving the current crisis and building beyond it.* Because it is precisely the opening up of Marxism to reflection, both on the errors of recent past practice and the release of the productive errors of a de-bureaucratised collective praxis, that will enable a new party to carry the flag of workers, self-emancipation forward under the repressions of Thermidor. Hence, in an early letter to Trotsky written in 1934, Serge argues candidly that the exiled revolutionary Left is largely divided now into two tendencies: 'those who think that everything must be reconsidered, that errors were committed from the outset of the October Revolution – and those who consider that the Bolshevism of the first years is beyond criticism.'[59] And clearly it is the former tendency, he insists, that must prevail.

In a synthesis of these re-positionings between 1934 and 1937, published in 1938 in the *Partisan Review*, Serge writes what amounts to a provisional document on error theory, 'Marxism in Our Time'.[60] In this article he not only brings his differences in the correspondence with Trotsky and his reflections on Bolshevism to a point of theoretical clarity, but, as if in an unconscious echo of Marx in 1871, and Lenin during the First World War, uses a Hegelian language to draw out the immanent creativity of Marxism's relationship to the proletariat.

> Can science be anything except a process of continual self-revision, an unceasing quest for a closer approach to truth? Can it get along without hypothesis and error – the 'error' of tomorrow which is the 'truth' (that is, the closest approximation of the truth) of yesterday?[61]

For Serge, if Marxism is a theory of worker's self-emancipation it is also by definition a 'science' of error; the *longue durée* of workers' self-emancipation and the errors of praxis go hand in hand. Praxis, then, is that which both *overcomes error and is made in error*. 'Marxism will go through many vicissitudes of fortune, perhaps even eclipse. Its power, conditioned by the course of history, none the less appears to be inexhaustible. For its base is knowledge integrated with the necessity for revolution.'[62] Accordingly, Serge is perhaps the first Marxist writer to explicitly assimilate the error into Marxism as a condition of Marxism's truth-claims. Again and again in the last writings he draws on this understanding in order to heighten the error's critical functions. Thus there are errors that need to be borne productively, and errors that need to be exposed and acknowledged as the necessary truth condition of revolutionary praxis itself – as opposed to the perfidious and Stalinist *confession* of errors (the theme of one of his last great novels, *The Case of Comrade Tulayev*):[63] 'it is better to remain erect and proud in error than to give an example of such abasement [the abasement of the Revolution] even for the best of causes.'[64] '[B]y not recognising old errors, whose gravity history has not ceased to bring out in relief, the risk is run of compromising the whole acquisition of Bolshevism.'[65] And, in the words of Captain Potapov during the Siege of Leningrad, in the novel *Unforgiving Years*: 'An error is sometimes the product of a flawless but excessively linear calculation which fails to allow for the unstable, the unknowable, the irrational, call it energetic or mindless folly.'[66] As such, if Marxism is a historical science in these terms – that is, the product of reflection on its own history and conditions of possibility – the historical consciousness of the revolutionary subject for Serge is expressly one that is *formed* by mistakes and the unwilled, providing the birth of a new rationality. In this sense the revolutionary subject exists in a permanently deposed state (in the decentred sense we have already discussed in relation to the subject in psychoanalysis). But it is this state of deposition that is precisely what characterizes the historically productive condition of the proletariat as a revolutionary subject. In these terms – as we will analyze below – the putative 'third voice' of Serge becomes here cognate with a kind of *'third subject'*: the revolutionary subject who is neither identical with Universal Historical Progress, nor a mere effect of anonymous historical forces (the revolutionary subject-who-is-*not*-a-subject), but a subject who lives and struggles in the interstices, gaps and contingencies of the historical process. In this position, in which praxis *is* error, the revolutionary subject, even in the midst of the worst tragedies and the worst kind of political de-subjectivization, 'feels himself enlarged by his ability to understand.'[67] This is why, echoing the language that Guérin and Jellineck adopted during the same period, Marxism, Serge insists, is 'able to find nourishment in its own defeats'.[68] Indeed: 'Do you wish to understand your defeat? You will be able to only by means of the Marxist analysis of history.'[69]

These brief selections reveal a further deepening of the presence of Hegel in the post-Thermidorian condition of Marxism. Marxism's attempt to theorize the shift from 'first Thermidor' to 'second Thermidor' in the late 1930s is absolutely congruent with Hegel's politicized model of truth-in-error. In the wake of the programmatic ideals of the Enlightenment and the French Revolution, reflection on historical development is inseparable from the reflection and assimilation of defeat and failure. With the move of the error-in-truth into the realm of proletarian politics, questions of culpability, of failure, of truth-in-defeat, now become not just the crisis-language of the workers' movement, but the language of Marxism's renewal.

LEFEBVRE'S IRONY

Another Hegelian Marxist thinker whose theoretical work is also explicitly shaped by the post-Thermidorian condition of Marxism is Henri Lefebvre. As a writer on politics and history, however, Lefebvre was not defined by the left-oppositionalist and Trotskyist milieu of Serge. Lefebvre was a member of the Partie Communiste Française (PCF) from the 1920s to 1956, and as such was the product of a culture that was violently opposed to the language of counter-revolution, before and after the Second World War. For the PCF, anything that smacked of a break with, or questioning of, the USSR as the culmination of a long and steady revolutionary road was anathema. Yet, despite his allegiance in this period to the USSR as the uncontested leader of the 'world progressive bloc', he was sufficiently independent-minded and creative to produce a range of heterodox writing on culture, history and politics that was indebted to Hegel and the growing intellectual crisis of Stalinism – as if he were accumulating clandestinely the necessary critical resources to make an eventual break with the Party, which he did after the Soviet invasion of Hungary.[70] In this sense, his reliance on Hegel in his critique of orthodoxy before and after he leaves the PCF is equally as compelling as Serge's work that precedes it: that is, he doesn't turn his exit from orthodoxy to an exit from revolutionary politics, and to apostasy, but as an opportunity to *re*historicize and *re*theorize. Accordingly, in the post-war period, he addresses the big question Serge was to face: *What political and critical language is appropriate to Marxism in the extended period of the counter-revolutionary defeat of the workers' movement?* Or, in other words, if Marxism is a theory of historical emergence and transformation, how is it able, in the period of extended Thermidor, to assimilate the unwilled outcomes, involuntary actions, and zigzags of history?

The task Lefebvre sets himself, then, is to breach the progressivism and historicism he was trained in. In this task, he turns, on the one hand, to that orthodoxy 'against the grain' that, as I have stressed, will play an increasing part in post-Thermidorian Marxism: 'Engels and Lenin are completely in agreement in rejecting a simplistic representation of *progress*: a linear evolution, uninterrupted, equal for all sectors and advancing on all fronts, and advantageous right down the line';[71] and on the other hand, in order to ground this anti-historicism in a philosophically adequate setting, he turns to a classical language of irony, uncertainty, and maieutic. We are recalled again to the historical ironies and ironizing history of the *Phenomenology* as the predeterminate language of historical truth: namely, dialectic reveals, 'the objective irony of world history, which brings men *something other*, than that which they expected or wanted'.[72] But this is not quite the defence of irony in Hegel that it would seem to be. Although Hegel 'recognized with irony the ironic cunning of history',[73] Lefebvre argues that he tends to leave the textual and critical functions of irony to the Romantics: if History is in and of itself the realm of ironic displacement – in its restless sublation of identity – then there is little room for the irony that *makes a difference*.[74] As such, Lefebvre is primarily concerned, via Hegel, with two interconnecting versions of irony: the Hegelian cunning of history that Marx – certainly after 1871 – transforms into the objective irony of proletarian self-emancipation; and the notion of irony as a form of self-reflexive destabilization of power and the claims to knowledge. This is perhaps closest to the 'existential' content of Serge's error theory (it is important to *honour* one's errors, in defiance of being asked to confess one's errors or, worse, falling into silence), and to the liberatory risk inherent to the pursuit of knowledge that we met at the end of the last chapter in our discussion on the post-Kantian subject: irony is that which sets out to displace, undermine, and unmask power and ideology. And it is this active function of irony, of course, largely secondary in Hegel – as Lefebvre notes – that Marx and the later development of ideology critique releases as an autonomous political and cultural force. 'Without irony we all become embroiled in acts of faith.'[75]

As a result of the subordination of the textual functions of irony in Hegel, Lefebvre turns to Socrates in order to make irony speak not just *in* history, but *as* a historicizing, critical practice. 'The Socratic ironist does not chose between "knowing everything" and "knowing nothing". He knows something, and first and foremost that he knows nothing; therefore he knows what "knowing" is.'[76] This is why irony and maieutic cannot be separated, Lefebvre declares, because the ironist (or the revolutionary subject) is an actor in a drama of not-knowing, uncertainty and false knowledge. The aim of Lefebvre here, then, is certainly close to that of Serge's error theory: *the collective revolutionary subject must speak and act from a position of critical weakness*. (That is, what distinguishes Socratic irony and makes it an excellent candidate for a post-Thermidorian Marxism, for

Lefebvre, is that it does not raise the thinker above the world, into the world of the ego). But this is not because weakness (and here Lefebvre echoes the later Badiou) is a more realistic or circumspect description of the actual conditions and possibilities of revolutionary praxis given this drama of misrecognition, but because the crises and defeats of the working class are internal to praxis and progress itself. Thus, 'today [in the post-Thermidorian world] Marxist irony cannot limit its attacks to the bourgeois world alone. It must also be directed at those who claim to be Marxist, but who ignore Marx's irony.'[77] Indeed, the greatest irony is that maybe Marxism currently is in possession of the wrong map altogether: 'it might well be that history has ironically taken a path other than that of the revolutionary transformation of everyday life.'[78] So, Hegelian error-in-truth and truth-in-defeat are exercised in Lefebvre not simply as the ironic outcomes of the historical process, but as the ironic work of revolutionary praxis itself. That is, as I noted in my comments on the use of historical irony in Marx's writing on the Commune, praxis in its unwilled outcomes is itself the work *of* irony. And this is why the Marxist self-reflexiveness that Serge calls for, rather vaguely, in 'Marxism in Our Time' becomes methodologically more explicit and robust in Lefebvre. Writing outside of the intense conflicts and ideological confines of the high Thermidorian drama of 1930s Europe, Lefebvre is able (in 1962) to be far more direct about how Marxism is now itself an aspect of the ironic drama of history, and, therefore, how it must bring irony to its own ironical reflections on its own defeats. 'To understand the significance of Marxist irony, we must understand the history of Marxism itself ironically, seeing it as a fragment of the prehistoric era of man and a transition towards history.'[79] It is 'only Marxist irony [that] can expose the becoming of Marxism.'[80]

ERRORS AND FAILURES

Lefebvre's critical relationship to Serge's error theory and the error theory inherited from the French Revolution is therefore primarily one of adjacency. Lefebvre doesn't so much adopt a version of error theory in any specific sense – at least in the way Serge intuits it – but assimilates its key post-Thermidorian and Hegelian figures – truth-in-error, truth-in-defeat – into historical materialism: 'the path of truth passes via dissimulation and, even worse, via defeat.'[81] This lack of specific focus on errors is partly to do with the determining place that irony plays in his post-Thermidorian theory, but also the greater emphasis Lefebvre places on 'failure' over and above 'error', as a way of mediating truth-in-defeat. His introduction of the concept of failure into his writing during this period – as a supplement to his concept of irony – presents a slightly different conception of praxis under post-Thermidoran conditions. It is important, therefore, that we spend a little time distinguishing between 'error' and 'failure', given the tendency for them to be confused, or at least made interchangeable, particularly as we will meet 'error' and 'failure' in quite different circumstances in the next chapter.

Whereas errors are identifiable with the missteps, omissions, oversights and mistakes involved in the execution of a particular activity, or pursuit of a set of ideals or programme, failures imply the dissolution, collapse, breakdown of a given programme, project or systematic endeavour. The execution and recognition of 'errors' implies correction and continuity, failure implies cessation, and perhaps, at a later point, the basis for new beginnings. 'Errors', of course, can lead to the 'failure' and cessation of a particular project or systematic endeavour, indeed errors consistently produce failures, but errors in themselves are not specifically identifiable with the collapse of a given project or endeavour overall. This is why the productiveness of the error, as it has been discussed so far in this book, has been discussed primarily in terms of continuity, renewal, sublation (certainly in relation to the philosophy of science); and this principally is what I mean by the productiveness of errors being contiguous with the need to *live with errors*. Living with failure doesn't sound quite the same. Consequently we need to distinguish the productiveness of errors from the productiveness of failure. The former implies the constant repossession and reassimilation of a given process, the latter implies the reassimilation of what has been lost as the basis for a continuation of the old project in new form, or the development of a new project altogether. Indeed, the assimilation of the consequences of failure here implies working on something that has been left behind, or more properly that has left you behind. Thus, although Lefebvre's use of failure is adapted to serve a similar function to Serge's 'error theory' – to reposition proletarian self-emancipation within the *longue durée* of its creative struggles – the reassimilation of a break implied by the understanding that is brought to failure stresses a different relationship to praxis as the mediation of political defeat. As a breakdown of a given project or endeavour, failure signifies that something supplemental has been risked in struggle, and as such *needs to be acknowledged and recovered as praxis.* At one level this is precisely what Serge means by the need to honour errors as the basis for future praxis. But, at another for Lefebvre, assimilating failure in these terms is attached to something that is politically and philosophically more sharply defined, which pushes his post-Thermidorian Marxism into an expressly existential and decisionist direction. (Serge's writing speaks to error, invites the speech of error as the authentic speech of revolutionary action, but not as a theory *of* action.) That is, on the back of his discussion of irony, truth-in-defeat and failure, Lefebvre draws on the Engels of *Anti-Duhring* and Lenin's theory of the zigzag, to attach revolutionary praxis to an explicit subjectivist position. The influence of Sartre here is not surprising. There is no promise of the actual – in Hegel's sense – without recognizing the necessary risk that is immanent to the realization of the possible. 'We must take account of the fact that every possibility contains risks, otherwise it would no longer be a possibility.'[82] As such, there are weak failures and strong failures. The failure that has involved a considerable risk is very different from the failure that results from indecision, indifference or incuriousness.[83] This is the difference, say, between the egalitarianism that is won from a strike, and the egalitarianism of the spontaneous attack against property, as in the Gordon Riots in the London of 1780, that ended up in mass drunkenness and self-immolation. The poor 'rose up incoherently in protest, unprepared and inarticulate, unsure even themselves of what they wanted or hoped to attain'.[84] Consequently it is the quality and ambition of a given plan or endeavour or sequence of actions that separates the productive failure from all the failures that make future actions impossible or unlikely, and, in turn, separates it from all the routine failures that make up everyday activity. 'In the narrative of every endeavour, what counts is the combination of failure and what has been won prior to failure, rather than failure per se.'[85] What is distinguishable as productive failure is that which has prepared the ground well for failure, and is, therefore, able to sustain the renewal of praxis after such a failure has been assessed and assimilated. 'The quality of failure is more significant than the fact of having failed. Therefore, if everything in the everyday ends in failure, since everything comes to end, the meanings differ. Could not successes sometimes be the worst failures.'[86]

This reversal of success into failure is something we will meet again in the next chapter, as a way of figuring the special intimacy between error and failure in art. But, overall, Lefebvre's use of failure here is quite

192 of E NECE

conventional: it is only those failures that have contributed directly to the continuation of struggle that have use value. Yet what of those failures that, in their seeming weakness, opaqueness, incoherence, remain productive despite their invisibility, that are lying in wait for better days? Lefebvre doesn't seem to acknowledge that failures have different kinds of productive afterlife, and, therefore, that the effects of failure are non-synchronous. Nevertheless, Lefebvre's introduction of risk through failure remains a significant move within post-Thermidorian 'error theory'. It introduces into 'error theory' – via Engels and Lenin – a horizonless conception of revolution that will come to dominate post-Thermidorian Marxism down to the stochastic Marx of Daniel Bensaïd and to the 'subjective' turn of the revolutionary anti-historicist political philosophy of today (Žižek, Badiou, Agamben). 'The new birth, this possibility or possibilities, this horizon of horizons is exactly what we are unable to include in our conception of what is possible.'[87] This is why this concept of the horizonless horizon is the key ironic motif of Lefebvre's concept of productive failure. For it is precisely the horizonless horizon as the outcome of what cannot as yet be named in the present, or shaped by the present, that defines the necessary ironic separation of the present from the immediate future, and therefore allows failure and error, as the productive supplemental logic of praxis, to flourish in the interregnum.

BENSAÏD'S STOCHASTICS

Daniel Bensaïd, like Victor Serge, is a product of the founding Trotsykist tradition (the Fourth International). But he is the most unlikely product of this milieu, in so far as his work brings a depth and sophistication to some of the key problems and issues associated with what I have so far been calling Marxist 'error theory'. Indeed, his work represents a kind of a synthesis of many of the themes and issues I have discussed in relation to Serge and Lefebvre; and, therefore, I would place his work as a continuation of this post-Thermidorian tradition. This places his writing theoretically at a kind of heterodox distance from orthodox Trotskyism, given his creative reliance on notions of anti-historicism, anti-positivism, stochasticism, the asymptotic, multi-temporality, the aleatory and risk. Moreover, his writing is conducted within a theoretical engagement with Marx and the Marxist tradition that draws on a wide variety of theoretical and philosophical sources – as indeed, admittedly, befits all vital political theory and philosophy after 1968. Thus his most ambitious work, and the work I will focus on here, *Marx For Our Times: Adventures and Misadventures of a Critique* (1995),[88] is not simply a defence of a shiny and relevant Marx for inauspicious times (the Marx of 'falling rates' of profit and the impact of globalization, that even the *Financial Times* can applaud), but a reckoning with history and politics in Marx and Marxism that are scarred as much by their hubristic revolutionary interlocutors as by their legions of Leftist and bourgeois *mystificateurs*. It is a work on Marx and Marxism, therefore, that is dug out of that long and dark road of counter-revolutionary retreat. In this light, *Marx For Our Times* is not to be seen as a redoubtable defence of Marx against neo-liberal chisellers and postmodern cynics who have forgotten what Marx actually said, but, rather, as an extended set of reflections on why what is rarely said about Marx *is* rarely said: that the self-emancipation of the proletariat is a long, arduous, broken, eclipsed, self-pathologizing struggle. This is why *Marx For Our Times* is important for our narrative. Not only is it one of the best books written on Marxism for some time; it is also, in the spirit of Serge and Lefebvre and 'error theory', a book on Marx that lets Hegel breathe again through the 'scientistic' portals of the critique of political economy, allowing the fractured and self-ironizing formation of the revolutionary subject to take centre stage. But, in a way, if Bensaïd is writing a book from within the confines of the long post-Thermidorian deposition of the proletariat, it is not a book that actually looks at its own political counter-tradition at close quarters. The title gives this away: a Marx for *our* times. To be honest, there is no Marx *for* our times, as if we have all been missing the real Marx, veiled and scaled over by decades of Stalinist and post-Marxist contusions. There is only the Marx who in the 1840s, 50s, 60s and 70s, experienced, analyzed and raged against the post-1794 counter-revolution, a counter-revolution that in its deep forms of attachment to hierarchy is still with us; and, therefore, the 'relevance' of Marx today remains so given that it is based precisely on the continuing realities of this counter-revolution. What we bring to Marx in our own period has to acknowledge this. This is not being obtuse. But a way of saying that it is the continuity of counter-revolution, under its various and changing capitalist forms, that makes Marx relevant, now, yesterday and tomorrow. So, after 140 years, the continuing significance of Marx also lies in the continuity of his prescient revolutionary 'third voice' after 1871: the truth-in-defeat of the *longue durée* of proletarian self-emancipation – a Marxism worthy of the future has to assimilate this. The attraction of Bensaïd's Marxism, then, is it sits strikingly within this historical purview – a book produced from defeat but in defiance of defeat.

But Bensaïd doesn't quite say why, philosophically, it sits there, or needs to sit there. And this has something to do with the fact that his defence of Marxism as a 'profane'[89] Hegelian science of social struggle doesn't, at least in *Marx For Our Times*, stretch to any wider reflections on the post-Thermidorian political tradition itself. This is not to devalue Bensaïd's achievement, but to merely point out that there is a disconnection between his use of notions such as the stochastic and asymptotic and the 'error-theory' that lies politically behind his thinking within the revolutionary tradition. So, we need to clarify what kind of theoretical place Bensaïd's writing occupies within the legacy of post-Thermidorian Marxism.

NECESSITY, CONTINGENCY AND ERROR

Marx For Our Times is organized around a set of negations in order to define what Marx and Marxism are not: Marx's account of history promises no salvation; 'ends' never finish ending; the historical present is not a link in a mechanical sequence of cause and effect; the present and the future are not the goal of the past; Marx's theory of capitalism is not a positive science; Marx does not reduce science, as in the natural sciences, to a physical model of explanation; Marxism is not a philosophical determinism; Marx is not an apologist for capitalist 'progress'; different forms of production do not proceed at the same rate of development; there is no single and socially neutral development of the productive forces that might enable the transition from capitalism to socialism; explanatory necessity does obviate the decisive role of chance in history; the prematurity of revolution is structural and essential; future revolutions cannot be reduced to pre-established schemas based on past revolutions; the negation of the negation tells us what needs to disappear, but not what must occur. The accumulated effect of this is to shift the focus of theoretical attention very decisively to a version of Marx that is at war, essentially, with two things: Universal History (historicism) and linear Progress. This quite rightly pulls the rug from under the Popperian and Carnapian critique of Marx and Hegel, and the whole legacy of historicist defenders of Marx, which see Marx as an advocate of 'historical necessity'. The truth is the exact opposite; and it is there in various guises and voices, in the *Grundrisse*, *The German Ideology* and *Capital*. But Bensaïd's intention is not so much to win non-Marxist sceptics, or old diamat Stalinist plodders, over to a view of Marx as a non-deterministic and 'anti-historicist' thinker. There are many Marxists who have done this, and continue to do this kind of work, with greater or lesser success. Rather, and more importantly, what Bensaïd wants to do is place Marx and Marxism within the liberatory framework of Hegel's critique of positive science as that which *qualitatively defines* Marxism as a critical methodology and a politics. 'The idea of a "philosophical science" that does not yield before the sacred positive sciences: that is Hegel's inuadible thunderclap, echoed by Marx.'[90] Hence the critique of positivity in Marx involves a different way of doing science, in which the pursuit of knowledge also involves a continuous labour on the forms in which this knowledge is produced, disseminated and naturalized. In other words, without Hegel's critical historicization of the claims of natural science, there 'would be no possible third way between vigorously demarcated camps of truth and error, good science and bad ideology.'[91] Facts, in other words, are always contested values. So, under a capitalist system whose inner function is to reproduce its own naturalization and evolutionary identity as a system, there is no way of founding a science that would dispel ideology, false consciousness, fetishization and reification, simply through the sovereign acts of reason itself, and their enlightened institutionalization. This is because false consciousness, fetishization and reification are not things produced by consciousness at all, but are the subjective and unconscious outcome of the reproduction of the commodity form. Science in Marx, therefore, inaugurates a different notion of emancipation under these conditions: the effects of violence, the illusions and pathologies of the commodity system, remain immanent to continuous labour of the critique of the system as a whole, and therefore require a language of science that is coextensive with errancy, and the unwilled and involuntary. Hegel's insistence, then, that history *steps worst foot forward* is structurally determinate for Marx's critique of scientific positivism. Yet contrary to what might be expected at this point Bensaïd does not introduce a discussion of the intimacy between Marx's methodology and historical irony (or error in any specific sense). In fact, the discussion of irony is surprisingly absent from Bensaïd's account overall. But, nevertheless, in making the connection between Marx and Hegel in these terms he offers something similar, that aligns his anti-historicist and anti-positivist thinking productively with the 'error theory' and Marx's irony that I have sketched out: he makes Marx speak, more clearly and more directly, in the language of the broken and shattered rhythms of detemporalization and disequilibrium. At one level, this involves a return to the Hegelian discussion of the actual, contingency and necessity, but, at another level, he recognizes that this language is immanent to Marx's thinking itself as it is confronted with the arhythms of history and capital, and as such, represents a decisive move beyond Hegel.

Bensaïd begins his argument by establishing, as we have already discussed in Chapter 2, that Hegelian teleology is fundamentally opposed to evolutionary necessity, and quotes, to this effect, from the *Scientific Logic*: 'The antinomy between *fatalism*, along with *determinism* and *freedom*, is likewise concerned with the opposition of mechanism and teleology; for the free is the Notion.'[92] This quotation is important because Bensaïd rightly wants to draw attention to the crucial distinction Hegel makes between absolute necessity and hypothetical necessity, which Hegel borrows from Leibniz. In Leibniz, what is absolutely necessary is that which cannot be otherwise, in other words that which is predetermined. That which is hypothetically necessary is that which involves a choice, in other words that which is open to different outcomes. But intermediate between these two positions, for Leibniz, is the work of divine action, which combines God's law with moral necessity, absolute necessity with hypothetical necessity. That is, an outcome may well be predisposed to occur, but it is certainly not *assured* of occurring given the multiply determinate actions of agents. 'We are thus not necessitated, but only "predisposed". This crucial difference sanctions "conditional events" between "certain futures" and "necessary futures."'[93] This freedom that predisposes without necessity is the freedom that Hegel develops through his distinction between the formal and the actual (or formal necessity and actual necessity): the potentiality of the actual exceeds its immediate determinateness – as we noted in Chapter 2. In these terms, the contingent actually disappears as a discrete category as a result of this multideterminatedness immanent to the actual. For if the actual is open to multidetermination then it of course disappears *into* necessity, making that which is strongly predisposed no longer oppositional to the contingent. The actual and the possible are thereby united in their contingency. This is Hegel's great philosophical advance.

For Hegel, there is a necessity of contingency, the two mutually determining each other while constantly vanishing into each other. The contingency of a thing consists in its isolation, hence its submission to an external constraint . . . whereas free necessity is the perfect connection of autonomous determination. Necessity is no longer the relational concept of an external, strict determinism but the index of the sufficiency of a *causa sui*. The task of science (and philosophy specifically) then consists in attaining knowledge of the reality concealed beneath the appearance of contingency.[94]

Hence the importance of the conceptual release of the error in Hegel's *Phenomenology*. In disconnecting the error from mere contingency, from the domain of ideological non-determination, its truths are rendered comprehensible and necessary. To these ends Bensaïd refers to the Hegelian scholar Eugene Fleischmann's *La Philosophie de Politique de Hegel*, one of the few works on Hegel that touches explicitly on this connection between error, contingency and necessity. Error and contingency are necessary from the standpoint of reason, Fleischmann asserts, because without contingency there would be no such thing as critical reason. Reason would simply be the necessary outcome of a predisposition: a version of the pure percipience scenario I outlined at the beginning of the Introduction. Unfortunately, though, as Fleischmann stresses, despite Hegel's 'categorial position on the necessity of contingency, [he] is still treated as a panlogicist and a purely deductive philosopher'[95] (by philosophers, as we have seen, who should know better).

For Bensaïd, what distinguishes Marx's critique of positivism is that it inherits the Hegelian/Leibnizian critique of absolute necessity, by raising up contingency to the level of hypothetical necessity. That is, if the actual in its contingency is both appearance and possibility, conscious possession of the actual-as-possibility changes necessity into freedom. And this is why Marx is not just the philosopher of this rationality of the actual and the contingent, but its scientific theorist and revolutionary critic. Thus if we have brought Hegel and Marx closer together in the main body of this book, in order to separate them and then reconnect them in this chapter, we need to separate them once more. Marx's critique of positivity is certainly inconceivable without Hegel's critique of mechanical causality and absolute necessity, and as such he draws on Hegel's immanent methodology. But in breaking with a linear model of uniform temporality, Marx's analysis of the rhythms and arhythms and lulls and catastrophes of capitalism, becomes, in its reflection on history, something that Hegel's thinking is not: an analysis and critique of capitalism as an empirically bounded system of production with its own laws and tendencies. Thus when Marx brings an analysis of contingency into the realm of necessity in his critique of capitalism, he brings with it a distinctive political imperative: the disequilibriums of the system are not random and therefore continually sublatable as mere contingencies, but determinate evidence of the internal contradictions of the system and its historical limitations. Therefore, for Marx, capitalism needs to be studied empirically as a historical system in which its tendencies and laws of motion are shaped by the system's contradictions, and, as such, whose future will be defined ultimately by their negation and transcendence. This is a science of the concrete – of the *capitalist* particular – unavailable to Hegel. For Bensaïd, this makes Marx's methodology in *Capital*, with its different temporal circuits of production, distribution and consumption, and multi-dimensions of the commodity form, clearly compatible with the stochastic tendencies of twentieth-century science, in which the parameters of a given system are unpredictable without being indeterminate. But if it is possible to identify stochastic insights in *Capital*, nevertheless, Marx is not a disequilibrium theorist. His sense of capitalism as an unstable system is countermanded by a sense of it also being a homeostatic whole, in which when crises and ruptures are resolved or displaced, the system is able to return to a stable state; indeed, it is precisely the function of these crises to secure the long-term dynamic continuity of the system. Thus if Marx was never an advocate, pure and simple, of 'historical necessity', he is not on the basis of this evidence now suddenly the master of stochastic thought. On the contrary, the singularity of Marx as a dialectical thinker is that he is neither a historicist nor an anti-historicist. As Bensaïd himself acknowledges, Marx 'sought to combine the dynamic stability of cyclical reproduction with the structured instability of the system.'[96]

With this interface, therefore, between a stochastic notion of contingency as structurally constitutive, and the notion of the system as an unfolding structured instability, Bensaïd presents a Marx whose sense of progress and historical development is mediated by the force and clash of discordant temporalities (what we called, in Chapter 2, a theory of deflected progress). And consequently, to Bensaïd's merit, this represents a far better way of showing the constitutive, but displaced, function of Hegel in historical materialism. Marx doesn't simply invert Hegel – according to his own famous formulation – but transforms Hegel's historicizing, immanent method into an empirico-science as a way of explaining, geneao-theoretically, why the disordered-order of capitalism takes the forms that it does. Thus, in response to the structured instability of capitalism, Marxism, for Bensaïd, requires a *politics* of the stochastic, for if contingency passes into necessity, then the actual is the unstable site by which necessity *comes into being*. 'For Marx . . . the antinomy of necessity and freedom is resolved in the aleatory process of struggle.'[97] Chance is not subordinate to necessity, but its determinate agent. 'Determinate, historical development remains full of junctions and bifurcations, forks and points.'[98] In fact this bridging of necessity and the aleatory, via Hegel, is also something that Lefebvre develops in his *Introduction to Modernity*. As with Bensaïd, the intractable struggle of revolutionary politics lies in uniting the maturity of historical circumstances with the aleatory demands of action. 'The aleatory is not the event which arrives out of the blue, unconnected with the past, absurd and irrational. By the *aleatory* we mean the dialectical unity between necessity and chance, where chance expresses a necessity and necessity expresses itself via a network of chances.'[99] I would argue, therefore, that in Lefebvre and Bensaïd, the aleatory functions expressly as a post-Thermidoran political category. Under post-Thermidorian conditions the aleatory is brought into the heart of revolutionary politics as the political form of the capitalist system's extended and self-stabilizing disequilibrium. And this is why, finally, we might also point to the links between Bensaïd's stochastic Marx and Marx's political 'third voice'. Given that both are premised on the violently discordant temporalities of a post-Thermidorian epoch, they both demand a politics that requires both the patience of the *longue durée* and a realist vigilance of the conjuncture.

ERROR, THE COMEDIC AND THE 'THIRD SUBJECT'

As is evident from the above, despite their differences in intellectual formation, Serge, Lefebvre and Bensaïd are all remarkably close on the question of a post-Thermidorian 'third voice', in Marx, and what I have called, in addition, a proletarian 'third subject': the subject who is neither an 'effect' of exoteric forces, nor the embodiment of history's reason itself, in the classical sense. This subject, therefore, is crucial to what we have discussed so far about 'error theory' in post-Thermidorian Marxism, for it is the disconnection between the proletariat and its 'mission' that continues to shape its future revolutionary identity. As the defeats of the working class have shown from 1794 to 1989, the proletariat is not revolutionary by ontological form or by absolute structure, but is revolutionary in certain and propitious circumstances; and these circumstances, in turn, when successful and propitious, are highly unstable. Lefebvre sees this kind of thinking as a way of 'relativizing' Marx. On the contrary, though, it is a way of bringing historical experience to the vicissitudes of Marx's own experience as a revolutionary (certainly after 1871), and, as a consequence, honouring what Marx honoured at the end of his life: the indefatigable power of Hegel to think progress as misstep, mistake, unwilled outcome. Thus the 'third subject' is a particular kind of subject-who-is-not-a-subject. The proletariat does not – unlike the individual subject of philosophical discourse – imagine itself as acting autonomously in its own interests, and thereby, in the process, denying its social determination. Indeed, the proletariat, outside of certain intense moments or periods of social and political crisis, is not able to imagine itself collectively as an autonomous subjectivity at all, and as such gives no consistent thought to any conflict between its reality as a class and its own misrecognition of this reality. It is a subject-who-is-not-a-subject, therefore, on very specific grounds: that is, in its day-to-day existence it is a subject whose subjectivity is in abeyance; and, as a consequence, is united as a class via its negative identity as a subject, its subjectless social determination as an atomized congregation of producers, individuals and consumers. Thus we might ideologically invert the notion of the subject-who-is-not-a-subject here: the self-understanding as a class experience of the subject-who-is-not-a-subject (the autonomously self-directed subject) is, in this instance, mediated by the proletariat's inversion of the autonomous subject into the socially determined subject of its atomized class identity. This implies a closed loop of consciousness, and of course, in these terms, this kind of approach (post-Lukács) has constituted much apocalyptic thinking on the disappearance of the proletariat under the reified conditions of its own reproduction. But this reproduction of subjects-who-are-not-subjects (i.e. autonomous subjects), through the reified social category of atomized subjects-who-are-not-subjects, is not stable, and has never been stable. This is because the proletariat, despite its subjectlessness, is able to threaten, confront and break down, in its daily labouring existence as a class, the ostensibly smooth reproduction of its own subjectless condition. Immanent to the proletariat as a subject-who-is-not-a-subject is also its identity as a subjectless subject who *is* a subject: the moment when, in struggle, class consciousness, collective identity and politics moves outwards to connect with the historical process. So, the notion of a 'third subject', one that is neither external to history nor internal to its necessities, rests on this sense of class subjectivity, as in dormant formation and struggle. Thus, as I have stressed in my reflections on the post-Thermidorian condition of revolutionary politics generally, this 'third subject' is by definition one of reflection on error and failure. But if we have analyzed the political trajectory of this 'third voice' and 'third subject', we have yet to subject it to a broader philosophical assessment. This means drawing on what we have touched on already in passing: the links between the recognition and possession of error, the pursuit of knowledge, emancipation and the comedic. In other words, what form of historical consciousness might be of the creative struggles of the proletarian 'third subject' and universal emancipation?

A good place to begin this discussion, then, is by asking: are truth-in-failure and truth-in-error essentially figures of the comedic? For, as we have noted already, reflections on error, the contingent and the unwilled in Hegel turn on a comedic imperative to history: history proceeds by way of a kind of falling, indeed of prat-falling. This is why Lacan sees the *Phenomenology* as a highly comedic text, for what is funnier than people acting and speaking in ways that they have little control over? Indeed, when Lacan says: 'the subject cannot be simply be identified with the speaker or the personal pronoun in a sentence',[100] we hear the Hegelian echo of outrageous humour: the subject, quite literally, at the moment of enunciation, cannot 'hold things together'. Hegel's concern with the gap between intention and outcome, action and event, therefore, posits an alinearity and waywardness that has the humour of maladroitness, of getting things wrong and wrong again. Gillian Rose, in an attempt to bring this Hegelian maladroitness back into the realm of dialectic, has called this 'the comedy of absolute spirit'.[101] And, as such, what draws out the comedy in the *Phenomenology*, is the recognition that this Spirit is essentially haunted by its own misconstruals and misrecognitions.

> *spirit* in the *Phenomenology* means the drama of misrecognition, which ensues at every stage and transition of the work – a ceaseless comedy, according to which our aims and outcomes constantly mismatch each other, and provoke yet another revised, aim, action and discordant outcome.[102]

Struggle, the pursuit of reason, is a comedic activity, in so far as the positing of truth and the recuperation of error, in order to posit truth and recuperate error again, is an endlessly humorous business; positing and repositing never seem to stop, a bit like bickering spouses. In the light of these insights, then, we might say that the subject in struggle takes on two comedic Hegelian identities: on the one hand, the subject is *itself* the comedic outcome of a process of comedic misrecognition – that is, the subject is caught up in an endless process of misidentification with its other, leading to all kinds of confusions – and on the other hand, the subject in its historical subjectlessness is the comedic aftermath of history's involuntary and unwilled outcomes – hence the notion that the self-revisions of the creative *longue durée* of the self-emancipation of the proletariat is, essentially, a self-ironizing (comedic) process. But how can the comedic in these terms, as creative *Bildung*, carry the full, pathologized weight of a post-Thermidorian politics? Moreover, how can the comedic, as a reconciliation with the pathological dimensions of history, provide the right conditions of enunciation for a revolutionary politics that discharges itself from the burdens of inflexible righteousness and betrayal? Is such a step one step too far for the Aristophanic subject of struggle that I discussed earlier: the figure who returns to the beginning and defeat without being dragged down by the motley of tragedy? In these terms, truth-in-error as a comedic figure is rightly a problem: it is unable to face the absolute horrors and losses of this counter-revolutionary period in a state of terse *equanimity*. Consequently, the comedic here falls into that trap that Alenka Zupancic has expertly critiqued, in which ironic laughter functions to humanize the demons of history;[103] everything is rendered pliant for redemption, and nothing as a result gets dumped into the hells of damnation. It sustains 'the very oppression of the given order or situation, because it makes it bearable and induces the illusion of an effective interior freedom.'[104] As Paul Ricouer has stressed, from this perspective, the justice of forgetting – of irony's necessary distance – is one step away from the injustice of forgiveness;[105] and comedy, in its reconciliatory voice, loves to forgive and purge the abstract and dogmatic.

Now, this ambivalent status of the comedic, is I believe, what makes truth-in-error the productive category it is. For, if on one level comedy allows and urges reconciliation and redemption, on the other, in its creative self-reflection, it provides an unfolding space for the critique of finitude. And it is the critique of finitude that importantly links our two figures of truth-in-error and truth-in-failure. Thus comedy may encourage us to empathise with our human frailty and particularity in the face of the

impostures of the universal (abstract ideology), but it also, in its mockery
or displacement of power and authority, allows the life of the particular to
grasp or move *towards* the universal, and the infinite. That is, the comedic is
a kind of reflective training in sustaining a goal, an ideal, through mishap,
miscalculation, misrepresentation and misunderstanding. The upshot of
this is that, contrary to appearances, Hegel was the greatest advocate of
comedy (his *Aesthetics* ends with a discussion of the comedic), and this is
why his reflections on comedy bear close comparison to his reflections
on dialectic and history, because what distinguishes comedy from tragedy,
for Hegel, is that it brings into sensuous form the very coming to being
of the contingent into necessity. In his *Aesthetics* he divides comedy into
three fundamental categories, or forms of action:[106] (1) those forms in
which characters and their aims are demonstrably pathetic or slight and
therefore cannot possibly succeed according to the intentions of their
authors; (2) those forms in which the aims and ideals of the hero are
palpably correct and virtuous, but are betrayed by the limited means at the
hero's disposal, so the hero is overwhelmingly defeated by his good intentions; and (3) those forms – the comedies of coincidence – that emphasize
chance and the contingent as the means by which a satisfying resolution to
the action is brought about. Of all the comedic forms that might possibly
sustain Hegel's interest in comedy and the infinite, the latter would hardly
seem to be the most rewarding, given the resolution of such comedies in
Hegel's time, and our own, in a kind of witless or fanciful denouement.
Yet for Hegel such comedies, in principle, are the most profound. For in
these works, the characters may imagine themselves to be the (striking
or effervescent) agents of their own actions – indeed, the pleasure they
take in themselves is the pleasure they provide for the audience – but
during the course of the action, their words and actions are revealed to
have no determinate say in the final outcome. Or rather their subjectivity
is always being displaced by chance and external determinations outside
of their immediate control. Now, of course, this is where tragedy and
comedy connect: the discrepancy between action and outcome, desire and
satisfaction, that leads to failure or irresolution. But in the comedy of
coincidence, the structuring of this discrepancy is based, not on the individual failings or misjudgements of the hero, but on the insubstantiality of
subjectivity as such.[107] The subject fails not because he himself possesses
inadequate means to realize his goals, or suffers from fatal psychologistic
flaws (hubris, naivety, overweening righteousness), but because his efforts

and desires are shown to be part of a historical process that ultimately is discontinuous with his actions; and we see this in the 'coincidences' that occur in the drama despite the perceived autonomous actions of the protagonists. Comedy, in this form, in spite of its seeming lightness and jollity, is the exemplary home of the 'depossessive' subject and an emancipatory desubjectivication. Reflection on the unintended consequences of events is deflected away from the perceived weaknesses or strengths of the hero, and his inability to control his destiny, to focus on the interrelational parts the hero and other protagonists play in a process that exists external to their complete understanding and that will continue without them. From this perspective, the reason on view in this kind of comedy is not the expression of a sovereign subject that is always being thwarted, but a kind of distributive intelligence that is the (culpable) possession of the many, and whose vitality and strength is grounded in misrecognitions, errors and misconstruals. Hence the laughter that arises from things going awry, being out of sync, contradictory, identifies the gap between intention and action, desire and satisfaction, not with the limitations and foolish excesses of humans – with the touching finitude of human maladroitness – but with the 'comedy of return': the endless capacity of humans to work through misrecognitions, errors and misconstruals, as a condition of the recovery and renewal of truth. If the dominant function of comedy is to reassure us in our finitude, its other function, the function that Hegel is so compelled by in the comedy of coincidence, is to re-establish the social and historical continuity of this truth, after its palpable collapse or fading in the actions of one individual or group of individuals. This is also Zupancic's primary concern in her strong Hegelian reading of comedy. As she says: 'the flaws, extravangences, excesses, and so-called human weaknesses of comic characters are precisely what accounts for their *not* being "only human". More precisely, they show us that what is "human" exists only in this kind of excess over itself.'[108] Consequently the comedic as a structure of action and reception provides a specific kind of sequencing or temporality, which is quite separate from the individual life of the joke and the somatic effects of the comedy generally; and it is this, following Hegel, that Zupancic draws our attention to.

Essentially, the comedic works through the recognition, advance, and assimilation of discontinuity, in so far as not only do the protagonists of comedies not get what they asked or hoped for, but they get something that they didn't ask or hope for. The expectations of the protagonists are defeated at the point at which their desired objects are within tangible reach of their grasp. Hence in comedy the discrepancy between intention and action, desire and satisfaction, incarnates – as a matter of the form's very legibility – the impossibility of a smooth teleology or an unimpeded sense of progress. The protagonists and audience are always having to find their satisfactions in new and unexpected places. But it is this very need to assimilate new satisfactions and draw up new challenges that characterizes the dynamic form of comedy, and, as such, why Hegel ascribes an advanced role to its forms as a manifestation of human 'maturity'. Which is not to say that Hegel does not have a critique of comedy. For Hegel, comedy is also the home of the capricious, particularly in the comedy of coincidence: the inflation of chance events into mere decorous effects. But comedy is also, by far, the space of the mutual implication of the subject and historical forces, chance and necessity, continuity and discontinuity, possession (culpability) and depossession (process), misstep and progress. It 'constructs with discontinuity, a continuity, whose very stuff is a discontinuity'.[109] And, as such, this focus on comedy as comedic sequence, as opposed to comedy as a compendium of comedic effects, enables us to avoid the pitfalls of comedy as reconciliation and redemption. In its logic of continuity-discontinuity-continuity, it provides what Zupancic calls the comedy of the undead, and what I have been describing as truth-in-error: that is, the indestructible 'persistence of something that keeps returning to its place no matter what'.[110] This, then, is the (comedic-sequential) function of the reflection on and assimilation of error in revolutionary political praxis: it captures the indefatigable return of praxis as the discontinuous-continuous, continuous-discontinuous renewal of truth as proletarian self-emancipation. But this is not just the renewal of desire as 'resistance', as if tragedy castrates desire, and comedy releases it from its burdens of social obligation, enabling us then to freely 'get on with things' unburdened by the past. In a way, this model of the 'comedy of return' as resistance is another version of comedy as assimilation. Look, see how desire persists against all odds! Rather, the renewal of praxis is what is produced *by* the pathologies, reversals and contradictions of history. What is productive is not the immutability of desire, but the miscalculations, misrecognitions and errors of praxis itself.

FIVE

ERROR, REASON AND ART

In the previous chapters the analysis of the error has, for all its theoretical opacities and detours, been pretty much tied to a straightforward proposition: for truth-in-error to signify beyond the most elementary relativism it has to be embedded in a theory of realism. Without the notion of realism as a theory of truth that is independent of mere supposition, the role of the error simply collapses into the pragmatic realm of 'what works' and 'what doesn't work' under a preferred description or conceptual scheme. This is why reflection on 'errors' in Marxist politics has such prejudicial ramifications in bourgeois political theory, because they are seen to be wholly conditioned by what the theory sees as the irredeemable subjectivism of Marxism as a political philosophy; and this is why specifically there is no category of counter-revolution for bourgeois political theory, because the moral authority and historical valency of such a category dissolves once the errors of Marxist politics are treated principally as the pathologized failure of an abstract ideal. The counter-revolution does not exist because the revolution itself did 'not' properly exist in the first place – that is, had no lasting implications beyond its first idealistic triumphs and effusions.[1] Thus bourgeois political theory sees (as does most current post-Marxist leftism) the commitment to an abstract ideal as invalidating the supplemental character of the error-as-productive. For to be haunted or driven by 'errors' as the outcome of unwarrantable ideals is to produce a kind of endless delirium that delimits the political. And, therefore, if errors are to have any generalizable value at all, they should be guided by the localized and perspectival conditions of judgement – the daily toing and froing of our finite practical reason – and not the metaphysical work of universal abstraction. Burke's critique of abstract reason, then, continues to stalk the contemporary political imagination.

But the errors that arise from theoretical incompleteness – a lack of predictive capacity, or a diminishment of explanatory power – do not necessarily presuppose evidence of *false* belief. Positivism and pragmatism, consequently, share a political history here in their general resistance to abstract reason: they *presumptively* assume falseness instead of provisionality. Hence my claim in this book to connect dialectics to error theory is precisely the opposite of this presumption: the renewal of truth is a condition of the attachment of the supplemental work of errors *to* the work of abstract reason (rather than, in the comforting spirit of our maladroit finitude, to the facticity of the actual). And this is why, despite the heuristic function of the error, and the fact that much of what we claim as knowledge is in error – and without us being able to grasp why it is in error, in Hegel's sense – the culpable or inadvertent character of mistakes have real existential consequences, in so far as the failure to meet a given set of programmatic, systematic, totalizing or ideal truth-conditions both obviously *limits* the capacity for cognition and action, and also produces the need to question and challenge these limits. Thus, as a condition of understanding what progress and historical development might be – or fails to be – truth is necessarily attached to examining and understanding how these limits (and the limits of self-consciousness) are to be defined, negated and superseded.

But if this notion of the productiveness of errors has real advantages in the areas of the formation of the Western philosophical subject, the philosophy of science, psychoanalysis and revolutionary political praxis, it seems to stall when we address the question of art. For there is no dialectic of truth and error in art that might attach the supplemental work of the error to a programme, system or ideal, that might install a sense of unrealized or deflected progress. From Kant and Schlegel to Adorno, what is necessarily valued in art – as art – as a universal realm of freedom and truth is, crucially, its indeterminate identity and function. Art in the modern period is not evidence of an accumulation and transmission of a shared set of intellectual and cultural skills that practitioners inherit and collectively build on, but a vast shifting, self-negating, transmuting constellation of aesthetic particularities that are defined one against the other as a condition of what gives them value: the singularity of the artwork as the singular expression of the artist or group of artists. To call on the productiveness of errors in art, therefore, as further evidence of a non-positivistic heuristic that has been hard won in the face of inflexible methodologies, bureaucratic practices and unpropitious intellectual circumstances is to presuppose a certain philosophical redundancy. That is, errors have nothing to prove 'scientifically' in art at all, certainly in the modern period; and therefore, in relation to the way I have so far analyzed and modelled errors – as the productive supplement of truth, which refuses to be speedily expelled from reason – they just don't fit this prevailing model of knowledge. Indeed, the particularities of art presuppose the very reversal of this model of the expansion of reason through error: rather than the error being assessed and assimilated into art as a measure of the progress of knowledge (of the refining of a methodology), or offering a correction to the limits of an ideal scientific reason, the productiveness of the error in art operates *in defiance* of the programmatic, systematic or unitary ideal (in other words, to science itself). Whatever particular errors it encourages, assimilates, rationalizes and invests in are designed to distance the values of art from the very notion of progress and system-thinking. Errors of execution and form, in art, therefore, are not supplemental to artistic practice but *definitional*: they define art, in and of itself, as an indeterminate and stochastic enterprise, *all the way down*. As Adorno says: 'Radical modern art is hated [or we might say now loved, precisely] . . . because it reminds us of missed chances but also because by its sheer existence it reveals the dubiousness of the heteronomous structural ideal.'[2] This is why if the productiveness of the error would seem to have any common characteristics with the disciplines and practices I have already discussed, it is with psychoanalysis. For what links art and psychoanalysis, in these terms, is the fact that they both work through the error first and foremost as a condition of its resistance to the stabilization and systematic codification of method as a guide to practice. Just as truth in the psychoanalytic session cannot be won through the imposition of a ready-made schema, art is driven by the neurotic condition of its own resistance to precedent and academic template (which is not say that the values of art are driven by 'newness' in and of itself, but, as in psychoanalysis, by the possible creativity of the singular encounter). Hence this does not mean that artistic practice is at base antipathetic to strict systematic methods, or indeed system building – as the history of modern art quite obviously shows, as I discuss below – but that such system building is itself the outcome of a singular demand: each systematizer is also a would-be systematizer of a *new type*.

In this chapter I want to examine both how this model of the error singles out art as a critique of heteronomy and unitary system-thinking and, as such, an exception to the critique of positivism in science, but also how, in reshaping the critique of positivism, art itself falls short of this critique of positivism. Thus, if art – in particular modern art – is at the heart of the critique of pure reason, scientific reason, philosophical abstraction, where does the heuristic role of the error actually sit within this? And, perhaps more pertinently, what positive metafunction, if any, might its role in the critique of heteronomy in art serve? In these terms there is also an additional debate about the error in relation to art which the recent history of art's engagement with art, as an indeterminate and aleatory realm of creativity, fails to address: the recurrent sense that art *is itself constitutively an error*, or evidence of a long decline into a dispiriting errancy. There have been many periods, of course, where this notion of errancy as cultural crisis has prevailed – indeed it is perhaps possible to locate such thinking in every historical period stretching back to the Greeks themselves. But today it has reached another crisis point, as the notion of art as a set of ideal judgements and experiences derived from their socially purposive realization in the world is further and further removed from its actualization.

Consequently, in this chapter I want to look at three interrelated areas: the connections and differences between error and the languages of chance, indeterminacy and the aleatory (for error and chance, indeterminacy and the aleatory are not the same thing in art) as a discussion more generally about modern art as a form of non-positivistic reason; the methodological links between psychoanalysis and art and the emergence of a new reason in art; and the ontological definition of art as a possible errant activity in and of itself.

THE ERROR AND THE RISE OF SYSTEMATIC ANTISYSTEMATICITY

In the 1850s, 1860s and 1870s something radical happens in the production and reception of art in Europe, particularly in France. What had hitherto been the two great pillars of aesthetic value and judgement, neoclassicism and naturalism, began to destabilize and dissolve quite rapidly. The reasons for this are manifold – we will touch on some of them below – and have been endlessly debated. Yet what is agreed is that at some point during these decades art undergoes a profound shift in orientation and ideals that finally propels artists into the modern world of capital and industry. The immediate outcome in the visual arts – specifically painting – is a protracted divorce of artistic technique and subject matter from the prevailing academic models of competence best represented by neoclassicism and naturalism. Into this new world of technique enters a whole array of strategies, practices and modes of perception, that now identifies achievement and authenticity in art with the adulteration or breakdown of professional skills and academic hierarchies. As a consequence there is an increasing sensitivity to, and the pursuit of, an image that resists the demands of pictorial transparency, academic finish, and propitious or sedate subject matter. In this sense the new techniques draw on the Realism of the 1840s and 1850s and the Romanticism of the early part of the century, to open up painting to the expressive demands of painterly suggestiveness and inchoateness and to the themes of modern urban life. One of the significant outcomes of this is that there is an increasing cultivation and foregrounding of mistakes and errors of execution and subject matter, as part of the new art's general deflation of academic techniques. In Manet and Impressionism, for instance, the failure to harmonize colour with pictorial space, and, certainly in Manet, the tendency to de-idealize genre subjects (to introduce diverse themes taken from non-bourgeois experience, as in *Olympia*) links errors and execution and subject matter to quality and the 'realism' of modern life. As such, deliberate mistakes in execution and technique become markers of value and purpose, thereby reversing the technical demands and expectations of neoclassicism and naturalism, where errors in execution and the deviation from customary and authorized subject matter were subject to high levels of ideological scrutiny and to condemnation by private and state patrons and religious authorities alike. Indeed, taking note of 'errors' and 'mistakes' in the content and technical execution of paintings and sculptures was a primary means of protecting or asserting cultural progress or ideal standards. But in the modern period, where fidelity to an aesthetic system, a religious tradition, or a set of inherited cultural conventions is in decline, there is corresponding diminution of the heuristic value of error and mistake as a way of measuring the attainment of these standards and sense of cultural progress. So, in this we see the error lose its old ideological bearings, and find a new and advanced identity. And it is this new identity that emerges at the heart of the new painting in the French Salon system of the 1860s. Here the invasion of the ugly, adulterated and disproportionate into the confines of the neoclassical and of naturalism represents a crucial moment in the transformation of the 'error' from a mark of scorn to a mark of ambition. No longer are 'errors' of execution to be chastised as a failure of technique or tone; they are to be recognized as the marks of a new expressiveness, in line with the sensory demands of 'modern life'.[3] Thus it is precisely what are judged to be failures of tone and mistakes in execution in the new painting of 'modern life' – in short, its vulgarity and disorderliness – that serve notice on the attachment of the error under neoclassicism and naturalism as a marker of subservience to formal hierarchy and academic technique. Technique becomes self-conscious and weakens the pursuit of these ideal standards or decorum. Now this is not to say that the arrival of modernism meant that art had no stake in a classicizing ideal of progress, or was unwilling to embrace the programmatic, but, rather, that the function of the error under these conditions reverses what is meant by progress and the programmatic. The diminution of a classicizing ideal of progress or programmatic cultural values is now measured by how well or how poorly the new art – principally the new painting – lives up to these new heterodox conditions. Thus failure of standards is now adjudged to lie in those works where the reliance on old 'stable' academic techniques and received subject matter *prevent* the entry of the new modernist conditions of experience and the modernist sensorium into painting. This means that errors and mistakes become expressly identifiable, not with the swerve away from a normative model of practice but with its actual replication or endorsement. Thus, it is precisely the marks and strategies of an academic professionalism that now identify the breakdown of cultural progress and programmatic cultural values. The reversal of the function and status of the error is crucial, therefore, in a number of respects. First, under the auspices of the shift, the artist becomes alert to the processes of making art, as latent with, or indeed *productively laden with, the promise of the mistake and error.* Second, as a consequence of this, the mistake and error – or the swerve away from the normative – becomes identifiable with art's powers of immanent self-critique and self-articulation. And third, as modernism breaks altogether with naturalism, the error becomes immanent to this logic of art's unfolding itself and to the specific value claims of a given work of art.

But the mistake and error as markers of value and authority are themselves subject to modification, once the full force of the new antisystematic tendencies immanent to the modernist revolution open up further subjective pathways in the 1880s and 1890s. As Impressionism passes into post-Impressionism and post-Impressionism into late-century Symbolism and the beginnings of abstraction, the error and mistake are subsumed by the wider requirements of chance, the aleatory and the indeterminate, which take over, develop and magnify the antisystematic tendencies of early modernism. By the 1880s–90s the deliberate error and mistake no longer appear to be supplemental to the old classicizing and naturalistic regimes of representation, but emerge as the basis for a new *antisystematic* regime (of the indeterminate and aleatory). Now, this is not to say the error is subsumed by chance, the indeterminate and the aleatory, but that it disappears as a discrete realm of judgement and as sign of modernity under this new regime. As the pictorial framework of naturalism and neoclassicism weakens, so does the contrast between normative model and its deviation. By 1910 (at the point of cubist painting and collage) chance, indeterminacy and the aleatory take on an autonomous identity at variance with the dying regulatory regimes of neoclassicism and naturalism; and, as such, antisystematicity takes on the characteristics of all new regimes: *it strives for systematicity itself.* This is why, over a period of sixty years, antisystematicity in art is definable not just in terms of a new set of aesthetic strategies and modes of attention, but as a new way of understanding the artist's skills and competences and art's place in the world. Thus, we can see how the emergence of modernism not only represents the arrival of new forms of subjectivism in art, but also a struggle to define new forms of reason or reasoning – or rather to rethink reason *through* art. For systematic antisystematicity is, above all else, a way of making what art does comprehensible to itself as a meaningful activity in a world that has little place for it. But if the new regime of systematic antisystematicity is indivisible from the struggle to find a process of reasoning outside of the bounds of classical standards and the discipline of naturalistic values, one of the paradoxes of this period is that much of the early reflection (1850–1905) on modernism is driven by the need to make the making of the modern understandable in terms of the achievements of the classical past. This is largely because the ideals of classicism, as opposed to the academicism of neoclassicism, is still the defining context, for good or ill, in this period, of modernism's ambitions and newly forged ideals – what modernism declares itself to have left behind, or, conversely, what it seeks to continue in the spirit of. There is a distinctive sense, then, that the demands involved in the making of a radically new culture come with responsibilities that are defined not just by measuring the new art against the achievements of the recent past, but in relation to the 'birth' of Western culture itself (ancient Greek art). As a result, if the birth of a new concept of artistic reason is in this period represented by the struggle against the legacy of neoclassicism and naturalism, this struggle is also mediated through the principles of classical culture.

THREE GATEWAYS TO MODERNIST REASON

On this basis, before I go onto discuss the development of antisystemicity into a fully blown hegemon in the post-Second World War world and the accompanying repositioning of the error in art via the figure of the errant artist, I want to focus here on three manifestations of modernist thinking that represent different 'classicizing' responses to the antisystematic tendencies already in place in modern culture at the end of the nineteenth century. These manifestations provide a snapshot of the struggles that accompany the formation of this new artistic subject of reason, and which will come to play a large part in the development of modernism in the first half of the twentieth century, and therefore are of particular interest to us: August Strindberg's 'On Chance in Artistic Creation' (1894), a key transitional text of the new antisystematicity, Friedrich Nietzsche's reflections on classical Greek culture and artistic vanguardism in *Untimely Meditations* (1873–1876) and George Santayana's jaundiced view of the new modernist subjectivism in his discussion on utility and modern art in *Reason in Art* (1905). Nietzsche's reflections on modernism, history and the 'strong artist' are well known, Strindberg's short essay on his own sculpture and painting and Santayana's book on modern culture less so. But they all share one thing: the desire to shape a new model of reason in art out of the flux, contingencies and heteroclite conditions of the new modernist culture. Yet if all defend the impetus and (some of) the demands of the modern, all three are unable to do so without the mediations and exemplars of classical culture. Consequently, all three authors think of modernism less as the emergence of new aesthetic tendencies that bear on the work of the recent past, than as an opportunity to think or rethink the question of reason in art. This is because all three authors are writing after the decline of the modern forms of neoclassicism, and the rise of subjectivism after Romanticism, and, therefore, accept a fundamental distinction between the inherited academic forms of classical culture and classical culture's formative principles. Thus, if there is nothing simplistically restorationist about these writers' thinking, this is because their reflections on classical culture represent how new forms in art might author a 'new reason' comparable to that of the ancient Greeks. So classicism represents a space for the discussion of reason, in a period when reason in art itself is being transformed, modified or abandoned.

Strindberg's elusiveness

Strindberg's essay brings together his passing thoughts on two of his own artistic works: an earlier clay neoclassical model of a male figure, and one of his late paintings, *Wonderland* (although it is not named in the piece), completed at the artists' colony Marlotte in the year the essay was written. In his discussion of the clay figure, a sculpture that was presenting him with many problems in its execution, he makes an allusion to a key classical reference on unintentionality and creativity: Pliny's description of the artist Protegenes, who, frustrated by his attempts at replicating the saliva of a dog, throws a sponge at the offending area of the painting, and finds that it disperses the paint in exactly the way he wanted.[4] Strindberg doesn't mention Pliny or Protegenes by name but the reference is certainly unmistakeable in his own solution to the problem of the clay figure's execution:

> I once had the notion to make a clay model of a supplicant, patterned on a model from antiquity. There he stood arms raised, but I became dissatisfied with him, and in fit of pique I brought my hand down on the poor wretch's head. And lo! A metamorphosis that Ovid could not have envisioned. His Greek looks were flattened by the blow, made into a kind of Scottish tam-o'-shanter covering his face with just a few additional touches, and the statue was perfect.[5]

That Strindberg alludes to Protegenes here reveals less evidence of modernist anxiety about cultural status than a fledgling modernist reconnection with a long, but marginal, pre-modern tradition of thinking on nature as the spontaneous creator of images. It is the artist's job to use, where necessary, the chance effects, indeterminate forms and delightful accidents of natural form and process, in order to create 'like nature' or 'with nature', for to create 'like nature' or 'with nature' is to create precisely in the manner of nature. That is, the artist creates *natura naturans* (without affect) rather than *natura naturata* (with affect). This is a crucial distinction from Greek culture, through to Leon Battista Alberti and Leonardo da Vinci, Giorgio Vasari, Albrecht Dürer and Andrea Mantegna, and on to Gustave Courbet. At one level this can be traced out straightforwardly in the extraordinary number of references made to the mutating patterns and images produced by cloud formations as a model of 'free creativity' in the work of artists and writers across these periods. The cloud signifies the perfect space of identification between nature's immanent powers of creativity and the spontaneous capacity of the artist to create something ostensibly from nothing. Rock formations also serve this function. But, at another level, this reflects the recurring effort on the part of artists to find ways of resisting their own inherited skills and mastery in order to 'see spontaneously' and to encourage others, spectators, pupils, to develop such skills. And it is this connection that is highlighted in Strindberg's essay: modernism, for him, is the recovery of creativity as *natura naturans*, as a way of both releasing the non-determinate capacities of the artistic process, and the interpretative 'imaginative perception' of artist and spectator alike. As he says: 'This is a natural art, where the artist works in the same capricious way as nature, without a set goal.'[6] This notion is continued in his reflections on his painting *Wonderland*, a small oil painting on paper which depicts, at the centre of a mass of dark green foliage, an opening that could either be the sky or a lake. Far from being worried about this ambiguity, Strindberg accords it the highest value for his painting and for modernism generally, in the same way that he rationalizes and celebrates the involuntary success of his flattening blow to his antiquarian figure. For what is compelling about this ambiguous central space of the painting, like the sculpted figure, is that it is not the direct outcome of his primary intentions. Indeed, he recognizes in its involuntary production a crucial truth supplied by the unconscious processes of modernist painting: that the production of meaning is ultimately a retroactive process based on the imaginative recovery of the details of the work. He steps back in the final stages of *Wonderland's* completion to discover he had put something down on paper that did not match his own interior conception of the work's progress and what he wanted at its conclusion, but nevertheless, on reflection, felt represented a satisfying outcome to his efforts. In fact this gap, between interior conception and the actuality of what gets committed to the paper, is precisely the truth of the process of painting, because what is not calculated for then acts as a possible trigger for new creative adjustments and developments. 'At first you see nothing, but a chaos of colors; then, it begins to look like something.'[7] Here in this meeting of the operations of the unconscious and an indebtedness to classical reflections on creative indeterminacy we see a direct connection to a pre-modern tradition of the latent image as one of the motors of creativity, most famously represented in the post-classical world, of course, by da Vinci's advice to young artists to look at stains and shadows on walls for imaginative direction in their painting, and infamously by Vasari's report on the working methods of Piero di Cosimo, who reputedly took great pleasure and pride in examining the spit and vomit left on walls for inspiration.[8] Yet if, like da Vinci and de Cosimo, Strindberg insists on the artist working with chance, through chance (allowing the work to transform and complete the work of chance), his use of the concept here serves a very different function than under classical and Renaissance culture. Chance in art is no longer a demonstration of enhanced felicity on the part of the artist, but it is now a definition of practice. It no longer serves to vivify the creative dexterity of the artist as a kind of exercise in pictorial fancy (that is, as a means of testing his powers of imaginative improvisation and construction), but acts as the constitutive force of art-making as such, and, consequently, it comes attached to a very un-classical and un-Renaissance sense of subjective destitution: loss of conscious deliberation is what is demanded of art, because this is what is required of the artist, in a world where 'felicity', 'dexterity', 'imaginative perception' have been rendered servile to the exoteric forces of capital, industry and the modern reproductive image. Strindberg is not alone in this kind of thinking in the 1870s, 1880s and 1890s, but his short essay has the merit of being one of the first attempts to think, or reason, through the concepts of chance and indeterminacy as a critical stance, as a way of reconciling what the modern world requires of the artist with the artist's own sense of loss of mastery. Effectively, then, Strindberg's essay is at the beginning of the modern and modernist association between chance, indeterminacy and the accidental, and the truth of the margin, the contingent and unformed, those areas of experience that modernism will come to invest with a heightened emotion in its challenge to the prevailing instrumentalities of bourgeois culture. Hence, if classical culture provides a port of call for Strindberg, it cannot furnish chance in art with a new model of reason that will make sense under these new conditions. This is because if the artist of the classical age and the Renaissance recognises the gap between intention and outcome, as the stage to perform certain acts of dexterity or sprezzatura, the modern artist has to plunge into this gap as a matter of self-definition. For whatever classical culture and Renaissance culture made of this gap aesthetically, technically, the modern artist has to live it subjectively. The knowledge of what eludes consciousness has to become the very practice of *elusiveness*, for elusiveness is what makes the coercions and repressions of modernity inhabitable and liveable. And this is why the 'new reason' in art is so amenable to psychoanalysis, just as psychoanalysis is so amenable to the new artists. Both invite chance and the aleatory into consciousness as a way of *resystematizing* reason, not abandoning it. And this is what is noteworthy about Strindberg's essay. It represents one of the assembly points of the new thinking, where the antisystematic tendencies of pre-modern art are transformed into the systematic antisystematicism of the modern epoch in art itself (1910–1970). That is, in this essay, Strindberg is one of the witnesses to, and actors in, the birth of a new, and now highly familiar artistic subject: *the subject who is at home in contingency*.

Nietzsche's forgetting

In one respect, in *Untimely Meditations*, Nietzsche is concerned with precisely the same problem as Strindberg: the relationship between the forgetfulness required of the modern artist in order to bring the new into being, and the demands and responsibilities of cultural memory. For crucial to Strindberg's argument is the recovery of heterodox tendencies within the classical past and within the Renaissance that allow the formulaic and academic doxa of neoclassicism and naturalism to be bypassed. The discoveries of modernism are rediscovered in the pre-modern past as a means of establishing an authentic tradition of creative perception. But for Nietzsche the possible technical continuities between modernist art and classical culture are not his concern. Rather, a far bigger picture emerges. The modernist artist must dispose of the recent past at the *behest* of the ideal conditions of classical art. In this light it is not the job of the modern artist to pay homage to the Greek ideal, in a kind of academic or technical subservience, but to use its powers of aesthetic and ethical disclosure for the very renewal of life itself. 'If you are to venture to interpret the past you can do so only out of the fullest exertion of the vigour of the present.'[9] Thus far from subordinating the modern artist to the greatest of past art, looking to the past should impel the modern artist towards the greatness of the future.[10] Consequently, the role of forgetting in Nietzsche's reflections on the condition of the new artist serves a particular purpose: to facilitate a systematicity that is in key respects antithetical to the emerging systematic antisystematicity. This is because it is the job of the modern artist not to identify with the contemporary, or the recent past of art at all, given that in modern culture man is split between an exterior that fails to respond to an interior and an exterior that fails to respond to an interior. Modern culture 'is not a real culture at all but only a kind of knowledge of culture'.[11] The new artist has to bear in mind that his work, for all the claims it might make for newness and appropriateness in its renewal of life, functions in a world dispossessed of 'unified inwardness'.[12] Indeed, under modern culture, inwardness is misled and poorly educated. Modern culture, therefore, if it is not to collapse back into decadence and academicism must strive towards a higher unity in which the split between inner and outer 'must again vanish'.[13] It must grasp, following the Greeks, that culture can be something other than decoration or entertainment. But if this higher goal is implicitly critical of the alienation of the artist and his or her public under capitalism, it is not set by the demands of democracy or class emancipation. On the contrary, 'unified inwardness' and the higher goal of culture (on the Greek model) can only be the work of the 'strong artist' and the cultural elect, who possesses the wherewithal for the production of an integral subjectivity. The masses, in contrast, possess no resources for autonomous subjectivity and therefore 'deserve notice' in three ways: 'first as faded copies of great men produced on poor paper with work-out plates, then as a force of resistance to great men, finally as instruments in the hands of great men.'[14] Nietzsche's meeting of modernism and Hellenic revivalism is made incoherent, then, by its ugly reduction of 'unified inwardness' to the work of a clerisy. And this is reflected most keenly in the subtext of the *Untimely Meditations* as a whole: an attack on Hegel. Bourgeois culture is not able to prepare anything but its own demise, let alone the future conditions that might produce a 'unified inwardness'; as such, the work of liberation must lie with those who purposefully bend the past to the demands of the future. That is, it must lie with those who are prepared to step outside of the present to become fighters against their age, in order to struggle against the notion that cultural progress or enlightenment is anything but a benign or inevitable process. Hegel, naturally – in a classic misreading of the philosopher that we are now very familiar with – is held to be the most corrupt advocate of this kind of historicist cultural thinking. Hegel's philosophy 'leads to an idolatory of the factual',[15] in which 'every success is a rational necessity',[16] 'every event is a victory of the . . . "idea"',[17] leading, understandably enough for Nietzsche, to the 'total surrender of the personality to the world process'.[18] That Nietzsche takes Hegel to be an advocate of 'thus it is so' as 'thus it shall be' is certainly misconceived, as we have shown. But his criticisms of the contemporary do have the merit of drawing attention to how questions of the actual, past and the future are played out in the early years of modernism. Who is to say that the modern, or the pursuit of the modern, is anything but the self-images of the age, particularly in the light of the subjective disarray of modern art? Thus, by implication, Nietzsche establishes an important point: in what ways does the current antisystematic subjectivism actually encourage the alienations of a 'disunified inwardness'? This is a question that haunts modernism, and is something that the early-modernist Hellenism is clearly very preoccupied with. Modernism simply capitulates to the flux of the moment, when it fails to encourage and support the strong artist as the exemplary subject of the collective subject-as-subject. Nietzsche, accordingly, is a modernist who is *not* at home in contingency, and sees the new subjectivism as a threat to the ambitions of his 'strong artist', who can rebuild the past in the present as an act of collective solidarity. But, if Nietzsche notes how the freedoms of subjectivism in art threaten a deeper subjective unity, he is wrong to suggest that such subjectivism is merely the self-image of the age. Here Hegel's 'necessity' is absolutely essential: the rise of antisystematic systematicity in art from the 1880s is no more nor less the democratic dissolution and dispersal of artistic form and spectatorship and the concretization of non-positivistic reason in the period of the subject's loss of subjective mastery. And, as will become clearer from our discussion of post-war art, then, chance, the indeterminate and aleatory, and the error, provide the coordinates for this productive dissolution of the artistic subject and release of the creativity of the artistic spectator to take place. Systematic antisystematicism represents the conditions of support and enablement of this subject. That Nietzsche seeks to establish a strong subject-who-*is*-a-subject, in defiance of this – that is, defend a modernist subject without the mediations and detours of history (what he disparagingly calls the realm of 'passion and error'[19]) – produces a modernism that actually fails the necessities of the age.

Santayana's utility

George Santayana was the teacher of T. S. Eliot, Gertrude Stein and Wallace Stevens at Harvard, and was a correspondent with Ezra Pound, who greatly admired his writing (Pound refers to Santayana in *Canto* LXXX1 and *Canto* XCV). I mention this because, as another anti-Hegelian, Hellenic conservative modernist, it shows how close Santayana was to the making of modernism in the USA in the latter part of the nineteenth century and the beginning of the twentieth century. *Reason in Art*, his (highly abstracted) assessment of the new modernism, represents another significant attempt to mediate the new artistic conditions through the ideal lens of classicism. But if, like Nietzsche, he was keen to distance himself from modernist subjectivism, he took no comfort from Nietzsche's notion of the 'strong artist'. Indeed, Santayana' antipathy to Hegel is matched by his antipathy to Nietzsche. As he was to say in his later book *Egotism in German Philosophy* (1915),[20] Nietzsche was incapable of any interest in things except the vehemence of the solitary will, leading to a consistent impoverishment in his writings of the actual. Santayana's critique of the Nietzschean 'strong artist' as a transcendental figure, therefore, is as much apparent in *Reason in Art* as is his critique of modernist aestheticism and subjectivism. One of his recurring criticisms is the 'transcendental pose' and the affecting of spontaneous inspiration, reserving his greatest contempt for those artists and writers who assume a metaphysical or mystical indifference to the actual. 'Romanticism, vitalism, aestheticism, symbolism are names this disease has borne at different times.'[21] 'The spontaneous is the worst of tyrants, for it exercises a needless and fruitless tyranny in the guise of duty and inspiration.'[22] The greatest threat to art, then, is precisely its resistance to reason, not the reason of calculation and deduction, or of transparent semblance, but the reason enshrined in the construction of the arts as integrated presence in the world of our everyday habitus, best represented, of course, by the achievements of classical Greece. What Santayana admires, as does Nietzsche, is that under this habitus the arts are integrated into the environment and therefore invisible as discrete, individual practices. 'When sculpture and painting cease to be representative they pass into the same category [the decorative]. Decoration in turn merges into construction; and so all art, like the Life of Reason, is joined together at its roots, and branches out from the vital processes of sensation and reaction.'[23] But this 'unified inwardness' for Santayana is exemplary for reasons quite different to those advanced by Nietzsche: for what marks out classical culture is not just the integration of the arts, but the interconnection of science and art as part of a cumulative and progressive tradition. Modernism's subjectivism and Nietzsche's prefiguration of the coming community through the 'strong artist' are characterized, therefore, by the very opposite: the expulsion of the languages of science, and the valorization of irrationality and subjective irresponsibility above collective endeavour. At one level this is a highly conservative template, and would seem to exclude Santayana from the framework of modernism itself; and, indeed, Santayana's model of reason pushes modernism to its very limits here. Santayana pretty much breaks wholesale with the notion of art as a form of non-positivistic reason, drawing little or no sustenance from antisystematicization as a way of inhabiting the growing instrumentalism of capitalism. But this is because – albeit in a politically unformed and idealist way – he has his mind on revolution. For this integrated model of the arts to prevail, a 'great revolution would have to be worked in society. We should have to abandon our vested illusions, our irrational religions and patriotisms and schools of art and to discover our genuine needs.'[24] Consequently, on the one hand, his writing uncannily looks towards the thinking of the post-revolutionary avant-garde. And indeed the conclusions of the book are taken up with a theory of utility that is strikingly similar to the Soviet and German avant-garde's contextual and situational application of art. The job of the artist is to give 'practice everywhere the greatest possible affinity to the situation.'[25] Under the breakdown of the traditional division of labour, '[T]here would need to be no division of mankind into mechanical blind workers and half-demented poets.'[26] And, on the other hand, his writing looks towards the Werkbund, in which the cultivation of beauty in functional objects becomes, for artist, technician and architect alike, a matter of practical efficiency. Now this is not to turn Santayana's Hellenism directly into a prefiguration of the revolutionary avant-garde. Santayana was not a man of the Left, although he did say a few supportive things about the early years of the Bolshevik revolution. For, the latter part of his career, his model of modernist utility was largely subsumed by a vehement critique of philosophical abstraction and systematic thought. But, nevertheless, his critique of subjectivism in *Reason in Art* is quite clear about where he doesn't want modernism to go, or to continue to go: in opposition to action and the coexistence of art with 'rational practices' in situations that enable the concrete enhancement of life. And in this respect his model of reason is one of the few classicizing responses to modernism in the period that re-ontologizes art's commitments and ideals. At the time this is a profound challenge to the growing systematic antisystema-ticity, precisely because it displaces the artistic subject, and, therefore, the unconscious and the unwilled outcome, from the primary scene of artistic production. His anti-historicist challenge to modernism, then, lies in stepping outside of the disorders of the new artistic subject altogether. And this is why his writing makes hard reading today: there is no invest-ment in *artistic subjectivity* as part of an emancipatory project, and as such no investment in the ways that art might be best placed to challenge scientific positivism as a critique of what capitalism makes of reason. This makes his 'revolutionary' model quite bloodless. It may advocate utility, but it is, in fact, frustratingly vague and strangely epicene with regard to specific artistic outcomes and admired precedents. Yet, despite the generality of his model, a hundred years on *Reason in Art* reads like a forewarning of aesthetic calamity, as if the emerging modernist histories of the artistic subject of the twentieth century are marked down from the beginning as destructive of 'unified inwardness'. This means that for Santayana, ultimately, there is no 'reason' to be sustained in contemporary art, in so far as the division of art into discrete practices perpetrates art in a fundamental state of errancy.

These three models of reason and the artistic subject have suffered very different fates under modernism. Strindberg's nascent formulation of antisystematicity, of course, diversified and readapted, became hegem-onic in twentieth-century Western art; Nietzsche's 'strong artist' became an elite notion of artistic brinkmanship at various points of modernism, quite against the collective spirit of the concept, and therefore shorn of its classicism (Clement Greenberg's support of Jackson Pollock is touched by this); and Santayana's modernist utility became a marginal entry point to the 'situational' aesthetics of the avant-garde, divorced of its predilection for a classicizing 'rational decoration'. One needs to ask, therefore, why modernist systematic antisystematicity became the force it did, encompassing both the painterly traditions of modernism, represented by Strindberg, and the pre-war and post-war avant-gardes? One would have to say that, for all Nietzsche's and Santayana's and others' hopes, classical systematicity, even in modernist guise, was unable to think the future of art as anything other than a form of *reparation*. In the case of Nietzsche and Santayana, because of their anti-Hegelianism (soon to become anti-Marxism in the hands of their classicizing epigones), they were unable to accord any value to the historical dissolution of art as a productive occurrence, preferring the 'making good' of the future of art, as a remodelling of the past as ideal image. So, for all their distaste for historicist abstraction and 'progressivism', they both fail to give due worth to the actual and the contemporary as the emergent site of 'another rationality'. The new is that which is won from the past in the present (which thereby acts as a kind of placeholder for the future), and not from the transformation of the present by the past and the transformation of the past by the present – what we might call the dialectic of the avant-garde. This is why we need to distinguish reparation from restorationism in classicizing modernism.

Nietzsche and Santayana are not Hellenic nostalgists intent on situating the harmony, proportions and detailing of Greek form within a modernist setting. Rather, in their respective ways they envisage modernism as a making true of the ideal unities of Greek culture as a modern enterprise; that is, one subject to the techniques of modernity. But, even so, they share with a restorationist classicism a horror of the artist as a figure of wayward or untrustworthy, or recalcitrant, subjectivity, in the manner of Plato. This is because they believe, as with Plato, that the prospect or ideal image of unity is threatened once the artist exercises his subjectivity over his social and historical fidelity to technique as a part of a collective enterprise. A loss of reason in art arises, then, when the artist moves away from his indebtedness to a pre-given or primordial unity. But, also, let us not forget that this image of wayward subjectivity is not evidence of a 'classical artistic subject'; if the modern subject can be said not to exist prior to the post-Cartesian formation of the self, for the Greeks there was no sense that the skills and reasoning of the 'artist' were based on any special characteristics attributable to a notion of artistic selfhood at all, and therefore to some independent sense of artistic identity. Artistic waywardness may define the unpredictable sparks of creativity, as in Pliny and Protegenes, but only as evidence of the maker's perspicacious adaptation of technique. Thus, for Nietzsche what is liberatory about Greek 'unified inwardness' is essentially its 'subjectless' status, as in the spirit of Novalis: 'A cultured Greek was only indirectly and only in very small part his own creator.'[27]

The emergence of modern aesthetics from the middle of the eighteenth century, then, is precisely the emergence of art from naturalistic technique and the formation of the artistic self from the Renaissance legacy of the 'independent creator'. For, if the Renaissance begins the process of formation of the artist as a figure of intellection and subjective autonomy, this is still limited to the strictures and discipline of Church and State, and to the higher rationality of the natural philosophic concept of *disegno*: the unification of intellect and emotion in the artist's immersion in the copying of natural form. This regime, as I have already suggested, may have been subject to all kinds of creative interruptions and displacements, from Leonardo da Vinci onwards, but as the technical basis of 'independent creativity', mimeticism represented the dominant means by which artists *thought* of themselves as artists, and thought of themselves as making sense of the world; mimeticism shaped the limits of the imagination, and not the other way around. The post-Renaissance world of art, therefore, is shaped by a particular struggle: to define art as a realm determined by its own special laws and modes of reasoning, thereby releasing the maker's subjectivity not just from the proscriptions of patrons, but from *disegno* as the disciplinary subjection of the artist to nature and to natural science. And, not surprisingly, this develops an increasingly explicit class content as artists of bourgeois, and lower bourgeois, origin seek to detach their skills from the subordinating function of neoclassicism and naturalism as aristocratic ideals. For these artists, classicism and naturalism's moral attachment to the notion of making as mimetic intimacy with nature increasingly feels like a form of servitude. In this respect, the resistance to naturalistic technical constraints in the late eighteenth century, from Alexander Cozens' prioritization of 'suggestiveness' over copying to William Blake and Henry Fuseli's 'subjective contours', expresses a resistance to the material circumstances that drive artists to function as servants of an Ideal externally embodied in academy and salon, despite the glorious achievements of art's embrace of natural philosophy in the Renaissance. This is why Romanticism at the end of the eighteenth century is the explicit entry point of the modern into aesthetics, in so far as it transforms the occasional moments of formal indetermination in classicism and naturalism into the critique of classicism and naturalism as systems of ideological *persuasion*. And this turns essentially on the very 'subjectless' character of classical culture, and the subordination of 'revealed creation' to the mentality of the copyist in naturalism. Thus classical culture may provide the conditions for the stabilization and continuity of natural beauty, but, in so doing, it subordinates artistic beauty to natural beauty, and as such mortifies the role of the artist as mere servant of nature. The notion that the classical ideal is, paradoxically, a celebration of death and inertia, under the guise of life and beauty and 'unified inwardness', is central to Gottfried Lessing's famous essay, 'Laocoön: An Essay on the Limits of Painting and Poetry' (1766),[28] one of the earliest texts of Romanticism and one that would influence the high-Romanticism of Schlegel.

Lessing is the first writer to explicitly devalue natural beauty as a constraint on the resources of the artist. And this critique is focused precisely on the naturalistic limitations of painting and sculpture. Painting and sculpture are delimited because of the complicit link they establish between the inertia of natural beauty and the frozen representational function of painting and statuary. Painting and sculpture are arts of arrested movement, hence their claim to aesthetic unity functions as a kind of deceit, given that the action or moment represented is incomplete, only one part of an imagined whole. The effect on the artist is to weaken, or even remove, his capacity to produce an autonomous and indeterminate beauty. This leads Lessing to demote painting and sculpture altogether, turning to poetry as the only viable means of securing this autonomous beauty and, as such, the infinity of creativity. This is because, whereas painting and sculpture succumb to the immediate sensuousness of the sign, poetry, in its motile capacity for succession and conjunction – for thinking imaginatively through time and space – renders the sign intellectually complex, and therefore increases the imaginative capacity of the reader. Moreover, this capacity for abstraction establishes quite a different sense of aesthetic unity. As J. M. Bernstein states: 'Because linguistic signs [in poetry] occur in succession, no one sign aesthetically dominates, thus allowing the ugly and terrible to be represented without ruining the aesthetic unity of the whole.'[29] This point is crucial, because it reveals the emerging correspondence between the modern artistic subject and the broader de-idealization of the pure subject of reason that Hegel's philosophy after the French Revolution calls for. That Hegel is rarely discussed in this context is down to his poor reading of German Romanticism, and as such his premature secession of painting and sculpture as practices of ideas. Romanticism may attack contemporary painting and sculpture for failing to live up to the new ideational conditions of art, but this is not an attack on art as such. One of the paradoxes of Hegel's writing, then, is that he is unable to fulfil his own dialectical commitments to a post-Cartesian subject and the critique of scientific positivism in his writing on the visual arts. But, in a sense, we don't need Hegel's thinking on the visual arts in order to establish the necessary connection between Romanticism's critique of classicism and naturalism and a theory of the errant subject; as we have seen, something like this is available in his writing on comedy. As a result, it is more productive to connect to Hegel's openness to contingency, error and the post-revolutionary democratic subject, to the democratic subject of Romanticism more generally. Consequently, despite Hegel's antipathy to what he calls Schlegel's Absolutization of the subject,[30] there's something to be gained, at least provisionally, from bringing Hegel's thinking on the subject into alignment with Schlegel's theory of artistic autonomy. This turns, fundamentally – as adumbrated in Lessing's writing above – on both authors' retemporalization of the subject.

With the post-Enlightenment connection between freedom and the emergence of subjectivity as a historical category, the subject of reason is now made and remade through the disorganizing forces of experience. This means that the post-Enlightenment reason brought into being by modernity – a reason split between the ideal and the actual – is founded principally for the Romantics, as for Hegel, on the passage through disunity. In Schlegel and Hegel, contingency and error (or indeterminacy principally for Schlegel) are expressly incorporated into the workings of reason. This is why both Hegel and Schlegel favour the written word over the 'worldly' or plastic image, for writing extends in time and therefore is capable of a greater intellectual subtlety and multivalence of interpretation, and therefore allows greater openness to contingency, ugliness and errancy, and the prospect of a 'modern beauty'. But where they differ is on what might be furnished from this temporal extension of the linguistic sign. Hegel, notoriously, positions philosophy against the plastic image, on the grounds that it is precisely philosophy where the work of infinite thinking might be secured, demoting modern art as a consequence. Schlegel, by contrast, favours poetry, but favours it for good philosophical and artistic reasons, on the grounds that it secures the greatest capacity for freedom. For Schlegel, poetry – as for Lessing – allows for a universalizing hybridity that oversteps the reflective powers of philosophy. Or rather, poetry's endless capacity for the inmixing of signs allows philosophy and art, scientific reason and artistic reason, the thinking of men and women, and the experiences of different classes, to live together. This is why: 'Poetry is republican speech: a speech which is its own law and end unto itself, and in which all the parts are free citizens and have the right to vote.'[31] And: 'The French Revolution, Fichte's philosophy and Goethe's *Meister* are the greatest tendencies of the age. Whoever is offended by this juxtaposition, whoever cannot take any revolution seriously that isn't noisy and materialistic, hasn't yet reached a lofty, broad perspective on the history of mankind.'[32] So, Schlegel's greater faith in poetry is not simply that the greater freedom is to be attained and secured through art, but that in a world split in two by the French Revolution, and, as such, subject to the divorce of the ideal from the actual under modernity, poetry is as an infinite speech that becomes, in its very unfolding, the infinite, democratic making of the self. Hegel's distaste for the absolutizing of the artistic subject in this way is thus short-sighted (although Schlegel's later penchant for abstruse mystification and general philosophical silliness would have certainly put Hegel off Schlegel's thinking for good reason). For Schlegel's position truly represents a radical advance beyond classicism's 'subjectless' creativity, and as such a greater advance on Hegel's subordination of art to philosophical enquiry, for it allows Hegel's post-revolutionary, post-Cartesian subject to find a productive place *in* art, in all its restless, contingent messiness. Indeed, Schlegel develops what Lessing only hints at: a theory of a modern autonomous artistic subject whose autonomy is grounded materially as the outcome of this split between the ideal and the actual. Art and its successful judgement are not given in the reproduction of empirical appearances, in natural beauty, or through the skilful inheritance of genre, but through uncompromising commitment to the 'transcendental condition' of the authentic work of art, the fact that the artwork itself, in its singularity, is that which is exemplary. Thus the authentic work of art imposes a new sense of what a work is, or might be, through its struggle to impose a unity on its heteroclite materials.

Now, if Nietzsche claims to see where this critical 'subjectivism' has led or leads, to the subjection of art to the actual, and therefore to the general disunity of culture, Strindberg, and late nineteenth-century modernists, take German Romanticism in some sense as axiomatic: that the 'transcendental' condition of art represents the democratic distribution of art's possibilities. But, of course, the emergence of systematic antisystematicism in late nineteenth-century modernism is not a revival of Romanticism as such, for its very commitment to indeterminacy is premised on what Romanticism disqualifies from this new realm of democracy and freedom: *painting*, the fact that Romanticism's entry onto the world-historical stage is premised upon the failure of painting and the visual arts to live up to the new transcendental conditions of art. This is why Strindberg's essay on chance, and the emergence of abstraction at the beginning of the twentieth century, may fulfil the demands of Schlegel's autonomy at some level, but this work is also premised on a confrontation with German Romanticism's logophilia. The celebration of indeterminacy is precisely that which is generated by the unconscious effects of painting. Yet we need to be careful here; this mediation of Romanticism is no return *to* painting as such, or to early Romantic painting, or to those moments of indeterminacy in painting from Protegenes to da Vinci, Dürer and Mantagena. That is, when Strindberg calls up the distant classical past in order to think of the technical advances of modernism as continuous with the achievements of the past, he is also by implication calling up Romanticism's critique of classicism and naturalism as a critique of the transparent painterly sign. And this is something that the histories of indeterminacy in art, such as Dario Gamboni's ambitious *The Potential Image* (2002), tend to gloss over. For the new life of art in the late nineteenth century is premised on the mediation of the painterly poetic sign in painterly form, in order to restore what German Romanticism claimed to be the absence of intellectual abstraction in painting. But if this represents the replacement of the painterly poetic sign into painting, it is not a *restoration* of this sensuousness to painting, as if indeterminacy in painting (those ambiguous effects pre-Romantic painting could only hint at) provides painting with a new and glorious poetic destiny. Thus the effects of chance and the accidental provide no more than a makeshift and transitory framework for the painterly sign, for indeterminacy in painting is, itself, no less subject to Schlegel's law of art's self-transcendence or negation. As early twentieth-century art shows, the dissolution of the sensuous (post-naturalistic) painterly sign is soon in evidence, as indeterminacy moves outside of the frame of painting altogether in order to move art forward conceptually. So, in this sense, Lessing's reflections on the limits of painting return to haunt modernist painting at the point that modernist painting imagines itself to have escaped from the constraints of classicism and naturalism. In this sense, the retrieval of painting as poetic sign acts a bit like a virus, in so far as under the guise of painting's sensuous revival, painting is itself subject to the pressures of art as a realm of infinite ideation. Painting exists merely as one source of indeterminacy, and not its univocal voice.

Thus this mediation of classicism and naturalism as empty poetic signs in the new painting in the form of the recovery of the full painterly (sensuous) sign inherent to poetry, is a crucial way of distinguishing twentieth-century systematic antisystematicity from its origins in Schlegel and German Romanticism. For autonomy in art, in the post-Romantic epoch of modernism's expansion and diversification, is not an expression of free creativity released from, or continuous with, the past, but is the disfigured and self-negating result of modernity's split between the ideal and the actual, and, therefore, is necessarily riven by critical self-consciousness. And this is why the classicizing reason of Nietzsche and Santayana and others ultimately couldn't compete with the systematic antisystematicism of the modernist anti-classicists that followed in the wake of Strindberg and Schlegel. For classicizing modernism inhibits modernism, misunderstands its subjectivism, and as such puts a break on modernism's emancipatory work, by disconnecting art from the wider social and political forces that propel led artistic autonomy into being after the French Revolution. Thus the task now is to explain what this new artistic subject promises, and how it manifests itself, as a fully self-conscious account of aesthetic reason.

MODERNISM, ERRANCY AND THE FORMATION OF THE MODERN ARTISTIC SUBJECT

What is clear from our discussion of Lessing and Schlegel is that prior to the artistic subsumption of the error under chance and the accidental at the end of the nineteenth century, German Romanticism had an emerging sense of the artist as an errant figure, someone, indeed – particularly in Schelegel – whose skills lay in the admixing of forms and discourses. This proposes, as a condition of modern artistic autonomy, that the artist is at his most authentic not just when he adulterates the pre-given aspects of genre and pictorial tradition, but when he moves between and across signs, systems and materials, as the very ground of his subjectivity and identity as an artist. Given that this was an essentially literary view of modern artistic subjectivity, it is not surprising that this appears quite different from, and in advance of, Manet and Seurat's sense of themselves as modern artists working at the margins of the genres of classical representation. Yet, by the early twentieth century, this sense of the artist as errant, as someone who is working on and with errancy, becomes pronounced. By 1915, in the wake of Duchamp's development of the ready-made and rejection of painting, it is now possible to talk about the artist as a figure who is as much at home in errancy as in contingency. As Duchamp was later to declare, in response to this shift, art is the 'arithmetical relationship between the unexpected but intended and the unintentionally expressed'.[33] For Duchamp, artisticness is essentially knowing how to make something of the unforeseen. Now this is not to say that this post-classical sense of the artist as a figure of errancy is the inevitable outcome of sixty years or more of modernism and the systematization of indeterminacy, as if indeterminacy is the inexorable and progressive development of art beyond painting in the epoch of art's naturalistic crisis. The crisis of classicism and naturalism does not represent the crisis of mimeticism *tout court* as a way of modelling the world, but of the way mimeticism, under the demands of tradition, authority, and institution, prevented art and the artist from entering and acting on the unassailable gap between the ideal and the actual under modernity. Systematic antisystematicization can be said, then, to offer one of the best routes for art under the emerging conditions of capitalism, which in the 1880s and 1890s was quite happy to continue supporting aspects of classicism and naturalism as the univocal voices of reason in art. Classical modernism's own response to these conditions, therefore, does not penetrate the academicism of neoclassicism and salon naturalism deeply enough, confusing the release of subjectivity through the effects of indeterminacy, ultimately, with the loss of reason in art. And this is why what is at stake for the generation of modernists that follows Manet, Seurat, Strindberg, Gustave Moreau and the Symbolists, is the codification (and politicization) of modernism as a form of reason that sits askance, or in opposition to, the prevailing positivistic accounts of reason. Thus, if Schlegel, Fichte and the French Revolution initiate this logic, so to speak, capitalism completes it for this generation of artists. Chance, indeterminacy, the accidental and errancy are variously pursued, presented, absorbed into the very being of the artist's identity, as forms of resistance to, and ultimately critique of the bourgeois triangulation of reason: religion, science and the state. Specific political positions, of course, mediate this triangulation (social democracy, conservatism, socialism, anarchism, religious pre-capitalist pastoralism, communism), and at times direct the production of artworks, but generally the sense of what makes the artist modern in this period is the fact that art's job is to operate as far away from this bourgeois triangulation of reason as possible. Elusiveness is the watchword. The result is that, for defenders of the new art, art allows us access to modes of perception and the workings of the empathetic imagination that expose these forms of reason for what they are: positivisms of the soul and mind.

Consequently, in this period, Schlegel's concept of autonomy is opened up to a framework of reception that will eventually provide modernism and the later avant-garde with its own revolutionary account of chance and indeterminacy: psychoanalysis. The links between early modernism and the emergence of psychoanalysis have been well mined, and indeed have become something of a commonplace in discussions of modernism's bid to separate itself from the workings of bourgeois reason: namely, how indeterminacy is given form by the concept of the unconscious. I'm not so interested in rehearsing this link here, or least not in any mechanical sense. What concerns me, rather, and has been little discussed, is how psychoanalysis furnishes the figure of the modernist artist with a conception of being at home in errancy as a condition of the new autonomous artistic subject. In this sense I want to look at how the construction of non-positivistic reason, formed from artistic indeterminacy and the workings of the unconscious, extends and deepens the post-Hegelian figure we are already familiar with: the subject-who-is-not-a-subject. For the demise of classicism and naturalism, and the rise of aesthetic autonomy, and the 'transcendental', self-negating function of art, releases an artistic subject that is in a sense at *war* with itself. The productive notion of errancy, then, comes to fill out and eventually displace the stable notion of artistic reason underwritten by classicism and naturalism, shaped as it is by the artists' increasing sense of conflict between the ideal and actual.

ERRANCY, PATHOS AND THE AESTHETIC UNCONSCIOUS

Jacques Rancière has drawn attention to how much Freudian psychoanalysis relies on art, and early modernism specifically, to ground its own shocking sense of truth: that knowing is not necessarily knowing, and that not knowing can put us on the path to truth.[34] When artists in the 1870s, 1880s and 1890s began to speak about chance, accident and the indeterminate there was a sense in which they were providing some of the psychic and material evidence for these paradoxes: the artist makes or speaks in the name of his or her intentions, but is surprised by the discrepancy between these intentions and their outcome. As I have suggested, Strindberg's essay is paradigmatic of this insight and its increasing significance for modernism. The effect of this is that, because of artists' historical and practical familiarity with the productiveness of their own unconscious processes, psychoanalysis sees artists as best placed to reflect on this gap between intention and outcome. This is why Freud draws many of his clinical insights from literature (admittedly, fewer from art), for there is a tacit sense in Freud that artists accept there is an undisclosed rationality to the accident, to fantasy, nonsense and the indeterminate. So, if psychoanalysis is not an art in itself (see Chapter 3), nevertheless, art and psychoanalysis do work over the same subjective materials. And this is why modern art and psychoanalysis share the same errant voice or intimacy with errancy: for both psychoanalysis and modern art, no thing, no matter how insignificant or marginal, fragmented or mistaken, is without signification or effect. Furthermore, in an echo of Schlegel's poetics, this process of assimilation represents a radical equalization or distribution of meaning and signs. As Rancière argues, when everything has the capacity to signify, the great hierarchical orders of representation no longer prevail. 'The great Freudian rule that there are no insignificant "details" – that, on the contrary, it is the details that put us on the path to truth – is in direct continuity with the aesthetic revolution. There are no noble and vulgar subjects, no important narrative episodes . . .'[35] Rancière, then, in a sense, supplies a psychoanalytic addendum to Lessing and Schlegel and the debate on classicism and naturalism: post-Romantic aesthetics and psychoanalysis offer comparable deflations of classicism and naturalism, converging over the issue of where meaning in art might be legitimately located. But if, for Schlegel, aesthetic reason is the dialectic partner of non-aesthetic reason, for Rancière, writing at the beginning of the twenty-first century, after the global domination of capitalism, the post-1970s defeat of the workers' movement, the stabilization of the counter-revolution, the technological coupling of perception and experience, and the demise of the historic avant-garde, Romanticism's hopes for the rationalization of aesthetic reason, are utterly enfeebled.

The dialectics of art and psychoanalysis, in his writing, therefore, dove-
tail to act as outriders of a critique of the interchange of non-aesthetic
and aesthetic reason, and ultimately art's relationship to revolutionary
transformation. Rancière still accords a place to non-aesthetic reason in
the workings of art, after the Fall of Modernity, so to speak, but it is
peripheral, a faint memory of revolution, and therefore a source now of
massive pathos. It is the job of authentic art, then, to respect the pathos
of this separation, for not to do so is to fall into the sins of heteronomy
and the transparent realm of art's effectivity (and, as such, to allow art to
get above itself). Effectivity lies, far more robustly, in how spectators and
readers use the work to their own ends within democratic, self-forming
communities of reception.[36] This is why the particular pathos uncovered
by the convergence of the aesthetic unconscious and the psychoanalytic
– the loss of a mastering reason – becomes, for Rancière, not so much
part of the great deracination of bourgeois order but the 'demastering'
code of Enlightenment reason in its entirety, in so far as it brings the split
between the actual and the ideal under a kind of pragmatic post-Romantic control. In this his position shares much with Jean-Francois Lyotard,
but without the need to frame this within the category of postmodernism. As in Rancière's other writings, this is in keeping with his general
post-Marxist, post-Hegelian, post-dialectic and anarchist themes, and his
exhortation of a politics of micro-agency, indivisible from the political
thinking of most of his generation.

Now, Rancière's recognition of the entry of pathos into debates on
aesthetic reason after Romanticism is without doubt important. This is
because the entry of the pathos of modernity into the development of
modern art is further reinforced and deepened by the logic and impact of
counter-revolution, deeply so after the destruction of the Soviet avant-
garde under the second Thermidor. But if Rancière sees why pathos was
productive for modernism before and after this defeat, he is not interested
in its continuing challenges today. The pathos of the gap between intentions and outcomes, the pathos of failure, is a kind of *fait accompli*. This
leads ultimately to a theory of the artistic subject that separates aesthetic
reason from dialectic, errancy and non-aesthetic reason: an emancipation
of the spectator at the expense of a continuing defence of the *emancipatory demands of the artist*. Our understanding of pathos is quite different:
how have modernist artists actually worked with and taken control of this
pathos as an expression of emancipatory reason, and how is this reason,

in the figure of the errant artist, still functional and transformative? In what ways, therefore, have artists tried to make themselves, and continue to try and make themselves, critically at home in contingency, errancy and the indeterminate?

Artists in the first three decades of the twentieth century treat the loss of conscious control over the artistic process as essentially transformative and emancipatory, albeit from various perspectives. Cubist painting incorporates the accidental mark as a kind of intellectual recovery of appearances deadened by naturalism; Cubist collage uses the incorporation of found scraps as a metonymic recovery of the real as a way of bypassing painterly illusionism; Dada produces improvised performances, nonsense poetry and scurrilous, sardonic montages, as the disorganizing force of an anti-bourgeois rationality that brooks no quarter with traditional artistic forms, or with bourgeois politics. 'There is a great negative work of destruction to be accomplished. We must sweep and clean . . . Dada Dada Dada, a roaring of dense colors, and interlacing of opposites and of all contradictions, grotesques, inconsistencies: LIFE';[37] Duchamp rejects painting in order to surrender the subjectivity of the artist to forces outside of the strict control of the artist's hand, transforming the artist into a surrogate or medium, and as a result opening a new intellectual life for the artist; Soviet Constructivism rejects painting in order to subordinate 'art' to extra-artistic skills and the collaboration of art with other disciplines, freeing the artist from the tyranny of 'expressiveness', and, as a result, 'putting the artist to work' on the revolutionary rebuilding of the environmental fabric of the world; Surrealism develops strategies of automatism and chance effects into drawing, painting, photography and writing as the primary material of the unexpected encounter and 'explosive' effect. All these highly familiar moments of twentieth-century modernism and the avant-garde possess and transform the new artistic subject in various ways, and as such are not strictly the same in intent; each proposes a different response to the question of indeterminacy and the disintegration of classicism and naturalism. Yet all impose or construct an artistic subjectivity that challenges the notion of a free expressive artistic subjectivity as the cornerstone of art's autonomy, even Surrealism, whose commitment to automatism was not a commitment to the 'visionary' artist at all, but, on the contrary, to the artist – in the spirit of Strindberg – who recovers meaning from the gap between intention and outcome after the unconscious has done its work, and, therefore, as a practitioner who is no more in control of the meaning of the finished artwork than the critic. No artist can or should know his or her work during its making, or immediately after its completion. 'Illumination comes *afterwards*,' as André Breton declares in 'The Automatic Message' (1933).[38] In this respect, the passage from Strindberg and Moreau to Duchamp and Breton is one in which artistic subjectivity is increasingly positioned or arraigned against the notion of the artist as a privileged subjective category. And this is wholly unprecedented in Western art. No artist in the pre-modern and early modern periods before Duchamp thought of themselves as being in the business of dissolving their own identity as an artist in order to practice as an artist. Yet this paradox is central to modernism under the transformation of indeterminacy into systematic antisystematicity. Through various strategies of self-distancing and expressive delimitation, the artist absents himself from any sense of 'unified inwardness' in the artistic process, defining himself or herself as anything but an artist (technician, engineer, intellectual, surrogate, medium, anamnesis). And this arises because the pathos of the split between the actual and the ideal makes the gap between aesthetic reason and non-aesthetic reason something that 'art' in its aesthetic powers of redemption appears wholly ill-equipped to heal, leaving the aesthetic identity of the artist hollow and bereft, and therefore incapable of unifying in imagination, in the form of the work, the actual and ideal. Now this is precisely what Nietzsche and Santayana might say would happen once artistic subjectivism is not grounded in strict formal and aesthetic protocols: subjective freedom in the end destroys art and the artist and the imaginative unity of the artwork. As a result, art doesn't just need the 'strong artist' but the strong state. But when the counter-revolution of the second Thermidor enables this strong state to do its corrective work on modernist disunity and attack subjectivism directly, it produces a catastrophe far deeper and of greater magnitude than Surrealism and Dada's excursions into disorganized thinking could ever imagine. What fascism and Stalinism do is destroy the pathos of freedom in a premature accession to cultural self-identity and stability. No doubt Nietzsche and Santayana would not recognize their Hellenism in these forms of premature reconciliation (although Santayana did live quite happily under Italian fascism in the 1920s and 1930s). Yet the returns to neoclassicism and academicism, in this instance of counter-revolutionary violence, reinforce my early criticisms of modernist classicism: blocking subjectivism in art in the name of cultural stability, tradition, populism, reason, the 'end of art', prevents the pathologies of history finding correlative artistic forms. In other words, there can be no hegemonic classicisms or naturalisms at ease with themselves under capitalism, for classicism and naturalism under these conditions are the ontological enemy of dialectic, the pathos of freedom and errancy. All they in fact can produce, as state ideology, are the atavistic remainders of classical order.

After the Second World War, and the destruction of the historic avant-garde, what remains of the avant-garde recognizes that for art to survive it has to continue to establish a place where these atavisms have no home: the self-negations of art and artistic identity. The errant status of the artist in this period, therefore, is defined by a sharpening of counter-revolutionary pathos: the destruction of the political culture of the avant-garde, and of systematic antisystematicism as non-positivistic reason, is compensated for by Western capitalism's increasing assimilation and valorisation of modern art as a testament to its post-war democratic vision. And the various cultural atavisms of the recent past, then, clearly had no part to play in this new settlement. As a consequence the errant identity of the artist enters a third modernist space: if in the 1860s and 1870s it represented a semiotic encounter between the new painting and classicism and naturalism, and between the 1890s and 1930s it represented the multifarious work of the deconstruction of artistic egoism and 'expressive unity', after 1945 the critique of egoism and the artistic self transforms systematic antisystematicism into a working methodology of resistance to modernist state ideology, as if modernism now needed to put into place, as a set of practices, what pre-war modernism had taught artists in order to keep open a space for aesthetic reason. On this basis, on the one hand, the relationship between indeterminate, chance and the accidental, are subject to an extensive theorization and development as exemplary practices, and on the other hand, the relationship between errancy and the indeterminate, chance and the accidental are reversed. That is, as a figure committed to the risks of errancy, and to its rationalization as practice, the development of strategies of indeterminacy, chance and the accidental increasingly fall in under this identity. The artist is, in a sense, now possessed *of* a strong errancy, rather than a figure that practices its indeterminate strategies. This is reflected in the large number of practices, painterly and otherwise – but mainly otherwise – between 1945 and 1970 that are driven by the artist as a kind of researcher in the indeterminate, and therefore by a sense of the artist as someone who needs to be out of control in order to be in control, or by the idea the artist as someone who, in working outside of the realm of the conventional forms of expressive intentionality, makes art and meaning from out of what he or she is not directly in control of. The first position, of course, is represented by Jackson Pollock, who produced paintings of classical scale through a radical destitution of expressive means. This is why the paintings are persistently confused with an aesthetic of 'expressive interiority'. On the contrary, the painterly evidence of expressiveness, the effervescent language of drips, gloops, scatters, loops and splatters, is the work of someone who does not want to identify making with the exteriorization of an expressive self, invested with stable sign-making attributes. And this is the great paradox of Pollock's painting and the source of its continuing power: it divests itself of the evidence of a stable, expressive self, in the delirious signs of an aleatory, expressive interiority.[39] Abstract painting, for Pollock, was, as for other painters of his generation, a way of disinvesting art of the metaphysics of the artistic self in a culture dominated by the terrible pathos of post-war art's rising public acclaim and aestheticization, and as such a way of maintaining fidelity to the pre-war notion of the artist as technician, medium, even artisan. This is why Pollock's work has one foot inside the history of painting and one foot outside, and why he was such a crucial figure for later American modernists, coming to understand and assimilate the lessons of systematic indeterminacy. His work offers a productive route outside of the high cultural confinements of painting into practical, everyday work on chance and the indeterminate, in performance, in dance, on the street, at the interface between art and mathematics. Hence, for younger artists who had no interest in painting, and saw its final conceptual demise in Pollock himself, the tension in his work between system and contingency, incoherence and coherence, represented a profound shift in what might be made from modern art's intimate relationship with chance and contingency.

Thus, after 1950 there is a huge expansion of work in the visual arts and music on the aleatory and the indeterminate in the US and Europe (tachisme, art informel, the literary/art group Oulipo),[40] but particularly in the US, where systematic indeterminacy sweeps all before it. Fluxus, John Cage, Allen Kaprow, the new 'post-painting' painting (Robert Rauschenberg) and early conceptual art, all invest in strategies of chance and the accidental as a means of sustaining the pathos of the artistic-subject-who-is-not-a-subject; and, as a consequence, all see the promotion of this relationship as a way of defending a notion of the artist as a kind of a researcher into indeterminacy and the aleatory. The theoretical positions, arguments, statements, works, experiments, come in a flood: 'the reason for the importance of randomness for purposes of scientific inference will be the same as the reason for its importance in the arts, that is, the elimination of bias' (George Brecht, 1957);[41] in the production of indeterminacy 'the ego no longer blocks action. A fluency obtains which is characteristic of nature' (John Cage, 1958); [42] 'a conscious use of chance bypasses failure by building non-control into the work as a desideratum. Whatever happens by definition happens as it, should. Theoretically, every occurrence is as a "good" as every other.' (Allan Kaprow, 1966);[43] 'I love Chaos; it is the mysterious, unknown road. It is the ever unexpected, the way out; it is freedom: it is man's hope' (Ben Shahn, 1966);[44] 'art itself is an activity of change, of disorientation and shift, of violent discontinuity and mutability' (Robert Morris, 1969);[45] 'irrational thoughts should be followed absolutely and logically' (Sol Lewitt, 1969).[46] And there are many more reflections from this period of a similar nature. What unites these quotations is twofold: the liberatory nature of an art that operates outside of an intentional, expressive base (and, therefore, the liberatory nature of the 'egoless' artist) and the new knowledge and aesthetic experiences to be won from the creation of a system of relations, which produces effects and outcomes not predicated by the artist, and therefore outside of his or her immediate control (although, of course, the artist or artists 'sets up' the system). As Rauschenberg defines this approach in 1965: 'even though chance deals with the unexpected and the unplanned, it still has to be organized before it can exist.'[47] So 'egoless' art is not an art without subjective investment, or even expressive intentionality (the intention to produce a system that generates interesting, unexpected effects); there is no assumption on the part of this work that 'egoless' is the same as subjectless. Rather, 'egolessness' here represents a formal recognition of the gap between intention and outcome as a consistently productive mechanism for innovation. What Strindberg was astounded by is now a matter of daily research and practice. Moreover, the shift to systematic indeterminacy is a shift to the notion of the artwork as an *open* system, in which, the withdrawal from the signs of a unified authorship allow the participation, and possible collaboration, of the audience. In the writings of Brecht, Cage and Kaprow, the diminishment of the free conditions of intentionality, and as such the subordination of the artist to a self-created system, allows indeterminacy actually to enter into and shape the relationship between artist, work and audience. In the performance of a live work no piece is the same, and each active response and contribution from the audience gives the work its final shape – the moment, that is, when the work (provisionally) ends. As Cage says in a discussion of the introduction of such indeterminate techniques into musical performance: 'The ending, and the beginning, will be determined in performance, not by exigencies interior to the action but by circumstances of the concert occasion.'[48] Systematic antisystematicity, therefore, has both a precise technical and critical meaning in US art of this period: on the one hand, it is that which is defined as the random production of meaning within an open system of relations, materials and positions; and, on the other hand, it is the framework through which the artist as a subject-who-is-not-a-subject brings this tension into creative focus, as a continuation of the modernist defence of art as infinite ideation. That the US becomes the advanced theoretical home of modernist infinite ideation after 1945 is, of course, not a quirk of fate but a consequence of the mass exodus of modernists and avant-gardists from Europe to the USA before the Second World War, and the eagerness with which that American generation of the 1930s and 1940s assimilated its lessons, initially through painting. Nevertheless, this does not account for how deep the development of systematic antisystematicity went in the USA after 1945, as if the rapid development of systematic antisystematicity was what was required as a defence mechanism in a foreboding cultural climate. And, indeed, whatever its aesthetics origins, it pragmatically became this, for despite all the attempts of the anti-communist right, during the Cold War and after, to taint it with subversion, it managed to out-manoeuvre both its retardataire and conservative critics, and the constant exhortations for a national popular art.[49] This is why I included in the selections above a quote from Ben Shahn, a figure not normally associated with the rise of indeterminacy in American art. A photographer with the FSA (Farm Security Administration) in the 1930s and a fellow traveller of the American Communist Party (CPUSA), his previous commitments were to some version of realism, and to the notion of representation as the stable agent of art as social praxis. His commitment to the productive notion of 'chaos', therefore, shows how deeply systematic antisystematicity penetrated American post-war culture as a means of allowing artists to think and practice beyond the pincer movement of the Cold War. The defence of systematic antisystematicity in the

US in between 1945–1970, then, carried an implicit, and sometimes explicit, political agenda: to continue the artistic debate on aesthetic reason into the very heart of bourgeois rationality. As a result, there was something greater at stake: to close this notion of the artist down, or to devalue it, was to reinstate a subjective identity for the artist that no longer carried any authority, and, furthermore, was now associated with the state coercion of the arts. But by the early 1970s it was possible to see the creeping academicism, and enfeebled liberalism, of this position, as indeterminacy and the accidental became the common sense of the age.[50] Cage, Brecht, Kaprow and others contributed to this, by failing to rethink and position the stochastic in art as in dialectical relation with non-aesthetic reason, but in many ways the assimilation of systematic indeterminacy was long out of the control of these artists, once it had become a state ideology. As T. J. Clark was to say of the strategies of Pollock and this generation of modernists: 'But in so far as this "outside" has been posited and organized as a new territory with its own rich sources of supply – what resulted was to the bourgeoisie's advantage rather than otherwise.'[51] Now we have to be careful here: Clark's view comes freighted with a Situationist account of how bourgeois culture has consistently locked down the meanings and potentialities of modernist art, whilst at the same time supporting the widest of artistic manifestations (as a source of its own intellectual renewal), 'locked down', in my view, being highly tendentious. Yet, nonetheless, a crucial point is being flagged up: post-war systematic antisystematicity was to be confronted by the limits of its powers of motility and creative disorganization – certainly by the late 1970s – once it came to be the official language of cultural renewal and the culture industry. Therefore systematic antisystematicity as a system was itself sublated by the logic of art's post-Romantic drive to autonomy: the need to secure and articulate a space for art at variance or 'out of sync' with the rationalities of bourgeois culture. By the 1970s, vanguard modernism's commitment to art's infinite ideation was faced with two pressures: the continuing need to defend systematic antisystematicity as the best means of securing a future for aesthetic reason, but at the same time a recognition that systematic antisystematicity had to submit itself to negation and scrutiny.

And this is the context in which Adorno writes *Aesthetic Theory* (1970), the key theoretical engagement in this period with the late modern pathos of art's 'self-transcendentalising' condition. Adorno's work, in substantive ways, is a recapitulation of Schlegel's Romanticism, but under the expanded logic of art's entry into commodity culture. Under the vast expansion of the commodity relations of art, post-war (state and public institutions; art market dissemination and promotion; the return, via modern forms of media, to reified images of artisticness) art's sense of its own autonomy, has to be produced out of an increasingly mobile sense of non-identity with those forces of social legitimation and critical approbation that would, in their attempts to explain or direct art, limit its capacity for infinite ideation. Authentic aesthetic experience is only won from art's continued resistance to its own exoteric and immanent logic of normalization. This means that aesthetic experience, in a world in which certain kinds of aesthetic experience are easily associated with certain kinds of socially agreed pleasure and their conformity with socially agreed conceptions of aesthetic reason, modern art has to be critically conscious of the falsely reconciliatory powers of aesthetic experience *tout court*. Particularly so in a world, as I have stressed, in which enlightened bourgeois culture now has a well-upholstered place for its own critique, and, indeed, is quite happy at housing the new art in its museums and institutions. Thus Adorno establishes an explicit connection between aesthetic experience and the requirements of self-negation, or aesthetic negation, if aesthetic experience is not to stand in conformity with its own past and the explanatory pressures and taxonomies of the dominant culture. In order for aesthetic experience to satisfy the concept of artistic autonomy, it has to resist, subvert, adulterate the socially agreed conventions of aesthetic experience; in other words, open up aesthetic experience to the forms, practices and signs of non-aesthetic signification and experience. For if aesthetic experience is highly susceptible to social and interpretative closure, then it is precisely art's assimilation of, and reflection on, non-aesthetic experience that has the capacity to remake or expand the boundaries of aesthetic judgement.

The history of modern art, of course, is the very history of this assimilation of the non-aesthetic or heteronomous sign and materials. But if Adorno notes that modernism's drive to autonomy is made, and continues to be made, from the non-aesthetic, his theory of the sign identifies autonomy, in the last instance, with the demand for aesthetic experience *as* aesthetic, that is, as an experience that is not to be confused with the cognitive and deductive processes of non-aesthetic reason, but is disruptive of these processes. Adorno's elaboration of this concept of autonomy is well known: to redefine and finesse the necessary distancing techniques and strategies of modernism through various strategies of semiotic and linguistic withdrawal, silence and non-communication, so as to make modernist elusiveness a critical imperative. Such elusiveness is not a way of enforcing impenetrability, but of encouraging reflection as an extended process of judgement, in contradistinction to the rush to judgement and interpretation that operate under the positivisms of both scientific enquiry and a hermeneutic science of the text. In one sense this is a position that is profoundly indebted to the culture of indeterminacy I have mapped out, stretching back to Protogenes and to the liberation of the spectator. And this is why, although Adorno pays relatively little attention to the visual arts in *Aesthetic Theory*, systematic antisystematicity does have a correlative in Adorno's identification of the authentic artwork with its (Schlegelian) immanent drive to processual self-transcendence. But in Adorno this processual drive has a far stronger sense of the demands of aesthetic negativity than post-war American systematic antisystematicity and its liberation of the spectator. This is because, although Adorno comes down on the side of aesthetic reason against the social gains that might be won for art from its partnership with non-aesthetic reason, he recognizes that there are no stable predicates that will produce a secure aesthetic experience; all kinds of non-aesthetic experience can be claimed legitimately for aesthetic reason. Accordingly, because there are no stable predicates for aesthetics, aesthetic judgement is not to be confused with aesthetic pleasure itself; or rather, what might be designated aesthetically pleasurable can be made from what is precisely unpleasurable, discomforting or disagreeable. So if art cannot assume its aesthetic place in the world in any pure or direct sense, the autonomy of art therefore has to produce itself *from* the heteronomous materials and processes of the world. This is why we should not confuse Adorno's specific judgements on the processual requirements of modern art with his actual judgements on the modernist art of this period, (abstract painting, serialism in music and non-naturalistic theatre). (Adorno recognises that the experience of modernism and negation in art does not stop with his own judgements on his favoured works.) Art's ideation is far larger than 1960s modernism. Hence Adorno brings an unprecedented theoretical sensitivity to the Romantic concept of infinite ideation: aesthetic reason is only sustainable through its mediation and negotiation with the signs and forms of heteronomous (commodified) experience. The result is that Adorno gives a new dialectic identity to the pathos of the artistic subject in the period of systematic antisystematicity's diffusion: the artist becomes a figure that operates permanently in the space between aesthetic reason and non-aesthetic reason, as a condition of his or her critical role within the advanced relations of artistic production. But in *Aesthetic Theory* this is developed without a precise sense of what this means as a definition of the artistic subject after Schlegel and Hegel.

If US systematic antisystematicity remains overly identifiable with an egoless infinite ideation, Adorno remains in a way too attached to the figure of the artist as a sovereign presence in the relations between aesthetic and non-aesthetic reason. For like Nietzsche he has a dread of non-aesthetic reason diminishing the artist as an exemplary stand-alone figure. Consequently, Adorno pays little attention to the productive interrelationship between the modern artist's subject status as a creator, and his or her depossessive status as one part of a knowledge process or technical process, or social contexts external to his or her own specific activity. Thus if he develops a concept of art's critical autonomy that is adequate to the pathos of aesthetic reason's diminished function under capitalism, this is not accompanied by a theory of artistic subject that is actually adequate to this concept of autonomy and art's new relations of production. And this rests, in my view, on how Adorno fails to assimilate the errant status of the artist into aesthetic reason. In these terms, what would a post-Adornian defence of infinite ideation look like? How would a defence of infinite ideation in art hold together in a situation where the liberatory functions of systematic antisystematicity have to continually adjust to its academicization and institutional endorsement?

INFINITE IDEATION, REASON AND ERRANCY

As we have seen, a defence of infinite ideation in art has involved the development of a depossessive or egoless artistic subject – for 'inwardly centred' subjects tend to get in the way of this process. And, as we have also seen, post-war systematic antisystematicity has best represented this position in its commitment to the displacement of 'strong intentionality' and the interdependence of artist, artwork and audience. In this respect, in terms of the aesthetic reason/non-aesthetic reason dialectic, these practices tend to come down on the side of aesthetic reason. But systematic antisystematicity also produces a form of infinite ideation in this period that is indebted to non-aesthetic reason: the emergence of a temporal, discursive, determinate, extra-gallery, activist post-object practice that embodies infinite ideation in art as an intellectual, knowledge-centred process (for example environmental art, land art, community art and eco-art). This work barely existed when Adorno was writing *Aesthetic Theory*, but its early avant-garde precursors (Constructivism, Productivism, early Activist Art), were clearly in mind in his judgement about the perils of non-aesthetic reason in a post-revolutionary culture. In this kind of work, then, infinite ideation takes the depossessive form of art's capacity to bring context-sensitive knowledge and skills to the solution of a problem or the amelioration of a given situation. Moreover, this dispossessive process represents a democratic shift from artist to non-artist; that is, the artist places his or her subjectivity in the service of an artistic identity in which the labour of what the artist does is placed in the same category as that of the non-artist (someone whose skills and knowledge are not defined by the privileges of self-expression). On this basis a large number of artists in the twentieth century have pursued, or imagined themselves in, the role of the non-artist. Many wanted to become, or envisaged themselves as, engineers, technicians and factory workers, or, post-1970s, as social workers or community activists. In Soviet Russia in between 1917–1927 such a process was indeed successful, challenging the historical division between intellectual and manual labour, and the Romantic pathos of art's alienation. The cultural achievements of the Russian Revolution are inseparable from this restructuring of artistic technique and the social relations of the artist, and at one level represent the extraordinary cultural achievement of the revolution. But if this generation of artists imagined themselves to be taking on the role of engineer or technician or activist, and indeed took on the attributes of the engineer or technician or activist, at no point did their imaginary identification ever *coincide* with such roles, even under sanguine revolutionary conditions. For to do so would have dissolved their identity as artist *into* that of the non-artist, aesthetic reason into non-aesthetic reason; and this would have made it impossible for the artist to bring the enlightened reason of aesthetic process to the labour process or to the technical/professional skills of non-aesthetic disciplines. Because with this dissolution comes the requirement to fulfil one's tasks as an engineer, technician or activist *as* an engineer, technician or activist, and not as an artist reflecting on these roles, or operating through them at a distance. Productivism's factory experiments suffered from this; the artist either had to find ways of being directly useful – that is, submit himself to the discipline of the labour process and the factory managers – or leave the factory. For instance, Karl Ioganson, a geometric Constructivist sculptor, found himself improving the dipping process in a Moscow metal factory.[52] The idea, then, that the artist should fill non-artistic roles in a technically professional way is deeply misguided. For if the process of identification is successful – and if it is to be successful then it should fulfil its practical and functional criteria to the letter – then there is no supplemental space for artistic reflection. If the process of identification is unsuccessful – if the artist fails to fulfil the job criteria – then it may open up a space of reflection, but it is unsuccessful as a practical and functional action. So, if practical and functional criteria are to be pursued successfully and in good faith, then it is best to train as an engineer, technician, and so on, in the first place – as indeed some Productivists suggested, calling for the training of artists to bypass art school altogether. For why subsume art under functional criteria if you are not able to fulfil these criteria properly?

THE FREEDOM OF DIFFICULTY MASTERED

A paradox attends the subsumption of aesthetic reason under non-aesthetic reason, then: for it to be successful on its own given terms it has to dissolve its relationship with aesthetic reason altogether. This is why under post-war capitalism, where the pathos of modern art remains determinedly in place, such a position performs a premature *de*-aestheticization of aesthetic reason, and as such is profoundly anti-Hegelian as a strategy: it imagines that direct action can overcome the pathos of the gap between the actual and the ideal, through eliminating the actual altogether. Adorno's defence of aesthetic reason, therefore, is very much premised on this rejection of the premature submission to non-aesthetic reason, although his target is not specifically post-object art, but political interventionism in art more generally. The defence of aesthetic reason may sacrifice 'effectivity', 'functionality', 'knowledge', but in its resistance to the forces of instrumental reason, it actualizes a place for a reason beyond the antinomies of the actual and ideal.[53] But what Adorno doesn't note about the defence of aesthetic reason in these terms, as is the case with US systematic antisystematicity, is that there is a third and more instructive position that lies between aesthetic distance and the dissolution of aesthetic distance altogether: the notion of the artist as someone who, in moving into the realm of the non-aesthetic, *performs* its limits and the limits of positivism and bourgeois culture more generally as the working space of art's pathos. And it is precisely this lack of attention to this place of negative ideation, of experimentation, that weakens both Adorno and Rancière's defence of aesthetic reason. The artist works with, and in, the realm of heteronomous action and experience, but in a sense does not *inhabit* it, or assume that the primary work of the artist is best given over to developing various kinds of technical expertise. The precise opposite occurs: the artist, in his or her encounter with, or adaptation of, non-aesthetic reason, operates as a kind of displaced amateur or non-professional, using the knowledges and skills from other disciplines when and where he or she can as a system of reference or negative criteria that refuses to submit to the instrumental demands of practical success and transformative 'outcomes'. There is, therefore, no pretence at wanting to build bridges, dig wells, grow crops, develop new strains of wheat with scientists, or heal the conflicts of a community (with police backup!), but, rather, a desire to act in ways that deflate the ambitions of non-aesthetic reason, in order to expose the shortfall between the hubris of non-aesthetic reason and its ruling means-end logic. So, what I discuss above as the failure of the artist to properly adapt to non-aesthetic reason by embracing its demands as an artist, actually becomes the artist's strength. This is because one of the few critical functions left to the artist is to attach himself, or herself, to a non-artistic discipline or skill *without* fully investing in it as an activity and a social identity; indeed, there is a comparable disinvestment from these social identities as there is from that of being an artist itself. That is, artists need to invest creatively in their privileged powers of negation. But if this means embracing the productive consequences of failure, it does not mean embracing the artist as a reified figure of failure. And as such we need to remind ourselves of our earlier discussion on the difference between failure and errancy. The transformation of the artist into a weakened figure of flight or self-denial simply abandons the pathos of the modern to impotence and self-abnegation – a prevailing tendency in 1990s 'pathetic art'. There is nothing to be won critically from unambitious failure or nihilism. Similarly, there is little to be won from the formal recovery of the poorly conceived or executed artwork, as if all the assimilation of failure commits the artist to is picking up on the 'leftovers' of abandoned production in order to 'do things better'. There's something of this in Niklas Luhmann and George Dickie's aesthetic approbation of failure. 'Failed works of art are still works of art, if unsuccessful ones. This is why it makes sense to take on difficult projects, to incorporate things that do not fit, and to experiment with possibilities of failure' (Luhmann).[54] 'Many works are failure in an attempt to produce art, and I would suppose that philosophers of art should be just as interested in artistic failure as moral philosophers are in moral failure.' (Dickie)[55] In contrast, however, a *political practice of failure*, as a critical reflection on 'the used-up, the embarrassing, the misguided and foolhardy who wagered much and lost',[56] has some viability, in as much as it links the Lefebvrian sense of productive failure to a project of cultural reclamation and construction. My understanding of errancy is closer to this, but operates, more emphatically, in the space where the pathos of the modern and the destitution of the subject mediates the relationship between negation and experimentation. And so this is where the errant function of the artist in the period of art's systematic antisystematicity is perhaps most purposefully engaged: not as the advocate of pure aesthetic reason (the aesthete, or the abstracted 'egoless' unit in the unfolding space of art's infinite ideation) or the defender of non-aesthetic reason as praxis (the technician or activist), but as a wayward and ironic figure of ideological disinvestment and disengagement and imaginative non-reconciliation. For what artists are particularly good at is not just formulating strategies of withdrawal or distanciation – modes of non-communication – but performing failure and errancy as activities that sustain a productively destabilizing relationship to knowledge and power.

Errancy, of course, is a condition, that always exercises the anxiety of the artist. No artist wants to produce work that is palpably incompetent, academic, or without the mark of authenticity. The notion of the errant artist, therefore, is not an invitation to produce work that is deliberately poor or off-key, or that sets the artist up as an idiot savant. I am not advocating passivity or stupidity as modes of enlightenment – although acting stupid, as we have seen in the context of psychoanalysis, has its occasional diagnostic and corrective moments of lucidity. Errancy here, rather, is a recognition of the dereliction of the subject, and the 'expressive self', as a primary condition of negotiating the pathos of modern art and modernity, and therefore a way of utilizing that which modern art has made its own: *the artist as a figure whose mistakes and errors are necessarily productive because they are free of externally imposed forms of justification.* Quite simply, modern artists are free to make mistakes. And this is because one of the consequences of art's autonomy is that, just as artists do not need to justify what they do against a system of normative values, they do not need to make good the validity claims of the extra-artistic disciplines they adapt or borrow from. They may spout nonsense, or make fools of themselves with impunity and in good faith *across aesthetic reason and non-aesthetic reason.* Admittedly, such mistakes are not wholly cost-free – mistakes impact on the quality of the work itself and the creation of a public – but the result of making a mistake does not require blame to be apportioned, and the claims of the work to be rejected. This is why the error in art has very different consequences to that of political praxis, philosophical reflection, science and even psychoanalysis. If, as I have suggested, in these practices, the error is the *daily language of that which has not arrived,* the error in art is that which *has arrived,* so to speak. Whereas in revolutionary political praxis and psychoanalysis, and the philosophy of science, the recognition and assimilation of error proposes the future resolution of a particular problem, errancy in art – and by this I mean the fundamental unwilling-ness of the artist either to *be* an artist or *not* be one, as the cornerstone of infinite ideation – becomes the daily language of art's incompatibility with bourgeois society. In existing in this cross-border state between aesthetic reason and non-aesthetic reason, and thereby in a state that refuses to sustain a stable aesthetic or non-aesthetic identity, the artist is free to be in error as a condition of producing an infinite number of 'thought experi-ments' that may or may not be meaningful or purposive. The use-value of art in this liminal position between aesthetic reason and non-reason, then, lies in its productively prefigurative and suspensive capacity; there is no sense that art's job is to heal or redeem the world, just as there is a refusal to accept that all art might offer is a form of aesthetic reconciliation or solace. Thus it is misconceived to assume that in the period of capital-ist decline art itself is in decline. The limits that artists work under – to borrow the thinking of the Oulipo group – are productively derived from the limits of the commodity system itself, and therefore constitute 'the freedom of difficulty mastered'.[57] This is why it is not art that has a pecu-liarly sovereign position within the broader economy of the critique of scientific positivism and the market ideology of bourgeois society. To reit-erate Adorno's argument: there are no secure aesthetic predicates (derived either from aesthetic reason or non-aesthetic reason) that can secure this critique. Rather, what characterizes art's sovereignty, and therefore has the capacity to maintain art's critical distance from scientific positivism, is the capacity of the artist to open himself up to errancy and art's infinite ideation, as a condition of art's rational self-preservation, and the preservation of the artistic subject. On this basis, the sovereignty of the artistic subject is a heightened version of the errant subject-who-is-not-a-subject we have met already: the subject of truth who possesses and repossesses error as a condition of his subjection to forces outside of his or her immediate control. Consequently, it is not constructive to identify post-1960s art with errancy and failure *tout court*, as Paul Virilio has done, the latest in a long line of conservative catastrophists. Virilio rehearses a version of modernist classicism that establishes the crisis point in the modern period with the post-Impressionists. After the post-Impressionists – that is, after the First World War – art falls into a permanent and nihilistic state of errancy as a result of the disastrous entry of 'theoretical abstraction' and technology into art. At this point art loses an unmediated sense of joy. 'Never again will there be a sunset, never again will we enjoy the beauty of the mountains.'[58] Indeed the production of modern art in the twentieth century has been an unmitigated failure. 'The arts of the twentieth century are a disaster, and they don't acknowledge it. They continue to walk on nothing . . .'[59] This clearly has echoes of Nietzsche and Santayana (even if its historical cut-off point seems quite arbitrary): modernist subjectivism is one long disaster for the sensuous balance between art and nature, and therefore is ruinous of our empathy with natural and artistic beauty and the arts' environmental habitus. Now, in one sense, we have to acknowledge the perspicacity and power of Virilio's refusal of the modern experience of art, as we also need to do with Nietzsche and Santayana. The critique of capitalism is a critique of modernity and its accelerationism, or it is nothing, and conservative and classical modernists have perhaps been best at doing this – with the exception of the strange case of the conservative Marxist Mikhail Lifshitz, who proposed a restorative communist classicism against Stalin's ugly and brutal neoclassicism and Western modernism.[60] But at the same time the critique of modernity, without a dialectical praxis of modernity, is itself nothing, an ideologically feeble husk, in which moralism, aestheticism and endism prevail. (Virilio's nod in the direction of the limitations of his own critique towards a 'renewed' artistic praxis of modernism – art must 'explode' and 'dismantle' the new technologies from inside – however, does nothing to ameliorate this.)[61] Hegel, therefore, continues to remain our best guide to the question of praxis and artistic subjectivity, despite his aesthetic shortcomings: there is no disaster or catastrophe that might be picked out as exemplary of a fall or break with the past, because modernity is the disaster and catastrophe we have to pass through in order emerge, transformed, on the other side. Errancy, and the productiveness of the error, then, are the necessary building blocks of this process of emergence, the means by which infinite ideation in art can continue to be secured.

CONCLUSION

Imagine a world in which everything you said and did was wrong, and everything everyone else said and did was wrong, a world, in fact, in which there was no consistency of meaning, or successful outcomes to any actions, only endless waywardness, dissolution and failure. Well, of course, such a world could not possibly exist, for we would not be in a position to observe or experience it: we would simply not be around. This is because our inability not to commit errors and mistakes in this instance, and, as such, our incapacity to sustain any form of natural continuity, would effectively mean that what we are talking about here is a form of life that is without a history: in short, our evolution as a species would never have got off the ground. I mention this in order to remind ourselves that after a book on the productiveness of errors, errors and mistakes do not, in themselves, guarantee our wellbeing, our intelligence or our humanity. On the contrary, errors of judgement and omission, failure to act correctly because of poor or incorrect knowledge, can cause pain, havoc and disaster, as we have discussed. If engineers get their calculations wrong, planes fall out of skies and bridges collapse.

Yet, without the presence and work of errors, it is hard to imagine that thinking and praxis and the continuity of being could sustain themselves, with any sense of futurity and purpose: instantaneous and transparent truth or the immediate and lasting solutions to problems would, as I have suggested in the Introduction, reduce thinking and practice to endless self-confirmation, and human temporality to a succession of dead and discontinuous moments. So, the error is something of a conundrum. It destroys continuity in being and purposeful action, and as such is to be avoided at all costs, but at the same time it secures and reproduces being, and as such is to be embraced and assimilated. In these terms it functions as a dialectical pivot between the requirement that humans need to reproduce themselves in a state of continuity and equanimity, and at the same time recognizes how this state of continuity and equanimity is insufficient and unsustainable. For if humans need to reproduce their conditions of existence in a state of stable continuity (that is, without the structural reoccurrence of error) continuity is not possible or conceivable without the heuristic and productive function of error (that is, the role of error as that which secures the freedoms of non-identity, misrecognition, and the failure or refusal to adapt). But if this is another way of saying, with Freud, that humans live in errancy as a condition of living in a state of continuity, it also a way of stating more dialectically that continuity and discontinuity, reproduction and excess, are locked into a mutually defining embrace. Thus to defend the 'error' is a fruitless task separate from the social, scientific and subjective and artistic conditions, and ultimately material conditions, of its emergence and possibility.

As we have noted, errors are required to do certain things, or achieve certain things, under their specific conditions of production and reproduction. In the philosophical formation of the subject, to register subjective or existential culpability, or the claims of sense experience. In the philosophy of science, to register the transmission of knowledge and truth-claims of the scientific subject as part of a process of judgement and assessment objectively external to the subject's individual powers of judgement. In psychoanalysis, to register the non-correspondence between the self-professed truths of the analysand and the undisclosed truth of his or her speech, and therefore the fact that the speech of the analysand says more than what he or she claims to be saying. In revolutionary political praxis, to register the discrepancy between intentions and outcomes, will and destiny, as a means by which revolutionaries are able to reflect, historically and critically, on political agency and strategy. In art to register the productive non-correlation between intentions and outcomes, actions and results, as a basis for a defence of infinite ideation and aesthetic reason. Now, as we have seen, these specific conditions of production and reproduction of the error, and as such the conditions of reflection and assimilation, operate under very different pressures and temporalities: reflection on and assimilation of errancy in revolutionary politics is invariably the outcome of the *longue durée*; reflection on and assimilation of errancy in relation to the indeterminacies of cognition is exercised through a far shorter period of time. Similarly the affective consequences of errors differ considerably. The consequences of the political error of judgement can be disastrous, a matter of life or death; the unforeseen outcome of indeterminate artistic practices a matter for creative assimilation; the error discovered through hard-won inductive experimentation a cause for celebration; the error in knowledge, risked by those without access to the relevant knowledge, a cause of shame. There is, therefore, no easy way of theoretically conjoining errors of omission and judgement across these different practices and disciplines, conditions and contexts: to do so is to de-register the different existential impacts and critical outcomes of the error across these domains, leaving us with a theory of error that is vague and underdetermined. Yet, as we have also seen, errors are not just locked into their specific disciplinary cycles of truth: they touch on the very conditions of being and non-being and, as such, touch on what it is to possess and renew our epistemological and ontological relationship with truth. To reiterate Hegel: errors and 'other being', when superseded, are still the necessary dynamic of truth. The error is not just where truth is absent, but where it is resourced and produced.

The very productiveness of the error as a supplemental logic across these disciplines and practices emerges, therefore, as a consequence of the non-positivistic relationship of these disciplines and practices to the social totality. Locating and defining errors, risking errors, assimilating errors, living with errors, being the means by which philosophy, philosophy of science, psychoanalysis, revolutionary political praxis, produce the negation of positivist science as the language of false totality. Thus, it is precisely when we make the direct connection between the reproduction of being and the reproduction of capitalism that the error, in this sense, takes on a metafunction. For, if the error is constitutive of the reproduction of being as a state of non-continuity in continuity, the metafunction of error becomes the speech and praxis of a historical *open-endedness* (historical open-endedness here being opposed to the continuity-as-repetition of the operational cycles of capitalism). The positing of the error as the exposure of untruth, and the pursuit and assimilation of the error as means of non-compliance, and negation as the production of truth, defies, resists and disrupts the stable conditions of this process of repetition-reproduction. Now this does not mean that scientific positivism and bourgeois culture have no space or use for the error. But science's way of understanding the error is to find it and expel it as soon as possible in order to bring the system under which it appears under control – hence the anti-positivistic argument represented by Mayo's work on scientific method that errors contain resources that are removed too fast in the interests of scientific efficiency and theoretical symmetry. Similarly, in the bourgeois social sciences the defence of political economy is, of course, premised on the cycles of production and consumption 'breaking down'. Indeed, such errors are seen as essentially constitutive of the creative life of the operational cycles of capitalism. But just as bourgeois Universal History has the capacity to assimilate all anomalies and discrepancies in the interests of progress, scientific positivism sees the errors immanent to political economy as endlessly reinscribable *in the same terms*. Consequently, this is where the productiveness of the error experiences a fundamental bifurcation: there is the error that re-establishes the untruth of the whole through discontinuity in continuity, in the interests of system transformation, and the error that reinforces the whole, through continuity in discontinuity, in the interests of system stabilization or expansion. Thus, it is not that bourgeois culture and Universal history are opposed to the truth-logic of the error, but rather that the place that they allot to it surrenders the actual to absolute necessity. And this is why the errancy of the artist is particularly significant to this metafunction of errancy within bourgeois society, for errancy in art is, above all, that which is defined, as we have seen, by its critique of absolute necessity.

But to establish artistic errancy as a crucial part of the critique of absolute necessity is not to place aesthetic reason over and above non-aesthetic reason. Aesthetic reason, in this sense, does not assume any kind of explanatory priority *over* the truths of political praxis, just as it cannot solve the problems of the scientific laboratory or the psychoanalyst's couch. But it is a condition of aesthetic negativity that, in its capacity to live with errors as a specific condition of art's infinite ideation, it is able to confront non-aesthetic reason, and thereby bourgeois society, with a powerful and continuous sense of noncompliance that subjects the positivization of non-aesthetic reason to its own limited rationality and positional crisis within the totality of capitalist social relations. Art, then, in the current period, is not that which allows us an image of our real selves, but that which *exposes the limits of the thinking of the system of as a whole*, and, as such, the predominant forms it presently takes, will surely dissolve when this system is superseded. As such, aesthetic reason is not an argument for abandoning philosophical realism, but rather offers, in its sovereign negation of the uses of positivism, a critique of non-aesthetic reason that the revolutionary critique of non-aesthetic reason is only able to demonstrate, not actually embody. In this way aesthetic reason allows the productiveness of the error to flourish in all its improbable, experimental and creative forms.

BIBLIOGRAPHY

Adereth, *The French Communist, A Critical History (1920–84): From Comintern to 'The Colours of France'*, Manchester University Press, Manchester, 1984

Adorno, Theodor W., *Negative Dialectics*, trans. E. B. Ashton, Routledge & Kegan Paul, London, 1973

Adorno, Thedor, W., *Aesthetic Theory*, trans. C. Lernhardt, Routledge & Kegan Paul, London, 1984

Adorno, Theodor W., *Hegel: Three Studies*, trans. Shierry Weber Nicholson, MIT Press, Cambridge MA and London, 1993

Ahearn, Barry, ed., *Pound/Zukofsky: Selected Letters of Ezra Pound and Louis Zukofsky*, New Directions Books, New York, 1987

Alembert, Jean de Rond de, *Essai sur les elements de philosophe, ou sur les principles of connoissances humanies*, in *Oeuvres de d'Alembert*, 5 vols, Editions Slatkine, Geneva, 1967

Althusser, Louis, *Writings on Psychoanalysis: Freud and Lacan*, trans. Jeffrey Mehlman, Columbia University Press, New York and Chichester, 1996

Antebi, Nicole, Dickey, Colin, and Herbst, Robbie, eds, *Failure: Experiments in Aesthetics and Social Practices*, published in conjunction with the *Journal of Aesthetics and Protest*, AK Press, Edinburgh and Los Angeles, 2008

Aristophanes, *Assembly of Women (Ecclesiazusae)*, trans. with introduction by Robert Mayhew, Prometheus Books, Amherst, New York, 1997

Arisotophanes, *Frogs and Other Plays*, trans. David Barrett, revised translation with an introduction and notes by Shomit Dutta, Penguin Books, London, 2007

Augustine, *On Free Choice of the Will*, trans. with introduction and notes by Thomas Williams, Hackett Publishing, Indianapolis and Cambridge, 1993

Bachelard, Gaston, *The Psychoanalysis of Fire* [1938], Routledge & Kegan Paul, 1964,

Badiou, Alain, *Being and Event*, Continuum, London and New York, 2005

Badiou, Alain, 'Three Negations', *Cardozo Law Review*, Vol. 29, No 5, 2008

Badiou, Alain, *The Theory of the Subject*, trans. Bruno Bosteels, Continuum, London and New York, 2009

Badiou, Alain, *Logics of Worlds: Being and Event 11*, trans. Alberto Toscano, Continuum, London and New York, 2009

Balibar, Étienne, 'Subjection and Subjectivation', *Supposing the Subject*, edited by Joan Copjec, Verso, London and New York, 1994

Barruel, Abbé, *History of Jacobinism*, 4 vols, trans. Robert Clifford, T. Burton, London, 1798

Baudelaire, Charles, *Art in Paris 1845–1862: Salons and Other Exhibitions*, trans. and ed. Jonathan Mayne, Phaidon Press, Oxford, 1981

Bates, David W., *Enlightenment Aberrations: Error & Revolution in France*, Cornell University Press, Ithaca and London, 2002

Brassier, Ray, *Nihil Unbound*, Palgrave, London, 2006

Bensaïd, Daniel, *Marx for Our Times: Adventures and Misadventures of a Critique*, trans. Gregory Elliot, Verso, London and New York, 2002

Bensaïd, Daniel, 'Theses of Resistance', *International Viewpoint*, No 362, December 2004

Bernstein, J. M. ed., *Classic and Romantic German Aesthetics*, Cambridge University Press, Cambridge, 2003

Bhaskar, Roy, *A Realist Theory of Science*, Harvester Press/Humanities Press, Brighton and New Jersey, 1978

Bhaskar, Roy, *Dialectic: The Pulse of Freedom*, Verso, London and New York, 1992

Bienvenu, Richard, ed., *The Ninth of Thermidor: The Fall of Robespierre*, Oxford University Press, Oxford, 1968

Black, Max, *The Prevalence of Humbug and Other Essays*, Cornell University Press, Ithaca and London, 1983

Bobbio, Noberto, *Studi Hegeliani*, Einaudi, Turin, 1981

Bonald, Louis de, *Oeuvres Completes*, 3 vols, J. P. Migne, Paris, 1858

Brecht, George, *Chance Imagery*, A Great Bear Pamphlet, Something Else Press, New York, 1957, in *Chance: Documents of Contemporary Art*, ed. Margaret Inverson, Whitechapel, London and MIT, Cambridge MA, 2010

Breton, André. 'The Automatic Message' [1933], trans. Antony Melville, in André Breton, Paul Eluard, Philippe Soupault, *The Automatic Message, The Magnestic Fields, The Immaculate Conception*, trans. David Gascoyne, Antony Melville and John Graham, Introduced by David Gascoyne and Antony Melville, Atlas, London, 1997

Burke, Edmund, *Reflections on the Revolution in France*, ed. L. G. Mitchell, Oxford University Press, Oxford, 2009

Cage, John, 'Indeterminancy' (1958), from *Silence: Lectures and Writings*, Wesleyan University Press, Middleton Connecticut, 1961

Cage, John, 'Interview with John Cage' by Silvy-Panet Raymond and John Roberts, *Performance Magazine*, No 7, 1980

Callinicos, Alex, *Theories and Narratives: Reflections on the Philosophy of History*, Polity Press, Cambridge, 1995

Canguilhem, Georges, 'A New Concept in Pathology: Error', *The Normal and the Pathological*, trans. Carolyn R. Fawcett in collaboration with Robert S. Cohen, with an introduction by Michel Foucault, Zone Books, New York, 1991

Caper, Robert, *Building Out Into the Dark: Theory and Observation in Science and Psychoanalysis*, Routledge, London and New York, 2009

Carey, Sorcha, *Pliny's Catalogue of Culture: Art and Empire in the* Natural History, Oxford University Press, Oxford, 2003

Carnap, Rudolf, 'Truth and Confirmation' in H. Feigl and W. Sellars eds, *Readings in Philosophical Analysis*, Appleton-Century-Crofts, New York, 1949

Carnap, Rudolf, *The Unity of Science*, trans. with introduction by Max Black, Thoemmes Press, Bristol, 1997

Caron, Pierre, *Paris Pendant la Terreur. Rapports des agents secrets du Ministre de l'Interieur*, Société de l'histoire de France, Paris, 1940

Cascone, Kim, 'The Aesthetics of Failure: "Post-Digital" Tendencies in Contemporary Music', *Computer Music Journal*, 24:4, pp12-18, MIT, Winter 2000

Castilhon, Jean-Louis, *Essai sur les erreurs et les superstitions anciennes et modernes*, 2 vols, Knoe & Eslinger, Frankfurt, 1766

Certeau, Michel de, *The Writing of History* [1975], trans. Tom Conley, Columbia University Press, New York, 1988

Cetina, Karin Knorr *Epistemic Cultures: How the Sciences Make Knowledge*, Harvard University Press, Cambridge MA, 1999

Clark, Andy, *Being There*, MIT Press, Cambridge MA, 1997

Clark, T. J., *Farewell to an Idea: Episodes from a History of Modernism*, Yale University Press, New Haven, CN, and London, 2001

Clifford, William Kingdon, 'The Ethics of Belief' [1877] in, *The Ethics of Belief and Other Essays*, Prometheus Books, Amherst, New York, 1999.

Cominel, George C., *Rethinking the French Revolution: Marxism and the Revisionist Challenge*, with a forward by George Rudé, Verso, London and New York, 1987

Condillac, Etienne Bonnott de, *An Essay on the Origin of Human Knowledge, Being a Supplement to Mr. Locke's Essay on Human Understanding*, trans. Thomas Nugent [1756], Scholars Fascimiles, Gainesville, Florida, 1971

Condorcet, Maquis (Nicolas) de, *Sketch for a Historical Picture of the Progress of the Human Mind* [1795], trans. June Barraclough, Weidenfeld & Nicolson, London, 1955

Critchley, Simon, *Infinitely Demanding*, Verso, London and New York, 2007

Davidson, Donald, *Essays in Actions and Events*, Oxford University Press, Oxford, 1980

Debray, Régis, *Revolution in the Revolution?: Armed Struggle and Political Struggle in Latin America* [1967], trans. Bobbye Ortiz, Penguin, Harmondsworth, 1968

Denning, Michael, *The Cultural Front: The Laboring of American Culture in the Twentieth Century*, Verso, London and New York, 1997

Descartes, René, *Meditations on First Philosophy: with selections from the Objections and Replies*, ed. John Cottingham, with an introduction by Bernard Williams, Cambridge University Press, Cambridge, 1986

Devitt, Michael, 'Minimalist Truth', review article Paul Horwich, *Truth*, Basil Blackwell, Oxford University Press, 1990, *Mind and Language*, 6, 1991

Dicker, Georges, *Kant's Theory of Knowledge: An Analytical Introduction*, Oxford University Press, Oxford and New York, 2004

Dickie, George, *Art and Value*, Blackwell, Oxford, 2001

Diderot, Denis, *Pensées sur l'interpretation de la nature*, in *Oeuvres completes*, ed. Herbert Dieckmann et al., Hermann, Paris 1975–95

Dolar, Maden, 'The Phrenology of Spirit', in *Supposing the Subject*, ed. Joan Copjec, Verso, London and New York, 1994

Duchamp, Marcel, *The Essential Writings of Marcel Duchamp*, eds M. Sanouillet and E. Peterson, Thames & Hudson, London, 1975

Earman, John, 'Carnap, Kuhn and the Philosophy of Scientific Methodology' in Paul Horwich ed., *World Changes: Thomas Kuhn and the Nature of Science*, MIT Press, Cambridge, MA and London, 1993

Edgley, Roy, *Reason in Theory and Practice*, Hutchinson, London, 1969

Endnotes, No 1, Preliminary Materials for a Balance Sheet of the Twentieth Century, October 2008

Engels, Fredrick, *Anti-Dühring: Herr Eugen Dühring's Revolution in Science*, Progress Publishers, Moscow, 1977

Engels, Frederick, *Ludwig Feuerbach and the End of Classical German Philosophy*, Foreign Language Press, Peking, 1976

Errorist Internacional, 'Notes on De-Education and Errorism', *Newspaper of the Platform "Chto Delat/What is to be Done?"*, Issue No 14: Self-Education, September 2006

Fauré, Christine, *Les declarations des droits de l'homme de 1789*, Text réunis et présentés par Christine Fauré, Editions Payot, Paris, 1988

Feyerabend, Paul, 'Consolations of the Specialist' in *Criticism and the Growth of Knowledge*, eds Imre Lakatos & Alan Musgrave, Cambridge University Press, Cambridge, 1970

Feyerabend, Paul, *Against Method: Outline of an Anarchist Theory of Knowledge*, Verso, London, 1978

Fichte, Johan Gottlieb, 'Reclamation of the Freedom of Thought for the Princes of Europe, Who Have Oppressed It Until Now', in James Schimdt ed., *What is Enlightenment? Eighteenth-Century Answers and Twentieth Century Questions*, University of California Press, Berkeley, Los Angeles, 1996

Field, Hartry 'Deflationist Views of Meaning and Content', in Simon Blackburn and Keith Simmons, eds, *Truth*, Oxford University Press, Oxford, 1999

Field, Hartry, 'Stalnaker on Intentionality' in *Truth and the Absence of Fact*, Oxford University Press, Oxford, 2001

Fleischmann, Eugene, *La Philosophie de Politique de Hegel – Sous Forme D'un Commentaire Des 'Fondements De La Philosphie Du Droit'*, Gallimard, Paris, 1992

Foucault, Michel 'Introduction', Georges Canguilhem, *The Normal and the Pathological*, trans. Carolyn R. Fawcett in collaboration with Robert S. Cohen, Zone Books, New York, 1991

Freud, Sigmund, 'Psychoanalysis and Legal Evidence' [1906], in James Strachey ed., *The Standard Edition of the Complete Psychological Works of Sigmund Freud*, Vol. IX, trans. James Strachey in collaboration with Anna Freud, and assisted by

Alix Strachey and Alan Tyson, Hogarth Press and the Institute of Psycho-analysis, London, 1959

Freud, Sigmund, 'Recommendations to Physicians Practising Psychoanalysis' [1912], in James Strachey, ed., *The Standard Edition of the Complete Psychological Works of Sigmund Freud, Volume XII (1911-1913): The Case of Schreber, Papers on Technique and Other Works*, trans. James Strachey in collaboration with Anna Freud, and assisted by Alix Strachey and Alan Tyson, Hogarth Press and the Institute of Psychoanalysis, London, 1958

Freud, Sigmund,'Beyond the Pleasure Principle', in *On Metapsychology: The Theory of Psychoanalysis*, trans. under James Strachey, Penguin Books, Harmondsworth, 1991

Freud, Sigmund, 'Errors', *The Psychopathology of Everyday Life*, in Alix Strachey and Alan Tyson eds, trans. James Strachey in collaboration with Anna Freud, Hogarth Press and the Institute of Psychoanalysis, London, 1991

Furet, François, *Interpreting the French Revolution*, Cambridge University Press, Cambridge, 1981

Gadamer, Hans-George, *Hegel's Dialectic: Five Hermeneutical Studies*, trans. with introduction by P. Christopher Smith, Yale University Press, New Haven and London, 1976

Gamboni, Dario, *Potential Images: Ambiguity and Indeterminancy in Modern Art*, trans. Mark Treharne, Reaktion Books, London, 2002

Giere, Ronald N., *Understanding Scientific Reasoning*, Holt, Rinehart and Winston, New York, 1984

Giere, Ronald N., 'Distributed Cognition Without Distributed Knowing', *Social Epistemology*, Vol. 21, No 3, July-Sept 2007

Godechot, Jacques, *The Counter-Revolution: Doctrine and Action 1789–1804*, Princeton University Press, Princeton, New Jersey, 1981

Gouges, Olympe de, *Déclaration des droits de la femme at de la citoyenne*, Mille et une nuit, Paris, 2003

Gough, Maria, *The Artist as Producer: Russian Constructivism in Revolution*, California University Press, Berkeley and Los Angeles, 2005

Grice, H. P., 'Logic and Conversation', *Syntax and semantics 3: Speech Arts*, 1975

Guérin, Daniel, *Class Struggle in the First French Republic: Bourgeois and Bras Nus 1793–1795*, trans. Ian Patterson, Pluto Press, London, 1977

Gupta, Anil, 'A Critique of Deflationism', in Simon Blackburn and Keith Simmons, eds, *Truth*, Oxford University Press, Oxford, 1999

Michael Devitt, 'Minimalist Truth', review article Paul Horwich, *Truth*, Basil Blackwell, Oxford University Press, 1990, *Mind and Language*, 6, 1991, pp. 273–83

Guérin, Daniel, *Class Struggle in the First French Republic: Bourgeois and Bras Nus 1793–1795*, trans. Ian Patterson, Pluto Press, London 1977

Gutov, Dmitry, 'Learn, Learn and Lean', in Grant Watson, Gerrie van Noord and Gavin Everall, eds, *Make Everything New: A Project on Communism*, Bookworks/Project Arts Centre, London and Dublin, 2006

Habermas, Jürgen, *The Theory of Communicative Action, Vol. 1: Reason and the Rationalization of Society*, trans. Thomas McCarthy, Beacon Press, Boston, 1985

Hacking, Ian, *Representing and Intervening: Introductory Topics in the Philosophy of Natural Science,* Cambridge University Press, Cambridge, 1983

Harré, Rom, *The Philosophy of Science: An Introductory Survey*, Oxford University Press, Oxford, 1974

Hegel, G. W. F., *Phenomenology of Mind,* trans. J. B. Baillie, Allen & Unwin, London, 1931

Hegel, G. W. F., *The Philosophy of History*, trans. J. Sibree, with a preface by Charles Hegel, and a new introduction by C. J. Friedrich, Dover, New York 1956

Hegel, G. W. F., *Hegel's Philosophy of Right*, trans. T. M. Knox, Oxford University Press, Oxford, 1967

Hegel, G. W. F.,*The Science of Logic*, [1830], trans. William Wallace, with a foreword by J. N. Finlay, Oxford University Press, Oxford, 1975

Hegel, G. W. F., *Hegel's Logic*, trans. William Wallace, with forward by J. N. Findlay, Oxford University Press, Oxford, 1975

Hegel, G. W. F., *Aesthetics: Lectures on Fine Art*, trans. T. M. Knox, 2 vols, Clarendon Press, Oxford, 1975

Hegel, G. W. F., *Phenomenology of Spirit*, trans. A. V. Miller with analysis of the text and foreword by J. N. Findlay, Oxford University Press, Oxford, 1977

Hegel, G. W. F., *The Encyclopedia Logic*, trans. T. F. Geraets et al., Hackett Publishing, Indianapolis, 1991

Hegel, G. W. F., 'Preface' to the *Phenomenology of Spirit*, trans. and running commentary by Yirmiyahu Yovel, Princeton University Press, Princeton and Oxford, 2005

Hegel, G. W. F., *Lectures on Logic: Berlin 1831*, transcribed by Karl Hegel, trans. Clark Butler, Indiana University Press, Bloomington and Indianapolis, 2008

Heidegger, Martin, 'On the Essence of Truth', in *Basic Writings*, ed. David Farrell Krell, Routledge, London 1996

Hibbert, Christopher, *King Mob: The Story of Lord George Gordon and the Riots of 1780*, Longmans, Green & Co, London, 1958

Holtermann, Martin, *Der deutsche Aristophanes. Die Rezeption eines politischen Dichters im 19. Jahrhundert. Hypomnemata, 155*, Vandenhoeck & Ruprecht, Göttingen, 2004

Horwich, Paul, *Truth*, Oxford University Press, Oxford, 1990

Hübner, Karl, *Critique of Scientific Reason*, University of Chicago Press, Chicago, 1985

Huson, Timothy, 'Truth and Contradiction: Reading Hegel with Lacan', *Lacan: The Silent Partners*, ed. Slavoj Žižek, Verso 2006

Hurwitz, Brian and Sheikh, Aziz, *Health Care Errors and Patient Safety*, John Wiley, London, 2009

Hutchins, Edwin, *Cognition in the Wild*, Harvard University Press, Cambridge MA, 1995

Inwagen, Peter Van, 'Is it Wrong Everywhere, Always, and for Anyone to

Believe Anything on Insufficient Evidence?' available at http://comp.uark.
edu/~senor/wrong.html

Israel, Jonathan I., *Radical Enlightenment: Philosophy and the Making of Modernity 1650–1750*, Oxford University Press, Oxford and New York, 2001

Iverson, Margaret, ed., *Chance: Documents of Contemporary Art*, Whitechapel, London and MIT, Cambridge MA, 2010

Jellinek, Franck, *The Paris Commune of 1871*, Left Book Club/Victor Gollancz, London, 1937

Kant, Immanuel, *Perpetual Peace: A Philosophical Essay* [1795] trans. with introduction and notes by M. Campbell Smith, and a Preface by L. Latta, George Allen and Unwin, London, 1917

Kant, Immanuel, *Critique of Pure Reason*, trans. J. M. D. Meiklejohn, Prometheus Books, Buffalo, New York, 1990

Kant, Immanuel, 'On a Newly Arisen Superior Tone in Philosophy', in *Raising the Tone of Philosophy: Late Essays by Immanuel Kant, Transformative Critique by Jacques Derrida*, ed. Peter Fenves, John Hopkins University Press, Baltimore and London, 1993

Kant, Immanuel, *Prolegomena: To Any Future Metaphysics That Can Qualify as Science*, trans. Paul Carus, Open Court, Chicago and La Salle, Illinois, 1994

Kaprow, Allen, *Assemblage, Environments and Happenings*, Harry N. Abrams, New York, 1966

Kuhn, Thomas, *The Structure of Scientific Revolutions*, second edition, University of Chicago Press, Chicago, 1970

Lacan, Jacques, *The Four Fundamental Concepts of Psychoanalysis*, Penguin Books, Harmondsworth, 1979

Lacan, Jacques, *The Seminar of Jacques Lacan, Book I: Freud's Papers on Technique 1953–1954*, ed. Jacques-Alain Miller, trans. with notes by John Forrester, Cambridge University Press, Cambridge, 1988

Lacan, Jacques, *The Seminar of Jacques Lacan: Book II, The Ego in Freud's Theory and in the Technique of Psychoanalysis 1954–1955*, ed. Jacques-Alain Miller, trans. Sylvana Tomasell, with notes by John Forrester, W. W. Norton, New York, 1991

Lacan, Jacques, *Ecrits: A Selection*, trans. Bruce Fink, in collaboration with Héloise Fink and Russell Grigg, W. W. Norton & Company, New York and London, 2002

Lacan, Jacques, *The Seminar of Jacques Lacan, Book XVII: The Other Side of Psychoanalysis*, trans. Russell Grigg, W. W. Norton, New York and London, 2007

Lacan, Jacques 'Of Structure as an Inmixing of an Otherness Prerequisite to Any Subject Whatever' (Lacan talk at John Hopkins University, Baltimore, 1966), available at http://www.braungardt.com/Psychoanalysis/Lacan-Baltimore.htm

Lakatos, Imre, *The Methodology of Scientific Research Programmes: Philosophical Papers, Vol. 1*, Cambridge University Press, Cambridge, 1979

Laplanche, Jean, *Life and Death in Psychoanalysis*, trans. with an introduction by Jeffrey Mehlman, John Hopkins University Press, Baltimore and London, 1976

Laplanche, Jean, *Essays on Otherness*, Routledge, London and New York, 1999

Lecercle, Jean Jacques, and Riley, Denise, *The Force of Language,* Palgrave Macmillan, Basingstoke, 2004

Lecercle, Jean Jacques, *A Marxist Philosophy of Language*, trans. Gregory Elliot, Brill, Leiden and Boston, 2006

Lefebvre, Georges, *The French Revolution: From Its Origins to 1793* [1930], trans. Elizabeth Moss Evanson, with a foreward by Paul H.Beik, Routledge, London and New York, 2009

Lefebvre, Henri *Introduction to Modernity: Twelve Preludes* [1962], trans. John Moore, Verso, London and New York, 1995

Lefebvre, Henri, *Vol. II, Critique of Everyday Life: Foundations for a Sociology of the Everyday* [1961], trans. John Moore, with a preface by Michael Trebitsch, Verso, London and New York, 2002

Lenin, V. I ., *Collected Works*, Vol. 13, Progress Publishers, Moscow, 1972

Lenin, V. I., *Collected Works*, Vol. 27, Progress Publishers, Moscow, 1972

Lessing, Gottfried, *Laocoön: An Essay on the Limits of Poetry and Painting*, Farrar, Straus and Giroux, New York, 1969

Lewitt, Sol, 'Sentences on Conceptual Art', *Art-Language*, No 1, May 1969

Lifshitz, Mikail, *Krise des Häfslichen. Vom Kubismus zur Pop Art*, trans. Helmut Barth, VEB Verlag der Kunst, Dresden, 1972

Locke, John, *An Essay Concerning Human Understanding*, abridged and edited by John W. Yolton, Everyman, J. M. Dent, London, 1993

Losurdo, Domenico, *Hegel and the Freedom of Moderns*, trans. Marella and Jon Morris, Duke University Press, Durham and London, 2004

Luhmann, Niklas, *Art as a Social System*, trans. Eva M.Knodt, Stanford University Press, Stanford, 2000

Lukács, Georg, *History and Class Consciousness*, Merlin, London, 1968

Luxemburg, Rosa, 'Leninism or Marxism?' [1904], in *The Russian Revolution and Leninism or Marxism?*, introduction by Bertram P. Wolfe, University of Michigan, Ann Arbor, 1961

Luxemburg, Rosa, 'On the Situation in the Russian Social Democracy' [1911], trans. Mike Jones, in *Rosa Luxemburg, Selected Political Literary Writings, Revolutionary History*, Vol. 10, No 1, Merlin Press, London, 2009

MacDonald, Graham, 'The Role of Experience in Popper's Philosophy of Science and Political Philosophy', in *Karl Popper: Critical Appraisals*, Routledge, London and New York, 2004

Maistre, Joseph de, *Considérations sur la France*, avant-propos de Jean Boissel; texte établi, preésenté, et annoté pa Jean-Louis Darcel, Editions Slatkine, Geneva, 1980

Malabou, Catherine, *What Should We Do with Our Brains?* Forward by Marc Jeannerod, trans. Sebastian Rand, Fordham University Press, New York, 2008

Marcuse, Herbert, [1936], trans. as *A Study on Authority*, by Joris De Bres, New Left Books, London, 1972

Marx Karl, *Capital*, Vol. 1, Lawrence & Wishart, London, 1970

Marx, Karl, Lenin, V. I., and Fedorousky, Nikita, *The Civil War in France: The Paris Commune* [1871], International Publishers, New York, 1988

Mayer, Arno J., *The Furies: Violence and Terror in the French and Russian Revolutions*, Princeton University Press, Princeton, New Jersey and Oxford, 2000

Mayo, Deborah G., *Error and the Growth of Experimental Knowledge*, University of Chicago Press, Chicago and London, 1996

Mazauric, Claude, *Sur la Révolution française.*, Editions Sociales, Paris, 1970

McCarney, Joseph, *Social Theory and the Crisis of Marxism*, Verso, London and New York, 1990

MacGregor, David, *The Communist Ideal in Hegel and Marx*, University of Toronto Press, Toronto, 1984

Menke, Christophe, *The Sovereignity of Art: Aesthestic Negativity in Adorno and Derrida*, trans. Neil Solomon, MIT, Cambridge, Massachusetts and London, 1998

Menn, Stephen, *Descartes and Augustine*, Cambridge University Press, Cambridge, 1998

Milner, Jean Claude, 'The Doctrine of Science', trans. Oliver Feltham, *Umbr(a)*, No 1, 'Science and Truth', 2000

Mitchell, Stanley, 'Mikhail Lifshits: A Marxist Conservative', in Andrew Hemingway, ed., *Marxism and the History of Art: From William Morris to the New Left*, Pluto Press, London, 2006

Morel, Genevieve, 'Science and Psychonalysis', trans. Karen M. Fischer, *Umbr(a)*, No 1, 'Science and Truth', 2000

Morris, Robert, 'Notes on Sculpture Part 4'[1969] in *Continuous Project Altered Daily: The Writings of Robert Morris*, MIT Press, Cambridge MA, 1993

Namier, Lewis, *The Structure of Politics at the Accession of George III*, Macmillan, London, 1957

Nancy, Jean-Luc, *Hegel: The Restlessness of the Negative*, trans. Jason Smith and Steven Miller, University of Minnesota Press, Minneapolis and London, 2002

Nietzsche, Friedrich, *The Will To Power*, trans. Walter Kauffmann and R. J. Hollingdale, and ed. with commentary by Walter Kauffman, Vintage Books, New York, 1968

Nietzsche, Friedrich, *Untimely Meditations*, ed. Daniel Breazeale and trans. R. J. Hollingdale, Cambridge University Press, Cambridge, 1997

Nobus Dany, *Jacques Lacan and the Freudian Practice of Psychoanalysis*, Routledge, London, 2000

Nobus, Dany and Quinn, Malcolm, *Knowing Nothing, Staying Stupid*, Routledge, London and New York, 2004

Novalis 'Goethe', in J. M. Bernstein, ed., *Classic and German Romantic Aesthetics*, Cambridge University Press, Cambridge, 2003

Noys, Ben, Review article on *Revolution in Psychology: Alienation to Emancipation*, Ian Parker, Pluto Press, London, 2007 and *The Lacanian Left: Psychoanalysis, Theory, and Politics*, Yannis Stavrakakis, State University of New York Press, New York 2007 in *Historical Materialism* No 17, 2009

Noys, Ben, *The Persistence of the Negative: A Critique of Contemporary Continental Theory*, Edinburgh University Press, Edinburgh, 2010

O'Neill, John, ed., *Hegel's Dialectics of Desire and Recognition: Texts and Commentaries*, State University of New York Press, New York, 1996

Orwell, George, 'Looking Back at the Spanish Civil War', *A Collection of Essays*, Doubleday, Garden City, 1957

Parfit, Derek, *Reasons and Persons*, Oxford University Press, Oxford, 1984

Pateman, Trevor, *Language, Truth & Politics: Towards a Radical Theory for Communication*, Jean Stroud, Lewes, 1975

Peirce, Charles Sanders, *The Essential Peirce*, 2 vols, ed. Nathan Houser, Christian Kloesel and the Peirce Edition Project, Indiana University Press, Bloomington, Indiana, 1992 and 1998

Plato, *Theaetus*, ed. Bernard Williams, trans. M. J. Levett, revised by Miles Bunyeat, Hackett, Indianapolis, Cambridge University Press, 1992

Pliny, *Natural History*, Book 35: An Account of Paintings and Colours, available at http://www.perseus.tufts.edu/hopper/

Popper, Karl, 'Normal Science and Its Dangers' in *Criticism and the Growth of Knowledge*, eds Imre Lakator and Alan Musgrove, Cambridge University Press, Cambridge, 1970

Popper, Karl, 'Epistemology Without a Knowing Subject', in *Objective Knowledge: An Evolutionary Approach*, Oxford University Press, Oxford, 1979

Popper, Karl, *The Logic of Scientific Discovery* [1935], Routledge, London and New York, 1992

Rancière, Jacques, *The Emancipated Spectator*, trans. Gregory Elliott, Verso, London, 2009

Rancière Jacques, *The Aesthetic Unconscious*, trans. Debra Keates and James Swenson, Polity Press, Cambridge and Malden MA, 2009

Rauschenberg, Robert, 'Interview with Dorothy Seckler', Archives of American Art, Smithsonian Institute, quoted in Margaret Iverson, ed., *Chance*, Whitechapel Gallery and MIT, London and Cambridge MA

Reason, James, *Human Error*, Cambridge University Press, Cambridge, 1990

Reinhold, Karl Leonhard, 'Thoughts on Enlightenment', first published in *Der Teutsche Merkur*, 1784, in James Schmidt, ed., *What is Enlightenment? Eighteenth-Century Answers and Twentieth Century Questions*, University of California Press, Berkeley, Los Angeles, London, 1996

Rescher, Nicholas, *Error: (On Our Predicament When Things Go Wrong)*, University of Pittsburgh Press, Pittsburgh PA, 2007

Ricoeur, Paul *Memory, History, Forgetting*, trans. Kathleen Blamey and David Pellauer, University of Chicago Press, Chicago and London, 2004

Richardson, Al, 'Introduction', Al Richardson ed., *Trotsky and the Origins of Trotskyism: Alfred Rosmer, Boris Souvarine, Emile Fabrol and Antoine Clavez*, Francis Boutle Publishers, London 2002

Roberts, John, '21 Aphorisms', *Cabinet Magazine*, No 1, 2000

Roberts, John, 'The Practice of Failure', *Cabinet Magazine*,

Roberts, John, *Philosophizing the Everyday: Revolutionary Praxis and the Fate of Cultural Theory*, Pluto Press, 2006

Robespierre, Maximillian, *Robespierre: Textes Choises*, Introduction et Notes Explicatives, par Jean Poperen, Vol. 2, of 3 vols, Paris, 1973

Robespierre, Maximillian, *Robespierre:Virtue and Terror*, introduction by Slavoj Žižek, texts selected and annotated by Jean Ducange, trans. John Howe, Verso, London and New York, 2007

Roche, Mark-William, *Tragedy and Comedy. A Systematic Study and a Critique of Hegel*, Albany, New York, 1998

Roche, Mark-William, 'Hegel's Theory of Comedy in the Context of Hegelian and Modern Reflections on Comedy', *Revue internationale de philosophie*, No 221, 2002/3

Rockwell, W. Teed, *Neither Brain Nor Ghost: A Nondualist alternative to the Mind-Brain Identity Theory*, MIT, Cambridge MA & London, 2005

Rose, Gillian, *Mourning Becomes the Law: Philosophy and Representation,* Cambridge University Press, Cambridge, 1996

Rose, Margaret, *Reading the Young Marx and Engels: Poetry, Parody and the Censor*, Croom Helm, London and Totowa, New Jersey, 1978

Ross, Kristin, *The Emergence of Social Space: Rimbaud and the Paris Commune*, Verso, London and New York, 2008

Rotscher, Theodor H., *Aristophanes und sein Zeitalter: Eine philologischphilosophische Abhandlung zur Alterthumsforschung*, Vossiche Buchhandlung, Berlin, 1827

Rudé, Georges, *The Crowd in the French Revolution*, Oxford University Press, London, 1959

Sankey, Howard, 'Kuhn's Changing Concept of Incommensurability', *The British Journal for the Philosophy of Science*, Vol. 44. No 4. Dec 1993

Santayana, George, *Egotism in German Philosophy* [1915], Haskell House Publishing, Brooklyn, New York, 1971

Santayana, George, *Reason in Art: Volume Four of 'The Life of Reason'* [1905], Dover Publications, New York, 1982

Sajer, Guy, *The Forgotten Soldier*, Phoenix, Cassell, London, 1999.

Schick, Fredrick, *Ambiguity and Logic*, Cambridge University Press, Cambridge, 2003

Schlegel, Friedrich 'Critical Fragments' [1797], in *Classical and Romantic German Aesthetics*, ed. J. M. Bernstein, Cambridge University Press, Cambridge, 2003

Schlegel, Friedrich, '*Athenaeum* Fragments', [1798], in *Classic and Romantic German Aesthetics*, ed. J. M. Bernstein, Cambridge University Press, Cambridge, 2003

Schmidt, James, ed., *What is Enlightenment?: Eighteenth-Century Answers and Twentieth Century Questions,* University of California Press, Berkeley, Los Angeles and London, 1996

Schopenhauer, Arthur, 'On the Suffering of the World' in *On the Suffering of the World*, trans. R. J. Hollingdale, Penguin Books, London, 2004

Robert Rauschenberg, 'Interview with Dorothy Seckler', Archives of American Art, Smithsonian Institute, quoted in *Chance, Documents of Contemporary Art*, ed. Margaret Iverson, Whitechapel, London and MIT, Cambridge MA, 2010

Serge, Victor, 'Marxism in Our Time', *Partisan Review*, Vol. 5, No 3, 1938

Serge, Victor, *From Lenin to Stalin*, trans. Ralph Manheim, Pathfinder Press, London and New York, 1973

Serge, Victor, *Year One of the Russian Revolution* [1930], trans. and ed. Peter Sedgwick with a new preface by Paul Foot, Bookmarks/Pluto Press/Writers and Readers, London and New York, 1992

Serge, Victor, *The Serge–Trotsky Papers: Correspondence and Other Writings between Victor Serge and Leon Trotsky*, ed. and introduced by David Cotterill, trans. Peter Sedgwick and Maria Enzenberger with introductions by Philip Spencer and Susan Weissman, Pluto Press, London, 1994

Serge, Victor, *The Case of Comrade Tulayev*, introduction by Susan Sontag, trans. Willard R. Trask, New York Review of Books, New York, 2004

Serge, Victor, *Unforgiving Years*, translated with an introduction by Richard Greenman, New York Review of Books, New York, 2008

Serge, Victor, *Year One of the Russian Revolution* [1930], trans. and ed. Peter Sedgwick with a new preface by Paul Foot, Bookmarks/Pluto Press/Writers and Readers, London and New York, 1992

Shahn, Ben, 'In Defence of Chaos', in the *Aspen Papers: Twenty Years of Design Theory, from the International Design Conference in Aspen*, ed., with commentary by Reyner Banham, Pall Mall Press, London, 1974

Shalzi, Cosma 'Review of Deborah Mayo's *Error and the Growth of Knowledge*' available at http://www.cscs.umich.edu/-crshaliz/reviews/error/

Sieyès, Emmanuel Joseph, 'An Essay on Privileges' in *Emmanuel Joseph Sieyès: Political Writings, Including the Debate between Sieyès and Tom Paine in 1791*, ed. with an introduction and translation of 'What Is the Third Estate?' by Michael Somescher, Hackett Publishing Company, Inc., Indianapolis/Cambridge, 2003

Sieyès, Emmanuel Joseph, 'The Explanatory Note of M. Sieyès, in Answer to the Letter of Mr. Paine, and to Several Other Provocations of the Same Sort', *Emmanuel Joseph Sieyès, Political Writings, Including the Debate between Sieyès and Tom Paine in 1791*, ed. with an introduction and translation of 'What Is the Third Estate?' by Michael Somescher, Hackett Publishing Company, Inc., Indianapolis/Cambridge, 2003

Soboul, Alfred, *La Civilization et la Révolution Française*, 3 vols., Arthaud, Paris, 1970, 1982–83.

Spinoza, Baruch, *Ethics and On the Correction of the Understanding*, trans. Andrew Boyle, with introduction by T. S. Gregory, Dent, London and New York, 1959

Stavrakakis, Yannis, *Lacan and the Political*, Routledge, London and New York, 1999

Strindberg, August, 'The New Arts! on, The Role of Chance in Artistic Creation', in *August Strindberg: Selected Essays*, ed. and translated by Michael Robinson, Cambridge University Press, Cambridge, 1996

Tarski, Alfred, 'The Semantic Conception of Truth and the Foundations of Semantics', reprinted in *Truth*, eds by Simon Blackburn and Keith Simmons, Oxford University Press, 1999

Thompson, E. P., *Poverty of Theory: or an Orrery of Errors* Merlin Press, London, 1978

Thomson, Phil, 'Atoms and Errors: Towards a History of Aesthetics of MicroSound', *Organised Sound*, 9: 2, pp. 207–218, Cambridge University Press, 2004

Toulmin, Stephen, 'Does the Distinction between Normal and Revolutionary Science Hold Water?', in *Criticism and the Growth of Knowledge*, eds Imre Lakatos and Alan Musgrave, Cambridge University Press, Cambridge 1970

Trotsky, Leon, *Revolution Betrayed: What Is the Soviet Union and Where Is It Going?* New Park Publications, London, 1967

Trotsky, Leon, 'One More Kronstadt' in *The Serge–Trotsky Papers*, ed. and introduced by David Cotterill, trans. Peter Sedgwich and Maria Enzenberger, with introductions by Philip Spencer and Susan Weissman, Pluto Press, London, 1994

Trotsky, Leon, 'The Capture of Power was Possible in May', in *The Serge–Trotsky Papers*, ed. and introduced by David Cotterill, trans. Peter Sedgwich and Maria Enzenberger, with introductions by Philip Spencer and Susan Weissman, Pluto Press, London, 1994

Trotsky, Leon, 'The Hue and Cry over Kronstadt', in *The Serge–Trotsky Papers*, ed. and introduced by David Cotterill, trans. Peter Sedgwick and Maria Enzenberger, with introductions by Philip Spencer and Susan Weissman, Pluto Press, London, 1994

Tulloch, John, and Lupton, Deborah, *Risk and Everyday Life*, Sage, London, 2003

Turgot, Anne-Robert-Jacques, *Oeuvres de Turgot*, ed. Eugene Daine and Hyppoltyte Dussard, 2 vols, Guillaumin, Paris, 1844

Tristan Tzara, Tristan 'Dada Manifesto' (1918) in *Dadas On Art*, ed. Lucy R. Lippard, Prentice Hall Inc., Englewood Cliffs, New Jersey, 1971

Vallejo, César, *Trilce,* Sheep Meadow, ed. Stanley Moss, trans. Rebecca Seiferie, Riverdale, New York 1992

Van Duzer, Charles Hunter, *Contribution of the Ideologues to French Revolutionary Thought*, John Hopkins University Press, Baltimore, 1935

Vaneigem, Raoul, *The Book of Pleasures* [1979], trans. John Fullerton, Pending Press, London, 1983

Vasari, Giorgio, *Lives of the Artists*, ed. Marilyn Aronberg Lavin, trans. Jonathan Foster, Dover Publications, New York, 2005.

Vassalli, Giovanni, 'The Epistemological Transformations of Psychoanalysis', available at http://www.epf-eu.org/Public/Article.php?ID=3855&ancestor1 =3715&page=

Vattimo, Gianni, Girard, René, *Christianity, Truth, and Weak Faith*, ed. P. Antonello, Columbia University Press, New York, 2009

Watson, Stephen, 'On the Errancy of Dasein', *diacritics*, 19.3-4, Fall/Winter, 1989

Wee, Cecilia, *Material Falsity and Error in Descartes' "Meditations"*, Routledge, London and New York, 2006

Wittgenstein, Ludwig, *On Certainty*, eds G. E. M. Anscombe and G. H. von Wright, trans. Denis Paul and G. E. M. Anscombe, Blackwell, Oxford, 1969

Wittgenstein, Ludwig, *Culture and Value*, trans. Peter Winch, ed. G. H. von Wright, in collaboration with Heikki Nyman, Basil Blackwell, Oxford, 1980

Yolton, John W., *Locke and French Materialism*, Oxford University Press, Oxford, 1991

Yovel, Yirmiyahu, *Kant and the Philosophy of History*, Princeton University Press, Princeton, New Jersey, 1980

Žižek, Slavoj, *In Defense of Lost Causes*, Verso, London and New York, 2008

Zupancic, Alenka, *Ethics of the Real: Kant, Lacan*, Verso, London and New York, 2000

Zupancic, Alenka, *The Odd One in: On Comedy*, MIT Press, Cambridge MA and London, 2008

NOTES

INTRODUCTION: THE RENEWAL OF TRUTH

1 Nicholas Rescher, *Error: (On Our Predicament When Things Go Wrong)*, University of Pittsburgh Press, Pittsburgh PA, 2007, p. 97.

2 Despite reference to the error and its cognates in the widest range of twentieth-century authors (Gaston Bachelard, Georges Canguilhem, Daniel Dennett, Michel Foucault, Sigmund Freud, Martin Heidegger, Jacques Lacan, Henri Lefebvre, Niklas Luhmann, Rosa Luxemburg, Karl Popper, Richard Sennett, Ludwig Wittgenstein, Raoul Vaneigem), reference to errors or mistakes mainly pass as asides (the exceptions being Freud, Foucault, Lefebvre, Canguilhem, Lacan and late Wittgenstein).

3 Friedrich Nietzsche, *The Will to Power*, trans. Walter Kauffmann and R. J. Hollingdale, and ed. by with commentary by Walter Kauffman, Vintage Books, New York, 1968.

4 Martin Heidegger, 'On the Essence of Truth', in *Basic Writings*, edited with an introduction by David Farrell Krell, Routledge, London 1996, p. 133.

5 Ludwig Wittgenstein, *Culture and Value*, trans. Peter Winch, edited by G. H. Von Wright in collaboration with Heikki Nyman, Basil Blackwell, Oxford, 1980, p. 56e.

6 Ibid., p. 39e.

7 Sigmund Freud, 'Errors', *The Psychopathology of Everyday Life*, trans. James Strachey in collaboration with Anna Freud, eds. Alix Strachey and Alan Tyson, Hogarth Press and the Institute of Psychoanalysis, London, 1991, p. 218.

8 Ibid., p. 220.

9 Michel Foucault, 'Introduction', Georges Canguilhem, *The Normal and the Pathological*, trans. Carolyn R. Fawcett in collaboration with Robert S. Cohen, Zone Books, New York, 1991, p. 22–3.

10 Georges Canguilhem, 'A New Concept in Pathology: Error', *The Normal and the Pathological*, trans. Carolyn R. Fawcett in collaboration with Robert S. Cohen, Zone Books, New York, 1991, p. 278.

11 Georges Canguilhem, ibid., p. 278.

12 Interestingly the issues of error, disability and women's reproductive rights have become crucial to recent feminist debates in Italy. The Catholic church's resistance to abortion, in a sense, represents an absolutist position on sexual and biological error:

all errors of sexual misjudgement and all instances of chemical breakdown are to be embraced and assimilated. This love in the name of error, for error – embedded deeply within Catholic ethics – is a powerful argument against all utilitarian arguments directed towards the expulsion of disability as a social inconvenience. Yet, of course, to embrace all biological error, in situations where such errors are unbearable and overwhelming, is precisely to diminish or destroy the lives of those who take on the responsibility for caring for the disabled. Without backtracking, on the issue of abortion and women's reproductive autonomy, thus, the failure of modern reproductive rights ideology to take on, and discuss, the socially productive assimilation of biological error (as a measure of the profoundest commitment to human emancipation and love) nevertheless has been missing from the debate. Where do the limits to the assimilation of biological error – as a liberation from normativity – lie? Thanks to Ivana Bartoletti for our discussion on this question.

13 Michel Foucault, 'Introduction', p. 22.

14 Ibid., p. 23.

15 Denis Diderot, *Pensées sur l'interpretation de la nature*, in *Oeuvres completes*, ed. Herbert Dieckmann et al., 33 vols, Hermann, Paris 1975–95; Maquis (Nicolas) de Condorcet, *Sketch for a Historical Picture of the Progress of the Human Mind* [1795], trans. June Barraclough, Weidenfeld & Nicolson, London,1955; Etienne Bonnot de Condillac, *An Essay on the Origin of Human Knowledge, Being a Supplement to Mr.Locke's Essay on Human Understanding*, trans. Thomas Nugent [1756], Scholars Fascimiles, Gainesville, Florida, 1971; Anne-Robert-Jacques Turgot, *Pensées et fragments sur les progress at la decadence des sciences et des arts*, in *Oeuvres de Turgot*, ed. Eugene Daine and Hyppoltyte Dussard, 2 vols, Paris 1844; Jean-Louis Castilhon, *Essai sur les erreurs et les superstitions anciennes et modernes*, 2 vols, Knoe & Eslinger, Frankfurt, 1766; Jean-le-Rond d'Alembert, *Essai sur les elements du philosophe, ou sur les principles of connoissances humanies*, in *Oeuvres de d'Alembert*, 5 vols, Editions Slatkine, Geneva, 1967.

16 Bernard le Bovier de Fontenelle, *Encylopédie*, s.v. 'philosophie', 12.511, quoted in David W. Bates, *Enlightenment Aberrations: Error & Revolution in France*, Cornell University Press, Ithaca, New York, 2002, p. 31.

17 Karl Leonhard Reinhold, 'Thoughts on Enlightenment', first published in *Der Teutsche Merkur*, 1784, in James Schmidt, ed., *What is Enlightenment? Eighteenth-Century Answers and Twentieth-Century Questions*, University of California Press, Berkeley, Los Angeles, London, 1996, p. 66.

18 Karl Leonhard Reinhold, ibid., p. 71.

19 Johan Gottlieb Fichte, 'Reclamation of the Freedom of Thought for the Princes of Europe, Who Have Oppressed It Until Now', in *What is Enlightenment?*, p. 122.

20 Fichte, ibid., p. 121.

21 Abbé Barruel, *History of Jacobinism*, 4 vols, trans. Robert Clifford, T. Burton, London, 1798.

22 Joseph de Maistre, *Considérations sur la France*, avant-propos de Jean Boissel; texte établi, preésenté, et annoté pa Jean-Louis Darcel, Editions Slatkine, Geneva, 1980.

23 Louis de Bonald, *Oeuvres Completes*, 3 vols, J. P.Migne, Paris, 1858.

24 As Jacques Godechot writes, for de Maistre the revolution is a 'fight to the death between Christianity and philosophy . . . The counter-revolution will be accomplished at the hour willed by God; but it cannot fail to come.' Jacques Godechot, *The Counter-Revolution: Doctrine and Action 1789–1804*, Princeton University Press, Princeton, New Jersey, 1981.

25 David W. Bates, *Enlightenment Aberrations*, p. 193.

26 G. W. F. Hegel, 'Preface' to the *Phenomenology of Spirit*, translation and running commentary by Yirmiyahu Yovel, Princeton University Press, Princeton and Oxford, 2005.

27 David W. Bates, *Enlightenment Aberrations*, p. 249.

28 David W. Bates, ibid., p. 247.

29 Karl Marx, *The Civil War in France* [1871], Foreign Language Press, Peking, 1977.

30 Rosa Luxemburg, 'Leninism or Marxism?' [first published in *Neue Zeit*, 1904], in *The Russian Revolution and Leninism or Marxism?*, introduction by Bertram P. Wolfe, University of Michigan, Ann Arbor 1961, p. 108.

31 Victor Serge, 'Marxism in Our Time', *Partisan Review*, Vol. 5, No 3, 1938, pp. 26–32, reprinted in *The Serge—Trotsky Papers: Correspondence and Other Writings between Victor Serge and Leon Trotsky*, edited and introduced by David Cotterill, trans. Peter Sedgwich and Maria Enzenberger, with introductions by Philip Spencer and Susan Weissman, Pluto Press, London, 1994.

32 Henri Lefebvre, *Introduction to Modernity: Twelve Preludes* [1962], trans. John Moore, Verso, London and New York, 1995, p. 9.

33 Henri Lefebvre, ibid., p. 48.

34 Régis Debray, *Revolution in the Revolution?: Armed Struggle and Political Struggle in Latin America* [1967] trans. John Fullerton, trans. Bobbye Ortiz, Penguin, Harmondsworth, 1968, p. 24.

35 Raoul Vaneigem, *The Book of Pleasures* [1979], trans. John Fullerton, Pending Press, London, 1983, p. 105.

36 Frederick Engels, *Ludwig Feuerbach and the End of Classical German Philosophy*, Foewifn Language Press, Peking, 1976, p. 52.

37 On the projective and retroactive truth-content of events, see Alain Badiou's theory of the Event in *Being and Event,* Continuum, London and New York, 2005.

38 This is something of a historical platitude these days, but nonetheless it is still of supreme value in any critique of (vulgar) historicism. See Slavoj Žižek, *In Defence of Lost Causes*, Verso, London and New York, 2008, and Alex Callinicos, *Theories and Narratives: Reflections on the Philosophy of History*, Polity Press, Cambridge, 1995.

39 In the end this turns on what kind of theory of history Marxism subscribes to: a model of evolutionary and linear progress derived from the natural sciences, or a model of deflected progress derived from Hegelian dialectic. With the latter, defeat, loss and retreat supplies a truth of the remainder, of the remnant, indeed, of a truth-of-praxis as error.

40 Stephen Watson, 'On the Errancy of Dasein', *diacritics*, 19.3-4, Fall/Winter, 1989.

41 See the recent debates in the *British Medical Journal* (2000–) and the work, more generally, of Brian Hurwitz for a discussion of the place of error in medical ethics (Aziz Sheikh and Brian Hurwitz, *Health Care Errors and Patient Safety*, John Wiley, London, 2009). Yet this is not to say that the costliness of medical errors is not itself productive. This is the unacknowledged vector of medical science, which medical ethics is currently preoccupied with: the tragedy or discomfort of the error experienced by the patient is the 'advance' or 'boon' for the medical researcher. Productiveness, therefore, is a hidden 'grey' ethical area here. Similarly, the many errors produced by a relegated football team contribute to the reproduction of the league as a competition; no errors of substance committed across all teams, or all teams committing the same errors to the same effect, and no one, or all, would be relegated. So, those different relegated teams that consistently produce errors sustain the ability of the league to reproduce itself as a competition and as a spectacle. In this way the majority-errors of a few clubs sustain the productiveness – the competitiveness – of the league overall. Yet, productiveness or unproductiveness aside, this is not to say that errors with *severe consequences* do not

get committed for unconscious reasons. Thus a counter-intuitive argument, based on a psychoanalytic reading of error (see Chapter 3), can be applied to costly mistakes, such as medical error. The error of the surgeon may have been unconsciously willed: his carelessness killed his patient because he no longer wanted to be careful. That is, he wanted to leave his profession, but was unable to do so directly, because of his fear of the loss of his social status and income, and his guilt about turning his back on his long-accumulated life-saving skills. However, charged with malpractice, he is able to say that he deeply regrets his carelessness, and as such no longer feels able to continue to work without it happening again. He thereby allows himself to be cast out of his profession as someone who recognized and admitted his own mistakes, and was willing to act on them to protect the interests of his future patients.

42 The 'virtuous error' is something that affects artistic and musical discourse, perhaps more than any other discourse, positivizing the error's disruptive, creative and productive function. That is, the 'virtuous error' is the one that, if not exactly sought, is immediately incorporated into the work *at hand*, or used as the basis for a new avenue of exploration.

43 Plato, *Theaetus*, ed. Bernard Williams, trans. M. J. Levett, revised Miles Bunyeat, Hackett, Indianapolis, Cambridge University Press, 1992, p. 77.

44 See Roy Edgley, *Reason in Theory and Practice*, London, Hutchinson, 1969. '[I]t is logically impossible for anyone to think or know what he thinks is false' (p. 121). Thus it is impossible for me to say in the present tense, 'I mistakenly believe *p*'. See also Nicholas Rescher, *Error*, pp. 15–17.

45 Outside of mental illness in the present period, that is. Counter-intuitively it is possible to translate this proposition into something like, 'I have never been to Edinburgh – but I may be mistaken', on the grounds that I was once very drunk on the night train to Edinburgh, but have no memory of arriving or returning to London the following morning. In 10,000 years' time when trips to the moon may have become utterly commonplace, drunkenly forgetting you've been to the moon will clearly dissolve its 'idiocy' as a proposition. Ludwig Wittgenstein, *On Certainty*, ed. G. E. M. Anscombe and G. H. von Wright, trans. Denis Paul and G. E. M. Anscombe, Blackwell, Oxford, 1969, p. 88.

46 Even if I was planning to commit suicide, and therefore, was acting to deceive – 'but he knew turning right was the safe road' – does not alter this situation.

47 See, Joseph McCarney, *Social Theory and the Crisis of Marxism*, Verso, London and New York, 1990.

48 Perhaps the key text here is Georg Lukács, *History and Class Consciousness*, Merlin, London, 1968.

49 Rom Harré, *The Philosophy of Science: An Introductory Survey*, Oxford University Press, Oxford, 1974, p. 12.

50 See, William Kingdon Clifford, 'The Ethics of Belief', originally published in *Contemporary Review*, 1877, published in *The Ethics of Belief and Other Essays*, Prometheus Books, Amherst, New York, 1999. For a critique of the Clifford-Principle, see Peter Van Inwagen, 'Is it Wrong Everywhere, Always, and for Anyone to Believe Anything on Insufficient Evidence?' available at http://comp.uark.edu/~senor/wrong.html.

51 Paul Feyerabend, *Against Method: Outline of an Anarchist Theory of Knowledge*, Verso, London, 1978; Imre Lakatos, *The Methodology of Scientific Research Programmes: Philosophical Papers, Vol. 1*, Cambridge University Press, Cambridge, 1979.

52 Roy Bhaskar, *A Realist Theory of Science*, Harvester Press/Humanities Press, Brighton and New Jersey, 1978, pp. 197–198.

53 Thomas Kuhn, *The Structure of Scientific Revolutions*, second edition, University of Chicago Press, Chicago, 1970.

54 Plato, *Theaetus*.

55 Deborah G. Mayo, *Error and the Growth of Experimental Knowledge*, University of Chicago Press, Chicago and London, 1996.

56 See Alain Badiou, *Being and Event*, ibid.

57 For a discussion of aesthetic reason as a critique of non-aesthetic reason, see Christophe Menke, *The Sovereignty of Art: Aesthetic Negativity in Adorno and Derrida*, trans. Neil Solomon, MIT, Cambridge, Massachusetts and London, 1998.

58 For a discussion of this 're-centring' process and the assimilation of the alien-ness of the unconscious, see Jean Laplanche, *Essays on Otherness*, Routledge, London and New York, 1999.

CHAPTER 1: ERROR, TRUTH AND THE SUBJECT

1 Plato, *Theaetus*, ed. with an introduction by Bernard Williams, trans. M. J. Levett, revised by Miles Bunyeat, Hackett, Indianapolis, Cambridge University Press, 1992, p. 12.

2 Ibid., p. 60.

3 Ibid.

4 Ibid., p. 71.

5 Ibid., p. 77.

6 Bernard Williams, 'Introduction', *Theaetus*, p. xviii.

7 René Descartes, *Meditations on First Philosophy: with selections from the Objections and Replies*, ed. John Cottingham, with an introduction by Bernard Williams, Cambridge University Press, Cambridge, 1986, pp. 37–38.

8 Ibid., p. 38.

9 Ibid.

10 Ibid., p. 39.

11 Ibid., p. 40.

12 Ibid p. 41.

13 Ibid., p. 43.

14 Ibid.

15 René Descartes, *Meditations*, p. 87.

16 See in particular Stephen Menn, *Descartes and Augustine*, Cambridge University Press, Cambridge, 1998.

17 Augustine, *On Free Choice of the Will*, trans. with introduction and notes by Thomas Williams, Hackett Publishing, Indianapolis and Cambridge, 1993.

18 Cecilia Wee, *Material Falsity and Error in Descartes' "Meditations"*, Routledge, London, 2006.

19 John Locke, *An Essay Concerning Human Understanding*, abridged and ed. John W. Yolton, Everyman, J. M. Dent, London, 1993, p. 4.

20 Ibid., p. 15.

21 Ibid., p. 14–15.

22 For a discussion of Locke's critique of innate ideas, see John W. Yolton, *Locke and French Materialism*, Oxford University Press, Oxford, 1991.

23 John Locke, *An Essay*, p. 28.

24 Ibid., p. 304.

25 Ibid., p. 310.
26 Ibid., p. 315.
27 Ibid., p. 317.
28 Ibid., p. 320.
29 Ibid., p. 341.
30 Ibid., p. 321.
31 Ibid., p. 318.
32 Ibid., p. 319.
33 Ibid., p. 410.
34 Ibid., p. 409.
35 Baruch Spinoza, *Ethics and On the Correction of the Understanding*, trans. Andrew Boyle, Introduction by T. S. Gregory, Dent, London and New York, 1959, p. 246.
36 Immanuel Kant, *Prolegomena: To Any Future Metaphysics That Can Qualify as Science*, trans. Paul Carus, Open Court, Chicago and La Salle, Illinois, 1994, p. 51.
37 Immanuel Kant, *Critique of Pure Reason*, trans. J. M. D. Meiklejohn, Prometheus Books, Buffalo, New York, 1990, p. 6.
38 Ibid., p. 6.
39 Ibid., p. 183.
40 See Immanuel Kant, 'On a Newly Arisen Superior Tone in Philosophy', in *Raising the Tone of Philosophy: Late Essays by Immanuel Kant, Transformative Critique by Jacques Derrida*, ed. Peter Fenves, John Hopkins University Press, Baltimore and London, 1993, pp. 51–81.
41 Immanuel Kant, *Critique of Pure Reason*, p. 198.
42 Ibid., p. 186–87.
43 Ibid., p. 237.
44 Ibid., p. 273.
45 Ibid., p. 311.
46 Ibid., p. 214.
47 Ibid., p. 228.
48 Georges Dicker, *Kant's Theory of Knowledge: An Analytical Introduction*, Oxford University Press, Oxford and New York, 2004, p. 195.
49 For a discussion of Kant's subject within the 'pathological' determinations of psychoanalysis, see Alenka Zupancic, *Ethics of the Real: Kant, Lacan*, Verso, London and New York, 2000.
50 Étienne Balibar, 'Subjection and Subjectivation', *Supposing the Subject*, ed. Joan Copjec, Verso, London and New York, 1994.
51 Kant, *Critique of Pure Reason*, p. 398.
52 Ibid., p. 409.
53 Yirmiyahu Yovel, *Kant and the Philosophy of History*, Princeton University Press, Princeton, New Jersey, 1980, p. 13.
54 Kant, *Critique of Pure Reason*, p. 267.
55 Immanuel Kant, *Critique of Pure Reason*, trans. Werner S. Pluhar, with an introduction by Stephen Engstrom, Hackett Publishing, Indianapolis and Cambridge, 2002.
56 For an extensive evaluation of the bourgeoisie's and aristocracy's involvement in the origins and development of the Enlightenment, see Jonathan I. Israel, *Radical Enlightenment: Philosophy and the Making of Modernity 1650–1750*, Oxford University Press, Oxford and New York, 2001. See also James Schmidt ed., *What is Enlightenment?: Eighteenth-Century Answers and Twentieth Century Questions,* University of California Press, Berkeley, Los Angeles and London, 1996.

57 G. W. F. Hegel, *Phenomenology of Spirit*, trans. A. V. Miller with analysis of the text and foreword by J. N. Finlay, Oxford University Press, Oxford, 1977. My quotations from the Preface, however, are taken from Yirmiyahu Yovel's translation. See below.

58 G. W. F. Hegel, *Preface to the Phenomenology of Spirit*, trans. and running commentary by Yirmiyahu Yovel, Princeton University Press, Princeton and Oxford, 2005, pp. 98–99.

59 G. W. F. Hegel, *Phenomenology*, p. 139.

60 G. W. F. Hegel, *Hegel's Logic*, trans. William Wallace, with forward by J. N. Findlay, Oxford University Press, Oxford, p. 117.

61 G. W. F. Hegel, ibid., p. 293.

62 G. W. F. Hegel, ibid., p. 274.

63 For a discussion of this connection, see Yirmiyahu Yovel, *Kant and the Philosophy of History*, Princeton University Press, Princeton, New Jersey, 1980. Jean-Luc Nancy makes the same point, in *Hegel: The Restlessness of the Negative*, trans. Jason Smith and Steven Miller, University of Minnesota Press, Minneapolis and London, 2002, 'Hegel . . . sets out to think what Kant demands' (p25).

64 I cannot criticize my present beliefs as false, for then they are no longer my present beliefs but my previous beliefs. In other words whether we change our beliefs or not, in believing what we believe (at a given time) we are forced to act on them (or adopt another set of beliefs).

65 G. W. F. Hegel, *Phenomenology of Spirit*, trans. A. V. Miller with analysis of the text and foreword by J. N. Findlay, Oxford University Press, Oxford, 1977, p. 240.

66 G. W. F. Hegel, 'Preface' to *Phenomenology of Spirit*, p. 157.

67 Ibid., p. 194.

68 Theodor W. Adorno, *Hegel: Three Studies*, trans. Shierry Weber Nicholson, MIT Press, Cambridge Mass., 1993, p. xxix.

69 Hans-Georg Gadamer, *Hegel's Dialectic: Five Hermeneutical Studies*, trans. with an introduction by P. Christopher Smith, Yale University Press, New Haven and London, 1976, p. 58.

70 Jean-Luc Nancy, *Hegel: The Restlessness of the Negative*, p. 63.

71 However, this sense of Kant's subject as a 'stranded' subject is mitigated at points by his critique, like Hegel, of Natural Law; subjects need the enabling condition of institutions and state legislation in order to act autonomously. '[A] good constitution is not to be expected from morality, but conversely, a good moral condition of a people is to be expected only under a good constitution' (Domenico Losurdo), *Hegel and the Freedom of Moderns*, Duke University Press, Durham and London 2004, p. 130. See Immanuel Kant, *Perpetual Peace: A Philosophical Essay* [1795] trans. with an introduction and notes by M. Campbell Smith, and a Preface by L. Latta, George Allen and Unwin, London, 1917, and Chapter 2.

72 For a discussion of this point and the important notion of subjective 'indifference' in Hegel, see John O'Neill, ed., *Hegel's Dialectics of Desire and Recognition: Texts and Commentaries*, State University of New York Press, New York, 1996, pp. 10–17.

73 Yirmiyahu Yovel, 'Introduction', *Hegel's Preface to the Phenomenology of Spirit*, p. 33.

74 Ibid., p. 36.

75 Theodor Adorno, *Hegel: Three Studies*, p. 42.

76 Ibid., p. 55.

77 Karl Popper, *The Logic of Scientific Discovery*, Routledge, London, 1992.

78 Deborah G. Mayo, *Error and the Growth of Experimental Knowledge*, University of Chicago Press, Chicago and London, 1996, p. 4.

79 Mayo, ibid., p. 55.

CHAPTER 2: ERROR, SCIENTIFIC PROGRESS AND VERIDICAL TRUTH

1 Immanuel Kant, *Critique of Pure Reason*, trans. J. M. D. Meiklejohn, Prometheus Books, Buffalo, New York, 1990, p. 413.
2 Ibid., p. 410 fn.
3 Theodor Adorno, *Negative Dialectics*, trans. E. B. Ashton, Routledge & Kegan Paul, London, 1973 p. 63.
4 See Hans-Georg Gadamer, *Reason in the Age of Science*, trans. Frederick G. Lawrence, MIT Press, Cambridge MA and London, 1981.
5 Ibid., p. 25.
6 Rudolf Carnap, *The Unity of Science*, trans. with introduction by Max Black, Thoemmes Press, Bristol, 1997; Rudolf Carnap 'Truth and Confirmation' in H. Feigl and W. Sellars, eds, *Readings in Philosophical Analysis*, Appleton-Century-Crofts, New York, 1949.
7 Rudolf Carnap, *The Unity of Science*, p. 26.
8 Ibid., p. 87.
9 Ibid., p. 98.
10 Carnap did qualify his position in the 1960s after the Kuhnian revolution. In a letter he wrote to Kuhn in April 1962, he argues that science is 'not direct to an ideal [true] theory, the *one* true theory of the world, but evolution as a step to a better form, by selection of one out of several competing forms'. Quoted in 'Carnap, Kuhn and the Philosophy of Scientific Methodology', John Earman, in Paul Horwich, eds, *World Changes: Thomas Kuhn and the Nature of Science*, MIT Press, Cambridge, MA and London, 1993, p. 11.
11 Karl Popper, *The Logic of Scientific Discovery* [1935], Routledge, London, 1992, p. 8.
12 Ibid., p. 16.
13 Ibid., p. 72.
14 Ibid., p. 267.
15 Paul Feyeraband, *Against Method: Outline of an Anarchist Theory of Knowledge*, Verso, London, 1978.
16 Imre Lakatos, *The Methodology of Scientific Research Programmes, Philosophical Papers, Vol. 1*, ed. John Worrall and Gregory Currie, Cambridge University Press, 1979.
17 Alfred Tarski, 'The Semantic Conception of Truth and the Foundations of Semantics', reprinted in *Truth*, eds Simon Blackburn and Keith Simmons, Oxford University Press, 1999, pp. 114–143.
18 Karl Popper, 'Epistemology Without a Knowing Subject', in *Objective Knowledge: An Evolutionary Approach,* Oxford University Press, Oxford, 1979.
19 Ibid., p. 109.
20 For a discussion of experience in Popper's philosophy of science, see Graham MacDonald, 'The Role of Experience in Popper's Philosophy of Science and Political Philosophy', in *Karl Popper: Critical Appraisals*, Routledge, London and New York, 2004.
21 Karl Popper, *Objective Knowledge*, p. 118.
22 Ibid.
23 Ibid., p. 119.
24 Karl Popper, 'In spite of a certain superficial similarity between Hegel's dialectic and my evolutionary schema there is a fundamental difference. My schema works through error-elimination, and on the scientific level through conscious criticism under the regulative idea of the search for truth', *Objective Knowledge*, p. 126.

25 Ibid., p. 125.
26 Ibid., p. 126.
27 Ibid., p. 147.
28 Ibid., p. 119.
29 Ibid., p. 126.
30 Popper's scientific subject is subject to a process outside of the control of the subject. However, this process of submission to an objective realm of problems is not neutral or inexorable; the problems immanent to the practices of science produce unexpected or uncontrollable outcomes, which then generate further problems that the scientific subject must respond to. In this sense the creativity of the scientific subject is determined by the quality of its response to the problems generated by the generation of further problems. Accordingly, we might say that Popper's scientific subject is the producer and eradicator of errors subject to the exoteric logic of scientific discovery.
31 Deborah Mayo, *Error and the Growth of Experimental Knowledge*, p. xii.
32 Imre Lakatos, *The Methodology of Scientific Research*, p. 149.
33 I borrow the concept of accelerationism here – and from a very different context – from Ben Noys, *The Persistence of the Negative: A Critique of Contemporary Continental Theory*, Edinburgh University Press, Edinburgh, 2010.
34 Roy Bhaskar, *A Realist Theory of Science*, Harvester Press/Humanities Press, Sussex and New Jersey, 1978, p. 216.
35 Deborah Mayo, *Error and the Growth of Experimental Knowledge*, p. 4.
36 Ibid., p. 57.
37 Ibid., p. 8.
38 Karl Popper, *Objective Knowledge*, p. 14, also quoted in Deborah Mayo, ibid., p. 8.
39 Thomas S. Kuhn, *The Structure of Scientific Revolution*, University of Chicago Press, Chicago, 1970.
40 For a critical overview of Kuhn's changing position on paradigm change, see Howard Sankey, 'Kuhn's Changing Concept of Incommensurability', *The British Journal for the Philosophy of Science*, Vol. 44. No 4. Dec 1993, pp. 759–774.
41 Thomas S. Kuhn, *The Structure of Scientific Revolution*, p. 24.
42 Ibid., p. 102.
43 Stephen Toulmin, 'Does the Distinction between Normal and Revoloutionary Science Hold Water?', in *Criticism and the Growth of Knowledge*, eds Imre Lakatos & Alan Musgrave, Cambridge University Press, Cambridge, 1970.
44 Kurt Hübner, *Critique of Scientific Reason*, University of Chicago Press, Chicago, 1985.
45 Paul Feyerabend, 'Consolations of the Specialist' in *Criticism and the Growth of Knowledge*, eds Imre Lakatos and Alan Musgrave, Cambridge University Press, Cambridge, 1970.
46 Ibid., p. 209.
47 Karl Popper, 'Normal Science and Its Dangers' in *Criticism and the Growth of Knowledge*, p. 55.
48 Deborah Mayo, *Error and the Growth of Experimental Knowledge*, p. 57.
49 Ian Hacking, *Representing and Intervening: Introductory Topics in the Philosophy of Natural Science,* Cambridge University Press, Cambridge, 1983.
50 Peter Galison, *How Experiments End,* University of Chicago Press, Chicago, 1987.
51 Ronald N. Giere, *Understanding Scientific Reasoning*, Holt, Rinehart and Winston, New York, 1984.
52 Deborah Mayo, *Error and the Growth of Experimental Knowledge*, p. 128.
53 Ibid., p. 185.

54 Ibid., p. 191.

55 Ibid., p. x.

56 Ibid., p. 358.

57 Roy Bhaskar, *A Realist Theory of Science*, p. 147.

58 Ibid., p. 185.

59 Ibid., p. 187.

60 Edwin Hutchins, *Cognition in the Wild*, Harvard University Press, Cambridge MA, 1995; Andy Clark, *Being There*, MIT Press, 1997; Karin Knorr Cetina, *Epistemic Cultures: How the Sciences Make Knowledge*, Harvard University Press, Cambridge MA, 1999; Ronald N. Giere, 'Distributed Cognition Without Distributed Knowing', *Social Epistemology*, Vol. 21, No 3, July–Sept 2007, pp. 313–320.

61 W. Teed Rockwell, *Neither Brain Nor Ghost: A Nondualist Alternative to the Mind-Brain Identity Theory*, MIT, Cambridge MA & London, 2005, p. 39.

62 Ibid.

63 Ibid., p. 45.

64 Ibid., p. 161.

65 Indeed, we might say this is one of the consequences of the increasing adaptation of neural plasticity in the neurosciences and cognitive sciences. With the move away from a notion of the neural functions of brain as centralizing, stable and machine-like (or computer-like) to a notion of the neural functions of the brain as multiply interdependent and self-transforming and self-modulating, the new neurosciences produce a plasticity of the 'self' that, for all its emphasis on the *living* brain and the historical conditioning of our synapses, defines neuronal change through a model of flexibility and accommodation, rather than resistance. For an analysis and critique of the new plasticity, see Catherine Malabou, *What Should We Do with Our Brains?* trans. Sebastian Rand, with a foreword by Marc Jeannerod, Fordham University Press, New York, 2008.

66 Ronald N. Giere, 'Distributed Cognition Without Distributed Knowing', p.319.

67 Roy Bhaskar, *A Realist Theory of Science*, p. 198.

68 Roy Bhaskar, *Dialectic: The Pulse of Freedom*, Verso, London and New York, 1992, p. 84.

69 Ibid., p. 77.

70 Ibid., p. 341.

71 Ibid., p. 5.

72 Ibid., p. 74.

73 Ibid., p. 90.

74 Ibid., p. 73.

75 Ibid., p. 74.

76 Ibid., p. 110–111.

77 Ibid., p. 73.

78 Ibid., p. 195.

79 Ibid., p. 73.

80 Ibid., p. 340.

81 Which is not to deny the fact that Marx in 'moments' of crisis, and towards the end of his career, returns again and again to Hegel for sustenance.

82 Norberto Bobbio, *Studi Hegeliani*, Einaudi, Turin, 1981.

83 Karl Marx, *Capital*, Vol. 1, Lawrence & Wishart, London, 1970, p. 283–284.

84 G. W. F. Hegel, *The Science of Logic*, Oxford University Press, Oxford, p. 292.

85 David MacGregor, *The Communist Ideal in Hegel and Marx*, University of Toronto Press, Toronto, 1984, p. 26.

86 Ibid., p. 11.
87 Daniel Bensaïd, *Marx For Our Times: Adventures and Misadventures of a Critique*, trans. Gregory Elliot, Verso, London and New York, 2002, p. 224.
88 Domenico Losurdo, *Hegel and the Freedom of Moderns*, trans. Marella and Jon Marris, Duke University Press, Durham and London 2004, p. 36.
89 Domenico Losurdo, *Hegel and the Freedom of the Moderns*, p. 36.
90 Ibid., p. 59.
91 G. W. F. Hegel, *Philosophy of History*, trans. J. Sibree, with a preface by Charles Hegel, and a new introduction by C. J. Friedrich, Dover, New York 1956.
92 Alain Badiou, *Logics of Worlds: Being and Event 11*, trans. Alberto Toscano, Continuum, London and New York, 2009, p. 145.
93 Ibid.
94 Roy Bhaskar, *Dialectic*, p. 24.
95 Ibid., p. 29.
96 Ibid., p. 27.
97 Alain Badiou, *The Logics of Worlds*, p. 148.
98 Ibid., p. 151.
99 Alain Badiou, *Being and Event*, p. 163.
100 Alain Badiou, *The Logics of Worlds*, p. 513.
101 Ibid., p. 509.
102 Ibid.
103 Ibid.
104 Ibid., p. 33.
105 Roy Bhaskar, *Dialectic*, p. 25.
106 Ibid., p. 183.
107 Alain Badiou, *Logics of Worlds*, p. 22.
108 G. W. F. Hegel, *Die Vernunft in Der Geschichte*, ed. J. Hoffmeister, Hamburg,1955, pp. 15–52, quoted in Domenico Losurdo, *Hegel and the Freedom of Moderns*, p. 126.
109 Theodor Adorno, *Hegel: Three Studies*, trans. Sherry Weber Nicholson, MIT, Cambridge MA and London, 1993, p. 2.
110 Ibid.
111 G. W. F. Hegel, *The Encyclopedia Logic*, trans. T. F. Geraets et al., Hackett Publishing, Indianapolis, 1991, p. 236.
112 G. W. F. Hegel, *Phenomenology of Mind*, trans. J. B. Baillie, Allen & Unwin, London, 1931 p. 385.
113 Jean-Luc Nancy, *Hegel: The Restlesslessness of the Negative*, p. 9.
114 Ibid., p. 74.
115 We see this time and time again: critics of Hegel end up as idealists in a mirror of their critique of Hegel as idealist; and Badiou is no exception. Indeed, as Lacan puts it, in 'going beyond' Hegel, we invariably end up in the same place ('Freud, Hegel and the Machine' in *The Seminar of Jacques Lacan: Book 11, The Ego in Freud's Theory and in the Technique of Psychoanalysis 1954–1955*, ed. Jacques-Alain Miller, trans. Sylvana Tomasell, with notes by John Forrester, W. W. Norton, New York, 1991, p.71). Badiou's inflation of the inexistent over the existent traduces the realist postulates of the physical sciences. As Ray Brassier puts it in *Nihil Unbound* (Palgrave, London, 2006): with this traduction of realism, 'his philosophy simply stipulates an isomorphy between discourse and reality, logical consequences and material causes, thinking and being. Thinking is sufficient to change the world: such is the ultimate import of Badiou's idealism.' (p. 179)

116 Alain Badiou, *Logics of Worlds*, p. 152.

117 Jacques Lacan, *The Seminar of Jacques Lacan, Book II, The Ego in Freud's Theory and in the Technique of Psychoanalysis, 1954–1955*, p. 69.

118 One philosopher of science in the 1970s who did offer a critique of science as a system was Kurt Hübner. In *Critique of Scientific Reason*, he rightly critiques Carnap's and Popper's philosophy of science as proceeding in 'an unhistorical manner' (p. 70), leading to the epistemological inflation of scientific method: 'we hold science to be competent in all matters, and grant it the right to speak on behalf of everything' (p. 105). But in the Kuhnian and anti-Hegelian spirit of the times, he replaces a critique of the valorisation of scientific truth, the self-actualization of knowledge, and logical progression, with a relativist critique of the growth of knowledge as such. This leaves his legitimate critique of scientific methodology exposed to the vagaries of anti-historicism. He is unable to explain why it is possible to point to the growth of knowledge on the basis of the objective outcomes of earlier forms of knowledge. Moreover, as with many other philosophers of science, he misconstrues Hegel, only to end up endorsing a Hegelian position. Thus Hübner – in 'opposition to Hegel' (p. 114) – stresses the need for science to embrace '*contingency* in history', and therefore contingency in science (p. 114) without at all being aware that historical contingency for Hegel is the spark that announces qualitative historical change. Similarly, Hübner attacks the would-be progressivism of Hegelianism on the grounds that it is unable to think the past in the light of the present. 'After all no system is unveiled and revealed immediately. It can be developed only in the course of time (explication), thereby revealing its potentials' (p. 199). The task of the historian – and the historian of science – consists therefore in 'the continuous rewriting of history' (p. 201) – precisely Hegel's point. Hübner's critique, then, offers a symptomatic failure on the part of the philosophy of science in the period of its critical revision in the late twentieth century to embed scientific methodology in both dialectic and a dialectical critique of science as system. Scientific methodology is either fetishized at the expense of science-as-system, or the critique of science-of-system is fetishized at the expense of scientific truth and the growth of knowledge.

119 Gaston Bachelard, *The Psychoanalysis of Fire* [1938], Routledge & Kegan Paul, 1964, p. 100–101.

120 And of course these high levels of scrutiny are no guarantee of success. As Cosma Shalzi puts it sharply in a review of Deborah Mayo's *Error and the Growth of Knowledge*: first, Mayo's writing 'does not seem to distinguish scientific knowledge – at least experimental knowledge – from technological knowledge, or even really from artisanal know-how. Second, [it leaves] me puzzled about how science got on before statistics'. http://www.cscs.umich.edu/-crshaliz/reviews/error/

121 Hans-Georg Gadamer, *Reason in the Age of Science*, trans. Frederick G. Lawrence, MIT Press, Cambridge MA and London, 1981, p. 26.

CHAPTER 3: ERROR, TRUTH AND PSYCHOANALYSIS

1 Sigmund Freud, 'Errors', *The Psychopathology of Everyday Life*.

2 See in particular 'Truth Emerges From the Mistake' and 'The Concept of Analysis' in Jacques Lacan, *The Seminar of Jacques Lacan, Book I: Freud's Papers on Technique 1953–1954*, ed. Jacques-Alain Miller, trans. with notes by John Forrester, Cambridge University Press, Cambridge, 1988.

3 Sigmund Freud, 'Recommendations to Physicians Practising Psychoanalysis' [1912], in James Strachey, ed., *The Standard Edition of the Complete Psychological Works of Sigmund Freud, Volume XII (1911–1913): The Case of Schreber, Papers on Technique and Other Works*, trans. James Strachey in collaboration with Anna Freud, Alix Strachey, and Alan Tyson, Hogarth Press and the Institute of Psychoanalysis, London, 1958, p. 114.

4 Giovanni Vassalli, 'The Epistemological Transformations of Psychoanalysis', available at http://www.epf-eu.org/Public/Article.php?ID=3855&ancestor1=3715&page=

5 Charles Sanders Peirce, *The Essential Peirce*, 2 vols, ed. Nathan Houser, Christian Kloesel and the Peirce Edition Project, Indiana University Press, Bloomington, Indiana, 1992 and 1998.

6 Sigmund Freud, 'Psychoanalysis and Legal Evidence' [1906], in James Strachey ed., *The Standard Edition of the Complete Works of Sigmund Freud*, Vol. IX, trans. James Strachey, in collaboration with Anna Freud, and assisted by Alix Strachey and Alan Tyson, Hogarth Press and the Institute of Psychoanalysis, London, 1959, p. 108.

7 Jacques Lacan, *The Seminar of Jacques Lacan, Book I, Freud's Papers on Technique 1953–54*, p. 24.

8 Ibid., p. 21.

9 Jacques Lacan, *The Seminar of Jacques Lacan, Book II, The Ego in Freud's Theory and in the Technique of Psychoanalysis 1954–1955*, ed. Jacques-Alain Miller, trans. Sylvana Tomaselli, with notes by John Forrester, Cambridge University Press, 1991.

10 Dany Nobus and Malcolm Quinn go one step further in their excellent book on Lacan and technique, *Knowing Nothing, Staying Stupid* (Routledge, London 2004), in calling for an ignorance from the analyst that comes down on the critical side of 'stupidity'. 'What is the connection between going stupid and becoming critical' (pp. 186–87). In other words the truth of the cure in psychoanalysis can only operate in a condition of 'failure', in so far as the analyst uses his or her passion for ignorance – for 'not knowing' – in order to relieve the analysand of the desire to know (prematurely). The analyst then does not produce more or better knowledge for the analysand, but allows the analysand to come to terms with the gaps and fissures in their knowledge. This gives rise to the primary experience of the transference process for analysand and analyst: 'one' is 'not one'.

11 Jacques Lacan, *The Seminar of Jacques Lacan, Book I, Freud's Papers on Technique 1953–54*, p. 271.

12 Robert Caper, *Building Out Into the Dark: Theory and Observation in Science and Psychoanalysis*, Routledge, London and New York, 2009, p. 6.

13 Dany Nobus, *Jacques Lacan and the Freudian Practice of Psychoanalysis*, Routledge, London, 2000, p. 120.

14 Jacques Lacan, *Book I, Freud's Papers on Technique, 1953–54*, p. 283.

15 Sigmund Freud, 'Errors', *The Psychopathology of Everyday Life*, p. 219.

16 Jacques Lacan, *Book I, Freud's Papers on Technique, 1953–54*, p. 283.

17 Ibid, p. 263.

18 Ibid.

19 Ibid., p. 265.

20 Ibid.

21 Jacques Lacan, *Book II, The Ego in Freud's Theory and in the Technique of Psychoanalysis, 1954–1955*, p. 306.

22 Ibid., p. 307.

23 Ibid., p. 282.

24 Mladen Dolar, 'The Phrenology of Spirit', in *Supposing the Subject*, p. 76.

25 For a discussion of truth as the passage through error, see Timothy Huson, 'Truth

and Contradiction: Reading Hegel with Lacan', *Lacan: The Silent Partners*, ed. Slavoj Žižek, Verso 2006, pp. 67–69.

26 Jacques Lacan, *The Seminar of Jacques Lacan, Book II, The Ego in Freud's Theory and In the Technique of Psychoanalysis, 1954–1955*, p. 56.

27 Jean Claude Milner, 'The Doctrine of Science', translation of Chapter 2, 'Le Doctrinal de Science', trans. Oliver Feltham, from *L'Oeuvre Claire: Lacan la science, la philosophie*, Editions de Seuil, Paris 1995, published in *Umbr(a)*, No 1, 'Science and Truth', 2000, p. 34.

28 Jean Claude Milner, ibid., p. 40.

29 Genevieve Morel, 'Science and Psychonalysis', trans. Karen M. Fischer, *Umbr(a)* No 1, 'Science and Truth', 2000.

30 Slavoj Žižek, *In Defence of Lost Causes*, London and New York, Verso, 2008, p. 3.

31 Žižek, ibid.

32 Louis Althusser, *Writings on Psychoanalysis: Freud and Lacan*, trans. Jeffrey Mehlman, Columbia University Press, New York and Chichester, 1996, p. 114.

33 For a discussion of the current play in the debate between Marxism and psychoanalysis, see Ben Noys's review article on *Revolution in Psychology: Alienation to Emancipation*, Ian Parker, Pluto Press, London, 2007 and *The Lacanian Left: Psychoanalysis, Theory, and Politics*, Yannis Stavrakakis, State University of New York Press, New York 2007 in *Historical Materialism* No 17 2009, pp. 183–208.

34 Louis Althusser, ibid., p. 38.

35 See, for example, Yannis Stavrakakis, *Lacan and the Political*, Routledge, London and New York, 1999. See also Žižek's coruscating attack on Stavrakakis in *In Defense of Lost Causes*, pp. 304–31.

36 Master–pupil letters indeed are an epistolary genre all by themselves. See also, for example the shorter replies of Ezra Pound to Louis Zukofsky's prolixity, in *Pound/Zukofsky: Selected Letters of Ezra Pound and Louis Zukofsky*, ed. Barry Ahearn, New Directions Books, New York, 1987.

37 Louis Althusser, Letter to Jacques Lacan, 4 December 1963, in Louis Althusser, *Writings on Psychoanalysis: Freud and Lacan*, trans. Jeffrey Mehlman, Columbia University Press, New York and Chichester, 1996, p. 153.

38 Louis Althusser, ibid., p. 159.

39 Ibid.

40 Ibid.

41 Ibid., p. 161.

42 Jacques Lacan, 'The Instance of the Letter in the Unconscious' (1957) in *Ecrits: A Selection*, trans. Bruce Fink, in collaboration with Héloise Fink and Russell Grigg, W. W. Norton & Company, New York and London, 2002, p. 139.

43 Jacques Lacan, Letter to Louis Althusser, 1 June 1964, in Louis Althusser, *Writings on Psychoanalysis*, p. 168.

44 Jacques Lacan, Letter to Louis Althusser, 19 October 1965, in Louis Althusser, *Writings on Psychoanalysis*, p. 170.

45 Jacques Lacan, 'The Instance of the Letter in the Unconscious', *Ecrits: A Selection*, p. 156.

46 Louis Althusser, Letter to Jacques Lacan, 11 November 1966, Louis Althusser, *Writings on Psychoanalysis*, p. 172.

47 Louis Althusser, 'The Tbilisi Affair', in Louis Althusser, *Writings on Psychoanalysis*, p. 91.

48 Ibid., p. 97.

49 Louis Althusser, 'Letter to Elisabeth Roudinesco, 12 August 1976, in Louis Althusser, *Writings on Psychoanalysis*, p. 105.

50 Louis Althusser, 'Open Letter to Analysands and Analysts in Solidarity with Jacques Lacan', Louis Althusser, *Writings on Psychoanalysis*, p. 129.

51 Louis Althusser, 'Complementary Remarks on the Meeting of March 15, 1980, at the Hotel PLM Saint-Jacques, Louis Althusser, *Writings on Psychoanalysis*, p. 138.

52 Louis Althusser, 'Open Letter to Analysands and Analysts in Solidarity with Jacques Lacan', Louis Althusser, *Writings on Psychoanalysis*, p. 133.

53 Ibid.

54 Ibid.

55 Ibid.

56 Louis Althusser 'The Tbilisi Affair', in Louis Althusser, *Writings on Psychoanalysis*, p. 91.

57 Ibid., p. 92.

58 Jacques Lacan, 'The Impotence of Truth' in *The Seminar of Jacques Lacan, Book XVII: The Other Side of Psychoanalysis*, trans. Russell Grigg, W. W. Norton, New York and London, 2007, p. 176.

59 Alain Badiou, *The Theory of the Subject*, trans. Bruno Bosteels, Continuum, London and New York, 2009, p. 142.

60 Ibid., pp. 142–143.

61 Ibid., p. 143.

62 Ibid., p. 144.

63 Ibid., p. 115.

64 Arthur Schopenhauer, 'On the Suffering of the World' in *On the Suffering of the World*, trans. R. J. Hollingdale, Penguin Books, London, 2004.

65 Alain Badiou, *The Theory of the Subject*, p. 115.

66 Sigmund Freud, 'Beyond the Pleasure Principle', in *On Metapsychology: The Theory of Psychoanalysis*, translated from the German under the general editorship of James Strachey, Penguin Books, Harmondsworth, 1991, p. 307.

67 Ibid., p. 308.

68 Ibid., p. 336.

69 Jacques Lacan, *The Seminar of Jacques Lacan, Book II The Ego in Freud's Theory and in the Technique of Psychoanalysis, 1954–1955*, p. 84.

70 Jean Laplanche, *Vie et mort en psychanalyse*, Flammarion, Paris 1970, trans. with an introduction by Jeffrey Mehlman, as *Life and Death in Psychoanalysis*, John Hopkins University Press, Baltimore and London, 1976, p. 123.

71 Jacques Lacan, *The Seminar of Jacques Lacan, The Ego in Freud's Theory and in the Technique of Psychoanalysis*, p. 100.

72 Alain Badiou, *The Theory of the Subject*, p. 120.

73 Ibid., p. 124.

74 Louis Althusser, 'Letter of Elisabeth Roudinesco', *Writings on Psychoanalysis*, p. 117.

75 Alain Badiou, *The Theory of the Subject*, p. 166.

76 Ibid., p. 168.

77 Ibid., p. 168.

78 Lacan's interest in Aristophanes appears to be confined to his contribution to Plato's *Symposium*; see *The Four Fundamental Concepts of Psycho-analysis*, Penguin Books, Harmondsworth, 1979.

79 Arisotophanes, 'Wasps' in *Frogs and Other Plays*, trans. David Barrett, revised translation with introduction and notes by Shomit Dutta, Penguin Books, London, 2007, p. 10.

80 Aristophanes, *Assembly of Women (Ecclesiazusae)*, trans. with an introduction by Robert Mayhew, Prometheus Books, Amherst, New York, 1997, p. 80.

81 On this basis, the play has a long history of reactionary interpretation, particularly after the French Revolution and the Commune, when it became a 'warning' from the past. For a discussion of the counter-revolutionary reception of Aristophanes in Germany in the nineteenth century, see Martin Holtermann, *Der deutsche Aristophanes. Die Rezeption eines politischen Dichters im 19. Jahrhundert. Hypomnemata, 155*, Vandenhoeck & Ruprecht, Göttingen, 2004. For a left Hegelian reading of Aristophanes, see Theodor H. Rotscher, *Aristophanes und sein Zeitalter: Eine philologischphilosophische Abhandlung zur Alterthumsforschung*, Vossiche Buchhandlung, Berlin, 1827.

82 See Aristophanes' reflections on Aeschylus – who has a speaking part – in *Frogs*, in *Frogs and Other Plays*, ibid.

83 Alain Badiou, *The Theory of the Subject*, p. 182.

84 For example: the weakness of the philosophical supplicant, Gianni Vattimo (*Christianity, Truth, and Weak Faith*, Gianni Vattimo and Rene Girard, ed. P. Antonello, Columbia University Press, New York, 2009), and the weakness of the self-ironizing anarchist, Simon Critchley (*Infinitely Demanding*, Verso, London and New York, 2007). In this respect, I am completely with Badiou on this matter: weakness is, precisely and only, a strength when it is pursued from a position of *strategic* patience; and an incorrigible and reactionary liability when taken to be a virtue in and of itself.

85 Alain Badiou, ibid., p. 322. Something similar is argued by the Endnotes group in their defence of a 'post-historicist' Marxism. See 'Bring Out Your Dead', *Endnotes* No 1, October 2008: Preliminary Materials for a Balanced Sheet on the 20th Century, 'we have nothing to learn from the failures of past revolutions – no need to replay them to discover their "errors" or distil their "truths", p. 1.

86 Jacques Lacan, 'The Impotence of Truth' in *The Seminar of Jacques Lacan, Book XVII*, p. 170.

87 Ibid.

88 See for example, Donald Davidson, *Essays in Actions and Events*, Oxford University Press, Oxford, 1980.

89 Roy Edgley, *Reason in Theory and Practice*, Hutchinson, London, 1969, p. 121.

90 George Orwell, 'Looking Back at the Spanish Civil War', *A Collection of Essays*, Doubleday, Garden City, 1957.

91 Fredrick Schick, *Ambiguity and Logic*, Cambridge University Press, Cambridge, 2003, p. 6.

92 Ibid.

93 For an extraordinary account of soldiers 'seeing and shooting' under intense combat – and who the professional soldier spares or does not, if in a position to do so – see Guy Sajer's memoir of his time in the Wehrmacht, *The Forgotten Soldier*, Phoenix, Cassell, London, 1999. There are also many stories of radical and revolutionary German and British soldiers during the First World War on occasions shooting to wound when and where possible.

94 Frederic Schick, *Ambiguity and Logic*, p. 13.

95 Hartry Field's 'Stalnaker on Intentionality' in *Truth and the Absence of Fact*, Oxford University Press, Oxford, 2001, p. 96. 'Stalnaker cannot accept the idea that a single belief state has inconsistent content' (p. 101).

96 Derek Parfit, *Reasons and Persons*, Oxford University Press, Oxford, 1984.

97 Of course, we also might redescribe rational irrationality as a form of 'creative' lying. Lying, like error, is inconceivable without a generalizable account of truth. Yet it is the virtue of lying here – 'kill me and my children' – in the spirit of the productiveness of the error that destabilizes the situation, and releases the father and his children from the clutches of the burglar. Such a deception is a constitutive part of the

agonistic conditions of speech. Parfit's example, then, is polemically anti-Kantian in its character. For Kant no lie – creative or otherwise – is worth the damage it inflicts on the speaker's moral reasoning. Parfit has his imaginary father inflict a lie, then, as a supremely virtuous, if risky, thing to do. Thus in some sense, on the question of lying, as on the question of error, we are caught between Kant and Nietzsche: 'no lying' is morally and practically inefficient; 'all lying', as creative truth, is morally and practically insidious. For an unconvincing (sceptical) discussion of the possibilities of 'creative' lying, see Max Black, *The Prevalence of Humbug and Other Essays*, Cornell University Press, Ithaca and London, 1983.

98 Derek Parfit, *Reasons and Persons*, p. 13.
99 Jürgen Habermas, *The Theory of Communicative Action, Vol. 1: Reason and the Rationalization of Society*, Beacon Press, Boston, 1985; H. P. Grice 'Logic and Conversation', *Syntax and semantics 3: Speech Arts*, 1975, pp. 41–58.
100 Jean Jacques Lecercle, *A Marxist Philosophy of Language*, trans. Gregory Elliot, Brill, Leiden and Boston, 2006, p. 93.
101 Paul Horwich, *Truth*, Oxford University Press, Oxford, 1990, p. 131.
102 Ibid., p. 17.
103 Hartry Field, 'Deflationist Views of Meaning and Content', in Simon Blackburn and Keith Simmons, eds, *Truth*, Oxford University Press, Oxford, 1999, p. 376.
104 Paul Horwich, *Truth*, p. 11.
105 For a discussion of this distinction, see Anil Gupta, 'A Critique of Deflationism', Simon Blackburn and Keith Simmons, eds, *Truth*, p. 306.
106 For a critique of deflationism on these terms, see Michael Devitt, 'Minimalist Truth', review article Paul Horwich, *Truth*, Basil Blackwell, Oxford University Press, 1990, *Mind and Language*, 6, 1991, pp. 273–83.
107 Paul Horwich, *Truth*, p. 50.
108 Jean-Jacques Lecercle and Denise Riley, *The Force of Language,* Palgrave Macmillan, Basingstoke, 2004, p. 73.
109 Jean-Jacques Lecercle, *The Marxist Philosophy of Language*, p.182.
110 Ibid., p. 198.
111 Trevor Pateman, *Language, Truth & Politics: Towards a Radical Theory for Communication*, Jean Stroud, Lewes, 1975, p. 73.
112 Ibid., p. 46.
113 Ibid., p. 60.
114 Jean-Jacques Lecercle, *The Force of Language*, p. 118.

CHAPTER 4: ERROR, HISTORY AND POLITICAL PRAXIS

1 Frederick Engels, *Ludwig Feuerbach, and the end of Classical German Philosophy*, p. 52.
2 G. W. F. Hegel, *The Science of Logic*, [1830], trans. William Wallace, with a foreword by J. N. Finlay, Oxford University Press, Oxford, 1975.
3 For instance, Lewis Namier's *The Structure of Politics at the Accession of George III*, Macmillan, London, 1957. Nevertheless, to identify Namier's history as 'psychoanalytic history' is admittedly to stretch the point a bit. Namier uses Freud in an utterly formal way, simply to expose the actions and decisions of leading historical characters to the conflicts of an 'internal life' – something that of course the empiricism of nineteenth-century British history had forsworn – as an update on the Great Men of History approach to historiography.

4 Arno J. Mayer, *The Furies: Violence and Terror in the French and Russian Revolutions*, Princeton University Press, Princeton, New Jersey and Oxford, 2000, p. 588.

5 For a discussion of the contribution of the 'liberal' professions to the intellectual formation of the Revolution, see Georges Lefebvre, *The French Revolution: Form Its Origins to 1793* [1930], trans. Elizabeth Moss Evanson, with a foreword by Paul H. Beik, Routledge, London and New York, 2009.

6 This absence of the classical conditions of bourgeois revolution in France in 1789 has been at the centre of revisionist attacks on the social and political character of the French Revolution since the late 1950s. Because the French Revolution does not conform to a conventional account of bourgeois revolution – the industrial fraction of the bourgeoisie sweeping away the seigniorial rights of feudalism and liberating the peasantry from its dues, and thereby releasing the forces of industrialization (levels of productivity in France didn't return to their prerevolutionary levels until the early 1820s) – it is argued that the revolution's democratic progress after 1792 is in some sense illicit or fruitless, a wayward passage into the errors of violence, what the revisionists have called pejoratively, *dérapage*: a swerving off course. The implication, of course, is that the revolution could have achieved all it achieved by way of the transition to capitalism, without the popular democratic struggles from below. This is, indeed, history without 'error'. See Alfred Cobban, *The Social Interpretation of the French Revolution*, Cambridge University, Cambridge, 1964, the founding revisionist text; and *Interpreting the French Revolution*, Cambridge University Press, Cambridge, 1981, by one of his 'heirs', François Furet. For a defence of the heterodox conditions of bourgeois revolution, see Albert Soboul, *La Civilization et la Révolution Française*, 3 vols, Arthaud, [Paris], 1970, 1982–83. For a defence of the essential unity of the revolution (there was no *dérapage* in 1792; it was precisely the alliance between the *sans culottes* and the revolutionary bourgeois that held the revolution on course), see Claude Mazauric, *Sur la Révolution française*, Editions Sociales, Paris, 1970, and for a 'Marxist' account sympathetic to certain aspects of the revisionist case (the revolution was an intra ruling class conflict over surplus extraction), see George C. Cominel, *Rethinking the French Revolution: Marxism and the Revisionist Challenge*, with a forward by George Rudé, Verso, London and New York, 1987.

7 Daniel Guérin, *Class Struggle in the First French Republic: Bourgeois and Bras Nus 1793–1795*, trans. Ian Patterson, Pluto Press, London, 1977. This book has been attacked since its first publication, for treating the left leadership of the *san culottes*, and the *bra nus*, as if they constituted a self-consciously coherent working class, although Guérin expressly states that: 'Jacques Roux and Varlet did not represent the modern proletariat: the industrialisation which generated it was still embryonic at that period.' (p. 66). What this objection disguises is the fact that Guérin presents a beautifully clear account of the dynamics and vicissitudes of class struggle *internal* to the revolution. There is, therefore, an explicit critique of the 'errors' of Robespierre and the revolutionary bourgeoisie. But far from this being 'ultraleftist' – as if the leadership of the *bras nus* were in a position to step into the shoes of the defeated revolutionary bourgeoisie – it sharpens, historically, what the defeat of the *san culottes* and *bras nus* has meant for the struggle for proletarian democracy after Thermidor. This is something that critics of Guérin, such as Georges Rudé, miss. It is one thing to say that the wage earners lacked the characteristics of a distinct social class; it is another to ignore, on the basis of this, what can be learned from the defeat of the *bras nus* as a defeat for the working class more generally. Georges Rudé, *The Crowd in the French Revolution*, Oxford University Press, London, 1959.

8 Frederick Engels, *Anti-Dühring: Herr Eugen Dühring's Revolution in Science*, Progress Publishers, Moscow, 1977.

9 David A. Bates, *Enlightenment Aberrations*, ibid.

10 Abbé Barruel, *History of Jacobinism*, p. 4.

11 Ibid., p. vii.

12 Joseph de Maistre, *Considérations sur la France*, avant-propos de Jean Boissel; texte établi, preésenté, et annoté pa Jean-Louis Darcel, Editions Slatkine, Geneva, 1980.

13 Edmund Burke, *Reflections on the Revolution in France*, ed. L. G. Mitchell, Oxford University Press, Oxford, 2009.

14 Jacques Godechot, p. 58.

15 Joseph de Maistre, *Considérations sur la France,* ibid.

16 Louis de Bonald, *Oeuvres Completes*, 3 vols, J. P. Migne, Paris, 1858.

17 For a discussion of the multiple positions internal to counter-revolutionary thinking (historical conservation, enlightened despotism, integral Absolutism), see Jacques Godechot, ibid.

18 Jacques Godechot, *The Counter-Revolution Doctrine and Action 1789–1804*, p. 94.

19 For a discussion of the Ideologues, see Charles Hunter Van Duzer, *Contribution of the Ideologues To French Revolutionary Thought*, John Hopkins University Press, Baltimore, 1935.

20 Ibid., p. 73.

21 G. W. F. Hegel, *The Philosophy of History*, trans. J. Sibree, with a preface by Charles Hegel, and a new introduction by C. J. Friedrich, Dover, New York 1956.

22 Emmanuel Joseph Sieyès, 'Essai sur les privileges' was first published as a pamphlet in November 1788. Translated as 'An Essay on Privileges' in *Emmanuel Joseph Sieyès: Political Writings, Including the Debate between Sieyès and Tom Paine in 1791*, edited with an introduction and translation of 'What is the Third Estate?' by Michael Somescher, Hackett Publishing Company, Inc., Indianapolis/Cambridge, 2003.

23 Emmanuel Joseph Sieyès, ibid., p. 71.

24 See, *Les declarations des droits de l'homme de 1789*, "Text réunis et présentés par Christine Fauré," Editions Payot, Paris, 1988. Of course the attack on privileges is itself split open in 1791, in Olympe de Gouges's 'Declaration of the Rights of Women and the Female Citizen', exposing its own error: the conflation of 'citizen' solely with 'man'. Olympe de Gouges*, Déclaration des droits de femme et de la citoyenne*, Mille et une nuit, Paris, 2003.

25 Emmanuel Joseph Sieyès, 'The Explantory Note of M. Sieyès, in Answer to the Letter of Mr. Paine, and to Several Other Provocations of the Same Sort', *Emmanuel Joseph Sieyès*, ibid., p. 171. Sieyès ends up as one of the stodgiest of monarchical constitutionalists.

26 Maximillian Robespierre, speech to the Jacobin Club, 21 Messidor, 1794 (9 July), first published in *Le Moniteur universal*, XX1, pp. 239–41, and reprinted in Richard Bienvenu, ed., *The Ninth of Thermidor: The Fall of Robespierre*, Oxford University Press, Oxford, 1968, p. 127.

27 Maximillian Robespierre, 'On the Principles of Political Morality That Should Guide the National Convention in the Domestic Administration of the Republic', 5 February 1794, 18 Pluviose, Year *11*, in *Robespierre: Virtue and Terror*, Introduction by Slavoj Žižek, texts selected and annotated by Jean Ducange, trans. John Howe, Verso, London and New York, 2007, p. 119.

28 Maximillian Robespierre, *Robespierre: Textes Choises,* Introduction et Notes Explicatives Par Jean Poperen, Vol. 2, of 3 vols, Editions Sociales, Paris, 1973, p. 121. 'Malheur a celui qui confondant les erreurs inévitables du civisme avec les erreurs calculées de

la perfidie, ou avec les attendants des conspirateurs, abandonne l'intrigent dangereux pour poursuivre le citoyen pasible!'

29 These reports were collected in *Paris Pendant la Terreur. Rapports des agents secrets du Ministre de l'Interieur*, ed, Pierre Caron, Société de l'histoire de France, Paris, 1940, p. 64.

30 Report by 'Pourvoyeur', from *Paris Pendant la Terreur*, quoted in Richard Bienvenu, ed., *The Ninth of Thermidor: The Fall of Robespierre*, Oxford University Press, Oxford, 1968, p. 77.

31 Maximillan Robespierre, 'Discours Prononcé Dans La Séance Du 8 Thermidor An 11', published in English from the pamphlet 'The Last Discourse of Maximillian Robespierre' (1867, trans. James Bronterre O'Brien) in Richard Bienvenu, ed, *The Ninth of Thermidor: The Fall of Robespierre*, ibid., p. 150.

32 G. W. F. Hegel, *The Philosophy of History*, ibid.

33 G. W. F. Hegel, *Die Philosophie des Rechts: Die Mitschriften Wannenmann (Heidelberg 1817– 18)* and *Homeyer (Berlin 1818–19)*, ed. K. H. Itling, Stuggart 1983, p. 133, quoted in Domenico Losurdo, *Hegel and the Freedom of Moderns*, ibid., p. 104.

34 Daniel Guérin, *Class Struggle in the First French Republic: Bourgeois and Bras Nus 1793– 1795*, trans. Ian Patterson, Pluto Press, London, 1977, p. 285.

35 Ibid.

36 Frank Jellinek, *The Paris Commune of 1871*, Left Book Club/Victor Gollancz, London, 1937, p. 16.

37 There was very much a missed opportunity to produce an 'error-theory' in Marxist historiography during this period, particularly for those Marxist historians who might have been sympathetic to its problems and the problems of historical method, such as E. P. Thompson. But Thompson's *Poverty of Theory: or an Orrery of Errors* (the nearest English Marxist historiography gets to a creative engagement with Hegel in the 1960s and 70s) became a repetitive and monological battle with Althusser; and as such Thompson would have done better to address himself to the 'new historiography' more broadly in France at the time (Roland Barthes, Pierre Nora and Michel de Certeau) than Althusser *tout court*. His political critique of the reduction of Marxism to the critique of political economy, his insightful identification of Popper with Althusser, his use of the anti-historicist Engels, and realist insistence on the fallibility of the historian, could have generated a productive dialogue with the likes of de Certeau and his attack on Stalinist historicism, and what he called the structuralist 'monster' (*The Writing of History* [1975], trans. Tom Conley, Columbia University Press, New York, 1988, p. 80). Interestingly, de Certeau argues in the 'Historiographical Operation' (from this collection) that 'the formalization of [historical] research has its goal precisely the production of 'errors' – insufficiencies, lacunae – that may be put to scientific use.' (p. 78)

38 Karl Marx, V. I. Lenin and Nikita Fedorovsky, *The Civil War in France: The Paris Commune*, International Publishers, New York, 1988, p. 167.

39 Ibid., p. 61.

40 Ibid., p. 122.

41 Ibid., p. 67.

42 Ibid., p. 62.

43 For a discussion of irony and parody in Marx's early writing, see Margaret A. Rose, *Reading the Young Marx and Engels: Poetry, Parody and the Censor*, Croom Helm, London and Totowa, New Jersey, 1978.

44 Kristin Ross, *The Emergence of Social Space: Rimbaud and the Paris Commune*, Verso, London and New York, 2008, p. 24.

45 Rosa Luxemburg, 'Leninism or Marxism?' in *The Russian Revolution and Leninism or Marxism?* , p. 108.

46 Rosa Luxemburg, 'On the Situation in the Russian Social Democracy' (1911), first published in *Internationale Wissenschaftliche Korresondenz zur Geschichte der deutsche Arbeiterbewegung*, Vol. 23 No 3, September. English translation by Mike Jones, in *Rosa Luxemburg, Selected Political Literary Writings, Revolutionary History*, Vol. 10, Number 1, Merlin Press, London, 2009, p. 71.

47 Ibid., p. 71.

48 V. I. Lenin, originally published in *Zagranichnaya Gazette* No 2, 23 March 1908, reprinted in Lenin, *Collected Works*, Vol. 13, Progress Publishers, Moscow, 1972, pp. 475–478.

49 V. I. Lenin, ibid., p. 477.

50 V. I. Lenin, *Collected Works*, Vol. 27, Progress Publishers, Moscow, 1972, p. 131.

51 Arno J. Mayer, *The Furies: Violence and Terror in the French and Russian Revolutions*, p. 45.

52 Herbert Marcuse, *Studien über Autorität und Familie'* (1936), translated as *A Study on Authority*, by Joris De Bres, New Left Books, London, 1972.

53 Al Richardson, 'Introduction', in *Trotsky and the Origins of Trotskyism: Alfred Rosmer, Boris Souvarine, Emile Fabrol and Antoine Clavez*, Francis Boutle Publishers, London 2002.

54 Leon Trotsky, 'The Capture of Power was Possible in May', in David Cotterill, ed, *The Serge–Trotsky Papers*, p. 149.

55 Leon Trotsky, *Revolution Betrayed: What Is the Soviet Union and Where Is It Going?* New Park Publications, London, 1967.

56 Victor Serge, *Year One of the Russian Revolution* [1930], trans. and ed. Peter Sedgwick with a new preface by Paul Foot, Bookmarks/Pluto Press/Writers and Readers, London and New York, 1992.

57 Victor Serge, 'Letter 24: Serge to Trotsky', Brussels, 27 July 1936, in David Cotterill ed, *The Serge–Trotsky Papers*, p. 83.

58 Leon Trotsky, 'Letter 40: Trotsky to Serge', Coyoacan, May 6th, 1939, and Trotsky's articles 'The Hue and Cry over Kronstadt' and 'One More Kronstadt', all in David Cotterill, ed, *The Serge–Trotsky Papers*, ibid.

59 Victor Serge, 'Letter 12: Serge to Trotsky', Brussels May 27 1934, in ibid., p. 60.

60 Victor Serge, 'Marxism in Our Time', *Partisan Review*, ibid.

61 Ibid., p. 177.

62 Ibid., p. 183.

63 Serge's novel *The Case of Comrade Tulayev* is essentially about the inauthenticity of the confessed error. *The Case of Comrade Tulayev*, trans. Willard R. Trask with an introduction by Susan Sontag, *New York Review of Books*, New York, 2004.

64 Victor Serge, *From Lenin to Stalin*, trans. Ralph Manheim, Pathfinder Press, London and New York, 1973, p. 67.

65 Victor Serge, 'One More Kronstadt', in David Cotterill, ed, *The Serge–Trotsky Papers*, ibid., p. 192.

66 Victor Serge, *Unforgiving Years*, trans. with an introduction by Richard Greenman, *New York Review of Books*, New York, 2008, p. 128.

67 Victor Serge, 'Marxism in Our Time', ibid., p. 178.

68 Ibid., p. 179.

69 Ibid., p. 180. This 'nourishment through error' is replayed in the 1960s in Latin America. See Régis Debray, *Revolution in the Revolution? Armed Struggle and Political Struggle in Latin America*. 'All decisive revolutionary processes must begin and have begun with certain mis-steps . . . because the existing points of departure are those left by the preceding historical period, and they are used, even if unconsciously.' (p. 23.)

70   Although he certainly played an important role in the Party before his resignation. See, Max Adereth, *The French Communist, a Critical History (1920–84): from Comintern to 'the Colours of France'*, Manchester University Press, Manchester, 1984.

71   Henri Lefebvre, *Introduction to Modernity: Twelve Preludes, September 1959–May 1961*, p. 235.

72   Ibid., p. 20.

73   Ibid., p. 17.

74   The key Romantic text on irony is Friedrich Schlegel's 'On Incomprehensibility' (1800). See J. M. Bernstein, ed., *Classic and Romantic German Aesthetics*, Cambridge University Press, Cambridge, 2003, pp. 297–307.

75   Henri Lefebvre, *Introduction to Modernity*, p. 16.

76   Ibid., pp. 10–11.

77   Ibid., p. 21.

78   Ibid., p. 215.

79   Ibid., p. 25.

80   Ibid., p. 33.

81   Ibid., p. 9. For a further discussion of Lefebvre and irony, see John Roberts, *Philosophizing the Everyday: Revolutionary Praxis and the Fate of Cultural Theory*, Pluto Press, London, 2006.

82   Henri Lefebvre, *Introduction to Modernity*, p. 205.

83   The modern – post Ulrich Beck – discourse on risk is weak precisely in this sense: risk is to be minimized at all costs. For a 'sociological' overview of the debate, see John Tulloch and Deborah Lupton, *Risk and Everyday Life*, Sage, London, 2003.

84   Christopher Hibbert, *King Mob: The Story of Lord George Gordon and the Riots of 1780*, Longmans, Green & Co, London, 1958, p. 140.

85   Henri Lefebvre, *Vol II, Critique of Everyday Life: Foundations for a Sociology of the Everyday* [1961], trans. John Moore with a preface by Michael Trebitsch, Verso, London and New York, 2002, p. 65.

86   Ibid., p. 66.

87   Henri Lefebvre, *Introduction to Modernity*, p. 224.

88   Daniel Bensaïd, *Marx For Our Time: Adventures and Misadventures of a Critique*, trans. Gregory Elliott, Verso, London and New York, 2002. For an exploration of similar ideas, see Bensaïd, 'Theses of Resistance', *International Viewpoint*, No 362, December 2004.

89   Daniel Bensaïd, *Marx For Our Times*, p. 2.

90   Ibid., p. 220.

91   Ibid., p. 223.

92   G. W. F. Hegel, *Science of Logic*, trans. A.V. Miller, Oxford University Press, Oxford, p. 734, quoted in Bensaïd, ibid., p. 268.

93   Daniel Bensaïd, *Marx For Our Time*, p. 272.

94   Ibid., p. 276.

95   Eugene Fleischmann, *La Philosophie de Politique de Hegel – Sous Forme D'un Commentaire Des 'Fondements De La Philosphie Du Droit'*, Gallimard, Paris, 1992, p. 233, quoted in Bensaïd, ibid., p. 277.

96   Daniel Bensaïd, *Marx in Our Times*, p. 289.

97   Ibid., p. 211.

98   Ibid., p. 23.

99   Henri Lefebvre, *Introduction to Modernity*, pp. 202–203.

100 Jacques Lacan, 'Of Structure as an Inmixing of an Otherness Prerequisite to Any Subject Whatever' (Lacan talk at John Hopkins University, Baltimore, 1966), available at http://www.braungardt.com/Psychoanalysis/Lacan-Baltimore.htm.

101 Gillian Rose, *Mourning Becomes the Law: Philosophy and Representation*, Cambridge University Press, Cambridge, 1996, p. 71.

102 Ibid., p. 72.

103 Alenka Zupancic, *The Odd One In: On Comedy*, MIT Press, Cambridge MA and London, 2008.

104 Ibid., p. 217.

105 Paul Ricoeur, *Memory, History, Forgetting*, trans. Kathleen Blamey & David Pellauer, University of Chicago Press, Chicago and London, 2004.

106 G. W. F. Hegel, *Aesthetics: Lectures on Fine Art*, trans. T. M. Knox, 2 vols, Clarendon Press, Oxford, 1975.

107 For a discussion of this issue, see Mark-William Roche, 'Hegel's Theory of Comedy in the Context of Hegelian and Modern Reflections on Comedy', *Revue internationale de philosophie*, No 221, 2002/3, and more generally, Mark-William Roche, *Tragedy and Comedy. A Systematic Study and a Critique of Hegel*, Albany, New York, 1998.

108 Alenka Zupancic, *The Odd One In*, p. 49.

109 Ibid., p. 140.

110 Ibid., p. 217.

CHAPTER 5: ERROR, REASON AND ART

1 See, Alain Badiou's discussion of the 'invisibility' of revolution in the current period, in 'Three Negations', *Cardozo Law Review*, Vol. 29, No 5, 2008.

2 Theodor Adorno, *Negative Dialectics* trans. E. B. Ashton, Routledge & Kegan Paul, London, 1973, p. 95.

3 Charles Baudelaire, *Art in Paris 1845–1862: Salons and Other Exhibitions*, trans. and ed. Jonathan Mayne, Phaidon Press, Oxford, 1981.

4 The painting was a portrait of Ialysus, the son of Helios, and, having been removed to Rome by Vespasian, was lost in a fire in The Temple of Peace in AD64. See, Pliny, *Natural History*, Book 35: An Account of Paintings and Colours, available at http://www.perseus.tufts.edu/hopper/. For a discussion of Pliny and Protogenes, Roman imperialism and the legacy of classical culture, see Sorcha Carey's, *Pliny's Catalogue of Culture: Art and Empire in the* Natural History, Oxford University Press, Oxford, 2003.

5 August Strindberg, 'On Chance in Artistic Creation', first published in *Revue des Revues*, 15 November 1894, reprinted as 'The New Arts! on, The Role of Chance in Artistic Creation', in *August Strindberg: Selected Essays*, ed. and trans. Michael Robinson, Cambridge University Press, Cambridge, 1996, and as 'On Chance in Artistic Creation', trans. Kjersti Board, in the online edition of *Cabinet* Magazine, Issue 3 (Weather), 2001. All quotes are from the last of these sources.

6 Ibid., p.

7 Ibid., p.

8 Giorgio Vasari, *Lives of the Artists*, ed. Marilyn Aronberg Lavin, trans. Jonathan Foster, Dover Publications, New York, 2005. For an excellent discussion of the legacy of pre-modern techniques of indeterminacy, and of the ubiquity of the latent and accidental image, see Dario Gamboni, *Potential Images: Ambiguity and Indeterminancy in Modern Art*, trans. Mark Treharne, Reaktion Books, London, 2002.

9   Friedrich Nietzsche, *Untimely Meditations*, ed. Daniel Breazeale and trans. R. J. Hollingdale, Cambridge University Press, Cambridge, 1997.

10   Ibid., p. 65.

11   Ibid., p. 78.

12   Ibid., p. 82.

13   Ibid.

14   Ibid., p. 113.

15   Ibid., p. 105.

16   Ibid.

17   Ibid.

18   Ibid., p. 107.

19   Ibid., p. 106.

20   George Santayana, *Egotism in German Philosophy* [1915], Haskell House Publishing, Brooklyn, New York, 1971.

21   George Santayana, *Reason in Art: Volume Four of 'The Life of Reason'* [1905], Dover Publications, New York, 1982, p. 218.

22   Ibid., p. 38.

23   Ibid., p. 164.

24   Ibid., p. 225.

25   Ibid., p. 228.

26   George Santayana, *Reason in Art*, p. 215.

27   Novalis 'Goethe', *Classic and German Romantic Aesthetics*, p. 232.

28   Gottfried Lessing, *Laocoön: An Essay on the Limits of Poetry and Painting*, Farrar, Straus and Giroux, New York, 1969.

29   J. M. Bernstein, 'Introduction', in *Classic and Romantic German Aesthetics*, ibid.

30   G. W. F. Hegel, *Philosophy of History*, ibid.

31   Friedrich Schlegel, 'Critical Fragments' (1797), *Classical and Romantic German Aesthetics*, p. 242.

32   Friedrich Schlegel, '*Athenaeum* Fragments', (1798) *Classic and Romantic German Aesthetics*, p. 251.

33   Marcel Duchamp, *The Essential Writings of Marcel Duchamp*, eds M. Sanouillet and E. Peterson, Thames & Hudson, London, 1975, p. 139.

34   Jacques Rancière, *The Aesthetic Unconscious*, trans. Debra Keates and James Swenson, Polity Press, Cambridge and Malden MA, 2009.

35   Jacques Rancière, *The Aesthetic Unconscious*, pp. 35–36.

36   Jacques Rancière, *The Emancipated Spectator*, trans. Gregory Elliott, Verso 2009.

37   Tristan Tzara, 'Dada Manifesto' (1918) in *Dadas On Art*, ed. Lucy R. Lippard, Prentice Hall Inc., Englewood Cliffs, New Jersey, 1971, pp. 19–20.

38   André Breton 'The Automatic Message' (1933), first published in *Minotaure*, trans. Antony Melville, in André Breton, Paul Eluard, Philippe Soupault, *The Automatic Message, The Magnestic Fields, The Immaculate Conception*, trans. David Gascoyne, Antony Melville and John Graham, with an introduction by David Gascoyne and Antony Melville, Atlas, London, 1997, p. 29.

39   For a discussion of this tension, see T. J. Clark, *Farewell to an Idea: Episodes from a History of Modernism*, Yale University Press, New Haven, CN and London, 2001.

40   For Oulipo, see *Oulipo Compendium*, eds Harry Mathews and Alastair Brotchie, Atlas Press, London, 1998. As Jacques Roubaud argues in his introduction, 'The Oulipo and Combinatorial Art' (1991), the Oulipo writers and artists treated 'constraints as 'productive' (p. 42).

41 George Brecht, *Chance Imagery*, A Great Bear Pamphlet, Something Else Press, New York, 1957, quoted in *Chance: Documents of Contemporary Art*, ed. Margaret Iverson, Whitechapel, London and MIT, Cambridge MA, 2010, p. 41.

42 John Cage, 'Indeterminancy' (1958), from *Silence: Lectures and Writings*, Wesleyan University Press, Middleton Connecticut, 1961, p. 37.

43 Allen Kaprow, *Assemblage, Environments and Happenings*, Harry N. Abrams, New York, 1966, p. 174.

44 Ben Shahn, 'In Defence of Chaos', in the *Aspen Papers: Twenty Years of Design Theory, from the International Design Conference in Aspen*, ed. with commentary by Reyner Banham, Pall Mall Press, London, 1974, p. 183.

45 Robert Morris, 'Notes on Sculpture Part 4'[1969] in *Continuous Project Altered Daily: The Writings of Robert Morris*, MIT Press, Cambridge MA, 1993, p. 69.

46 Sol Lewitt, 'Sentences on Conceptual Art', *Art-Language*, No 1, May 1969, p. 11.

47 Robert Rauschenberg, 'Interview with Dorothy Seckler', Archives of American Art, Smithsonian Institute, quoted in *Chance*, ed. Margaret Iverson, p. 109.

48 John Cage, 'Indeterminancy', *Silence*, p. 39.

49 For a discussion of the dialectics of the modernism and the popular and the Cold War, see Michael Denning *The Cultural Front: The Laboring of American Culture in the Twentieth Century*, Verso, London and New York, 1997

50 For a indication of how precious and self-confirming Cage's systematic indeterminancy had become by the late 1970s, see 'Interview with John Cage' by Silvy-Panet Raymond and John Roberts, *Performance Magazine*, No 7, 1980. He distances himself from Surrealism, psychoanalysis, minimalism, conceptual art, and the notion that his practice of indeterminacy had become tainted by a certain kind of 'taste', of 'tastefulness'. For an overview of the adaptation of a post-Cagean indeterminacy in relation to the new post-digital microsound production, see Kim Cascone, 'The Aesthetics of Failure: "Post-Digital" Tendencies in Contemporary Music', *Computer Music Journal*, 24:4, pp. 12–18, MIT, Winter 2000, and Phil Thomson, 'Atoms and errors: towards a history of aesthetics of microsound', *Organised Sound*, 9: 2, pp. 207–218, Cambridge University Press, 2004.

51 T. J. Clark, *Farewell To An Idea*, p. 307.

52 For a discussion of these problems, see Maria Gough, *The Artist as Producer: Russian Constructivism in Revolution*, California University Press, Berkeley and Los Angeles, 2005.

53 For an extensive discussion of this tension in Adorno, see Christophe Menke, *The Sovereignity of Art: Aesthestic Negativity in Adorno and Derrida*, trans. Neil Solomon MIT, 1998.

54 Niklas Luhmann, *Art as a Social System*, trans. Eva M. Knodt, Stanford University Press, Stanford, 2000, p. 194.

55 George Dickie, *Art and Value*, Blackwell, Oxford, 2001, p. 97.

56 See 'Introduction', Nicole Antebi, Colin Dickey and Robbie Herbst, in Nicole Antebi, Colin Dickey and Robbie Herbst, eds, *Failure: Experiments in Aesthetics and Social Practices*, published in conjunction with the *Journal of Aesthetics and Protest*, AK Press, Edinburgh and Los Angeles, 2008, p. 12. See also the work of the artist-activist group the 'Errorist Internacional' founded in Argentina in 2005. 'Accepting the permanent presence of error in reality liberates, and it drives a new vision of, and a new participation in life. Error liberates. Error is a permanent source of inspiration', Erroristas Internationalle (& Etcetera . . .), 'Notes on De-Education and Errorism', *Newspaper of the Platform 'Chto Delat/What is to be Done?'*, Issue No 14: Self-Education, September 2006, unpaginated.

57 Jacques Rouboud, 'Introduction: The Oulipo and Combinatorial Art' (1991), in *Oulipo Compendium*, eds Harry Mathews & Alastair Brotchie, p. 41.

58 Paul Virilio, in Sylvere Lotringer and Paul Virilio, *The Accident of Art*, trans. Michael Taormina, Semiotext(e), Foreign Agents Series, New York, 2005, p. 36.

59 Paul Virilio, ibid., p. 60.

60 See in particular, *Krise des Häßlichen. Vom Kubismus zur Pop Art*, trans. from the Russian by Helmut Barth, VEB Verlag der Kunst, Dresden, 1972. For a discussion of Lifshitz, see Dmitry Gutov's, 'Learn, Learn and Lean', in Grant Watson, Gerrie van Noord and Gavin Everall, eds, *Make Everything New: A Project on Communism'*, Bookworks/Project Arts Centre, London and Dublin, 2006, pp. 25–37, and Stanley Mitchell, 'Mikhail Lifshits: A Marxist Conservative', in Andrew Hemingway, ed, *Marxism and the History of Art: From William Morris to the New Left*, Pluto Press, London, 2006, pp. 28–44.

61 Paul Virilio, ibid., p. 74.

INDEX